Fear is an emotion that we all deal with at some stage in our lives. I can remember often asking my children, "What are you afraid of?" I suppose we could all ask ourselves the same question. Anna Hampton has captured the essence of this question as she considers the global risks and dangers that we face today as we share the gospel in high-risk environments. By unpacking the biblical truths related to fear and courage, she guides the reader through a practical process of facing fear as we build our framework of trust in the Lord. I'm grateful that Anna takes a section of her book to address those in leadership. Barnabas International has greatly benefited from implementing various practices that Anna has outlined in her earlier book *Facing Danger*; *Facing Fear* has once again provided room for growth—it is a must-read for anyone serving in church leadership.

PERRY BRADFORD
Executive Director, Barnabas International

Everyone involved in modern gospel advancement knows the need for this book! The places yet to be reached by the Gospel are dangerous, risky, and require those who go to have mature courage and a vibrant life-sustaining and courage-promoting faith in God. But this book is not only for global workers as the reality of hardship and persecution invades the Church at large with new ferocity. In this book, Anna Hampton draws on her personal experiences serving in dangerous places, and her knowledge in subjects as diverse as neurosciences, theology, sewer rats, Hebrew and Greek etymology, and Awassi sheep to help the reader understand and prepare for the journey of courage that followers of Christ must walk. Well researched and written, this book is truly a seminal treatment of preparing for and facing risk and persecution. Every international worker (indeed, every Christ follower!) should read and meditate on it!

HAMILTON T. BURKE, PhD, Clinical Psychologist
Executive Director, Great Commission Consulting
Author, Serving in Hazardous Places book series

Safety, risk, and fear have dominated global headlines over the past few years. How we think about these topics has huge implications for how we carry out our tasks as Christ's ambassadors. While persecution is promised in the New Testament, we must see it through spiritual eyes with an understanding of appropriate risk-taking. This book raises the bar of our understanding of the challenges we face as kingdom activists in a dangerous world.

TED ESLER, PhD
President, Missio Nexus

Brilliantly written, deeply thought-provoking, and practicable, Anna Hampton has done it again! This sequel to *Facing Danger* is a must-read for anyone engaged in cross-cultural or intercultural witness work, and for the organizations that send and support those workers. In this guide to facing fear, Anna manages to combine profound spiritual truths, biblical realities, and hard-won personal experience. Page after page, she gives us practical guidance and inspired wisdom on risk, mature courage, Spirit-led discernment, and what it takes to face risk wisely amid persecution, laying out a model for witnessing for Christ from a place of peace, love, and trust. I couldn't put it down, and I can't wait to share this book with everyone in my organization.

Sarah Grainger
Executive Director, Family Missions Company

Facing Fear is a movingly spiritual pilgrimage which every believer must read. Anna Hampton traces with such compassionate audacity the deep heart transformation from fear to mature courage that I often just put the book down to reflect and worship. This book is like the "song of ascent" for our lives: the beginning point is our everyday life now but it prepares us for the hardest persecution. This practical book fills a void in our increasingly volatile world, as it spans from biblical basis and spiritual discernment to risk decision making and crisis management. *Facing Fear* draws from years of personal experience serving in a high persecution context; counselling, training, and equipping others in high-risk areas; and extensive and deep research. *Facing Fear* is a guidepost for our times.

Mary Ho
International Executive Leader, All Nations

What a rich and impactful book! Like a stone in the lake that creates ripples of resonance, Anna educates, challenges, and renews the reader's mind, with real-life stories, illuminating references, and in-depth theology. It's easy to write a book about courage, but it's strenuous to write about fear. Fear? No one likes it! We all have it! Many global workers face it daily and need to face it intentionally. As you read this book you realize that fear and courage are inseparable in the twenty-first century. As the coordinator of the Global Member Care Network (GMCN), it is my honor to endorse this book and recommend it as a must-read.

Harry Hoffmann
Coordinator, Global Member Care Network

Rooted in personal experience, comprehensive field research, and a thorough biblical analysis and understanding of risk, Anna Hampton once again invites us to live in deep and mature courage—one that undergirds a life that is lived with prudence, boldness, and conviction. It is no light task to tackle the issues of safety and risk, especially in a world where safety is so highly valued. As someone working in the anti-sex trafficking sector, the pertinence of Hampton's words cannot be ignored. I am walking away better equipped to ask the right questions for myself and my team in situations of risk, while still walking more deeply in the courage instilled through the Holy Spirit.

Andrew Larson
Anti Sex-Trafficking Specialist, Νέα Ζωή (Nea Zoi), Athens, Greece

I have been an avid devotee of Anna Hampton since reading *Facing Danger*. I have twice attended the Hamptons' RAM Training and now have been privileged to read *Facing Fear*. Anna has done the heavy lifting: bringing the various streams of research on risk management together with the theological framework with which to approach "witness risk" in a way that no one else has. Her own experience as a global worker and the risks that she has faced bring an element of real answers to serious risk questions in addition to the consultations that she and her husband have had with many sending organizations and churches. To say that I highly recommend this book is to discount its importance. I desire that every global worker, and even every believer, who chooses to enter into the inherent risk of following Jesus where he leads, would read and meditate on the contents of this book.

Edward Nye
Global Security Coordinator, Assemblies of God World Missions, USA

Facing Danger opened my eyes to a biblical process when faced with excruciating decisions, and *Facing Fear* opened my eyes even further and challenged my perspectives. Anna Hampton joins biblical scholarship with real-life experience. She has built for us a unique bridge that spans the chasm of the fears we face. The book is anchored in the bedrock of orthodoxy and provides a way across the chasm built with sound orthopraxy. *Facing Fear* is not a trite response or reckless approach to fear. It is an honest exposé of the reality of fear and the response of courage.

Rev. James Petersen, ThM
Executive Director, ReachGlobal Personnel, Evangelical Free Church of America

For years now I have incorporated principles from Hampton's *Facing Danger* into the training for our new kingdom workers. Now, with *Facing Fear*, Anna is challenging us to break down our own cultural constructs of fear, leaving our own biases at the door to explore how the ultimate authority, God's Word, addresses the subject. As many security professionals in global ministry are leaning heavily on a secular paradigm of risk, she has presented a holistic analysis of fear, courage, and risk; incorporating the fields of neuroscience and professional risk management, as well as an earnest dependence on the Holy Spirit and scripture. This work comes from a place of raw transparency, drawing on authentic past experiences and God-given insight. I am ecstatic that this resource is available and will be highly recommending it to leadership and field workers alike.

Rev. Michael W. Reeves
Captain, US Army, Director of Security, SIM USA

After equipping Christ's followers in *Facing Danger* with the much-needed concepts and decision-making skills to respond to intense risk in ministry, the author now focuses on the hearts and souls of the faithful as they experience a normal response to danger: fear. In this book, you will find thoroughly researched, biblically profound, and practice-relevant nuggets; a detailed and instructive study of the Hebrew and Greek words used for fear in the Bible; applied neuropsychological concepts of fear and attachment; an exploration of how to move from fear to courage; cross-cultural considerations of risk-related decision-making; and wise counsel about preparing for and managing risk. I recommend this book to all who seek to prepare their hearts and minds to courageously face fear with increasingly mature courage.

Frauke C. Schaefer, MD, Psychiatry
Barnabas International Christian Counseling and Therapy, Psychiatric Care

Facing Fear is a book for all believers. Author Anna Hampton dives deeply into the Hebrew and Greek words for fear and courage, explores the neuroscience of fear and attachment and their implications for our relationship with God, and shows us a better way to respond to the grief and suffering of others through her compassionate treatment of the wife of Job. For those living in dangerous situations, she also offers a roadmap for assessing risk and discerning the next right step. *Facing Fear* offers comfort, courage, and a way forward even in the darkest of circumstances.

Elizabeth Trotter
Editor-in-chief, cross-cultural website, A Life Overseas; Author, *Serving Well: Help for the Wannabe, Newbie, or Weary Cross-cultural Christian Worker*

FACING FEAR

The Journey to Mature Courage
in Risk and Persecution

Anna Hampton

Facing Fear: The Journey to Mature Courage in Risk and Persecution
© 2023 by Anna Hampton. All rights reserved.
Graphics Copyright © 2023 Neal & Anna Hampton

The Grief Process from the Sharpening Your Interpersonal Skills workshop. Used with permission from International Training Partners. © 2016.

© 2022 Joshua Project. Global map used with permission.

Global Terrorism Database used with permission. START (National Consortium for the Study of Terrorism and Responses to Terrorism). (2022). Global Terrorism Database 1970–2020 [data file]. https://www.start.umd.edu/gtd

No part of this book may be reproduced, stored in a retrieval system, or transmitted in any form or by any means—electronic, mechanical, photocopy, recording, or otherwise—without prior written permission from the publisher, except brief quotations used in connection with reviews in magazines or newspapers. For permission, email permissions@wclbooks.com. For corrections, email editor@wclbooks.com.

All Scripture quotations, unless otherwise indicated, are from the ESV® Bible (The Holy Bible, English Standard Version®), Copyright © 2001 by Crossway, a publishing ministry of Good News Publishers. Used by permission. All rights reserved.

Scripture quotations marked CSB are taken from the Christian Standard Bible®, Copyright © 2017 by Holman Bible Publishers. Used by permission. Christian Standard Bible® and CSB® are federally registered trademarks of Holman Bible Publishers.

Scripture quotations marked NASB are taken from the NASB® New American Bible®, Copyright © 1960, 1971, 1977, 1995, 2020 by The Lockman Foundation. Used by permission. All rights reserved. lockman.org.

Scripture quotations marked AMP are taken from the Amplified Bible (AMP), Copyright © 1954, 1958, 1962, 1964, 1965, 1987 by The Lockman Foundation. Used by permission.

Published by William Carey Publishing
10 W. Dry Creek Cir
Littleton, CO 80120 | www.missionbooks.org

William Carey Publishing is a ministry of Frontier Ventures
Pasadena, CA | www.frontierventures.org

Cover and Interior Designer: Mike Riester

ISBNs: 978-1-64508-468-6 (paperback)
       978-1-64508-470-9 (epub)

Printed Worldwide

28 27 26 25 24   2 3 4 5 6   IN

Library of Congress Control Number: 2023937371

This book is dedicated to those witnesses
wondering if they have enough courage and strength
to endure risks, persecution, and martyrdom with Jesus.

Contents

Foreword by Scott Brawner … xi

Introduction … xix

Part One: The Twenty-First Century Challenge
Chapter 1: When Your Back Is Against the Wall … 2
Chapter 2: The Squeeze, the Smash, and the Rhomphaia … 15

Part Two: Biblical Background
Chapter 3: An Introduction to a Grammar of Fear and Courage … 32
Chapter 4: Temptations, Idols, and Ancient Heresies in Risk … 63
Chapter 5: Anti-Fragile Faith … 76
Chapter 6: Put the Candy Jar on the Lower Shelf … 89

Part Three: Essentials of Decision-Making in Risk
Chapter 7: Shrewd as a Serpent … 100
Chapter 8: Thinking about Thinking … 121
Chapter 9: Witness Risk Axioms … 141
Chapter 10: Becoming Shrewd as a Serpent … 151
Chapter 11: Information and Death-Threat Analysis … 168
Chapter 12: Risk Decision-Making … 178
Chapter 13: Risk Communication and Trust … 187
Chapter 14: Embracing Grief and Loss … 200
Chapter 15: Standing in the Tragic Gap … 213

Part Four: Leadership
Chapter 16: Systems and the Liminal Moment … 224
Chapter 17: Ten Mistakes Leaders Make … 242
Chapter 18: It's Time to Member Care Job's Wife … 250

Part Five: Contagious Courage
Chapter 19: Hope Like a Sewer Rat and PTSJ … 262
Chapter 20: Mature Courage and Spiritual Nobility … 275

Appendix A: Thresholds for Departure/Benchmarks for Return … 284

Appendix B: Choosing to Stay … 291

Appendix C: Risk Assessment and Management Training (RAM Training) … 294

Acknowledgments … 297

Witness Risk Glossary … 299

Bibliography … 303

About the Author … 319

Index … 320

List of Figures

Figure 1: Theology of Risk	xxiv
Figure 2: Core Specialties	xxvi
Figure 3: Three Fear Responses	43
Figure 4: Avoidance and Attachment	47
Figure 5: The Path of Fear and Courage	56
Figure 6: Four Categories of Questions in Risk	79
Figure 7: RAM Flow Chart	168
Figure 8: Aspects of Risk Decision-Making Process	169
Figure 9: Types of Information	170
Figure 10: Aspects of Trust	188
Figure 11: The Grief Process	206
Figure 12: Risk Attitude Scale	227
Figure 13: Impact of Stress	247
Figure 14: The Grief Process	256
Figure 15: Cycle of Despair	268
Figure 16: Cycle of Hope	269

List of Maps and Tables

Map 1: Unreached People Groups	10
Map 2: Terrorism Map	11
Table 1: Persecution Terms in English and Greek	19
Table 2: Fear Verbs in Hebrew, English, and Greek	36
Table 2: Courage Verbs, Adjectives, and Nouns	40
Table 3: Two Modes of Thinking	123

When your fears overwhelm you,
> *Stand firm.*

When you are threatened,
> *Stand firm.*

When you are hated,
> *Stand firm.*

When you are hungry,
> *Stand firm.*

When you are cold,
> *Stand firm.*

When you are in pain,
> *Stand firm.*

When you have fallen,
> *Get back up and stand firm.*

When your spouse or mother or father is beaten because you are a Christ-follower,
> *Stand firm.*

When they torture your child in front of you,
> *Stand firm.*

When your family attacks you verbally, physically, sexually,
> *Stand firm.*

When your friend betrays you,
> *Stand firm.*

When your children turn their backs on you and Christ,
> *Stand firm.*

When you feel all alone,
> *Stand firm.*

When they are hitting you,
> *Stand firm.*

When you feel no one remembers you,
> *Stand firm.*

When it seems like God can't hear your prayers,
> *Stand firm.*

When your tears won't stop,
> *Stand firm.*

When you have no tears left,
> *Stand firm.*

When the knife is at your throat,
> *Stand firm.*

When you don't think you can stand any longer, your knees tremble, and you're ready to give up,
> *Stand firm.*

The ones who endure to the end will be saved.[1] He is worthy.

---

[1] Verses on endurance: Exod 14:13–14; Luke 21:19; 1 Cor 10:13; 15:58; 16:13; Eph 6:11, 13; Phil 1:27; 4:1; 2 Thess 2:15; 1 Pet 5:9; Jas 1:12.

Foreword

Typically, a Foreword for a book is intended to help "sell" the book. This is not that kind of Foreword. Why? In my opinion, this is not a book hocking ideas that are here today, gone tomorrow, or even three or four steps to a better something. Anna Hampton's follow-up to *Facing Danger* deserves better than that. Now more than ever, Christians are suffering for the gospel. Now more than ever, Christians are making hard choices to follow God in simple obedience *and* facing the realities of "witness risk." That is to say, Christians making a stand for Christ are facing real and tangible risks associated with being obedient followers of Jesus who share the Gospel with others.

As a follower of Jesus, I have a passion for sharing the gospel and helping Christians count the cost of obedience. As an adventurer and former Army Ranger, I have a passion for bringing others to hard places. Taken together, for nearly thirty years I have led or empowered Christians to sojourn to hard and often dangerous locations to authentically live and share the Gospel with the lost. However, as a Great Commission security professional and President of Concilium, I far too often find myself talking with Christians who, while on similar journeys serving the Lord, have succumbed to risk when serving in cross-cultural work and are now, at best, disillusioned with the gospel call. At worst, these poor souls have walked away from Christ altogether because of their traumatic experiences.

It is for this very reason that Christ-followers need to read *Facing Fear*. Anna Hampton knows personally and intimately of what she writes. Christ-followers need to understand the threats facing them as a consequence of gospel obedience—and Anna Hampton's latest book is a must-read for any believer serving the Lord in the West or the East. The experience that Anna brings in *Facing Fear* for Christians everywhere to consider is second to none. Her work is not rooted in an academic pursuit, written from the comfort and safety of a seminary professor's office. Instead, Anna's writing is gritty and the experiences from which she writes are messy and even bloody. She writes from a place of sacrifice, of both her and her husband, Neal, their children, and the many brothers and sisters in Christ that Anna has interviewed for her book. These facts alone make *Facing Fear* a must read.

An important point to make first is that *Facing Fear* is not just for those contemplating serving the Lord "over there." On the contrary, one encouragement Anna's writing has given me is consideration of what Holy God sees as right moral behavior—sharing the whole gospel and accepting the risk that personal obedience brings—while addressing the lack of moral courage that often interrupts the follow through in communicating the truth of God's salvation by grace alone, through faith alone, in Christ alone. That fear of repercussion for standing for the truth of Christ's salvation has undoubtedly kept many Christians from sharing the gospel to a lost world drunk on its own hedonism, entitlement, and desire for self-gratification. In these cases, moral cowardice has often won the day as Christians shy away from speaking the truth of the gospel to a lost and dying world. Anna says so herself when she declares, "*In contrast, moral cowardice knows what is right but will not do it. It lets evil prevail.*" I would submit to you the reality of moral cowardice on behalf of the elect has done more to inhibit the spread of the Gospel than the anti-Christian rhetoric that is often spewed in the public square today.

While not directly saying it in her book, Anna understands power and its application to the theologies of risk and suffering. To understand power in theology of risk, we must begin with epistemology. To that end, Catherine E. Althaus stated in her work, *A Disciplinary Perspective on the Epistemological Status of Risk*, that "understanding that the epistemological underpinnings of risk places the personal decision maker at the center of attention and decision making." With the power the decision maker possesses, he or she must distinguish between that which is justified belief and that which is personal opinion with regard to threat and risk. Anna does an excellent job of breaking this down in Part Three: Essentials of Decision-Making in Risk. The one taking the risk is required to concentrate on the nature of uncertainty in the risk, and to bring to bear any available knowledge to remove that uncertainty from the decision-making process. Anna and Neal's "Risk Axioms" in chapter 9 help give words to feelings and creates a process by which assessment can be done. This process forces the decision maker to "count the cost" of risk taking. While there are many different approaches to analyzing and processing risk, the power someone possesses both to mitigate and to *embrace* risk is an important consideration in analysis.

To put it another way, one's use of power has a direct impact on their understanding and practice of theology of risk. This is not only the wielding of physical power, but also of the power of knowledge ("knowledge is power"). In particular, a theology of risk cannot be complete without the power of knowledge to drive consideration. One cannot count the cost of obedience if they do not know what the cost is or could be. Anna successfully addresses this when she states that, "theology of suffering and theology of risk is not the same. Risk and suffering ask different questions, thereby requiring different answers. Responding to risk questions with suffering answers are unhelpful." In this way, one is not faithful before God for forsaking knowledge in decision making *or* confusing matters between what is a theology of risk vs a theology of suffering. To the contrary, not only is God not the author of confusion (1 Cor 14:33), but one may also be ridiculed and considered a fool for not assessing risk wisely and, thus, "counting the cost." Jesus even says this when he tells those who would follow him, "Whoever does not bear his own cross and come after Me cannot be My disciple" (Luke 14:27). Jesus goes on in Luke 14:28–32 to provide critical word-picture examples of those who, having power but lacking knowledge, did not count the cost and paid an extreme price.

With knowledge comes understanding; namely, under what conditions can risks be accepted? Wisdom, versus feelings, allows us to understand that there is a difference between incurring a risk and bearing the costs of risk. This can be especially poignant when taking risks on behalf of others is morally questionable, especially if those driving the risk taking have not thought through the consequences for others (this is critical to a comprehensive "duty of care").

Complementing necessary knowledge and power, when deciding to take risks that lead to suffering, one must believe and understand that suffering is purposeful. For it is in that purpose that the formation of Christ-like character becomes possible (Rom 8:28–29). Suffering, and even misery, provide opportunity toward God's glory and our good through the transformation of our mind, testimony, and ministry. Christians must nevertheless be careful in how they seek out suffering. This is because suffering is not a decision merely made by the individual; it is also a calling given by God. Suffering requires our cooperation and Christlike response if it is truly to accomplish God's purposes. In chapter 14, Anna speaks with great insight on the issues of risk, suffering, and persecution. While someone may be willing to suffer, and takes steps toward preparing to do so, needless or self-inflicted suffering is neither biblical nor holy. What's more, perseverance when facing needless suffering is all the harder, as a firm commitment is hard to maintain when this kind of suffering could have, (1) been avoided and (2) is not a privilege. When we suffer, we want it to have meaning because suffering from the consequences of witness risk gives us the opportunity to better understand who God is and why He cares so deeply for us.

Facing Fear helps the reader understand not only fear and suffering, but also hope. Anna addresses the disconnect between resilience and fatalism. She says, "An essential aspect of resilience is resisting a fatalistic attitude in situations of powerlessness. It takes courage to face reality, name it, and then accept what we can control and live in peace with that, even as we deeply grieve and move forward." This highlights the reality of personal agency in light of spiritual identity, and strength and weakness. Later, in chapter 19, she continues to flush out the truth of resiliency. If you desire to develop resiliency, look to develop hope like a sewer rat. In these pages, she speaks of the adaptability and resiliency of the sewer rat and its application to the human condition.

The need for adaptability and resilience in ministry are critical to thriving when serving in gospel advancement today, but this need is not just applicable to full-time overseas work. Adaptability and resiliency are critical resources for all people, especially Christians who are facing challenges and traumas, including persecution. I believe Anna does a great job of expounding on this as she balances the orthodoxy of faith and the praxis of living. Anna outlines "The gift of fear" and indeed it is. Anna says, "Fear is not an emotion like sadness or happiness, either of which might last a long while. It is not a state like anxiety. True fear is a survival signal that sounds only in the presence of danger." This is a powerful statement on the human condition and testimony to the Lord's lovingkindness. Most of all, as good stewards of all God has provided us (including the gift of fear), the Lord has given us permission *and* laid upon us an expectation to manage our fear and use it for God's glory and our good.

Allow me to remind you why any of this matters. First a reality check: The 10/40 Window, where much of the suffering facing Christians takes place, is not merely an area of lostness; it is an area of lostness that is characterized by terrible security challenges associated with reaching the lost in the region. Otherwise, the 10/40 Window would already be reached. Thus, the 10/40 Window is as much about the security threats and concerns of the area as it is about the lostness of the area. If you do not address or prepare for the security challenges of the 10/40 Window, you will not reach the lost who are in desperate need of the Gospel there. Anna's book is an important resource to empower ministry in the 10/40 Window.

Second, since 1998 I have been involved in developing biblically based, gospel-centered security, risk, and crisis management training programs, resources, and tools for Great Commission workers and their sending organizations. For twenty-five years I have seen far too many tragedies that could have been avoided. Please consider that in Great Commission sending, an organizational duty of care without a corresponding theology of risk is akin to discipline without direction. And according to

Don Whitney, my former spiritual disciplines seminary professor and author of *Spiritual Disciplines for the Christian Life*, "discipline without direction is drudgery!" A theology of risk that lacks a duty of care is at best poor stewardship; at worst, negligence. To that end, in chapter 16, Anna begins with this quote: "Nothing changes until blood is shed." Well, maybe ...

That quote is pretty intrinsic to the secular humanitarian world where aid workers are much more apt to sue their organizations than most gospel workers (I can answer the why of that statement another time). Sadly, some of the worst physical and moral injuries suffered by expatriate gospel workers and their children have happened in organizations that, while maintaining an articulated theology of risk, *lacked* a standardized duty of care. This, in turn, led these organizations and their people into "predictable tragedies."

Predictable tragedies are consequences resulting from a failure to acknowledge and mitigate known threats and vulnerabilities. Suffering consequences that are predictable, especially consequences having nothing to do with persecution, is not faithfulness; it is spiritual negligence. A biblical approach to stewarding risk begins where obedience meets calling and prepares for the consequences. This makes duty of care and the practice of biblical security principles an act of godly stewardship.

With the many predictable tragedies I have observed, organizations often failed to enact, manage, or enforce basic security policies, programs, or procedures (P3s) that should have minimized vulnerability to the threats faced in the more dangerous places of gospel advancement. That said, because gospel workers are less likely to sue than secular humanitarian workers, the result in some organizations has been a lack of accountability. This as allowed organizations to "dodge a bullet" of responsibility due to lack of legal and fiduciary consequences for their duty of care failures. Similarly, in some organizations I have also observed an unhealthy culture with a propensity toward answering theology of risk questions with theology of suffering answers. The result being that the ones asking hard questions can run the risk of being labeled unfaithful or even disloyal for their questions or risk, safety, and security. Sadly, in these kinds of organizations, it has been very hard for lessons to be learned so that the same tragedies are not repeated.

The good news is that many sending organizations take the development and implementation of a comprehensive duty of care seriously as an act of stewardship before the Lord. These Great Commission leaders acknowledge their duty of care as a moral, ethical, and even spiritual issue as they care for those sent by the organization. How do I know this is happening? Because Concilium has relationships with more than eighty evangelical mission and humanitarian organizations whose leaders I personally know. They invest significant amounts of money not only in security but also in member care to help workers and their families thrive on the mission field. For those leaders, reading *Facing Fear* will be a powerful encouragement as they develop a healthy orthodoxy/orthopraxy of theology of risk while leading their organizations to enact a duty of care that develops, implements, and empowers the organization's P3s. Most of all, they do this not to stifle the ministry but to empower it! I really do thank the Lord for my godly brothers and sisters who "get it." They are the ones making security an issue of stewardship for God's glory and the well-being of their people.

There is still much work to be done in the mission sending community, however. Please allow me to share my concerns.

Remember the shedding of blood Anna mentions? The worst duty of care abuses I have seen in the global missions community happened when there was shedding of blood and either no changes to the organization came about to better protect field workers and their families, *or* (worse) the organizational leaders attempted to spiritualize those critical incidents to justify negligence in order to protect the organization's reputation or members of the organization guilty of grievous sin.

These kinds of events are more akin to self-inflicted wounds than attacks by the enemies of God. These self-inflicted wounds appear most graphically when leaders (be they in the field or at headquarters) spiritualize the shedding of innocent blood in order to justify the actions, or lack thereof, in the organization. Appallingly, I have personally seen cases involving the spiritualizing of negligence in the duty of care of innocent adolescents and children. One such case involved the brutal sexual assault of teenage girls sent alone to conduct prostitute ministry in a redlight district. A lack of security P3s allowed for the isolation of teenage short-term gospel workers in the midst of sexual predators which, unsurprisingly, lead to their brutalization. In another case I investigated, a young lady on a semester trip was sexually assaulted because her team, lacking basic security training and possessing naivety to the security threats surrounding them in a Middle Eastern city, left their teammate vulnerable to be raped in her own bed after gates and doors were not only unlocked, but left wide open. A lack of training and compliance with even basic security protocols led to the brutalization of a young person not because she loves Jesus, but because her team, in their zeal for witnessing and lack of concern for security, left their teammate open to isolation and victimization because she was female, accessible, and alone. Other tragic cases I am aware of involved the ongoing molestation of children attending boarding schools where the perpetrators were themselves gospel workers! In several of these cases, organizations either spiritualized the situations or otherwise covered up wrongdoing to protect those responsible, the reputation of the organization, or both.

Not only does this kind of mismanagement damage the reputation of sending agencies, it also tarnishes the witness of all believers. Just as bad, children harmed on the mission field and who are now adults have gone to the courts for justice in light of the physical and moral injury caused by those who were tasked to protect them. As a result of the folly of leaders and perpetrators, many who have now passed away, the sins of the past are even now causing long term consequences for those organizations. Some have settled out of court with plaintiffs, but that did not end the problem. The reputational damage that has been done to these organizations, as well as the broader body of Christ, are documented to be, at best, a stumbling block to those who might otherwise follow Christ. Worse, I have met and spoken with parents of children who have fallen away from the faith as a result of their trauma on the mission field. I have often mused whether there might be a string of millstones ready to hand out at the Judgement for the necks of those who have either directly hurt children or whose poor handling and mismanagement of these incidents led to children leaving the faith as a result of their moral injury.

To be clear, I am so very thankful that the majority of mission organizations are not like what I have just described. Sadly, far too many of the good organizations are paying the price for the negligence of others. However, the global missions movement is filled with individuals who Anna describes in chapter 20 as "spiritual nobility." These are leaders who are defined as *"people with high moral character and a decorous manner of behaving."* If you must boast, boast in the Lord. I want to boast that these are the people who make me proud of their demonstrated Great Commission zeal and their stewardship of security in the context of ministry before the Lord. Likewise, I want to boast of the godly example of Anna and Neal Hampton. They both have made such a great impact on God's Kingdom around the world. In spite of all their hardships, traumas, and sacrifices on the mission field, they continue to say to the Lord, "Here am I, send me!" That witness is catalytic, blesses the Lord, and advances this Kingdom. I pray that those who read *Facing Fear* would not only be able to wisely count the cost of obedience but be empowered to have a similar boldness to take wise risks for the Lord as they count the cost of obedience. These are the people I hope one day to hear God say to them, "Well done My good and faithful servant." THAT DAY the ultimate consequences of risk and obedience will truly be WORTH IT.

In Christ,
Scott Brawner
Concilium President
Executive Director, Risk Management Network

Introduction

*If you want a religion to make you feel really comfortable,
I certainly don't recommend Christianity.*[1]
—C. S. Lewis

Graham Staines and his sons, Philip, age ten, and Timothy, age six, were sleeping in their old Willys four-wheel drive station wagon on January 22, 1999, outside the local church in the village of Manoharpur in Kendujhar, India. The night was quiet, and all three were asleep. Suddenly, angry, screaming men encircled their car. A thundering noise on the vehicle terrified them. A mob of over one hundred Hindus swarmed around them, yelling, pounding, and rocking the car. Graham could see there was no way to flee through the mob, and even if they did, they'd likely be beaten to death.

Then the mob did what mobs frequently do—malevolence which none would commit if they were just one person. They doused the car with gasoline. Acridity permeated the car; Graham and his sons saw the flames, and smoke began to fill the air. Fire engulfed the vehicle, blocking any attempt to escape. Graham realized he could not do what his father's instinct demanded of him: he could not protect his sons from the terror and pain. He wrapped his arms around them, embracing them tightly.

> I wonder
> did Graham pray out loud
> as he shielded his sons with his body?
> I reflect on
> what that was like,
> young Philip and Timothy,
> burying their heads in their dad's chest,
> fear filling their tummies,
> hearing,
> smelling,
> seeing?

"Even in death, they were inseparable. Charred beyond recognition and reduced to fragile frames of ashes, the three bodies lay clinging to each other in what must have been a vain attempt to protect each other."[2] Their killers were upheld as heroes by many in the Hindu community.

---

1 Lewis, *God in the Dock*, 58.
2 IBS, "Graham Staines Story."

"Gladys sang 'Because He Lives' at [their funeral]. She [forgave] those who had murdered her beloved husband and two sons," leaving her widowed and her daughter fatherless. "Because of these events, Christ [was] proclaimed [on the front pages of Indian newspapers]. In the face of persecution, many are coming to Jesus from families that have rejected the gospel for years."[3]

Violent occurrences like this one are not uncommon in areas of the world hostile to Christianity. As will be shown later, locations with active terrorist and jihadist groups[4] correlate with the greatest persecution.

Twenty-first century ministry in these places is characterized by uncertainty, risk, intensifying surveillance, targeted intimidation, complex conflicts, blended threats, and escalating persecution with exceedingly high numbers of Christian martyrs in the past century. Those advancing Christ's kingdom in such hostile and dangerous situations find themselves at the same time navigating a digitized, terrorized, globalized world. Fear is understandably present, so courage is essential in cross-cultural risk!

If courage is critical, what does it act, talk, and feel like when advancing Christ's kingdom in such high-risk situations? We think we know what courage is, but it's a bit disconcerting to realize that even Plato, the father of philosophy and one of the most brilliant minds in human history, could not identify it:

"For I fancy that I do not know the nature of courage; but, somehow or other, she has slipped away from me, and I cannot get hold of her and tell her nature."[5]

If we can define courage, then what are the critical elements of "mature courage," and how do we develop that courage in our own lives? Is it possible to "mother boldness"[6] instead of risk aversion so that we develop personal resiliency and endurance to keep pressing forward?

This book is a sequel to my first book, *Facing Danger: A Guide through Risk*, and builds on the discussion that began there. *Facing Fear: The Journey to Mature Courage in Risk and Persecution* develops and synthesizes additional elements of a practical theology of risk that works and is forged in the fires of my own real-world experience as a woman, wife, mother, and humanitarian organizational staffer living in a high-risk war zone. I also draw on my own research, years of providing risk-consulting to organizations and teams around the world, multi-disciplinary consultation with numerous experts, and my theological reflection over almost two decades.

---

3 IBS.
4 Gardner, "Jihadist Groups Around."
5 Plato, "Laches."
6 Harter, "Inmost Fear," 47.

In *Facing Danger*, I discussed two key concepts that laid the foundation for both books: the definition of a theology of risk and the three critical elements of a theology of risk. These two concepts struck a chord with many global workers seeking a holistic, biblical foundation to explain risking their lives for Christ.

I recall a veteran international worker—an older woman who had spent thirty years in service in the Middle East—coming up to Neal and me and thanking us for finally giving her the vocabulary to understand and explain her life. She spoke and acted like a woman liberated from the heavy burden of not understanding the meaning behind her and her family's suffering. Naming and vocabulary are sometimes all that is needed for soul freedom.

I admit being humbly surprised at how many have been touched by *Facing Danger* and the two-day Risk Assessment and Management Training (RAM Training) written by my husband Neal, which we have facilitated worldwide. Neal and I are honored to get to know so many Christ-followers and to teach the practical techniques and primary principles of a holistic theology of risk.

The primary intended audience of *Facing Fear* is the global family of Christ facing risk and persecution. International workers and local Christ-followers seeking to prepare themselves for enduring well through high risk and persecution will find this information valuable. Encouragement comes when we are given vocabulary to name the reality internally and externally. This book adds a useful resource to the ministry toolbox for those desiring to deepen their awareness of human tendencies and assumptions while decision-making under extreme pressure.

Risk Definitions and Limitations

Before diving deeper into managing our fears and cultivating mature courage, several definitions and a summary of the two key concepts I mentioned earlier are necessary. Firstly, cross-cultural risk (CCR) is "The potential for loss and gain when following Christ."[7] Notice that there is potential for loss *and* gain. Since sin's destructive force was unleashed, humanity's operating system frequently defaults to fear. While it's normal to focus on the loss, eternally substantial gains are always made when risking our lives for Christ. We want to keep that truth in mind throughout this discussion on fear, courage, risk, and persecution.

---

7 In *Facing Danger*, the definition of cross-cultural risk did not include "and gain." This definition is modified in *Facing Danger* 2nd Ed. (2024) We've been teaching the full definition in the RAM Training since 2016.

However, since writing *Facing Danger*, I've realized that the term "cross-cultural risk" is inadequate to fully encapsulate the global situation (see chapter one). It leaves out the experiences of a significant section of Christ-followers around the world: a foreigner experiencing cross-cultural risk faces different ramifications than a person in their own culture.

"Intercultural[8] Risk" (ICR) may also be used to describe the loss, threats, risks, persecutions, and gains (new Christ-followers) faced by our brothers and sisters living and ministering in home cultures. However, this term is also limiting in that it doesn't include those ministering cross-culturally. What term incorporates the entire global family of Jesus Christ in risk and persecution?

After consultation with personal friends from the global church, I've settled on the term "witness risk."[9] A witness is someone whose identity is in Christ, who bears witness to their relationship with Jesus, the Son of God. Witness risk is the potential for loss and gain when following Christ. It is what any Christ-follower faces while working in adverse, dangerous circumstances, especially when the gospel is proclaimed. This term is immediately and easily translatable into all cultures that already have the New Testament word for witness in their Bibles.

I also use the term "Christ-follower," which refers to anyone who walks in the way of Jesus as their Lord and Savior, no matter their church tradition or denomination. "Christ-follower" includes both global workers crossing cultures to share the gospel and local believers remaining within their culture groups who face risk and danger as they share the gospel. Thus, we have Christ-

> Witness risk is the potential for loss and gain when following Christ.

followers engaged in witness risk, defined as the potential for loss and gain when following Christ. For the remainder of this book, when I use "witness risk" I mean *both* CCR and ICR. Often, while there are some differences, the lived experience of Christ-followers in danger is similar.

This book is not a "theology" of persecution or martyrdom and does not systematically examine Scripture on topics discussed within this book. That work has been done by Ton (1997), Cunningham (1997), and Penner

---

8 Lewis, "How Cultures Work." The term "intercultural" was possibly coined by anthropologist Edward T. Hall in 1959. Dr. Lewis is an experienced expert on intercultural missions. Geert Hofstede developed it further. in his work on cultures.

9 Thank you to an individual on the Leadership Team at All Nations. Your input catalyzed our thinking and global discussion.

(2004), to name a few I'm aware of from Western research. While these studies provide an excellent service to the global church, my focus is to look more closely at the specific types of persecution and hostility in the Greek New Testament and offer a reasonable response. It's hard to mitigate[10] the general concept of persecution but easier to mitigate specific types of danger and persecution. To do so, I've organized persecution into categories. The primary Scriptural focus of this book is the early church experience of risk, persecution, and martyrdom as described in the New Testament.

A word on risk terminology: my work synthesizes a wide variety of thinking to push further the studies and understanding of witness risk. "[Synthesis combines] seemingly disparate and obviously related things into a [coherent] whole whose characteristics are greater than the sum of the individual parts."[11] I hope this book will contribute to the conversation on a practical theology of risk. In this book and in *Facing Danger*, I purposefully used or not used key industry terminology and concepts from the fields of risk and security. As in other industries that perform risk assessment, terms are not always used in the same way with the same definitions. A crucial distinction between witness risk and other types of risks (business risk, medical risk, etc.) is that witness risk does not have the same values and long-term goals as other risk endeavors.

This book is not intended to be comprehensive on the security topics discussed throughout. My goal is to introduce key issues and ground them within a framework of a theology of risk for the benefit of the global church. For security reasons, certain significant best practices have been purposefully left out (this is being shrewd as a serpent!). This book should not be considered a comprehensive resource for security practices best obtained through training by the experts.

The second primary concept to summarize from *Facing Danger* is the definition of a theology of risk. It includes people:

1. Whose solid foundation is a trust in God
2. Who have a clear and specific calling to that specific risk (chosen or selected by God)
3. Whose risks are acts of worship that lead to a sacrifice of worship.

See the next page for more on foundation, selection, and worship.

---

10 In both *Facing Danger* and *Facing Fear*, I use the term "mitigate" synonymously with "management."

11 Hall and Citrenbaum, *Intelligence Analysis*, 314.

Figure 1: Theology of Risk

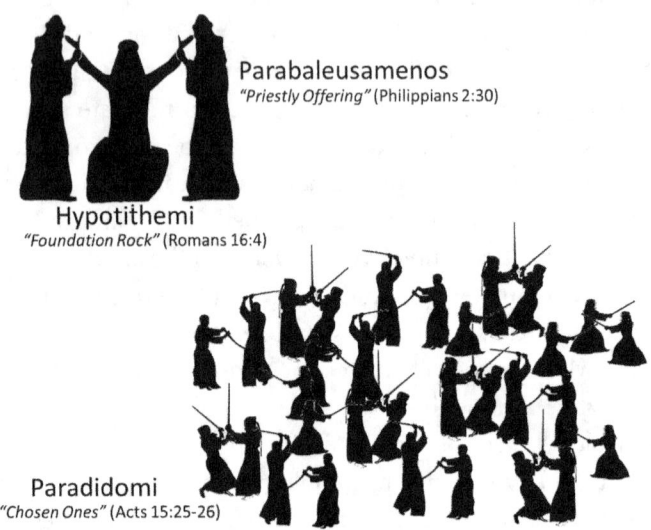

© 2022 Neal & Anna Hampton

1. Foundation

Our confidence in risk is upon our sovereign God, who is over all things and supports all things. We trust in, cling to, and rely upon him first and foremost. He is supreme.

2. Selection

God, who inspires and guides all things, directs our movement into or out of risk. Risk is primarily a situational question, not a conceptual one. God handpicks select people to move into specific risk for his particular purposes. It is a myth that God calls all people to all risks; in Scripture we see this isn't true.

Esther was called in her situation to do one thing. Shadrach, Meshach, and Abednego were called not to bow before the idol, but Daniel wasn't in that fiery furnace situation. Some believers risked their lives in Ephesus, but Paul, secreted out of the city, was not called to risk at that time. It's easy to judge outside appearances, but sometimes it is the least likely people that God calls to risk—not the one who looks so capable.

3. Worship

Our motivation toward risk is the adoration of God. He is worthy. Our devotion goes beyond negligible acts of admiration for God and draws us toward meaningful sacrifices filled with peril.

a) When we are motivated to risk our lives for our glory, what people will say or think about us, or the adrenaline rush of excitement, we are not risking out of a motivation to worship him.

b) If we risk our lives, but our relationships are characterized as constantly in conflict, we may not be risking out of worship.

c) If we are angry at the culture, suspicious of everyone, and can't find anyone to trust, we aren't risking from a motivation to worship him.

d) If we slander our teammates and refuse reconciliation even while facing death threats, our risks are not taken out of love and worship of God.

When we risk, our daily actions and relationships reveal an outworking of our love for God and others by keeping short accounts when we mess up. Risk motivated by worship means we love even those who are our enemies.

My husband was the country director of a humanitarian organization when we lived in Kabul. Once we grasped these solid elements of a theology of risk, he found that his understanding expanded the scope of his questions. Instead of primarily asking, "What's our contingency from a security standpoint?" he started with, "What's our foundation?" and "On what or whom are we (am I) relying?" Instead of asking, "Who on my team is best equipped to face this risk?" he asked, "Who is God choosing for this risk?" Finally, instead of "What can I preserve and protect?" he asked, "In what ways am I invited to risk as worship?"

Having a solid theology of risk increases resiliency in the face of danger. Resiliency is strengthened when we know what it means to have mature courage and we are equipped to manage fear.

Mature courage helps us know whether we need to stand firm, move forward, or retreat to fight another day. There is a difference between courageous retreat and cowardly retreat, between courageously remaining and cowardly remaining. When we act courageously, our souls are enlarged, and the fruit of the Spirit becomes increasingly visible in our lives. Our spirits become purified, full of power, and firm. In this, God is glorified, and the peace that surpasses human understanding descends and guards our hearts and minds.[12]

> Mature courage helps us know whether we need to stand firm, move forward, or retreat to fight another day.

---

12 Hampton, *Facing Danger*, xiii.

Figure 2: Core Specialties

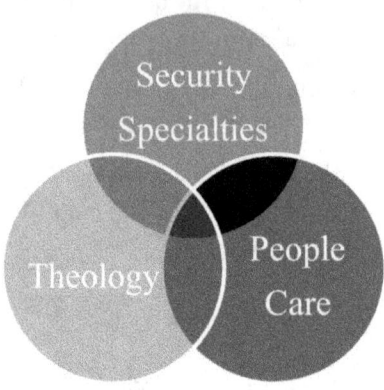

© 2022 Neal & Anna Hampton

Figure 2 depicts the three core areas of a practically applied theology of risk. "Security specialties" refers to all the security training topics relevant to Christ-followers ministering in dangerous situations. It includes learning such things as counter surveillance (the process of detecting and mitigating hostile surveillance),[13] avoiding and surviving kidnapping, how to handle government interrogation, etc.

"People care" includes counseling, critical incident stress debriefing, trauma resolution counseling, and pastoral counseling. Policies, standards of care, pre-field preparation, and training are also significant parts of people care and how well people are prepared for risk and persecution.

The theology circle includes all aspects of a theology of risk. This circle also touches on the theologies of mission, family, failure, uncertainty, the Holy Spirit, suffering, stewardship, emotions, and evil. Because needs vary, the Risk Assessment and Management (RAM) Training, *Facing Danger*, and this book try to equip Christ-followers to identify from which of these areas—Theology, Security Specialties, and People Care—they need more training and resourcing to prepare for their calling more effectively.

Training companies have sprung up in many countries, providing specialty security training to Christians working in places with elevated risk. The "Global Risk Resource" document tries to list all the pertinent training entities for each of these three areas and is updated regularly. It is found at www.theologyofrisk.com.

This book introduces significant critical areas of risk from a faith-based perspective, integrating how fear and courage operate in these situations.

---

13 Stratfor, *How to Look*, 7.

All the data points to much higher rates of martyrdom of Christ-followers in the past hundred years. The burgeoning available research enlightens us as to how we naturally operate in fear and danger and respond to risks. Men and women going out to serve our Lord "can no longer afford to remain ignorant of critical [risk] issues and questions that used to be only in the domain of psychologists, soldiers, and mathematicians."[14] That means some "translation" is required to take the best from secular research and security practice, view it through the lens of a Christo-centric understanding and motivation, and apply it to fear management and decision-making in high-risk areas while facing persecution. That's the aim of this book.

It is natural to feel fear when threats are breathing down our necks, and we daily experience intimidation and harassment from our communities, governments, and families. We may be ashamed to admit feeling overwhelmed by fears, threats, and continual loss. We often do not know what courage acts and feels like in such treacherous situations.

When we have ordered our fears, recognized and named the reality we find ourselves in, and focused the eyes of our hearts on him, we will at that moment see the next courageous step he is calling us to take. May the following discussion provide rich clarity on identifying and living out enduring mature courage *despite* our fears as we endeavor to faithfully persevere through risk and persecution for his kingdom.

He is worthy.

Anna E. Hampton
Minnesota, 2023

---

14 Williams, *Reflections from Plato's Cave*, 3.

Part One

The Twenty-First Century Challenge

Chapter 1
When Your Back Is Against the Wall

> *And given the elusive psychology of courage, it is often the case that the surer knowledge of our cowardice will give us some access to the uncertain knowledge of our courage.*[1]
> —William Ian Miller

"You're so courageous! I could never do what you do!"

I'd frequently hear this statement after sharing at supporting churches about our lives and work in the Middle East. Honestly, I'm sure some of my projected confidence included a sense of adventure that propelled me to jump on planes and travel halfway around the world. But if a sense of adventure is the motivation, can it be courageous? What *is* courage? Do I have enough of it? Must a person be fearless all the time, or sometimes brave and sometimes cowardly?

We want to *seem* courageous to others, so we say things that sound brave to society. Courage, connected to fear and cowardice, is more than being patient and enduring suffering. Is courage defined as a description of deeds, a character trait, or motivation that propels us to act?[2] Or do we need to ask different questions entirely?

Those who are innocent of battle terror speak blithely of fear and courage.[3] Tim O'Brien, a soldier in the Vietnam War, thought deeply about courage and how to explain it. From his experiences on the battlefield and his study of Plato in *Laches*, O'Brien realized that it is hard to precisely identify what courage is.

"It's the charge, the light brigade with only one man, that is the first thing to think about when thinking about courage. People who do it are remembered as brave, win or lose, and are heroes forever. It seems like courage, the charge [but] it's hard to be brave, and it's hard to know what bravery is."[4]

From Aristotle to the Twenty-First Century

Possibly more than any other virtue, the concept of courage has been debated for over two millennia. So much of modern-day thinking about risk, danger, fear, and courage stems back to Plato and Aristotle.

---

1 Miller, *Mystery of Courage*, x.
2 Miller, ix, x.
3 Inge, *Tour of Bones*, 6.
4 O'Brien, *If I Die*, 134.

In his book, *The Mystery of Courage*, Miller describes the shape and style of courage.[5] First, Aristotelian courage belongs only to male warriors ready to die and marching forward to the battlefield; they die in a forward attacking position. Aristotle found no virtue or courage in retreat, and he believed that the person who never struggles with fear is the most virtuous and courageous. Ethical courage (the good) is courage on the battlefield in defense of Greek cities.[6]

Secondly, since the time of the ancient Greeks, courage has implied specific physical characteristics. The man of courage is often represented physically by the youthful, blond Norse male body in Olympic shape. According to Plato, courage is the lynchpin that holds all four main virtues together, so overweight people are never depicted in writings or art as courageous. Assumedly, they are overweight because they lack temperance; therefore, they lack courage.

Thirdly, cowardice also embodies particular features—the skinny, spindly, short guy is rarely depicted as the courageous one. Even moral courage is displayed physically: we "Stand tall," "Stand up," "Stand firm," and "Don't take it lying down."

Finally, the primary picture of courage in Western thought for women is Joan of Arc (also depicted as ethnically white), with her Romanized metal battle attire as she sits on her warhorse. Miller says that "there is no favored body type that is both female and courageous that is not substantially masculinized."[7]

When it comes to courage, a vulnerable female image is rarely used. Consider the fearsome, physical, and spiritually courageous image of the twenty-two-year-old new mother, Perpetua, her breasts dripping with milk, rearranging her hair, disheveled from the bull's attacks (a modest woman's hair should not be down in public), in the middle of the arena in Carthage on the seventh of March, AD 203.[8] She refused to deny Christ even though it meant leaving her baby motherless, guiding the gladiator's sword to her own throat when the bull didn't kill her.

After Aristotle and Plato came the Stoics and Epicureans. Stoic philosophy extended Aristotle's teaching on fear even further, defining fear as an irrational emotion to be repudiated. For the Epicureans, no type of fear was acceptable, even the fear of death.

---

5 Miller, *Mystery of Courage*, 185–200.
6 Plato, "Laches."
7 Miller, *Mystery of Courage*, 189.
8 Moore, "Perpetua, An Early Christian."

When we consider Jesus and our humanity, fear seems so much a part of what it means to be human that to see Jesus as fully human, it's possible to consider him feeling fear. We may even have to see him afraid. In Christ, both human and divine, it is possible to have fear and not sin.

Three of the Gospels mention what sounds like his fear.[9] In Gethsemane: "Father, if it be possible, let this cup pass from me" (Matt 26:39). Scientists explain that when Jesus was sweating drops of blood, he was having a severe physiological response to a dread fear (horror).[10] The cup is his suffering of having the evil, vile sins of the entire history of the world placed upon him, the utter separation from his Father, and the horror of submitting to one of the most painful, shameful, and terrifying deaths[11] known. However, these passages of our Lord's passion threw Origen, an early church father, into a third-century uproar.

Origen denies that Christ felt fear in facing his crucifixion. Dr. Ernie Manges writes,

> Origen's view was influenced by his adoption of the four cardinal virtues of Plato: prudence, justice, temperance, and fortitude. Like several other early Christian writers, Origen adopted these four cardinal virtues from Aristotle and Plato: prudence (which Origen calls wisdom), justice, fortitude (courage), and temperance. And so, he says a Christian should let God reign over him, not fear, which is the counterpart to fortitude.[12]

In Origen's *Exhortation to Martyrdom*, he referenced Christ's prayer at Gethsemane (Matt 26:39). Origen says that some "may think that the Savior was in a way afraid." Origen then cites Psalm 27:1–3, and states Christ cannot be inferior to the Psalmist, and indeed that the Psalm refers to Christ:

> Who because of the powerful protection given him by God is afraid of no man. The heart of the Savior never feared when the whole camp of Satan was drawn up against Him. His heart, filled with divine knowledge, was confident in God when war rose against Him. It is therefore impossible that the same man should say in fear, "Father, if it be possible, let this cup pass from me"; and with fortitude: "*Though an army encamps against me, my heart shall not fear; though war arise against me, yet I will be confident.*" (Ps 27:3)[13]

---

9 Matt 26; Mark 14; Luke 22.
10 Jerajani, Jaju, Phiske, Lade, Nitin, "Hematohidrosis—A Rare Clinical," 290–92.
11 Roland Muller, *Honor & Shame*, Kindle Location 397.
12 Adamantius, *Homilies on Luke*, 152. And Author discussions with Dr. Manges, PhD, Early Church History.
13 Adamantius, *Homilies on Luke*, 152. Origen himself proved to be a person of fortitude and faithful to Christ to the end. As a teen, he wanted to join his father, arrested for the crime of being a Christian, but apparently, his mother prevented that by hiding Origen's clothes. At the end of his life, he was tortured during the persecution under Emperor Decius and probably died of those wounds a couple of years later.

While Origen's example of faithful endurance in serving Christ is exemplary, I differ from his interpretation and understanding of fear. The writer of Hebrews (vv. 2:17 and 4:15) makes it clear that Jesus was tempted in every way as we are, yet without sin. This includes the temptation to let fear paralyze and overtake us. Yet Jesus did not give in to fear and instead moved forward in obedience and courage to his calling to die a terrifying death on the cross.

In the thirteenth century, Thomas Aquinas transformed Aristotelian courage from simply being defined as a noble death on the battlefield to a broader definition. The one principal act of perfect courage is found in the ideal martyr, Jesus Christ, as the paradigm of a courageous person.[14] He stated that endurance is the chief act of courage since it is more challenging than aggression (in battle). He wrote, "The principal act of courage is to endure and withstand dangers doggedly rather than attack them."[15] While Aquinas offers a more helpful description, it is still limiting what may be considered courageous. What about those led by Christ out of danger? Is that not courageous?

Finally, here are some excerpts of sermons preached in 2020 in the middle of the COVID-19 pandemic on the topic of fear from Sermon Central:[16]

- *"Simply trust Jesus, and your fears will disappear."*
- *"True Christians don't fear death."*
- *"Think of some things tempting you to flirt with worry and disobey God."*
- *"I want us delivered from the spirit of fear."* (While the Bible speaks of a spirit of fear, this statement implies that all fear is from the devil.)
- *"If you are afraid today, you have forgotten who God is."*
- *"Faith is the opposite of fear; fear is sin so ignore your fear."*
- *"We need to live a life free of fear."*
- *"At the crossroads of faith and fear, choose faith."*[17]
- *"When facing fear, faith, or foolishness, choose faith."*

From this progression of thinking and teaching on fear and courage over the past twenty-five hundred years comes the false idea that courage is risking our lives for Christ without fear and not retreating from danger.

---

14 Qiaoying, "Aquinas' Transformation," 483.

15 Aquinas, *Summa Theologica*, IIb, 123–28.

16 Sermon Central, "Fear."

17 I just heard this preached again on a Sunday morning in an American church, February 2022. While it's true we want to choose faith, it implies the way to handle fear is to ignore it. It is a pithy statement that does not equip or clarify.

> The kind of people we designate as courageous or fearful reveals our cultural values.

When Christ-followers carry this perspective into dangerous situations, it often leads to confusion, discouragement, and disempowerment.

Mistaking Greco-Roman definitions and the resulting Western worldview for biblical teaching on fear and courage not only does violence to this topic and God's people while misrepresenting what the Bible teaches, but also results in poor shepherding of people who risk their lives for Christ daily. Life's most profound questions demand critical and thoughtful deliberation. The kind of people we designate as courageous or fearful reveals our cultural values.

Christ-followers living in hostile situations and daily encountering threats naturally feel fear. Howard Thurman, author of *Jesus and the Disinherited*, writes,

> The fear encountered daily at the root of the relationship] between the weak and the strong, between the controllers of the environment and those who are controlled by it … arises out of the sense of isolation and helplessness … in the perpetual threat of violence everywhere.[18]

Not being able or allowed to fight back, not understanding the meaning of the reality of what is happening, or being the recipient of personally targeted evil and violence often may cause paralysis and resignation. Thurman continues, "The masses of men and women live with their backs constantly against the wall. They are the poor, the disinherited, the dispossessed."[19]

Framing the Global Reality

Thurman, a pastor in the mid-twentieth century, wrote about the daily reality of oppression experienced by Blacks in America. Extending Thurman's description of "their backs against the wall" to Christ-followers worldwide suffering constant oppressive persecution, what are we facing if our backs are against the wall? It can be summarized with this simple quote: "Christianity has become, by far, the most persecuted religion."[20]

According to secular research by the non-partisan think tank, the Pew Research Center, about three-fourths of the world's population lives under a government that has extensively restricted religious freedoms.[21] According to Cochran,

---

18 Thurman, *Jesus and the Disinherited*, 37.
19 Thurman, 13.
20 Montgomery, "New Age."
21 Cochran, "What Kind of Persecution?" 34. The importance of Cochran's article should not be underestimated.

Of those restrictions, the vast majority are aimed at Christians. Some international humanitarian agencies have estimated that 80% of all religious persecution in the world today is aimed at Christians. The Catholic Bishops Conference estimates that number to be only slightly lower, around 75%. Whatever the actual percentage, the reality is undeniable: "Christians are the single most widely persecuted religious group today. This is confirmed in studies by sources as diverse as the Vatican, Open Doors, the Pew Research Center, *Newsweek*, and *The Economist*. The problem of Christian persecution is vast, involving more than 135 countries."[22]

Defining Persecution

Defining persecution is a subject of much debate. "There is, unfortunately, no universally accepted legal or theological definition of [persecution]."[23] How persecution is defined impacts how data is collected and reality is framed. Naming, a task given to humanity in Genesis 2:19, is still a task for us to engage in today. How we name and what we name, describes the reality we see. After wading

> How we name and what we name, describes the reality we see.

through numerous definitions and discussions of the definition of persecution, Charles Teiszen's definition seems to be the most helpful and thorough. In his book, *Re-Examining Religious Persecution: Constructing a Theological Framework for Understanding Persecution*, he combines both a religious, socio-political, and theological definition through a three-stage model.

First, Teiszen discusses aspects of the challenge of defining persecution. Some approach it as though it was an experience of the early church, so it doesn't exist today. Others, especially in the West, limit it only to eschatology; in other words, persecution is a sign-post of the end times but not really something that happens to all Christians. Others think of persecution only in terms of violence and brutality reported in the majority world.

Still others make the mistake of equating suffering and perecution. The problem with this is that suffering asks different questions than persecution does, although obviously, they are closely related. It's crucial to recognize that persecution includes martyrdom, and that martyrdom is a subset of persecution. The history and twenty-first century reality of martyrdom is aptly described by the Center for the Study of Global

---

22 Cochran, 34.
23 Penner, *In the Shadow*, 163.

Christianity (CSGC) at Gordon Conwell Seminary. Note that martyrdom is the second-to-last step in persecution, as the one final step occurs after death: Christians not being allowed to bury their dead, or the bones of those martyred dug up by their persecutors and scattered. Whether in death or life, Christians are hunted and pursued.

Teiszen also points out that persecution is not defined by the level of pain, not all persecution is religious, and Christ-followers are to have a theological expectation of persecution. Finally, he discusses the aspect that rarely is religon or any other single motivation the only factor in persecution and martyrdom.[24]

With these aspects and limitations in mind, Teiszen's expanded definition of Christian persecution:

> Any unjust action of mild to intense levels of hostility, directed at Christians of varying levels of commitment, resulting in varying levels of harm, which may not necessarily prevent or limit these Christian's ability to practice their faith or appropriately propagate their faith as it is considered from the victim's[25] perspective, each motivation having religion, namely the identification of its victims as "Christian," as its primary motivator.[26]

For the purposes of this book, this is the definition I am using and expand on in chapter two. Two significant Christian entities gather data on aspects of the global persecution of Christ-followers.[27] They each define persecution differently, resulting in widely diverging counts of martyrs.[28] Between Open Doors and the Center for the Study of Global Christianity (CSGC), the numbers of martyrs range from twelve hundred

---

24 Sauer and Howell, *Suffering, Perseuction, and Martyrdom*, 159–72.
25 In the U.S. in 2022, the word "victim" has come to mean something other than the traditional definition. I would assume Teiszen means those who are on the receiving end of the hostility are the victims, but not automatically victimized. We always have a choice of how we will respond to tribulation.
26 Teiszen, *Re-Examining Religious Persecution*, 47.
27 Open Doors International describes persecution using eight primary persecution engines in their Complete World Watch Research Methodology Paper on page 14. Three additional significant sources for research include (1) *The Global War on Christians* (John Allen, 2013); (2) Gender and Religious Freedom Organization (UK); and (3) The International Journal for Religious Freedom.
28 Open Doors definition of persecution: "Any hostility experienced as a result of one's identification with Christ. This can include hostile attitudes, words, and actions toward Christians. This broad definition includes (but is not limited to) restrictions, pressure, discrimination, opposition, disinformation, injustice, intimidation, mistreatment, marginalization, oppression, intolerance, infringement, violation, ostracism, hostilities, harassment, abuse, violence, ethnic cleansing, and genocide." See the CSGC definition in footnote 31 below.

to one hundred thousand people per year.[29] Because there is such a wide divergence of numbers, it seems the two data sets are not comparable (I discuss the dangers of using incomparable data sets in chapter 11). Open Doors research wholistically describes the reality of persecution country by country.[30] The CSGC research and reporting on persecution primarily focuses on martyrs, publishing the number of Christian martyrs globally every year.[31] "Since the Church's founding, nearly seventy million Christians have been killed for their faith. Even more remarkable than this statistic is that the great majority of these—nearly sixty-five percent—were martyred in the twentieth century alone."[32]

The Reality

According to the WWL 2022,[33] in 2021 there have been

- over 360 million Christians living in places where they experience high levels of persecution and discrimination,
- over 5000 churches and Christian buildings attacked,
- almost 6200 believers detained without trial, arrested, sentenced, or imprisoned, and
- over 3800 Christians abducted.

This data means that one in seven believers worldwide experiences high levels of persecution.

Keeping a "snapshot" of the Open Doors reporting on persecution and the CSGC research on global martyrs in our minds, we can add to our view on the global reality with additional research from the Joshua Project, Open Doors, and the Global Terrorism Database on the following maps.

---

29 See this discussion by Open Doors on why there is such incongruity in the reporting: "The Number of Christian Martyrs Continues to Cause Debate." Also, in *Sorrow & Blood: Christian Mission in Contexts of Suffering, Persecution, and Martyrdom* (2012), Chapter 5, Thomas Schirrmacher wrote the chapter, "A Response to the High Counts of Christian Martyrs Per Year," also addressing the discrepancy in the counting of martyrs.

30 Open Doors International, *Complete World Watch List Methodology* and "How the Scoring Works."

31 See Dr. Todd Johnson's report on "Martyrology: The Demographics of Christian Martyrdom" at the CSGC website, along with additional resources by Johnson and Zurlo. The CSGC short definition used for a Christian martyr is "Christian martyrs are defined as believers in Christ who have lost their lives prematurely, in situations of witness, as a result of human hostility." There are limitations of the Open Doors' definition of martyrs. For example, the five men killed by the Auca warriors in 1956 would not be classified as martyrs based on the Open Doors definition, nor would John Chau in 2018.

32 Sauer and Howell, *Suffering, Persecution, and Martyrdom*, 159.

33 Open Doors. The 2022 World Watch List.

The dots on Map 1 exhibit Joshua Project's geographical analysis of unreached, unengaged people groups. While not shown on Map 1, a simple review of the fifty countries where it is most dangerous to follow Christ (as revealed by Open Doors research) overlaps the areas where most of the dots are clustered. Map 2 reveals the global terrorist incidents and attacks of the past forty-five years. Even a cursory examination reveals a horrifying overlap of concentrated terrorist attacks in the same areas as higher concentrations of unreached people groups located in the most hostile and hard places. These pictures reveal what security analysts have known for a long time: the places left to reach for Christ are the most dangerous. *The physical world reveals the spiritual world.*

However, it's important to highlight what these maps are *not* saying. There is a difference between correlation and causation. These maps reveal an apparent correlation between where most remaining unreached people groups are located and where it is most dangerous to follow Christ. The cause of terrorism and persecution should not be mistaken for labeling whole people groups as terrorists. Neal and I have enjoyed warm hospitality from many people where unreached people groups are clustered.

Map 1: Unreached People Groups

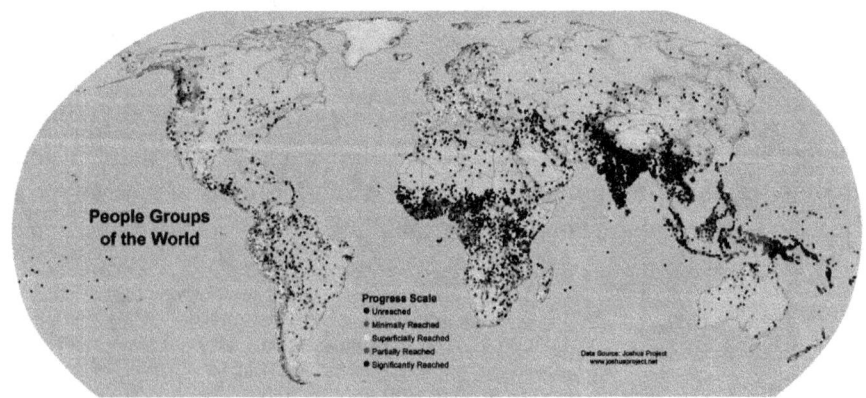

© Joshua Project

Map 2: Terrorism Map

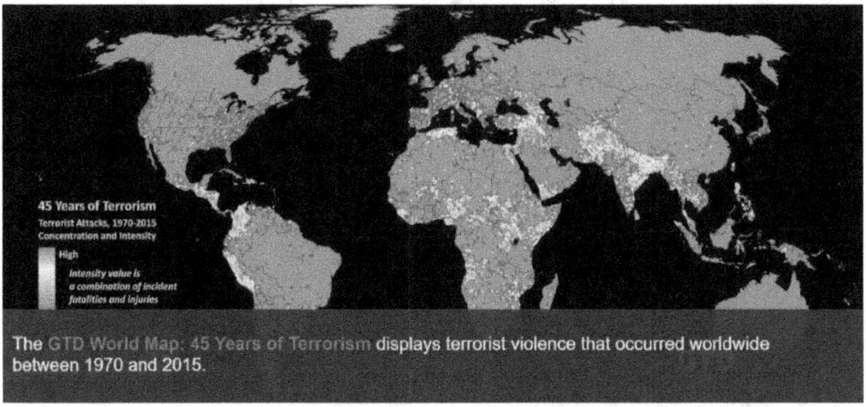

45 Years of Terrorism
Terrorist Attacks, 1970-2015
Concentration and Intensity

High

Intensity value is a combination of incident fatalities and injuries

The GTD World Map: 45 Years of Terrorism displays terrorist violence that occurred worldwide between 1970 and 2015.

Global Terrorism Database (used with permission)

To further see what is happening, we must look specifically at gendered persecution.[34] Open Doors has produced four annual "Same Faith Different Persecution Reports" on the reality of GSRP—Gender-Specific Religious Persecution. "The trends of increasing violence against women continue to grow unabated. GSRP occurs at a higher rate in countries experiencing conflict. Women and girls are more likely to be trafficked, seduced, sexually violated, forced to convert to Islam, forced to marry or flee the country and face an increased chance of abduction. Daughters of pastors are often targeted."[35]

Women's bodies as a battlefield—these "tools" are more and more widely used; the actual weaponizing of the female body to inflict harm on minority Christian communities and limit the church's growth.[36] Susan Brooks Thistlethwaite writes about women's bodies as battlefields. "Battlefields [are] places in a war where bodies are damaged, flesh is ripped apart, and minds and lives are destroyed." What do women's bodies as battlefields look like? She continues,

> All day long, all night long, every day and every night, the bodies of women and girls are turned into battlefields. Their bodies are penetrated against their will; they are burned, maimed, bruised, slapped, kicked, threatened with weapons, [drugged], confined, beaten with fists or objects, shot, knifed; their bones are broken, and they lose limbs, sight, hearing, pregnancies, and their sense of personal and physical integrity. They are terrorized, and they are killed.[37]

---

34 Open Doors has also begun publishing about targeted persecution against children of Christ-followers. For space, I did not discuss it in this book, but it is a current reality of global persecution.
35 Author's notes from a talk at the 2022 Refugee Highway Project Conference in Athens given by Helene Fisher, so I used both my notes and the GSRP paper to make this statement.
36 Brown, Fisher, Miller, Lane, Morley, "Same Faith Different Persecution," 2.
37 Thistlethwaite, *Women's Bodies as Battlefields*, 1.

This annual GSRP report also examines the specific violence against men. The primary forms of pressure against men and boys include "physical violence, economic harassment at work/job/business," forced inscription into the army or to take up arms, and imprisonment by the state. The report summarizes that the GSRP against women is "complex, hidden, and violent, and the GSRP of men is focused, severe, and visible."

> Every country (in the top fifty most hostile nations) is ranked as experiencing "very high" or "extreme" levels of persecution. Outside of the top [fifty, twenty-six] countries are [categorized] as having "very high" or "high" levels of persecution. The severity of persecution in countries on the list, demonstrated by the total points scored, has increased by more than [twenty percent] since 2014. This signifies an increased pressure in all areas of life for persecuted Christians.[38]

Avoiding the Global Reality

They are used to being sheep among sheep, not sheep among wolves.

Many global workers also do not want to face this reality. They often carry this same willful blindness to the existence of risks and persecution. One of the primary concerns of mission security personnel is summarized this way: "The most urgent concern is making security a priority in the minds of our people. They are used to being sheep among sheep, not sheep among wolves."[39]

Yet, what are some of the top fears global workers and their sending organizations listed simultaneously? In early 2022, I wrote an email to the Risk Management Network (RMN) members, asking three questions related to fear. RMN members represent approximately one-hundred North American missions security personnel. When asked, "What are the most common fears related to risk expressed in your organization?" The response included (in no particular order):

- Imprisonment
- Terrorism
- Crime
- Disease
- Preparation: Are we prepared well enough to manage a crisis?
- Armed muggings

---

38 Open Doors, "World Watch List."
39 Hampton, "Survey of RMN."

- Assault
- Gang threats
- Potential revolution (in the country of service)
- Fear of too much risk mitigation (too limiting for ministry work)
- Fear of knowing: "I don't want to know because then I might have to do something about it, which will hinder my ministry."
- Fear of putting children in harm's way due to the parents' missional calling.
- Fear of too-high risk: Where is the boundary between my call and being foolish?
- In some contexts, it is a concern about health, safety, and security. In a growing number of contexts, there are serious concerns about continued access.
- "I will be pulled out of my project and unable to return in a timely way." "Risk concerns are hindering me from productive work."
- There's fear that if we are too worried about the risks, it will cause us to shrink back from fulfilling our calling.
- From management/central office: Fears of limitations in caring for workers and communicating with family and churches in a crisis. Secondly are legal and reputational concerns. For expatriate workers, the most common fears are related to potential hostile actions from host country governments, surveillance of communication, and US-based office overreactions. For national workers, rumors of being targeted as an apostate.

It's a thought-provoking response. There are a variety of fears of violence listed, along with the fear of risk assessment and mitigation preventing or distracting from engaging in ministry and the stated preference not to know the reality. There seems to be fear of fear (what you imagine is almost always worse than the reality), unprocessed worries, and some irrational fears. The following chapter will delve further into the actual threats and realities of global workers' risks, which substantially overlap with the persecution categories described by Open Doors.

The problem remains: how can we bridge the gulf between our fears and the violent reality we face as a global body of Christ? Clarity on the issues surrounding our fears and how to manage anxiety in risk is beneficial. We must see and name the genuine dangers and prepare for them. But to see means to understand how we perceive and frame risk, and to see requires becoming more acutely aware of our biases and dangerous attitudes. Risk assessment and management are sacred acts of worship, and engaging in them equips global workers to make more effective decisions in the uncertainty and chaos of their situations. Naming reality, not only tames it, but also helps us cultivate greater endurance and resilience as we build relationships and demonstrate Christ's love to those who haven't yet heard. When we accomplish this aim, evil doesn't win. Righteousness wins. Christ wins.

The lived example of Jesus Christ still imbues us with power when we encounter ISIS, Boko Haram, a resurgent Taliban, Hindu militants, or any other evil group or regime. Jesus of Nazareth, a poor Jew from a minority group scratching existence and survival amid a dominating Greco-Roman super-power, sends us out in his name, love, and power, knowing we are vulnerable to attack, pain, suffering, and martyrdom. He intentionally taught a radical message of who to fear and how to order our fears as we learn to courageously serve him with a heart of love even when surrounded by a culture that hates him and him-in-us. He is worthy.

People will do to you exactly what they did to me.
—Jesus (John 15:21, CEV)

Chapter 2
The Squeeze, the Smash, and the Rhomphaia

O Lord my God, ... create in me the faithfulness that moves you.[1]
—Joseph Tetlow, SJ

The last chapter briefly surveyed the darkness of the reality of persecution facing the global church today. Jesus normalized persecution in Luke 21:12, "But before all this, they will lay their hands on you and persecute you." He frames what will happen when we are sent out like a "sheep in the midst of wolves" (Matt 10:16). In the animal world, the survival probability of a lamb surrounded by a pack of wolves is extremely low.

Likewise, a Christ-follower living in a situation where people and governments are hostile to the gospel has a much higher likelihood of experiencing threats, increased risks, and persecution (tribulation). We are not victims of evil—we always have a choice of how we will respond to tribulation. There is a lot of "distracting noise" in dangerous situations. The unnamed is terrifying. Clarity is needed to name what the reality is, which means defining our terminology. We can't address a risk we don't understand, and to understand it, we have to identify and name it. This takes time and energy, which humans naturally want to avoid for many reasons. Avoiding risk assessment feels expedient but often results in poor stewardship of the vulnerable in risk (people) and needless suffering. Avoiding risk assessment on purpose is a type of cowardice. There is no faith, courage, and sacrifice in doing what feels expedient.[2]

Often, a crisis may be mistaken for risk or a risk for a crisis. "A crisis is a time-limited traumatic event that demands a response or intervention."[3] Yet if everything is "risk," then it becomes impossible to prioritize the risks and steward the resources at risk. When we do not name reality correctly, we are not living in it, and therefore we cannot effectively mitigate real dangers. Naming, understanding, and preparing for these dangers reduces our fear and anxiety and helps us strengthen or guard our weak points. Then we have more space in our souls to consider and reflect on how God is working within the risk or persecution situation and what losses *and gains* may be ahead.

---

1 Harter, "You Have Called," 14.
2 Peterson, *12 Rules*.
3 Carr, "Crisis Response Training Manual."

Greek Terms

The New Testament uses numerous Greek words to name the various risks, persecution, and suffering familiar to the early church and to us. The words below are included under the umbrella of persecution. The words were selected from every place in Scripture where the difficulties experienced by Christ's disciples due to their witness are mentioned. This fits Teiszen's approach in his (short) definition: "Any unjust action of varying levels of hostility, perpetrated primarily on the basis of religion, and directed at Christians, resulting in varying levels of harm as it is considered from the victim's perspective."[4] He also makes the crucial point that "the experience of persecution is contextual, but the presence of persecution is universal."[5]

> The experience of persecution is contextual, but the presence of persecution is universal.

The list of terms below demonstrates that all Christ-followers do experience persecution at some level of hostility. While I've tried to place them on a generally increasing scale of intensity of impact or severity, others may order them differently.[6] A risk axiom we often share in our RAM Training is, "severity is as severity is felt." Not all synonyms and references in the New Testament are included in the list.

Greek Terms

General Words:

- Persecute, chase, pursue, oppress, afflict: διώκω (*dioko*), Matthew 10:23; 13:21
- Risks: Hand over—παραδεδωκόσι (*paradidomi*), Acts 15:26; Gamble one's life— παραβολευσάμενος (*parabalueosomos*), Philippians 2:30; Expose one's neck to being killed—hiέθηκαν (*hypotithemi*), Romans 16:3
- Suffer: πάσχω (*pasha*), Matthew 16:21

Specific Words:

---

4 Teiszen, *Re-examining Religious Persecution*, 47.
5 Sauer and Howell, *Suffering, Persecution and Martyrdom*, 171.
6 Psychologists have mapped out well that humans differ in how we experience a stressor. What impacts one person severely may hardly impact a different person.

English Translation	Greek Translation	References
Not hear	ἀκούω (akouo)	Matthew 10:14
Not receive	δέχομαι (dechomai)	Matthew 10:14; Luke 10:10
Excluded/ostracized	ἀφορίζω (aphorizo)	Luke 6:22
Mistreat/mistreat with arrogance	ὑβρίζω (hybrizo)	Acts 14:5
Insult/harshly criticized	ὀνειδίζω (oneidizo)	Luke 6:22; 1 Peter 4:14
Ridicule/mock/make fun of	ἐμπαίζω (empaizo)	Matthew 20:19
Hostility	ἀντιλογία (antilogia)	Hebrews 12:3
To be publicly disgraced/made into a show	θεατρίζω (theatrizo)	Hebrews 10:33
Slandered/gossip	καταλαλέω (katalaleo)	1 Peter 3:16
Slandered, denigrated	Βλάσφημος (blasphemos)	Acts 6:11
False witnesses/lies against	ψευδὴς μάρτυς (pseudes martys)	Acts 6:13
Property plundered	ἁρπαγή (harpage)	Hebrews 10:34
To be cheated	ἐμπορεύομαι (emporeuomai)	2 Peter 2:3
Scorn your name	ἐκβάλλω (ekballo)	Luke 6:22
Threaten/verbal abuse/slander	ἐεπηρεάζω (epereazo)	Luke 6:28
Verbal abuse	λοιδορέω (loidoreo)	John 9:28; Acts 23:4; 1 Corinthians 4:12; 1 Peter 2:23
To hold a grudge, have it in for	ἐνέχω (enecho)	Mark 6:19
Rise up against, revolt, rebel	ἐπαναστήσονται (epanistemi)	Matthew 10:21
Stirred up against (crowds)	συγκινέω (synkineo)	Acts 6:12
Agitating, troubling, stirring up	σαλεύω (saleuo) and ταράσσω (tarasso)	Acts 17:13
Formed a mob	ὀχλοποιέω (ochlopoieo)	Acts 17:5
To incite people against (stir up the minds)	ἐπεγείρω (epegeiro)	Acts 14:2
To embitter people against	κακόω (kakoo)	Acts 14:2
Distress	στενοχωρία (stenochoria)	2 Corinthians 6:4
Constricting distress/acute anxiety	συνοχή (synoche)	Luke 21:25

English Translation	Greek Translation	References
Pressure/distress/tribulation	ἀνάγκη (ananke)	Luke 21:23; 2 Corinthians 12:10
Treated shamefully/dishonored	ἀτιμάζω (atimazo)	Mark 12:4
Hated	μισέω (miseo)	Matthew 10:22; Luke 6:22
Threats/warn	ἀπειλέω (apeile)	Acts 4:17, 21, 29, 9:1; Ephesians 6:9; 1 Peter 2:23
Conspired/plotted against	συμβούλιον (symboulion)	Matthew 12:14; Acts 9:23
Rioting/violent opposition/tumults/disorder/upheaval/insurrection	ἀκαταστασία (akatastasia)	2 Corinthians 6:5; Luke 21:9
Physically seized with force/arrested	κρατέω (krateo)	Mark 6:17
Dragged away	ἑλκύω (helkyo)	Acts 16:19
Attacking the house/battering the door	ἐφίστημι (ephistemi)	Acts 17:5
Snatched/grabbed	συναρπάζω (synarpazo)	Acts 6:12
Drag away	σύρω (syro)	Acts 8:3
Arrested/brought to judgment	ἄγωσιν (ago)	Mark 13:11
Arrest/apprehend	συλλαμβάνω (syllambano)	Acts 12:3
Robbery/open violence	ἁρπάζω (harpazo)	Matthew 11:12
Afflict/harass/distress/pressure/oppression/tribulation	θλῖψις (thlipseos)	Matthew 13:21; Acts 11:19
Lay waste to/harm (the church)	λυμαίνω (lymaino)	Acts 8:3
Stand (before rulers as a testimony)	ἵστημι (histemi)	Mark 13:9
Interrogation/bring before rulers	εἰσφέρω (eisphero)	Luke 12:11
Lead away (to give testimony)	ἀπάγω (apago)	Luke 21:12
Brought to judgment in court	ἀχθήσεσθε (achthesesthe)	Matthew 10:18
Lay hands on (to bring to jail)	ἐπιβάλλω (epiballo)	Acts 5:18
Betray/deliver over	παραδίδωμι (paradidomi)	Matthew 10:17, 10:21
Bind	δέω (deo)	Acts 9:14

English Translation	Greek Translation	References
Shackled	δεσμός (desmos)	Acts 20:23
Imprisoned	φυλακή (pylake)	Mark 6:17
Left in prison indefinitely	καταλείπω (kataleipo)	Acts 24:27
Suffer violence	βιάζω (biazo)	Matthew 11:13
Harm/evil/badness done to	κακός (kakos)	Acts 9:13
Danger	κίνδυνος (kindynos)	Romans 8:35; 2 Corinthians 11:26
Scourge/flog	μαστιγόω (mastigoo)	Matthew 10:17, 23:34
Beaten up/beat without trial/beat to flay the skin	δέρω (dero)	Mark 13:9; Acts 16:37
Beat with club, stick, fist	τύπτω (typto)	Acts 18:17
Beaten with rods	ῥαβδίζω (rhobdizo)	2 Corinthians 11:25
Tortured	τυμπανίζω (tympanizo)	Hebrews 11:35
Make war with the saints	πόλεμος (polemos)	Revelation 13:7
Execute/destroy	ἀναιρέω (anaireo)	Acts 5:33
Kill	ἀποκτείνω (apokteino)	Matthew 20:19, 23:34, 37
Crucify	σταυροω (stauroo)	Matthew 23:34
Behead	ἀποκεφαλίζω (apokephalizo)	Matthew 14:10
To stone	λιθοβολέω (lithoboleo)	Matthew 23:37
Destroy	πορθέω (portheo)	Acts 9:21
Imprisonment	φυλακή (phylake)	2 Corinthians 11:23
Murder	φονεύω (phoneuo)	Matthew 23:31; Acts 9:1
Legal murder (state sanctioned execution)	ἀναίρεσις (anairesis)	Acts 8:1
Eliminate/put to death/death/fatal illness/pestilence	θανατόω (thanatos)	Matthew 10:21

Table 1: Persecution Terms in English and Greek

Risk and Threat Terms

In *Facing Danger*, I explain the mechanics of risk assessment and mitigation, and in the RAM Training we guide participants through performing risk assessment and mitigation, so I won't discuss those here. In the security world (secular and Christian), the terms "risk," "threat," "danger," and "hazard" are often used interchangeably. I encourage the standardization of terminology by providing a glossary at the end. I invite further discussion and refinement of this glossary by cultural anthropologists (skilled in bridging Eastern and Western thinking), theologians, security professionals, and anyone with risk savviness engaging in faith-based risk assessment and management. Though the terms "threat assessment" and "risk assessment" in secular practice are sometimes (but not always) used to describe the same process, I will differentiate them in this discussion.

Assessing witness risk is primarily a forward-looking activity. We use recent past events to inform our forward-looking risk assessment evaluation, but information gathered from historic incidents is only one data point in our risk assessment. Because risk is a changing environment, we want to look at what is happening right now, in the present. What is the emotional temperature around us, the tempo of the threats being issued? What is currently preached in the local mosque, temple, or national TV station? These help us better see what the genuine risks are at that moment.

Threats are a source of harm to our goals. Threats are external; we have little control over them. Their origin is often identifiable, and they may be targeted toward a person or entity. I use "threat" in terms of witness risk, and I use "threat" primarily related to verbal threats directed at an individual, family, team, or organization. Threats imply intentionality. An analyst I consulted with described the focus of threat assessment: "Threat assessment is done regarding geopolitical threats, conflict threats, terrorism threats, or the threat of a localized mass shooting."[7] It's crucial to remember that the goal of any threat is to create fear and paralysis, but the threat could be hollow, with no substance to it. The New Testament uses different words for threat and risk. Etymologically, these are not Greek synonyms in the New Testament. Receiving a death threat requires nuanced assessment, addressed in the discussion on information analysis.

Threats add to the uncertainty and fog of risk and result in more challenging decision-making. One way of thinking about these two terms is "Risks are where threats and vulnerability meet."[8] Here's an equation that may help:

RISK = THREAT PROBABILITY × VULNERABILITY IMPACT[9]

For those who have taken our RAM Training or looked at the risk assessment and mitigation process we teach (see the RAM Action Guide), the graphic of four quadrants analyzes this equation: frequency, severity, geographic proximity, and demographic proximity. We simplify the equation, although its meaning remains the same:

---

7   Author's personal discussion with a security analyst.
8   The author in discussion with Scott Brawner of Concilium and Neal Hampton, February 2022.
9   "Threat, Vulnerability, Risk?"

RISK = PROBABILITIES × IMPACT

In stewardship, we explore what is vulnerable and prayerfully discern what God is asking us to do to steward those vulnerable resources in the risk. We evaluate the threat, then perform a risk assessment.[10] Risks are not necessarily targeted toward an entity, and we can mitigate the causes and consequences of the risk. Another way to describe the relationship between risk and threat is: "Risk is a function of the values of threat, [impact], and vulnerability ... Risk management [aims] to create a level of protection that mitigates vulnerabilities to threats and the potential consequences, thereby reducing risk to an acceptable level."[11]

It would be impossible to list every form of hostility experienced by Christ-followers worldwide. However, I have tried to identify the most prevalent forms of hatred faced by those engaging in witness risk. Right expectation anticipates that hostility originates from three primary sources: the government, the community, and the family, and these are broken down further in chapter ten in the section on "Actor Mapping."

However, the sequence, intensity, and frequency vary from situation to situation. Categories also tend to overlap because they are interrelated, but a framework helps us name and see reality more effectively. Open Doors uses "the squeeze" (the pressure Christians experience in all areas of life) and "the smash" (targeted violence). The modified framework below expands to include: Threats, the Squeeze, the Smash,[12] the Rhomphaia and finally, Collateral Violence.

Threats

Purposes for threats range from revenge or punishment to instilling fear and anxiety and manipulating or forcing a desired reaction, excitement, or attention. Anonymous and direct threats may be masked by religious language (i.e. revenge for converting from one religion to another). Threats against Christ-followers include but are not limited to:

- Threats calling for the genocide of all Christ-followers (India in 2022 is an example)[13]
- The threat of deportation of expatriates

---

10 Hampton, *Facing Danger.*
11 Renfroe PSP, Smith PSP, *Threat / Vulnerability Assessments.*
12 Open Doors, "How the Scoring Works."
13 Religious Liberty Commission of the Evangelical Fellowship of India, "The year 2021 saw calls for genocide and threats of mass violence made from public platforms, and important political and religious figures on the stage."

- The threat of visa non-renewal
- The threat of police interrogation
- Threats to the honor of women and children of Christ-followers—the threat of rape and dismemberment if they don't denounce Christ.
- Threats of torture and death are given to the person being targeted; threats given to the husband of what will be done to his wife or children have a powerful impact.
- The threat of being stopped by police while driving
- The threat of state surveillance on phones or computers. There are best practices related to cybersecurity that should be followed. Assume your phone is being listened to by the police.
- Written and verbal death threats require a slightly different assessment from other threats.
- Virtual Kidnappings: An extortion-by-deception scheme where the kidnappers have not kidnapped anyone, and instead, they coerce victims to pay a quick ransom through deception and threats before the plan falls apart.[14] Typically, a ransom demand is made by phone, text, or email claiming to have taken the target's loved one hostage. As Artificial Intelligence (AI) technology improves, this risk will likely increase. "Kidnappers" can even make a person "feel kidnapped" and thus willing to do what they demand.[15]
- Insider Threats: A person with some combination of knowledge and access from inside the organization. It may be intentional or unintentional, violent or non-violent, including government-sponsored espionage, fraud, sabotage, unauthorized dissemination of information, or poor security practices.[16]
- Blended Threats: Threats against a person or team based on political unrest, terrorism, crime, gang activity, and religious persecution. It may be hard to sort out the primary reason for the threat.

From the front door of the home to anywhere in the community, Christ-followers living in hostile situations daily face the "squeeze" from numerous directions.

---

14 McCalister, "Insider Threats."
15 For insight and training, contact one of the Christian Security companies cited in "Global Risk Resource List" at the Theology of Risk website.
16 Gelles, *Insider Threat Prevention*, 3.

The Squeeze

- Frivolous and arbitrary "new" laws: These are reasons to hinder Christ-followers in something. For example, these laws are cited as the reason that Christians may not rent or purchase a building, or for why their structure will be torn down (i.e. "new" fire codes, government road-widening plans). This occurrence is a discretionary interpretation of the law used against the Christ-follower. For instance, while Turkey has "freedom of religion" in their constitution, churches are usually not able to get permission to build or own a building. In another country on the Open Doors list, "a temple can be built anywhere, at any time, even in inconvenient places. But a church? It will require three thousand permissions and five years of bureaucracy, escalating the cost. Then if the church is built, but gets damaged or burned down due to persecution, it's impossible to rebuild it."[17]

- General anti-foreigner hostility and discrimination: This discrimination is the general hostility in all spheres of life that makes it uncomfortable to be in a community.

- Anti-Christian hostility and discrimination: Hostility in all spheres of life. Everything related to daily life is challenging to do, or the Christian is not allowed to participate, to pay bills, get a bank account, be out in public without public harassment, enroll children in the local school, marry whom they'd like, etc. For example, when needing medical help, a person must write their religion on the hospital admissions form. Their treatment is often delayed if the word "Christian" is entered.

- Technological surveillance: Digital surveillance through a wide variety of means. Drone surveillance is reaching new levels of invasiveness. There are guidelines for mitigating drone surveillance not discussed in this book. Gospel workers should adhere to cybersecurity best practices.

- Surveillance of people and cars: Being watched constantly and being followed.

- Personal car as a witness: Christ-followers who park their vehicle outside of the church or house church have returned to find the tires slashed or the air let out. One pastor lost count—sixty to seventy times his tires were flat. His car has been keyed or dinged up so much it is a witness to Christ, and people continue to recognize the vehicle and add more scratches and dings.[18]

---

17 Quote from private conversation with a persecuted pastor.
18 Story related to me from a persecuted pastor.

- Paperwork harassment: The paperwork submitted (for anything) is never "correct" or complete, and something is always missing.
- Visa hassles: See paperwork harassment above!
- Vandalism of houses, churches, Christian community centers, etc.
- Detainment: Detainment can happen for fabricated reasons. The Christ-follower is accused of all sorts of things and detained. It can also occur for valid reasons—the Christ-follower was caught sharing the gospel, teaching the Bible, etc. Detainment has been known to go on for years without formal charges.
- Gendered persecution: "Christian men are most often subject to pressures related to work, military/militia conscription, and non-sexual physical violence. [In contrast,] Christian women are specifically and most frequently targeted through forced marriage, rape, and other forms of sexual violence."[19]
- Police raids of one's home and/or office. Bank accounts/assets confiscated.
- Interrogation: Sometimes, severe psychological stress from the mental and ethical challenge of responding to the good cop/bad cop interrogation.
- Psychological pressure tactics: One's choice of food, clothing, religion, and spouse is taken away; there is no access to the community water source.
- Heavy fines for various "offenses" or manufactured offenses
- False information: Authorities creating incorrect information about some group or loved one to discourage the person from standing firm in Christ. This practice is common.
- Temptations after torture: Tempt the tortured Christ-follower at their weakest with a formidable temptation that is hard to refuse, and that seems mostly good.
- Psychological torture:[20] One of the worst forms of torture and is often done in conjunction with drugs that unhinge the person from reality.
- False charges levied: Accused of being a traitor, an apostate (to dominant religion), false arrest.
- Artificial Intelligence is used to create a fake reality. For example, it could make a realistic video of a loved one talking, saying things they would never say to encourage you to do something against your convictions.
- Prison sentences: Long or short, often in brutal conditions.

---

19 Fisher and Miller, "Gendered Persecution."
20 Ton, *Suffering, Martyrdom, and Rewards*, 424.

The Smash

- Jail: In many cases, Christ-followers are sent to prison and never heard from again. This threat is genuinely frightening. Preparing oneself and one's family for this possibility seems critical if such persecution happens in your situation.
- Beatings
- Public flogging
- Torture: Many physical and psychological types. Humankind has continued to perfect what the Romans had already figured out.
- Gender-based violence: The increasing targeting of Christian women and girls for rape, sexual torture, forced marriage, sexual slavery, and sex trafficking.
- Entrapment: Christ-followers can be trapped into sharing the gospel. In Malatya, Turkey, in 2007, five supposedly earnest young men sought discipleship. Instead, they lured three pastors to a certain location, locked the door, tied them up, tortured, and murdered them.[21]
- Forced disappearance and never being heard from again.
- Religious terrorism: Violence in all forms as sacred duty legitimizes and justifies it.[22]
- Opposition to burials and attacks on the dead bodies of Christ-followers: Extreme costs to bury the dead; then bodies dug up, dismembered, and discarded.
- Martyrdom: Todd Johnson's forty-page "Martyrology" document includes a table that dramatically has 112 methods used to kill Christ-followers in the past two thousand years. Martyrdom can be divided into two primary categories:
  - ◊ Executions: These are intentional, targeted judicial killings. These are killings not necessarily by the state but by state actors. For example, killings in which the police are unofficially involved. "They beat you so badly, you don't recover."[23]
  - ◊ Killings: People are killed in a generalized attack on a church, family, or community center.

---

21 Klama, "Malatya Murders."
22 Tahir, "Role of Globalization," 3–17.
23 From private conversation with a persecuted pastor.

The Rhomphaia

In ancient Greece, there was a knife called a *rhomphaia*. The rhomphaia's straighter blade facilitated a short, quick thrusting motion up under the rib cage and could be used by tightly packed troops engaging in hand-to-hand combat. In Luke 2:35, Simeon uses it to describe to Mary what lay ahead for her. A *"sword will pierce through your own soul"* describes intense pain and sorrow resulting from following him.[24] Perhaps her primary pain came as the religious leaders rejected and killed her son. The difficult question to ponder is who drove the rhomphaia into her soul.

There are two ways that people identifying as Christ-followers tend to persecute their own. I describe these attacks as "wounds of the short knife."

1. Wolf in sheep's clothing: Matthew 7:15; Acts 20:29, 30; 2 Corinthians 11:13–15; 2 Timothy 4:3; 2 Peter 2:1

2. The church family and our biological families: Matthew 10:21, 36; Luke 21:16

Wolf in Sheep's Clothing

This kind of persecution requires careful discernment to recognize the wolf. A wolf is someone who appears to be very close to you or Christ. This person seems to be a person of peace but isn't. Their motivation is to destroy the church. They appear as anything but a wolf.

In Acts 20:29, 30, Paul, in his last speech to the Ephesian Christ-followers, said, *"I know that after my departure, fierce wolves will come in among you, not sparing the flock; and from among your own selves will arise men speaking twisted things, to draw away the disciples after them."* For example:

1. Misleading sincerity and entrapment: Street kids—"Please show us the Jesus movie!" In reality, it's a trap because the instigators know the Christ-follower is less likely to suspect children used as bait.

2. Betrayal: This person seeks to infiltrate the church and become a trusted person. Then they betray all the believers. Example: Judas betrays Jesus with a kiss.

3. False Christs, false prophets, false teachers, false apostles, false witnesses, false brothers (*pseudochristos, pseudoprophetes, pseudodidaskolos, pseudapostolos, pseudomartys, pseudadelphos*): Lead followers astray through signs and wonders and falsely "point" to Christ. Matthew 7:15; 24:24; Mark 13:22; Romans 16:17, 18; 2 Corinthians 11:13; 2 Peter 2:1; 1 John 4:1; Jude 1:4.

---

24 Louw and Nida, *Greek-English Lexicon*, 25.279.

4. Deceitful workers (*Ergatēs dolios*): 2 Corinthians 11:13–15; 2 Timothy 3:5. For example, those who molest Christian children in boarding schools.

Jesus teaches how to spot a wolf. He says, be watchful, stay alert! Look for the spiritual fruit of being a follower of Christ. Matthew 7:15–20; 24:23–27; 2 Peter 3:3.

Our Biological Families

Jesus made it clear that persecution can also come from our own families. "Those who persecute God's agents in Luke are ironically those who are supposed to be God's people."[25] This persecution happens even in Christian families and within the family of Christ. "*Brother will deliver brother over to death, and the father his child, and children will rise against parents and have them put to death.*"[26] (Matthew 10:21; Luke 21:16). And Matthew 10:36, "*A person's enemies will be ones from their own household.*"[27]

Being reoriented to his kingdom, we learn from Jesus that we are his sister, mother, and brother (Mark 3:33–35; Luke 8:21). In other words, Jesus did not deny the importance of our biological families. Still, he transforms "our perception of family away from our mere biological and adoptive heritage and toward the broader context of the household of God. Jesus greatly expands our lineage, calls us to new relationships with certain responsibilities and accountability to one another."[28]

We can describe the range of hostility from Christian families from discouragement and distraction from one's calling to verbal, physical, and psychological abuse. This persecution is hard to identify because it is hard to believe it's happening and to call it persecution. It's easier to understand hostility from relatives when one's family is not Christian. Some of the ways persecution from within our biological family occurs:

- Deserted (*Enkataleipō*): 2 Timothy 4:10, 16, 26; we will be deserted
- Betrayal (*Paradidōmi*): Matthew 10:21; insider threats
- Cause to put to death (*Thanatōsousin*): Matthew 10:21

Attacks within the church family can be incredibly debilitating and distracting for long periods. "When a [person] feels condemned, [their] creativity and power to love, joy in life, and sense of wholeness are blocked."[29]

---

25 Penner, *In the Shadow*, 117.
26 In Matthew 10:21, Jesus is providing insight into Micah 7:6.
27 A dynamic translation of Matthew 10:36.
28 Webb-Mitchel, "Open House," 250.
29 van Breemen, *As Bread That Is*, 69.

Curt Thompson elucidates, "Our lives will be abundant, joyful, and peaceful only to the degree that we are engaged, known, and understood by one another."[30] When we are known, we can more effectively engage in mission. Not being known by family and being attacked by one's family always seem to come right when ministry is fruitful or intense. This hindrance inhibits powerful ministry as it drains energy and reorients focus on these family relationships. Thus, creativity diminishes.

Collateral Violence

Sometimes, by simply being in another country for the sake of the gospel, we experience danger apart from persecution and become victims of violence by proximity. Exposure to additional violence occurs in countries where instability, criminality, wars, and coup d'états arise more frequently than we may be exposed to in our passport country. These dangers include:

- Bystander violence
- Gang or cartel violence, kidnapping, and murder
- Re-election violence
- Coup d'état
- Proxy wars
- Transnational criminality: International criminal groups coordinate with local gangs to conduct increasingly sophisticated operations.[31] Or criminal groups team up with religious terrorist groups to move into a new area
- Resource conflicts: Land, water, grazing land, crops

This exposure may be why the Apostle Paul made a point in 2 Corinthians 11:26 to list all the dangers he had experienced. He uses only one word for danger in the Greek manuscript: κίνδυνος (*kindynos*) eight times in this verse. He writes, "on frequent journeys, in danger from rivers, danger from robbers, danger from my own people, danger from Gentiles, danger in the city, danger in the wilderness, danger at sea, danger from false brothers." The only other place *kindynos* is used in the New Testament is Romans 8:35 where it is translated "peril," often used synonymously in English to danger.

I'm impacted by how many different Greek words are used in the New Testament for dangers, hostilities, and persecution. Our present twenty-first-century experience mirrors the early church, meaning we are not alone, and

---

30 Thompson, *Anatomy of the Soul*, 109.
31 OSAC, "Transnational Crime Fuels Spike."

what's happening is not new. Those who have gone before us and remained faithful are now cheering us on to stay steadfast in our race.

Looking at the darkness in this chapter can be overwhelming, because there are a lot of possibilities that arouse fear in us. Learning to recognize and respond to our fears is called fear management, which I will discuss next. Firstly, we'll orient ourselves in the Hebrew and Greek words and perspectives for fear and courage. I'll explain the physiology of fear and courage and list our options on the path to mature courage. Knowing this information will enable better witness risk decision-making and develop the resilience, endurance, and courage we long to demonstrate in our lives for our Savior. He is worthy.

Part 2

Biblical Background

Chapter 3
An Introduction to a Grammar of Fear and Courage

Fear is not the opposite of faith. Unbelief is.
Fear is the prerequisite to courage.[1]
—The last pastor of the International Church of Kabul, Afghanistan

We live in an age that demands certainty but seems to have the most uncertainty over what the future holds. We yearn for safety, but our world seems filled with fear. We have the most information but the least grip on reality. Our news about reality is algorithmically controlled to engender fear. At the same time, we are often taught incomplete truths or myths about fear. We are taught to ignore our fears, that our fears are not faith, that fear is sin, and fear is a liar. Is fear a sin? Does it lie?

What if we flip our approach? What if we approach our fears by recognizing that they can give us helpful information about ourselves if we pay attention? What if we allow ourselves to lean into fear, give ourselves permission to recognize our feelings, acknowledge them, to listen to what they are telling us, and dissect their source and object? As we sit with the fear, what does it tell us about ourselves and our view of God?

A grammar book in any language covers explanations of the rules of that language—the order of how words and phrases are put together in sentences, and what is allowed and not allowed in academic writing and speech. A grammar of fear and courage is an exegetical and practical inquiry into how fear and courage work bodily and spiritually throughout the Old and New Testaments and daily life. This chapter introduces some introductory basics of a theology of the grammar of fear and courage, but is not comprehensive.[2]

---

1 Private correspondence with the author, August 2017.
2 Space limitations required a generalization of key aspects of an introduction to Hebrew grammar and the grammar of fear and courage for the purposes of this book. Regretfully, I do not have space to discuss Jesus's imperative command in four places in the New Testament to "not fear." In Greek, he uses an imperative command with the strongest "not." However, careful study on any "fear not" verse requires a close look of which "not" in Hebrew and Greek, including which verbal tense or aspect is used, the differences between the New Testament and Old Testament on fear and courage, the context in which the command or wish was made, to whom, and for what time period. For example, Moses wishes the people of Israel to not be afraid in Deut 31:6, but in Deut 31:8, he strongly commands the leader, Joshua, to not be afraid. As a leader, Joshua must not act in fear, because then the people will follow him (see Randall Buth, 149).

Fear In Hebrew and Greek

Careful exegesis requires a close examination of individual words and the concept of fear and courage viewed in Hebrew from the Hebraic worldview. Fear has a wide range of meanings in the Hebrew and Greek Scripture texts. The first step in understanding the Old Testament view of fear is to understand a few of the unique characteristics of the Hebrew language.

Hebrew is an "action" language, using action verbs, describing what someone or something looks like or is doing. Hebrew verses average three verbs each. Hebrew has perfect (completed action, past) verbs and imperfect (incomplete action, future) verbs. The fear verbs are almost always found in a form[3] of the Hebrew imperfect (future) tense, which implies the end is not yet decided—it's not complete yet, so don't be passive. It will come, but what you do in the future is yet to be determined.

Biblical Hebrew never uses the imperative Hebrew command form to express negative commands.[4] The imperative command form is only used with positive commands.[5] While English translations often simply translate "don't fear," both Hebrew and Greek have different "nots" with ranges of strength and intensity. Rarely is the strongest "not fear" "lo" (לֹא) given, and when it is used, "it negates factual statements in all time frameworks."[6]

In the great majority of the cases in the Old Testament, the imperfect[7] (incomplete action) form of the verb "to fear" (and its synonyms) is used with the softer "not" (אַל) ("al") form of Hebrew. It means God is expressing his request (wish) that when we feel the emotion of fear, we volitionally[8] choose to not do the

> God is expressing his request (wish) that when we feel the emotion of fear, we volitionally choose to not do the action of fear and instead obey him.

---

3 Jussive form, which is a volitional form, a wish being expressed by the one speaking, requesting the person(s) hearing to choose to not do something.
4 Weingreen, *Practical Grammar*, 77.
5 Kutz and Josberger, *Learning Biblical Hebrew*, 194.
6 Weingreen, 77, Bowling, 463 *not* (לֹא) (lō'). Looking at the "nots" in Hebrew can be hugely encouraging. For example, in 2 Chr 20:15, the Hebrew actually says, "The battle is never yours, but God's."
7 Jussive.
8 The Jussive as a volitional verb (dependent on the compliance of the individual) and the imperfect as an indicative verb (indicating facts). By stating that an action will not take place (indicative), obedience is assumed and demanded. As a result, the imperfect (lō') לֹא is a more forceful manner of expression and is especially apparent in certain forms of divine legislation, including the Ten Commandments. Using a negated imperfect to indicate that an action is absolutely not allowed does not mean it will not happen. Consider the rhetoric of a parent emphatically saying to a child, "You will not talk back to me" (Kutz and Josberger, 196).

action of fear[9] and instead obey him. "Often, the phrase 'Fear not and be not dismayed,' though phrased in the English as an imperative, this formula usually expresses assurance (*sic*)."[10]

The Old Testament repeatedly talks about fear with nuance. Sometimes fear is an action verb and sometimes a noun. "In several passages, 'fearing' and proper living are so closely related as to be virtually synonymous ideas (Lev 19:14; 25:17; 2 Kgs 17:34; Deut 17:19)."[11] It comes down to what choice we will make in the face of feeling fear.

In the Talmud, Jewish Rabbis have described fear overtaking us like melting into wax, having no firmness, being malleable, paralyzed, or soft.[12] Fear does that to us when we let it consume us. It leads to disorder. We have no strength, boldness, or focus. We can't help it when we physiologically feel fear, but we can help how we respond. Will we respond by melting into wax? By being passive in the face of our fear of danger? By succumbing to paralysis? Or will we choose righteous action?

In Hebrew, there are ranges of words and meanings which can be used for one idea, and a Hebrew reader sees all the words under the umbrella of that word as acceptable based on context. Still, we are limited to whatever word the translator chooses for the language in which we read the Bible. When interpreting the Hebrew Old Testament's view of fear, we must take care not to oversimplify biblical teaching. According to Bowling, "At times careful exegetical judgment may be needed to decide whether a given passage refers to internal emotion or to an external object of terror. Some passages could refer to either."[13] Bowling goes on to say,

> *Yare'*, the primary Hebrew word for *fear* in the Old Testament, is used for a range of meanings of fear, and sometimes it may refer to five general categories of fear:
>
> 1. The emotion of fear
> 2. The intellectual anticipation of evil without emphasis upon the emotional reaction
> 3. Reverence or awe
> 4. Righteous behavior or piety
> 5. Formal religious worship[14]

---

9 Buth, *Living Biblical Hebrew*, 149.
10 Tigay, *Deuteronomy*, 15.
11 Bowling, *Theological Wordbook*, 399-401 (entry 907 אָרֵי *yārē'*).
12 Jastrow, *Dictionary of the Targumim*, עוּשׁ 1537, 1538. Ps 22:14 and Isa 41:10 are examples of not becoming soft, passive, melting like wax. These are all idioms for fear.
13 Bowling, *Theological Wordbook*, 721 (entry 1756, פָּחַד *pāḥad*).
14 Bowling, 399–401 (entry 907 אָרֵי *yārē'*).

Notice only the first use of *yare'* focuses on emotion. Old Testament synonyms of *yare'* include *pahad, hatat, harad,* and *gur.*[15] Fear is often described in physical terms in the Old Testament. Shaking, quaking, trembling, and heart-melting all describe fear. *Gur* also means feeling the fear of intimidation by a "more powerful or superior being or object."[16] "[The] noun form [of *gur*] (*megurot*) connotes horror."[17]

It is significant to note that *hatat*, while often translated as "dismayed" or "shattered" includes the meaning "to be demoralized." The basic sense is "to be broken" from which other abstract and secondary ideas are derived such as "be abolished" or "be in a panic." Bowling explains, "Four ranges of meanings are attested for this word and its derivatives: (1) literal breaking, (2) abstract destruction, (3) demoralization, and (4) terror."[18] Demoralization, in particular, is more common among Christ-followers when facing danger, fear, and risk, than cowardice. Spiritual demoralization is discussed with PTSD and hope in chapter nineteen.

The most common use of fear in the Old Testament is theological. It "connotes reverence, piety, or worship with God."[19] However, there is no particular word for holy fear.[20] The exact translation of *yare'*, in connection with God/Yahweh ("fear of God"), is difficult and potentially misleading because there is no exact English equivalent.[21] Respect is too weak, but the fear of God is not a horror that a person would want to run away from. This fear is not an "unhealthy dread but an attitude that leads to obedience to God's commands and the Holy Spirit in light of the coming judgment.[22]

Pahad is used as a synonym for "*yare'*" and is almost entirely found in the Hebrew Old Testament poetic sections. It is not used for abstract evil. Instead, it is often used to emphasize the immediacy of the object of fear or the resulting trembling, which may refer to terror.[23]

The Bible is well aware of the human emotion of fear and all of its ranges. The chart below shows fear words and their derivatives, all closely related. It's a bit hard to place the exact equivalents into a neat linear chart, but

---

15 Bowling, *Theological Wordbook*, 401.
16 Jones, "When I Am Afraid," 17, quoted from Stiger, *Theological Wordbook*, 157, (entry 332 מָגוֹר (māgôr).
17 Jones, 17.
18 Bowling, *Theological Wordbook*, 336 (entry 784 חָתַת *ḥātat*).
19 Jones, "When I Am Afraid," 17.
20 Spencer, "To Fear and Not," 229–49.
21 Longman III, "Fear of God," 13–21.
22 Longman III, 13–21.
23 Bowling, *Theological Wordbook*, 720 (entry 1756 פַּחַד (*pāḥad*)

the purpose is to show the wide range of Hebrew and Greek words for the increasing intensities of fear. Though we are putting the different Hebrew, English, and Greek words for increasing levels of fear on a scale from mild concern to complete horror, a number of the terms listed do not fit into just one category.

The most common words for fear in the New Testament include *phobos* and *deilos*, covering the entire range of fear from sluggishness to terror. There are at least twenty more variations of phrases for anxiety and fear in the New Testament with different intensity levels of feeling. Only once is the English "cowardice" used, in Revelation 21:8 translated from *deilos*. Synonyms for cowardice in the Bible include soft, anxious, weak, timidity, faintheartedness, and hearts melting.

HEBREW	ENGLISH	GREEK
Hatat/Hasok	Apprehension/Sluggish Demoralized	Nothros/Deilos
Deaga/Maset	Concern/Burden	Merimna
Pa'am/Shata/Yese	Anxiety/Worry/Timid	Merimna/Deilos/Melei Prosdokao
Pahad	Astonishment/Alarm Inflamed with Worry	Thombos/Piroo
Raasa	Extreme Agitation/Stirred Up	Seio
Yare'/Harad/Mora/	Fear/Cowardice	Phobos
Pahad/Harad/Harad	Panic/Trembling	Appolymi/Tromos
Hatat/Pahad/Zewaa/Aratz/Mora	Terror/Shattered/Dread Wrath/Terrible	Mega Phobos Phobos/Ptoeo
Ema/Gur	Horror	Ekphobos, Apollumetha

Table 2: Fear Verbs in Hebrew, English, and Greek

The Gift of Fear

What is fear? Fear is one of the eight major categories of emotions and includes shades from mild anxiety to paralyzing horror. It is a natural reaction to the unknown, uncertain, and uncontrollable danger that threatens to overwhelm us. All fear involves the threat of danger and the fear of what we cannot control.[24] In this way, it is a gift, as Gavin de Becker writes in *The Gift of Fear*, because it alerts us to danger. Our well-being, maybe even survival,

---

24 Allender and Longman III, *Cry of the Soul*, KL 671.

may depend on us paying attention to what our fear is trying to tell us.

In their chapter on "Unrighteous Fear" in *The Cry of the Soul*, psychologist Dan Allender and theologian Tremper Longman contribute a concise summary of the emotion of fear. Ignoring or allowing fear to paralyze us distorts reality, imprisons us, and destructively leaves us feeling impotent and helpless. Human fear ranges from mild anxiety to dread fear that paralyzes us. The difference is the intensity of the emotion, not necessarily the seriousness of the problem.[25] "Real fear is a signal intended to be very brief, a mere servant of intuition. ... Fear is not an emotion like sadness or happiness, either of which might last a long while. It is not a state like anxiety. True fear is a survival signal that sounds only in the presence of danger."[26]

> Our well-being, maybe even survival, may depend on us paying attention to what our fear is trying to tell us.

Fear is anger in reverse.[27] Anger tries to control by attacking the object of the fear, while fear retreats from it and limits our choices to respond to it. We want control, and we are fearful of failure (however we define it). The loss of control and fear of failure are two sides of the same coin. The more we sense the possibility of personal or physical death, of disintegration, or the terror of separation, the more impotent we see ourselves and the greater our fear. Feeling fear is not automatically a sin or a character issue.

Fear distorts our perception of ourselves.[28] Terrorists know this, and they know how to demoralize and play on human dread or fear of death. "Low-probability events in which many people are suddenly killed trigger an unconscious psychological [response]: If many people [are killed] at one time, react with fear and avoid that situation."[29]

Another dynamic occurs at the same time. Jones writes, "Often, those who seek control will attempt to heighten our fear and anxiety to prompt our compliance."[30] When all we can see and feel are our fears, the enemy seems overwhelming; we seem weak, inadequate, and alone. God seems nowhere to be found. We feel like we do not have the resources to cope with the situation. Ironically, we tend to blame ourselves for our fear because then we gain the illusion of having control over some perceived failure that we

---

25 Allender and Longman III, *Cry of the Soul*, KL 663.
26 Becker, *Gift of Fear*, 318-19.
27 Allender and Longman III, *Cry of the Soul*, KL 679-728.
28 Allender and Longman III, KL 765.
29 Gigerenzer, *Risk Savvy*, 2.
30 Jones, "When I Am Afraid," 23.

feel we can and must change. Jones continues, "When we recognize God as the only appropriate object of 'fear' and refuse to associate fear of God with terror [and] anxiety but rather base it on our trust [in] God, we become better able to recognize the truth that the real power in this world is God. We then recognize these attempts to manipulate us into thinking otherwise [are a] fallacy."[31]

Constructive, helpful fear, fear that is a gift, is fear that drives us to God. But first, we must recognize fear is *not* abnormal, and living without fear is inhuman.[32] We cannot escape it. But we can allow it to move us to a more profound capacity and awareness of what it means to stand in our fear before God but without shame.

When our intuition leads us to feel fear, don't disregard it or deny it. We deny it because we have difficulties facing reality and prefer to create a less threatening narrative. We see what we want to see instead of seeing reality. "Denial is a save now, pay later scheme. Denial will result in constant low-grade anxiety. Denial keeps [people] from taking action that could reduce the [risk] and the worry."[33] We do best if we honor the feeling and then assess the validity of our fear. Is it legitimate? Do we need to engage in a complete risk assessment? Is it time to flee without further thought? To ignore fear is to ignore a survival signal.

If we can never completely get rid of fear, how can we learn to manage it? Where is the line between fear that protects us and fear that paralyzes and imprisons us? It has to do with what or whom we fear and what we do in response to our fear.

Courage in Hebrew and Greek

Courage, in Scripture, is the willingness to take action; it is "heartedness" and often simply "strength." In the Old and New Testament, references to courage range from what you do to yourself to what God does. *Ametz* and *Hazak* are the primary Hebrew words for courage. The root of *ametz* is used fifty times in the Old Testament[34] and has numerous shades of meaning: "to make firm, strengthen, secure, harden one's mind, feel strong, persist in, make oneself alert, effort, obstinance, quality of endurance, strength of faith and hope, be resolute, prevail, grasp tightly, to repair, fasten with nails, keep hold of."[35] It is boldness, like "bold as a lion" in Proverbs 28:1.

---

31 Jones, 23.
32 Allender and Longman III, *Cry of the Soul*, KL 803.
33 Becker, *Gift of Fear*, 10.
34 Jenni and Westermann, *Theological Lexicon*, 157–59.
35 Feinberg, *Theological Wordbook*, 157–59 (entry 117 אמץ *ametz*).

Hazak is used 291 times and includes the idea of being "stouthearted and firm in your convictions, and then God will instill courage into your heart."[36] It means we are choosing the action of courage, and God is also putting courage in our hearts. It's not all up to me, and it's not all God's responsibility. Courage requires us to partner with God to act in it. Together with God, we act courageously. "To grow firm" means there is a growth and change process, and we can grow in courage. We grow in courageous action each time we choose to act courageously. It's a positive cycle that strengthens and deepens each time we choose to respond to fear with the action of courage in partnership with God. We collaborate with God (collaborative coping), leading to increased resilience!

In the Greek and resultant translation into English, courage takes on many idiomatic phrases and synonyms. *Tharsos*:[37] boldness, persevering, enduring, waiting patiently, being confident, taking courage, being bold, trusting, relying on, not moving, deaf to threats,[38] having a heart like iron, raising the head (to look up), behaving like a person of integrity, acting with honor and noble character, firm of purpose in the face of danger, to be of good cheer, of good courage, rely on, firm of purpose in the face of danger; *Tolmao*:[39] not to dread, to bear, endure, bring oneself to; *Parrhesis*: bold, openness, confident, skilled in rhetoric, "boldness is being able to say whatever needs to be said. It is to speak your heart and mind no matter what the consequences,"[40] preaching openly and eloquently to a hostile world; *Andrizomai*: to be courageous in the face of danger, act like men.[41]

Courage in the Bible is seen and expressed as an action: what we do, and what God does. It describes the Christ-follower as a quality (noun) and a characteristic (adjectives, adverbs). The verbs for courage are often written in an imperative command form, implying action. We are commanded to do the stated action. For example, what does boldness look like in action? What does waiting with patience look like when it seems like God is late to show up?

---

36 Weber, *Theological Wordbook*, 276 (entry 636 חָזַק *ḥāzaq*).
37 Grundmann, *Theological Dictionary*, 3:25–27.
38 Louw and Nida, *Greek-English Lexicon*, V 1, 305.
39 Fitzer, *Theological Dictionary*, 8:181–86.
40 Moen, "Backup."
41 Louw and Nida, *Greek-English Lexicon*, 25.165.

Verbs	Qualities and Characteristics
Do "Bold"	Boldness
Do "Strength"	Strength
Do "Endurance"	Endurance
Act in Confidence	Confidence
Persevering	Perseverance
Growing Firm	Firmness
Skillfully Speaking	Eloquent Speech (not remaining silent or concealed at the right time)
Prevailing	Prevail
Not Moving	Obstinance
Being Deaf to Threats	Resolute
Standing Firm in the Faith	Stouthearted
Relying	Reliance
Grasping Tightly	Secure
Making Oneself Alert	Alertness
Uphold	Daring
To Seize	Valiant
Wait	Calm

Table 3: Courage Verbs, Adjectives, and Nouns

How to Know When You Have Enough Courage

It is easier to have courage in some situations than others. For example, in Exodus, the Israelites had been rescued by God from a superpower, and he had done miracle after miracle. Yet once the Egyptians were destroyed in the Red Sea, and he led the Israelites into the wilderness, they immediately started complaining about everything. They complained about the water, then about the bread, then about the meat, then about the water again. Their faith crumbled in increasing levels of panic. You'd think they would fall apart when going to their first national war with the Amalekites.

In contrast, the chosen men under Joshua's command engaged in battle and defeated their enemy. We must be missing something in the type of faith we need to have courage in danger. It can't be more faith because the Israelites didn't demonstrate more faith after encountering God. And they had numerous experiences of God's loving care, so it can't be only the experience of God that engenders courage.

I wonder if it's more the idea that faith and trust in God are easier in some areas of our lives and harder in others. It's easier for me to trust God for certain big things that are somewhat removed or distant (to me), like the general "protection from my enemies," but a different issue of trust and faith that he will provide for me in my finances every month, even though he's been doing it month after month for twenty-seven years through faithful financial partners. Like the Israelites, my worries about my finances imply difficulty trusting God to provide me with meat, bread, and water. Does he care personally for me in that way? Is he there?

Fear, courage, and cowardice are complex, nuanced, personal to each of us, and bring different psychological implications. We struggle to trust various aspects of God's character, especially the side of God that cares about our daily needs. I wonder if this is why the Bible teaches us to encourage each other—because God knows that we are unique in what makes us fearful and what we more easily find courage in.[42]

Jesus *commands* us to be confident and courageous, to strengthen ourselves, to be bold, and to move forward trusting him. The question, "How do you know when you have enough courage?" is the wrong question. Courage requires a predetermined commitment to disciplined obedience, a willingness to pay the price because Jesus is Lord. It's not a matter of *more* faith, *more* courage, but cultivating a *type* of faith, a *type* of courage. It's not "not" feeling fear, either. It's not a matter of having enough courage, but of having wise, maturing courage. It's obedience with trust and hope.

Taking courage is not about my feelings, but my actions. Fear is contagious, but so is courage. We can help each other have courage! Courage requires discipline to do tasks, to keep moving forward on the path of courage. Bravery leads to purposeful, ordered, meaningful action even when we are not in control. It's taking the next small step in the present moment that gets us in touch with our senses. I did laundry when I was afraid, and it had a calming effect on controlling one aspect of my life as I lived through those (uncontrollable) threats and bombs.

Let's take a look at two examples. The first is Deuteronomy 31:6. "Be strong and courageous, do not (al) be afraid (al) or in dread of them, for the LORD your God is the One who is going with you. He will not (lo) desert you or (lo) abandon you." (NASB)

This one verse has seven Hebrew verbs! The first pair, strong and courage, *are verbal imperative commands of action.* If we examine the English "be strong," "be" makes "strong" sound like it's in the form of a predicate

---

42 Gal 6:2; Phil 2:4; 1 Thess 5:11; Heb 3:13; 10:24, 25; Jas 2:14–17, etc.

adjective; however, we see that the Bible is using an imperative command verb: (you) do the action of strong and (you) do the action of courage.

When we examine the fear words in this verse, *afraid* and *tremble*, we see these are action verbs, but not command verbs. The Bible knows we will feel fear—the text frequently assumes that reality. There is no shame in feeling the normal human response to danger. When the text says, "(*al*) don't be afraid, (*al*) don't tremble," the text is expressing God's wish that when you feel the emotion of fear come over you, when you begin to experience anxiety in the body, volitionally choose not to do the action of "afraid" or the activity of "trembling."

Significantly, these are the Hebrew imperfect verb tense—a not-completed action that is not yet in the past. The future isn't decided. You and I can always choose how to respond when we experience fear, and we can change at any point until the moment has passed. I love that last phrase of this verse. God will "never" fail us and "never" forsake us. This time, the text uses the permanent "not" form of Hebrew.

The second example is the story of Gideon's men in Judges 7:1–8. This story illustrates three different fear responses: too much, too little, and just right.

Too Much Fear

The Midianites, the most fearsome superpower at the time, had been harassing the Israelites, destroying their livelihood and attacking when possible. The Israelites cried out to God for deliverance. The Lord called Gideon to lead the Israelite army against the Midianites in response. When all the fighting men had gathered, the Lord said, "You have too many troops ... or else Israel might elevate themselves" (take credit for winning the battle). "Whoever is fearful, and trembling may turn back and leave Mount Gilead. So, twenty-two thousand of the troops turned back."[43] In this verse, "fearful" and "trembling" are adjectives, which means they were characterized by fear. They had too much fear. In this situation, for this one event, their fear disqualified them from service in battle. The troops were asked to go home, but nowhere does the text condemn them or imply sin (although many preachers do!).

To our surprise, God says again there are too many troops, even though only 10,000 Israelites remained to fight 135,000 Midianites (Judg 8:10), a 1:13 ratio! Now God does a second fear test that reveals the actions of fear and the actions of courage. He tells Gideon to invite the remaining 10,000 men to come to the edge of the nearby water and drink. Gideon's task is to separate those who lap the water (like an animal) from those who kneel and drink.

---

43 Judges 7:1–8.

Too Little Fear (Indifference)

Think about these two drinking positions.[44] The first drinking position required the men to put their weapons down, place both hands on the ground or even in the water, and then put their faces in the water. In this position, their eyes are down; they cannot see what is happening around them. They seem to be situationally unaware. They are the type of people who say, "Fear? Why should I be afraid? I'm not afraid; the situation is fine. There's nothing to worry about." They did not have enough fear. Their posture is un-alert; thus, they are not usable by God. They did not see reality correctly. They are sent home. But again, God does not condemn nor pronounce them in sin. How many times have I heard preachers condemn these thirty-two thousand men! I believe it highly likely they fought in future battles, but in this one, they were disqualified.

Figure 3: Three Fear Responses

© 2022 Neal & Anna Hampton

Just the Right Amount (Situational Awareness)

In the second drinking position, only three hundred men are upright. In this position, only one hand is required to drink by bringing their hand to their mouth. The other hand can still be holding a weapon. Their head and eyes are up, and their position remains alert. Their posture indicates situational awareness and an appropriate amount of concern in the situation, but they also choose to act in a position of courage.

The lessons from these two examples are clear. There is a difference between the experience of feeling fear and the action of acting in fear. Similarly, courage is often an action we choose, despite our fear. The Bible accepts and even presumes we will feel fear. So we, too, are wise to accept

---

44 Read the chapter on situational awareness, chapter 10, then re-read this section.

that we may feel fear in dangerous situations. The experience of feeling fear is a normal human response. However, once we become aware that we are feeling fear, we can choose to act the fear, or we can choose to act courage despite our fear. Acting in courage despite our fear is righteousness.

The main "ground" of fear lies in three primary areas: death, pain, and disgrace. We fear physical and non-physical death (dreams, hopes, aspirations). Pain comes to all of us, whether spiritual, physical, emotional, or psychological. And the shame of disgrace causes some to give in to fear; the extreme result of shame is to commit suicide.

There are at least six broad categories to consider when parenting our children and cultivating courage in our own lives: physical, social, moral, emotional, intellectual, and spiritual. Usually, we think of physical courage as "bravery at the risk of bodily harm or death." Social courage is the risk of social embarrassment, exclusion, or rejection; speaking truth to power requires immense courage. Intellectual courage is our willingness and strength of soul to speak up and "engage with challenging ideas, question thinking, and risk making mistakes. Moral courage is doing the right thing, particularly when [we risk] shame, opposition, disapproval of others," and persecution or death. Emotional courage is engaging in all our emotions at the risk of fully feeling the painful ones. And finally, spiritual courage is "when we grapple with questions about faith, purpose, and meaning."[45]

With fear and courage, one caution is that when fearful things become routine, courage may become foolish, unthinking courage. What is normal, and what should be expected? Awareness, observation, and taking the right action under the direction and power of the Holy Spirit requires constant communication with our Lord and alertness to what is going on internally and externally. In our humanity, it's easier to choose fear over courage, and one way we can overcome that tendency is by choosing to surround ourselves with others who help us choose courage.

Grammar is crucial, whether in English, Hebrew, or Greek. A feeling is not a verb; it's a noun. The action of fear, that's different. When you feel fear, don't do the action of fear. What does acting in fear look like in your risk situation? What does "doing strong" and "doing courage" look like? Don't let yourself be paralyzed or melt in the face of danger, but acknowledge your fear and choose to respond to the Holy Spirit's leading, whether to move further into chaos or retreat.

---

45 Swerdloff, "Six Types of Courage."

Too often, we believe that [being] fearless requires individual strength and courage; ironically, this hinders us from fully trusting God. Psalm 56:3 teaches that when we are afraid, our next action step is to put our trust in God. It is a purposeful, directed choice of action. It is when our strength and courage waiver and we choose to trust him; this is at the same time what it means to cultivate trust in God and overcome our fears.[46]

This is the beginning of mature courage.

Don't Export Fear

Fear is educated into us. Often, this education comes from sources like the media, church, parents, and our cultures; then, we export it worldwide. Karl Menninger wrote, "if we wish, [it can be] educated out."[47] When we don't discuss and process our fear, we may be demonstrating a fear of fear, escalating our fears by ignoring or repressing them. In the Bible, a couple of places could be translated as "fearing a mega fear." This practice is called "the avoidance pattern of response," also known as a flight from fear.[48] We spiritualize the statement, "I am not afraid," while our actions and words express the opposite. When we think experiencing fear (a normal human response) is immoral, and sinning, we believe ourselves to be more mature, godly, and righteous by denying our fear.

How do we export our fear to other places? In consultation and discussions with colleagues, I've tried to identify the ways we do this. First, Christ-followers may wrestle with what words to use in specific security risk contexts, e.g. prayer, God, Bible. Depending on the context, we could ask ourselves:

- Are our decisions in practical areas of communication based on fear or wise security practices?
- Is this language selection fear-driven, or have I recognized the risk and discussed it with God?
- Are we avoiding sharing our faith and instilling fear into words we genuinely want to be found guilty of?
- How do we discern which words could cause unnecessary misunderstanding and bring unwanted attention to Christ-followers?
- Are we hiding what should be revealed and revealing what should be concealed?

---

46 Jones, "When I Am Afraid," 22.
47 Becker, *Gift of Fear*, 277.
48 Frankl, *Doctor and the Soul*, 291.

- To what degree do we fear losing our visa more than we fear God and what he wants us to communicate in the risk situation?
- Are we modeling being "ashamed of Jesus and his words"? Jesus taught, "For whoever is ashamed of me and my words, of him will the Son of Man be ashamed when he comes in his glory and the glory of the Father and the holy angels" (Luke 9:26).

Daniel sets the example of practicing his faith in dangerous contexts: he prayed even when he knew it would cost him severely (Dan 6:10–28). Likewise, we want to be "found guilty" of being authentic Christ-followers who pray, read our Bibles, and identify as Christ-followers. I wonder if, instead, we sometimes appear to be working for a government rather than Jesus.

Secondly, when we have an underdeveloped theology of risk within a dangerous ministry context, we can tend to export our fears because they are unprocessed. We don't even realize we may be communicating this to local Christ-followers. Thirdly, we may also express our concerns without thinking of the impact on the locals listening. Anytime we express concerns with self-focus, without connecting and redirecting to God's presence and awareness in the situation, we export our fears.

Fourthly, when an NGO has preventative security strategies for foreigners and the organization but nothing for the locals, it can engender greater fear in locals because they begin to wonder what is so scary and whether they should also be doing something different in terms of their security. In risk and crisis management planning, don't leave out the locals! A fifth way we export Western fear is when we impose security protocols on locals that do not fit the cultural context. Are we quenching the Spirit in our "security consciousness?"

We export our fear because we don't even know we are culturally swimming in it. As long as we continue to ignore, deny, and repress our fear, "we will remain isolated and limited in our capacity to relate to others and the world in a compassionate way. We will continue to live in illusion rather than authentic love. As we drop our illusions and move into love, we don't have to deny our reality anymore."[49]

How can we help others manage their fears? Parents have a significant role in modeling fear management. David French wrote,

> I've only grown to more fully understand as I became a parent [that] in times of uncertainty, I first turned to my parents to understand how to react. I took many of my emotional cues from them. If they

---

[49] Crenshaw and Snapp, *Hidden Life Awakened*, 34–35.

were anxious, I was *more* anxious. If they were calm, I felt at peace. And when it came to the challenges of life, I can never remember a moment when they didn't face the future with faith and hope.[50]

Attachment Theory

French's experience is related to attachment theory. Fear and love, two of the most basic human emotions, are opposite yet intertwined. On the avoidance-attachment spectrum, fear leads us to avoid, and love leads us to attachment.[51] Attachment theory is the idea that infants and children seek socio-emotional support from their parents. Validated research reveals this theory also describes how we bond with others into adulthood, and how humans bond with God.[52] Thompson explains, "The way we attach shapes the neural networks that are the vehicles of the attachment process. Those neural networks then reinforce the same interpersonal dynamics, which leads us [to connect ourselves to others (spouse, kids, God) as we did to our parents when we were young.]"[53]

This is significant for the following section which discusses the neural networks fear runs on.

Figure 4: Avoidance and Attachment

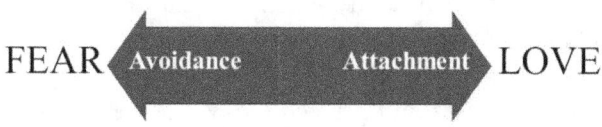

© 2022 Neal & Anna Hampton

"Attachment styles have been shown to predict depressive symptoms and other forms of psychological distress."[54] According to Thompson, attachment styles are secure, insecure, and avoidant.[55] "Secure attachment is characterized by feelings of love, approval, closeness, and warmth toward attachment figures."[56] Feelings of inconsistency and confusion describe anxious attachment which is when "attachment figures are perceived as warm, loving, and reliable at certain times [yet] cold, distant, and unreliable at

---

50 French, *Parenting Against the Spirit*, Newsletter.
51 Spencer, "To Fear and Not," 229–49.
52 Bradshaw, "Attachment to God," 130–31.
53 Thompson, *Anatomy of the Soul*, 110.
54 Bradshaw, "Attachment to God," 131.
55 Thompson, *Anatomy of the Soul*, 114–29.
56 Bradshaw, "Attachment to God," 131.

[other times.]"⁵⁷ "Avoidant attachment is ... the inverse of secure attachment—that is, potential attachment figures are perceived as consistently cold, [remote,] and unreliable."⁵⁸

Research has shown that "secure attachment to God is inversely associated with distress," which means a stronger secure attachment to God results in less distress. "Anxious attachment to God and stressful life events are positively related to distress" (more distress). "Both secure and anxious attachments to God [influence] individuals' psychological well-being regardless of whether they are coping with stressful life events."⁵⁹ Coping strategies also vary, depending upon the attachment style to God. Attachment-to-God style, coping strategies, and mental health are all related.

Secure attachment includes the confidence of God's personal presence within the trial (or risk), and the belief that God is intimately caring and emotionally present for his people. Since "styles of attachment to God are more potent and consistent predictors of distress,"⁶⁰ assessing someone's attachment style before sending them to a dangerous environment seems wise.⁶¹ Attachment to God happens more easily when we see him more clearly for who he really is, which sometimes requires teaching from Scripture about his character and his ways. But it also means recognizing our experience of God, our connection to him, our feelings about him, and what we think he feels towards us, filtered through the lens of what the Bible says about his character and how he acts and feels.

There is hope no matter our family of origin! Whatever style of attachment we bring with us into risk and persecution, we can shift it to a robust and secure attachment to God and others. Scientists have proven we can rewire our brain (neural networks) by the narrative we tell ourselves, our choices, and our lived experience of God.

In terms of fear and courage, when we choose attachment to God, turning to him in our fear and trusting in his loving-kindness and presence, our fear will gradually recede enough for us to act in courage. He is not ashamed or embarrassed by our fear, and he knows what we are going through and longs to help us. Talking to him about our fear strengthens both attachment and courage. We are deepening secure attachment neural networks when we turn to him.

---

57 Bradshaw, 131.
58 Bradshaw, 131–39.
59 Bradshaw, 140.
60 Bradshaw, 141.
61 Thompson, *Anatomy of the Soul*, 109–34. Curt Thompson explains the AAI–Adult Attachment Interview. It is used by therapists and provides a validated description of one's attachment style. This interview would seem to be a helpful tool for pre-field assessment to equip individuals to learn how to be more resilient in their significant relationships including with God.

But when we focus on our fears and sit in them without lifting our gaze to Christ, we spiral down into greater fear and paralysis mentally and physically and struggle to fathom courageous action. Our relationship with God is impacted. We may develop confusion about God and what he's like, and we may feel like we are waiting for him to act. We could lose trust and even begin to despair over our spirituality because of these confusing thoughts. Chronic fear that overwhelms us strengthens anxious or avoidant neural networks, and likely moves us further into disorganized and confusing emotions. We may have a greater mental and spiritual disordered attachment to our fear's object(s). An extreme result of this struggle is its potential to lead to a mental health crisis or PTSD; others may have a faith crisis of some sort, while still others make poor decisions in risk, further endangering their (and others') lives.

Fear in the Body

Just as we have neural networks for attachment, we have neural networks that our fear runs on. What does fear in the body feel like? We know generally, but how in tune are we with the specifics of what is going on? Our natural reaction to fear is to run from it, in the sense of avoiding the emotion or denying it. But if we have fears about a threat that is not yet present, we must manage our fears purposefully and honestly. Instead of "white-knuckling" our way through a fear, which usually makes it worse anyway, a quicker way to overcome the fear is to lean into it. Don't judge the feeling, but recognize you are feeling it, and watch with curiosity what it does inside you. Notice it. Become fully aware and tell yourself it's a normal physiological response to fear and is not bad or wrong. "There's a science behind [our] body's natural reaction to fear."[62] When we know what to expect, we have less anxiety about it, normalize it, and recognize we are not alone.

When we integrate what we know about our brains (neuroscience), emotions, bodily sensations, and spiritual resources and fully feel our feelings, they become less threatening and have less power over us. The following description of the physical response to fear takes only milliseconds in the body but much longer to read:

1. My brain focuses on a fear I have from a threat I just heard (i.e. from extremists). My body's alarm system goes off. I begin to feel the physical sensations I usually get with fear.

2. As the fast path to fear occurs, a slightly slower path (milliseconds) searches my sensory memories of past experiences (real or familiar from the news) and the emotions associated with them.

---

62 Quesenberry, *Spotting Danger Before*, 66.

3. In my limbic system (emotion brain), the hippocampus (store of sensory memories) sends a signal to my amygdala, a small bilateral almond-shaped bundle of neurons in my midbrain.
4. My autonomic system is activated automatically as a reflex.
5. My body responds with a fight, flight, or freeze response.
6. My adrenal gland releases the primary stress hormones of cortisol and adrenaline, and they heighten my alertness to my surroundings and create a hyper-focus on the threats. At this point, I am unable to notice neutral or assuring sensations.
7. My reasoning and thinking (the frontal lobe of my brain) go off-line when I feel overwhelmed by fear.
8. The unique signs that my body has in the stress response are triggered. Bodily stress responses may include any combination of the following:
    a. Shallow or rapid breathing;
    b. Feeling faint;
    c. Pupils dilate, and peripheral vision decreases;
    d. Pounding heart;
    e. Blood drains from one's face and becomes pale;
    f. Clenching teeth and tightness in the jaw;
    g. The body feels hot and sweaty, but the hands are cold and clammy ("the chills");
    h. Goosebumps (hair "standing up" on arms and back of neck);
    i. Muscles in the shoulders and neck tense up, readying for defensive movement;
    j. The mouth becomes dry, and the digestive system shuts down to conserve energy;
    k. A "pit" forms in the stomach, or a feeling of nausea sweeps over;
    l. Trembling, weakness;
    m. Headache.
9. When I notice the signs of stress response in my body—for me, it's that pit in my stomach—I realize that something must have triggered it. This realization empowers me to know to do something to reduce its intensity.

10. I realize I'm out of breath and have been focusing on my fear of the threat.
11. I ask myself, "Why am I feeling these things? My mind hasn't yet identified what's happening, but it's beginning to come back online as coherent words come to mind.
12. I pause and take a deep breath through my nostrils and force it out through my mouth. I focus my mind on my breath.
13. I begin to notice my body temperature and how unevenly it's distributed.
14. I look for the Lord and go to my calm place with him. It's quiet, beautiful, and warm, and I visualize leaning my head against his shoulder.
15. "Thank you for being with me." Focusing on him helps me experience my emotional attachment to him, which is calming.
16. I begin to notice my body and the tension throughout. Starting at the top, I picture more than two hundred muscles in my head and face that are tight and visualize them relaxing.
17. I feel the pain of my clenched teeth and relax my jaw. I smile to broaden my tightened, drawn face, which helps me relax more.
18. I call to mind my happy memory with my children and husband on the beach; the sun was warming the top of my body and the warm sand underneath me. I feel my back muscles begin to relax.
19. I picture myself calmly relaxing and sitting in silence with my Lord.
20. My mind wanders to David, who wrote in the Psalms that he "talked to his soul," so I'm going to talk to my soul.
21. I feel my feet beneath me and push down to let my body know I'm here.
22. I begin to pray, "Lord, thank you for your love. I need help because this fear threatens to overwhelm me. You care about me, know what is happening, and know those who want to harm me."
23. I ask myself what is most concerning me right now.
24. I recognize I'm focusing on my fear because of a threat of evil toward people like me. I remind myself he would be with me and help me.
25. I accept that my bodily reactions to this real fear are normal.
26. I picture the neural connections in my brain and permit them to calm down. I focus my mind on Christ's hands. Perfect love.

27. I tell my body to relax.

28. I begin to notice my surroundings. I see the dirty dishes in the sink. I hear the birds chirping and my children playing in the living room with Legos. I feel my feet on the floor. I take a sip of my coffee.

29. I go back to washing dishes, feeling calmer, and turn on some worship music. I mentally repeat my tasks of the day and focus my mind on "what's the next task."

30. Each time I feel signs of stress in my body throughout my day, I am reminded to talk to the Lord about my fear.

31. I picture how I will respond to a crisis with resilience and courage.

The body's response to fear is automatic. It happens without asking, but we can develop awareness that it is happening. When we notice our alarm that we are experiencing anxiety, our understanding helps us make a new decision. We have a choice: we can focus on fear or on God. We may choose to take an action that focuses on the object of our fear, which increases our worry. We may engage in catastrophizing, allowing our fear to paralyze us and forget to connect to God. Or, despite our fear, we can purposefully focus on God (an action) and connect with him in some meaningful way, then the experience (feeling) of fear will begin to recede. We are free to choose what we do with our worries—we can follow Christ, and not act enslaved to fear. When we choose to focus on God, we will notice a difference in our bodies. We will gain a different perspective and be reminded of his promises and presence. This practice makes us ready for the action of courage.

Brené Brown wrote in *Daring Greatly*,

> Vulnerability is not weakness, and the uncertainty, risk, and emotional exposure we face every day are not optional. Our only choice is a question of engagement. Our willingness to own and engage with our vulnerability determines the depth of our courage and the clarity of our purpose. The level to which we protect ourselves from being vulnerable is a measure of our fear and disconnection.

The Courage of Cowardice[63]

> I sigh, relax, and lean into the old familiar feeling, taste, and smell of well-worn grave clothes enveloping me.
> I slip easily into the embrace of cowardice
> recognizing the metallic taste of bitterness.

---

63 Hampton, "Warm Embrace."

The weariness of fighting settles over my mind, head, and heart.
I distract myself from my wounds and insecurities,
gathering the threadbare fabric around my spirit.

Those who heal wounds lightly,
offering trite phrases to unanswerable questions,
answers from those who've never experienced the answer they so blithely give,
answers to questions not being asked,
lollipop and cookie answers from those who've never been forced to grasp the thread of trust when drowning in the stormy merciless waters of chaos.

"Just have faith."
"You can overcome your fear if you'll just pray more."
"Trust God."
"Here's what Paul says …"

The way of "trust and vulnerability" … that's for others. It would be easier to face the Taliban, al-Qaeda, ISIS, or al-Shabab. "A bear robbed of her cubs is far less dangerous than a stubborn fool." (Prov 17:12)

I'll take the cowardly, silent way, thank you.

I read the "Christian" quotes on cowardice:
"cowardice is sin";
"cowardice is the greatest evil";
"cowardice is the unpardonable sin."

Courage, fear, and cowardice so easily explained and dismissed.
Who is perfectly courageous or perfectly a coward? Swimming in our procrustean[64] waters, we cannot see we've syncretized Plato and Marcus Aurelius with the Bible.

The non-suffering church elaborately frames simplistic pictures of what courage and cowardice look like … an easy game to play that takes no discernment, empathy, or wise application of the balm of Gilead.

I feel the cold lonely breeze as my tears fall, knowing how courageous I am to admit my cowardice …

---

64 Procrustes was the Greek god who cut off or stretched people's legs to make them fit the iron bed. Procrustean thinking is forcing answers to fit a specific ideological framework or theological interpretation.

NAME Fear[65]

We can work on our fears before we are ever in a dangerous situation. When we do the work of facing our real fears, not only do we begin a path of healing, but our souls are enlarged to be able to see and help others with more empathy. If instead we "deny and distract ourselves from fear and refuse to enter into suffering, we simply reopen and re-inflict wounds."[66] Here's a guided plan for doing it using the acronym NAME.

1. Name your fears:
   a. Fear has an object. "I'm fearful of *x*" or "I fear … " What or who comes to mind? Write them down.
   b. Order your fears from least to dread fear.
   c. Look at the fears. How do you feel about your fears?

2. Ask yourself:
   a. If it happened, what's the worst thing about it?
   b. What does that cause you to feel?
   c. When you start to feel _____, where does that take you? (List your emotions and physical responses.)

3. Meaning and Imagination:
   a. Meaning: If it happened, imagine where God would be in the situation. How could he work? What purpose would he assign to your pain and fear?
   b. Imagine: We trust the person we know, so what is he like? Imagine Jesus telling his Father about your fear. What would his countenance be like? What would he be saying? Imagine him interceding with the Father about your fear.

4. Entrust:
   a. Entrust the fear to God and ask him to help you with it and give you the courage to obey him. "Trust is the equivalent of fearing God with the subsequent result of obedience."[67]

In *The Hidden Life Awakened*, Dr. Cathy Snapp describes the growing field of neuroscience and how we can change our brains. She explains how

---

65 I have lost the source for NAME, but it is not original to me. I suspect it comes from Crenshaw and Snapp.
66 Myers, "Introduction: Fear and Faith," 8–12.
67 Jones, "When I Am Afraid," 23.

the area of "Neuroscience is growing in its capacity to map ... how our thoughts, emotions, and choices register in the brain by a cascade of physical and energetic changes in the structure of its cells. Scientists now affirm that how and where we focus our attention dictates the content of the brain structure we create."[68]

When a "neural structure [is activated], ... oxygen, blood flow, and energy are moving through them, strengthening them."[69] We can choose to strengthen our fear/anxiety pathway or weaken it by turning to God and asking for help (this choice is cultivating secure attachment habits).

We turn to God by

> choosing to focus our attention ... on uplifting emotional content (positivity and hope) [and our attachment to God], and sustaining that moment for twenty-five seconds (installation), we little by little change our brain structure, which changes mental activity, which changes biochemical communication in the body, which epigenetically changes gene expression, and thus our physical, mental, and emotional well-being. In other words, replacing anxious, worried thoughts with realistic, balanced thoughts physically impacts the synapses of our brain, "causing them to disconnect and make brand new connections," new pathways, and cells devoted to right thinking. It's called the process of neuroplasticity; a new brain is created to replace the old brain.[70]

The Path of Fear and Courage

When we combine all these elements, we see two paths in Figure 5. One leads to mature courage and hope, and the other to paralysis, despair, difficulty, or even the inability to follow Christ. It's likely our path will not be perfect, but we will experience progress as we work towards mature courage.

When we feel the experience of fear related to death, pain, or shame, we look to God or we look at our fearful circumstances. One choice leads to acting in fear, the other to acting in courage.

Looking at the fear, we often begin to focus on it and feel overwhelmed. This habit leads to avoidance and inability to do the works of God. Anxiety breeds more anxiety. The more I let my fear overwhelm me, the more I let my fears grow in size, and the more I fear my fears. It's a vicious cycle. I cannot take in the assuring parts of my surroundings and those around me, and I will likely miss an opportunity to serve him in my risk situation.

---

68 Crenshaw and Snapp, *The Hidden Life Awakened*, xiii.
69 Crenshaw and Snapp, 37.
70 Crenshaw and Snapp, xiii.

Instead, we should look to God and tell him about our fear (NAME it), we should ask for his help to respond with courage, recognizing that no matter what we feel, he loves us and is a compassionate, faithful, merciful Father God. In response, we find sufficient light to know what to do next, even if it's just doing a household task. This practice moves me step by step to mature hope and mature courage.

Figure 5: The Path of Fear and Courage

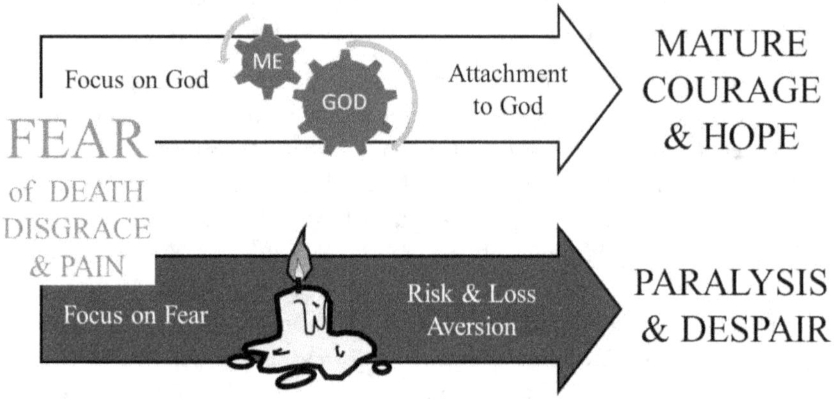

© 2022 Neal & Anna Hampton

We see Peter acting with impulsive courage when he sees Jesus walking on water and asks the Lord to call him to join him. Jesus calls, and Peter steps out of the boat, looks at Jesus, and walks on water! But when Peter looks down (action of fear)—looks at his fearful circumstances of giant waves—he experiences fear and begins to sink into the water. Then he does the right thing: he chooses to act in courage by calling out to Christ for help! Immediately Jesus rescues him from (his fear) the storm.

How Jesus Reorders Our Fears

"The dis-orderliness of life has the potential to produce fear; seeking the Lord of order appears[...]to be the antidote."[71] It is what trust looks like. Scripture is filled with examples of humans having fear directed at the right person (God) but for the wrong reason. Because humanity needed help to manage our fears, God himself came in the person of Jesus Christ to show us how to reorder our fears.

---

71 Jones, "When I Am Afraid," 18.

Throughout the Gospels, Jesus addresses our fears and gently shows his disciples who to fear and why. He teaches in Matthew 10:28, 31 "And do not fear those who kill the body but cannot kill the soul. Rather fear him who can destroy both soul and body in hell. ... Fear not, therefore; you are of more value than many sparrows." He is teaching that as we consider our fears and list them out, it's helpful to put them on a scale of increasing intensity, but make sure that our biggest fear, our dread fear, is oriented to him for the right reason—he, God, is the one who controls the essential aspect of our body and soul, destruction, or eternal life.

This truth is significant, but until it takes up residence in our hearts and touches our emotions, it remains an external spiritual truth. He is a courteous gentleman who does not force his will or thoughts on us but invites us to join him. When we accept his invitation to trust him with our fears, his supernatural peace and love fill us at that moment. There is no shortcut or simple step to this reality. Connecting our minds to our hearts is an individual path for each of us in relationship to Christ.

Facing fear in risk and persecution feels like facing fear in a first-century wooden boat in a storm.[72] Dr. Skip Moen does a masterful job of commentating on the types of fear in this text.[73] The following is used with the author's permission.

In Mark 4:35–41, Jesus said, "He said to them, 'Let us go over to the other side.' Leaving the crowd, they took Him along with them in the boat, just as He was; and other boats were with Him" (NASB). He purposely directed his disciples to go a certain direction. He knew the storm was coming.

If you are in the boat with Jesus, the first question in a storm is, "Where's the life preserver?" It's the last question we need to ask, but it's likely the first question in your mind. Jesus answers this question, but not in the way we expect.[74]

"And there arose a fierce gale of wind, and the waves were breaking over the boat so much that the boat was already filling up" (v. 37, NASB). The storm came up quickly and violently and was so bad the boat was filling with water. The waves were so high that they started splashing over the bow of the boat, filling it, until the boat was almost on the verge of sinking.

---

[72] Moen, "Stormy Monday" and "Calm Terror." The following section on the storm as told by the Gospel of Mark incorporates many direct quotes and thoughts from Dr. Skip Moen's writing. He graciously re-edited this section to his satisfaction and gave me permission to include it in this book. He has written over 7000 word studies. His writing may be accessed on his website.

[73] Moen's own translation of Mark 4:35–41.

[74] Moen, "Calm Terror."

"Jesus Himself was in the stern, asleep on the cushion" (v. 38, NASB). He's asleep! How could Jesus possibly sleep in this chaos?

> Without saying a word, Jesus still reflects an Old Testament perspective on life. To sleep during a storm reveals complete confidence in the sovereignty of God, just as the Scripture suggests in Leviticus 26:6 (lying down with no concern about trouble), Job 11:18, 19 (resting securely), and Psalm 3:5 (the Lord protects the righteous even in sleep). Jesus is the righteous Old Testament man even when he does nothing at all.[75]

Sleep is perhaps the actual indicator of our confidence in God, especially in a storm. A child sleeps with no cares, no worries, and no wrinkles on the face. Someone is in charge of the world, and it's not me.

"… and they woke Him and said to Him, 'Teacher, do You not care that we are perishing?'" (v. 38, NASB). The disciples began to panic. From the disciples' point of view, things were worsening by the minute. They might have said, "What's the matter with him? How can he sleep? Doesn't he know how serious this is?" The disciples didn't see the irony of their situation that day on the Sea of Galilee. If the storm was so bad that the disciples thought they would drown, what did they think Jesus could do? Jesus is also in the boat without a life preserver.[76] How do they think Jesus is going to save them? Furthermore, who is in the boat with Jesus? They're sailors. At least some of them were seasoned sailors. Who is Jesus? All they know is he's an ex-carpenter rabbi. What do they think he can do to save them when they can't save themselves?

They were probably wondering, "Why isn't he helping us?" The disciples could not imagine how Jesus could sleep in such danger. Jesus could not imagine how they could be so concerned when they were under God's care. It's a matter of perspective, isn't it? Jesus asleep during the storm also gives us a significant clue as to how we can begin to see spiritually: sleeping soundly directly contrasts the apparent panic of the disciples—he was at rest; they were in distress. In the presence of Jesus, things may not be as they naturally appear. There's always a different spiritual reality, and it takes practice to discern it.

The word for drowning is "*Apollumetha*!" It's a verb that means "to destroy, to lose, to perish," but with the added emphasis of emotional terror.[77] They were utterly terrorized! We would say, "Lord, we're going to die!" What is implied by what they said? "Are you just going to sleep? Are you just going to take care of your own needs? Do you not care if we perish?"

---

75 Moen, "Stormy Monday."
76 Moen, "Calm Terror."
77 Moen, "In the Boat."

The disciples failed to grasp that they were just fine as long as they were in the boat with Jesus. In a panic, men [and women] often don't think straight, but at least they noticed who wasn't worried.

Notice what sends them into crisis: "Jesus Himself was in the stern, asleep on the cushion; and they woke Him and said to Him, 'Teacher, do You not care that we are perishing?'" (NASB). Their crisis comes when they feel that Jesus doesn't care. What causes you to ask God, "Why don't you care about … ?"

If we are in the boat with Jesus, we can realize that we're riding through the storm together. While there is no guarantee of how bad it will get or when it will end, we can cultivate a "Jesus-is-present" perspective.

"And He got up and rebuked the wind and said to the sea, 'Hush, be still.' And the wind died down and it became perfectly calm" (v. 39, NASB). Jesus said nothing to them. Instead, he instantly responded to the threat before them: the sea. He got up, rebuked the wind, and said to the waves, "Hush, be still" (v. 39, NASB). Now put yourself in that boat. The disciples were not prepared for Jesus's solution. Has anyone you know ever reprimanded the wind and the sea and told them to behave? When you are about to drown in a violent storm, does talking to the ocean sound like a reasonable solution to you?[78]

"And the wind died down and it became perfectly calm" (v. 39, NASB). Amazingly, the elements obey him. Mark is careful to tell us that the miracle included the sea going from gigantic waves to completely calm, totally unruffled, serene. But that's not the way water works in ordinary life. After a storm, the water is usually choppy for a while before it calms down. But instantly, the wind dropped, and the sea went utterly calm. No wonder these men were overcome by awe. They were more frightened after the calm than before. What kind of man commands the earth and the sea? Only a man who is an agent of God. Sitting in the boat next to such a man must have been terrifying indeed.[79]

"And He said to them, 'Why are you afraid? How is it that you have no faith?'" (v. 40, NASB). Jesus's response to all this terror is so typical of God's perspective. He uses an entirely different word for fear than Mark used to describe the disciples' fear. Jesus is reframing and reordering their fears. Jesus changes the situation with another word—cowardly, timid, instead of dread or fear. He asks, "Why are you timid-cowardly?" The question may be more accurately translated as "Why are you running away from nothing?" Then the second question: the Greek sense of these questions can also be translated as "You little-faiths! Why are you so upset? I'm right here with you.

---

78 Moen, "Calm Terror."
79 Moen.

It's no problem." We could say that Jesus is helping them become aware they had lost sight of his presence. He was there with them. They focused on their dread fear, their terror of drowning in the storm and him not caring. He was helping them understand that their fears were misplaced. He rejected their fear of the storm for a different and more appropriate fear. Notice also that Jesus asked them questions, but he did not condemn them.

How often do we condemn those who have fear instead of walking through it with them? Scazzero writes,

> When we deny our pain, losses, and feelings year after year, we become less and less human. We transform into empty shells with smiley faces painted on them. Sad to say, that is the fruit of much of our discipleship in our churches. But when I allowed myself to feel a wider range of emotions, including sadness, depression, fear, and anger, a revolution in my spirituality was unleashed. I soon realized that a failure to appreciate the biblical place of feelings within our larger Christian lives has done extensive damage, keeping free people in Christ in slavery.[80]

"They became very much afraid and said to one another, 'Who then is this, that even the wind and the sea obey Him?" (v. 41, NASB). They ask a different question: *"Who is this?"* The Greek presumes a negative answer to the question, so a better way to translate this is, "What is he?" It implies an answer of "He is not a man." Here, "overcome with awe" has a different word for fear: they were "mega" *phobos*. They were filled with mega fear, or literally, "they feared a mega fear." Here in verse 41, finally, they have a more ordered fear. Jesus taught his disciples in Matthew 10:28, "Do not fear those who kill the body but are unable to kill the soul; but rather fear him who is able to destroy both soul and body in hell" (NASB). The idea of disordered fears and ordered fears becomes clear when Jesus tells his followers who to fear. "Little fears" emphasize a threat that is not as significant as the "big fear" that Jesus teaches is the most serious.

What are the crucial lessons for how we face fears in risks when our very lives are at stake? The first lesson is about the sovereignty of our Lord. He rules everything! When I am in the boat with Jesus, he is quite capable of doing something that is unpredictable and appears insane. Another fundamental spiritual principle is about what holds power. When Jesus asks his disciples in Mark 4:40, "Why are you afraid? How is it that you have no faith?" (NASB)? He says, "Why are you timid towards something so little with such little power and hold over you? Don't you see that I am greater, more powerful, and trustworthy?" Seeing him and fearing him for the right reasons teaches

---

80 Scazzero, *Emotionally Healthy Spirituality*, 44.

us that "big fears make little fears go away."[81] Next, I need to fear him far more than any circumstance in my life. "The solution to my problem is never a change in circumstances."[82] The solution is not about physical reality. It's about who loves me and cares for me.

There are several critical questions to ask ourselves here from Mark's story: With what perspective am I looking at this storm in my life? Jesus's perspective, or the disciples' perspective? As I reflect on my fears, what is my core fear underlying the presenting fear?

If you were in the boat, sopping wet and cold after a violent storm, and you had just experienced the raw, primal emotion of absolute and complete terror, what tone would Jesus be using to ask you, "Why are you frightened? Don't you have faith yet?" What tone do you hear Jesus using when he asks this question of the disciples? The tone playing in your mind gives you both spiritual and psychological awareness of what is going on in you in your relationship with Christ.

Finally, how is Jesus leading me to reorder my fears? He is the living and gracious God who longs for us to come to him with our fears. When we bring our fears to him, somehow, they are changed. There is mystery at work here. They may still be there, but his presence takes up more of the room in our hearts than our fears.

Corrie ten Boom, a concentration camp survivor, put it this way, "When you look death in the eyes, not once but often, you see the things, how they are, things in proportion ... the great things great and the small things small."[83] "I have seen what it means to have security in the Lord Jesus when all the security of the world had fallen away."[84]

Another more profound spiritual truth from Mark's story of Jesus calming the storm is less obvious to the modern hearer.[85] We enjoy the sea and lakes as a pleasure and places for vacation. In the Ancient Near East and into the first century, the sea symbolized evil, a source of chaos, the abyss to be feared. This story in Mark alludes to the abyss of Genesis 1:2. Just as God's spirit hovered over the deep and had the power to make order out of chaos, Jesus has the same power. Jesus's calming of the storm revealed him as Yahweh, the Creator God. "The message of Scripture is clear and consistent— the forces of evil are terrible, but our Lord is far greater. Jesus has authority over the forces of evil, chaos, and death."[86]

---

81 Allender and Longman III, *Cry of the Soul*, KL 893.
82 Moen, "Calm Terror."
83 TenBoom, *Amazing Love*, Kindle Location 1290.
84 Attributed to Corrie TenBoom.
85 Jethani, "Real Meaning of Jesus."
86 Jethani.

When the gun is to your head, and the pressure is on to witness for Christ, what is essential in fear and love becomes very, very clear. All the lesser fears and lesser loves recede in significance. And as our Father helps us order our fears and loves (it's a continual process over a lifetime), our souls calm and are led more by peace, trust, and love, no matter what storm is ahead. He is worthy.

Chapter 4
Temptations, Idols, and Ancient Heresies in Risk

Many, many people come to the altar, but few find their way to the foot of the cross.[1]
—Betty Walthour Skinner

We don't want to stare at the naked, bloodied body of Jesus stretched out on rough wood, hear him gasping for breath, and smell the stench of his dying body. It is horrifyingly uncomfortable. Only one man and three women from Christ's band of followers remained with him. What would it look, feel, sound, and smell like to go and comfort John, Jesus's mother Mary, his aunt, Mary (wife of Clopas), and Mary Magdalene at the foot of the cross?[2] Standing there was hazardous—standing there was to be seen as "one of them." Standing there meant risking being seen as subversive to the Roman state. Standing at the cross meant standing against the acceptable religious orthodoxy. Standing there with them was to be seen as a failure in the humiliation of his death. Standing with them was standing with a new type of family suffering with Christ.

What does "taking up your cross" mean? What does "not taking up your cross" mean? Not taking up one's cross implies an unwillingness to suffer or to enter the suffering of others. To assuage the discomfort of Christ's sufferings and our own, we numb ourselves, distract ourselves, give way to temptations, turn to idols, and allow comforting heresies to creep in unnoticed. Anything to make sacrifice feel less sacrificial, life feel controllable, and diminish the discomfort of doubt and uncertainty.

Temptations in Risk and Persecution

Penner points out four temptations identified in Matthew 10:33–42:[3]

1. The temptation to deny Christ (v. 33).

The ultimate and direct test of this temptation is discussed in chapter five. However, there are numerous "soft" ways a Christ-follower may be tempted to deny Christ.

---

[1] Crenshaw and Snapp, *Hidden Life Awakened*, 214.
[2] John 19:25, 26.
[3] Penner, *In the Shadow*, 106–8.

After days, months, and years of being kept off balance by persecutors and interrogators, offers may be made to the Christ-follower to get them to give in to a compromise which seems holy and right on the surface. It's extremely tempting to be persuaded by rational thought that isn't outright denying Christ, and releases one from torture. Our imaginations can be sanctified, but they can also be hijacked by fear and horror. The response in such an extreme moment of temptation is to follow the example of Richard Wurmbrand: "I have considered well, and weighed the dangers, and I rejoice to suffer for what I am sure is the last truth."[4]

2. The temptation to love one's family more than Christ (vv. 34–37).
3. The temptation to love one's life more than Christ, therefore not being prepared to lose it for Christ's sake (vv. 38, 39).
4. The temptation to refuse to receive those who, because of their witness, could put you in danger (vv. 40–42).

There are additional temptations (recognized from personal experience as well as listening to others and observing them in risk and persecution):

5. The temptation to minimize the danger and not prepare.

For example, between 2016–2022, the number of non-governmental organizations in India went from 43,000 to 4,000. Most of these organizations were unprepared and often responded, "We should have prayed more." They had no contingency plans for staying in the country to be able to continue their work, even though there were clear signs that the environment was changing and threats were increasing.[5]

6. The temptation to believe you are alone and isolated.

The first place "aloneness" is found in Scripture is in Genesis 2:18. The word "alone" in Hebrew is "*lĕbad*." When God said, "It is not good for man to be alone," he was referring to more than physical aloneness. We are meant to be in relationships with him and with others, connected to others, not isolated in all spheres of life.

However, we may feel isolated and alone not only externally, physically, but also in our interior life—we may feel that even God has left us. We feel isolated when walking through danger and persecution; we feel even more alone when people don't seem to understand what we are going through and have already gone through and the impact these experiences have on us. This sense of isolation is a scary and vulnerable place to be, and the enemy

---
[4] Penner, 267. Penner is quoting Richard Wurmbrand, *In God's Underground*, 265–70.
[5] Conversations with a pastor living in persecution and danger.

of our soul knows this and exploits it to his advantage.

The reality is that God describes himself as Emmanuel, "God with us." Emmanuel is the God who is always with us, even when it feels like he has abandoned us. We think we are abandoned because we cannot see, hear, or feel him in our usual ways. Instead, we *must* cultivate spiritual eyes and discernment to trust his presence, even when it feels like he has concealed himself in "darkness" or "opaqueness."

> Emmanuel is the God who is always with us, even when it feels like he has abandoned us.

7. The temptation to believe there is nothing you can do (resignation) and to accept whatever happens without resisting.

Stoicism is a philosophical approach to life that has been influencing Western thought since the time of the Ancient Greeks. According to the Stoics, the good is [the] "one in which reason, not passion, rules, and peace of mind and harmony with nature consequently prevail."[6] Accepting hardship and suffering calmly and without complaining is a good response and is a form of Stoicism. However, one stream of Stoicism can lead to the point of passivity. To not do anything in the face of danger contrasts with Proverbs 22:3 and 27:12: "The prudent sees danger and hides himself, but the simple go on and suffer for it." People resigned to whatever happens are likely to have a more challenging time with endurance, resiliency, and the ability to persevere in adversity and fight for survival because of this internal attitude of resignation and stoicism. The impact of resignation and stoicism is not merely personal and individual—these can cause a lack of empathy and care for others in dangerous situations. A lack of empathy and care does not enhance more intimate community and unity of the family of God walking through persecution. Thus, God's kingdom is not put on display (John 13:35). It's a terrible spiral that can result in disintegration and conflict.

8. The temptation to minimize and rationalize one's private sin. This happens when we face persecution and evil. We begin to compare the external evil as so much greater than our "small" private sin, we justify our sin to comfort ourselves. This is unrighteousness.

9. The temptation toward dissipation, numbing out, or anxiety.

---

6 Beitzel, "Stoics, Stoicism," v2, 2000.

In Luke 21:34, Jesus says, "But watch yourselves lest your hearts be weighed down with dissipation and drunkenness and cares of this life, and that day come upon you suddenly like a trap." Before he said this, he taught about all the horrifying events that would happen as "the day" draws near (the day of judgment). He warned us about what we should watch for and guard against.

First, "dissipation" means to be so distracted and busy we are unable to focus on the task at hand. Resources like time and energy are wasted. We fritter away our lives on acceptable "busy" tasks but avoid what God actually wants for us. Secondly, drunkenness, of course, can refer to alcohol, but many other things similarly "numb" the pain, such as social media scrolling, food, pornography, entertainment, until we are numbed out. Don't numb out of reality. Thirdly, he put "cares of this life" on the same level as drunkenness! Being drunk is being out of control and unable to discern accurately. When we are overly concerned about the cares of this life, we are being controlled by them, unable to discern reality correctly, and not living prayerfully, as wise stewards of the Lord.

10. The temptation to want God's omnipotence more than his sovereignty.

God's omnipotence (all-powerful) and sovereignty (his will and reign) are not the same as Greco-Roman gods or human sovereigns. His power is constrained to allow humans free choice to accept and love him or reject him. This reality obliges us to see that evil and chaos are permitted in the world, and we should not be indifferent or apathetic. His sovereignty, his will to act or not act, is not like a sovereign ruler of a nation. His sovereignty is "an authority given for the express purpose of conferring eternal life."[7] His authority is given to Christ to convey life through his death and resurrection. Christ exercised his authority to bring all humanity to life and in right standing with his father by "reigning from the tree."[8]

In situations of risk and persecution, we want his power to rescue us more than his sovereignty to leave us subjected to suffering. However, when we are invited to follow him and then do so, we follow him into his suffering, which even his Father did not prevent.

Yet we often pray and ask God to protect us from evil and keep us safe. That's not wrong, but that's not all, nor is that even primary. How did Jesus pray for us, and how did the early church pray amid persecution?

---

7 Morris, *New International Commentary*, 716–39.
8 Morris, 716–39.

How Did Jesus Pray?

Let's examine the last prayer Jesus prayed for his disciples and all of us who would follow him. In John 17, he says the following:

- v. 11: "They are in the world ... keep them in your name, which you have given me, that they may be one, even as we are one."
- v. 12: "While I was with them, I kept them in your name ... I have guarded them"
- v. 14: "I have given them your word, and the world has hated them because they are not of the world."
- v. 15: "I do not ask that you take them out of the world, but that you keep them from the evil one."
- v. 17: "Sanctify them in the truth; your word is truth."
- v. 18: "As you sent me into the world, so I have sent them into the world."

We want to retreat from the world, but Jesus prays not that his father would take us out of the world but keep us in it. The world hates us; he asks his father to keep us in his name and from the power of the evil one. The prayer of Jesus reveals the father's sovereign will for us—that we go into the world which hates him in us, and as we are going that the father would protect us from the power of the evil one because "we are 'in Christ' and therefore 'out of' the evil one. [We] have such a weighty task to do in the world that we should be in the world but kept from evil, for evil is fatal to the discharge of [our] task."[9]

How Did the Early Church Pray?

In Acts 4:24–30, the first recorded prayer after our Lord's ascension results from Peter and John being jailed because they "greatly annoyed" the religious leaders. After a night in jail, Peter and John were brought in for interrogation. The religious leaders told them not to speak or teach in the name of Jesus again, threatened them, and let them go. Peter and John went home to their friends and reported everything and then prayed a fascinating prayer that combines both God's power and sovereignty:

> Sovereign Lord, who made the heaven and the earth and the sea and everything in them, who through the mouth of our father David, your servant, said by the Holy Spirit, "Why did the Gentiles rage and the peoples' plot in vain? The kings of the earth set themselves, and the rulers were gathered together

---
9 Morris, 730.

against the Lord and against his Anointed." For truly in this city, there were gathered together against your holy servant Jesus, whom you anointed, both Herod and Pontius Pilate, along with the Gentiles and the peoples of Israel, to do whatever your hand and your plan had predestined to take place. And now, Lord, look upon their threats and grant to your servants to continue to speak your word with all boldness, while you stretch out your hand to heal, and signs and wonders are performed through the name of your holy servant Jesus.

The very first two words in the Koine Greek are not "Sovereign Lord" but the Greek word "*Despota*," which is the source for the English noun, "despot." There are ten places in the New Testament this word is used for Lord instead of the typical "*Kyrios*." However, only three of these are used to address the Lord directly in prayer.[10]

Using the appellation "*Despota*" signifies his power as master over all with authority to reign. His sovereignty to do as he wishes is emphasized in the middle: "to do whatever your hand and your plan had predestined to take place."

> In Jewish thought, *doulos* [slaves] has two critical but opposite distinctions. First, it is a term for human oppression, but second, it is a term of divine-human commitment. The determining factor is *choice*. If I am *doulos* by compulsion, the term is derogatory and hateful. But if I am *doulos* by choice, then the term expresses deep, emotionally positive commitment. It's all up to the subject. If we were to translate *doulos* in this verse as "slave," we might have the same adverse reaction as any first century Roman. We think being a "slave" means losing our most important characteristic of humanity—*freedom*! The two-sided nature of *doulos* means I am always free to choose, but the result of my choice must mean total commitment if I am going to be a servant of the Most High.[11]

There are two significant aspects of this early New Testament church prayer. While theologians state that "*Kyrios*" and "*Despota*" came to be used interchangeably, it is noteworthy that in this passage, in response to persecution and the decision to continue proclaiming Christ in a risk situation, the disciples' recognized God's absolute power and sovereignty while also stating their position as slaves who are choosing to obey. Second, their only request for themselves is that he would grant them as his servants (slaves) to speak with boldness. Notice they did not ask for protection, safety, or for God to do something to their enemies. They trusted the Lord to take care of their enemies.

---

10 Luke 2:29; Acts 4:24; Rev 6:10.
11 Moen, "Kingdom Status."

Two additional temptations we face in fear and persecution are:

11. The temptation to spiritual pride.

When we suffer for Christ, it is tempting to compare our suffering with another's and to consider ours greater; in a sick way, we can view ourselves as a more holy sufferer. The enemy will do anything to remove the closeness we experience with Christ when we have endured torture or persecution or suffering for him in any way. But he is sneaky and subtle in how he does it. We may have a thought about how much we have suffered for Christ, and how righteous we are (true), but our heart is immediately roused to thinking of ourselves as great, and others as ... not so much. Instead of thinking of others as better than ourselves (Phil 2:3), we begin to think we are better than others. This attitude infects how we talk to and about others and eventually how we treat them (disdainfully). Spiritual pride is a temptation that is almost always present when risking our lives for Christ and suffering for him.

12. The temptation to fixate on our enemies.

A vicious cycle often takes place without our awareness. "The more effort we exert labeling others as enemies, the more we actually take on the traits of our enemies ... In fear and with a lack of trust in God's justice, we begin to judge based on our criteria (often driven by fear) ... [we conflate our 'enemies' with 'God's enemies,'] and we begin to create a god in our image."[12]

While the prophets modeled what it is to "denounce enemies of justice, whether structural, communal, or individual, [it's imperative we realize] with humility that we regularly participate in unjust systems."[13] How do we resemble our enemies?

Idolatry in Risk

I stated earlier that evil is not logical in the way we normally think; it has its own logic. With idols, evil follows the logic of idols. Idols enslave and dehumanize: "As fear grows, it 'disorders' our loves and drives us to serve idols."[14] What is idolatry? We can identify it in our lives by asking ourselves, "What am I trusting in, clinging to, or relying upon over God?" Idols are means of control that demand sacrifice for the wrong thing.[15] Psalm 135:18 teaches, "Those who make them [idols] become like them, so do all who trust in them." It is not uncommon for a Christ-follower to inconsistently use Scripture to defend whatever they want to support.

---

12 Jones, "When I Am Afraid," 24.
13 Jones, 24.
14 Brackley, *Call to Discernment*, 44.
15 Brackley, 27.

We identify what has become an idol if we react very angrily or are undone if that thing is criticized or taken away. If we are betting our future on that thing being part of our lives, or we are desperately trying to hold on to that thing, we should ask ourselves if we have an idol in our life.

> Idolatry is a significant topic in the Bible—much neglected by contemporary evangelical Christians partly because we are unconsciously involved with and sometimes dominated by the false gods of the people around us. One reason for the slow but accelerating collapse of Western civilization is the profoundly syncretistic and idolatrous nature of Western Christianity, combined with the idolatry of the culture that surrounds us. Like Israel of old, we, God's people, are in uncritical collusion with the false gods of our ambient cultures.[16]

What are some idols in risk? Here are ones I've identified with Neal that are not uncommon among Christ-followers in dangerous situations.

Security

We know that security has become an idol when we assuage our fears by putting our ultimate trust in security practices. We become angry or immobilized when we do not have a certain level of security mitigation practices in place. Lange wrote, "It is when our fear overtakes our trust in God, and when our fear blocks the exile from heading home, and when our fear overwhelms us to the point that we are willing to rest our ultimate security in something that is not ultimately able to comfort us or protect us, then both our fear and our security have been misplaced and made into idols."[17]

We can justify how safety is achieved when we worship this idol, which implies ethics derived from idolatry, not kingdom culture.

One example of security as idolatry is when a Christ-follower, working in dangerous places for kingdom purposes, weaponizes themselves using Nehemiah as the example. Nehemiah 4:18: "Each of the builders had his sword strapped at his side while he built." However, unlike a twenty-first century gospel worker, Nehemiah's men were building defensive fortifications. It's a dangerous hermeneutic to use Bible stories as prescriptions for how we are to act and make choices. According to the Gospel writers, the disciples of Jesus were sent out without even an extra cloak, certainly not with a sword.[18]

---

16 Wright, *Here Are Your Gods*, 93.
17 Lange, "Exploring the Idol."
18 Some Christians use Luke 22:36 as proof text for arming themselves even when they go out in cross-cultural work. I believe this is an example of eisegesis and proof-texting. The context of this verse is in light of the events leading to the arrest and crucifixion of Jesus, not with the Great Commission in mind, which wouldn't happen for weeks. The clear example throughout the Gospels is Jesus sending out his disciples unarmed, in a position of vulnerability.

Individualism

This idol leads people serving it to do what seems right to them without considering the impact on the team or community. Selfish decision-making in risk is individually-focused and does not consider others (both expatriates and locals involved in the situation) whether Christ-followers or not. While God speaks and leads individuals, individualistic cultures tend towards this type of decision-making far more than communal-based cultures.

Christian Nationalism and Exceptionalism

This mindset is the idol that says, "It can't happen to me because I'm from ____ country." Or, "The government of my passport country is powerful and will rescue me." This thinking also infects our theology. "Our" theology is the right one, not the one from the less powerful nations.

Christian Functionalism and Organizational Expertise[19]

This idol states that we can depend on an idea or approach if it is materially successful and if we do it the right way (correct behavior). (And by the way, our organization does it the right way, not like that one over there.) Or, "if it's not working for us, then we just have to bring in the correct training entity, read the right books, and function correctly, and once we do that in this dangerous environment, we will have success." (Because doing it "right" is what we are clinging to.) Those serving this idol believe that their project is so essential that they must keep going no matter the risk level and impact.

Of course, there is nothing wrong with doing things right. But if we are clinging to, trusting in, and relying upon proper execution instead of God, it's likely an idol. This idol of functionalism includes methodology and numbers. The focus is on Western church metrics of success, even in dangerous and challenging areas resistant to the gospel. Churches have gone into conflict over which approach to reaching Muslims is correct. "Certainly, this method is the biblical one, and we have the 'inside expert' telling us and the numbers to prove it."

In crucial contrast, we want to faithfully obey where the Spirit is at work, follow his leading in risk and persecution, and leave the results up to God.

Comfort and the Cult of Success

Paul discusses how the Corinthians were living their best life; they had all they wanted. He said, in 1 Corinthians 4:8–12:

---

19 McBride, "Sociological Imagination."

Already you have all you want! Already you have become rich! You have become kings! You are wise, you are strong, you are held in honor! But we are like last of all, like men sentenced to death, we have become a spectacle to the world, we are fools for Christ's sake, we are weak, we are held in disrepute, we hunger, thirst, are poorly dressed, buffeted, and homeless. We labor, working with our own hands. We have become and are still, like the scum of the world, the refuse of all things.[20]

This passage is a description of the prosperity gospel. It may rear its ugly head in times of suffering. The person who follows this idol believes the suffering implies something wrong in their relationship with God. Perhaps they've sinned or are not praying enough, reading enough, etc., so God is not blessing them. It is easier for those living in comfort to buy into the prosperity gospel and believe they have the proper theology, true Christianity, and power. They mistakenly believe their wealth, success, and comfort automatically means everything is good between them and God.

But the prosperity gospel impacts even those of us who utterly reject it. For example, we might believe that when we sacrifice so much and risk our lives, God will answer by providing spiritual "fruit" that we can report back to our donors. We believe that he will respond like a puppet on a string that we can manipulate by our actions.

Ancient Heresies in the Twenty-First Century

Why discuss ancient heresies with risk and persecution in the twenty-first century? As the author of Ecclesiastes wrote, "there is nothing new under the sun" (Eccl 1:9). Just as heresies arose in the early church times, there are heresies today. The heresies of the twenty-first century are just the same old ones but with different nuances, names, and intensities. Paul taught about dissensions, divisions, and rivalries in Galatians 5:20. This idea is one "party" being correct over another.

Peter wrote in 2 Peter 2:1, "But false prophets also arose among the people, just as there will be false teachers among you, who will secretly bring in destructive heresies." Peter wrote this warning to Christ-followers because these false teachings can creep in, and we might not realize it. Discernment is needed.

The word "heresy" should be used carefully. "May it not be the case that at least some of today's so-called heretics are really following the example of Jesus himself, by questioning conventional orthodoxies which have grown up round his truth and have hardened like old wineskins round the

---

20 My rearrangement for emphasis.

new wine of the gospel?"[21] However, today, there's a tendency to elevate a heretic as someone heroic, someone who has the courage to rebel and stand up to the institutional church or refuse to agree with a particular version of Christianity. I am not using this definition.

Heresy has traditionally been defined as "a choice to deviate from traditional teaching in favor of one's insights ... A heretic has compromised an essential doctrine and lost sight of who God is [usually by oversimplification]."[22] This choice has always had a negative implication and resulted in significant church councils and creeds.

To be clear, I am not saying that Christ-followers compromise essential doctrines in risk and persecution. However, some tendencies and attitudes are echoes of heretical doctrines that take the focus off of (1) fully identifying with Christ's physical and spiritual sufferings; and (2) walking in obedience to him with our whole heart, mind, and soul; as (3) our invitation by the Holy Spirit into risk and persecution *or* invitation by the Holy Spirit to flee risk and persecution. Ancient heresies that rear their heads in twenty-first century witness risk include the following:

Pelagianism (fifth century)

This is moralist theology that teaches salvation is up to us and not dependent on God's grace. It teaches that God gave us the tools to respond to him, and we have unconditional free will and moral responsibility. God commands only to our ability. Perfection is achievable since Jesus commands us to be perfect, and he would not ask us to do something we can't. It's all up to us.

In risk, we see echoes of Pelagianistic thinking when people believe that the risk event they feared happened because they did not do enough righteous acts (moralism) in the risk. Echoes of Pelagianistic thinking are when we think we earn Christ's approval by "rightly" handling the risk situation. What does "rightly" mean? Most ask "What is the correct way?" instead of asking "How do I discern his leading in this risk?" This is most closely aligned to Risk Myth Nine: If something bad happens, it's because I didn't pray, work, or do a proper risk assessment or enough risk management. It's all up to us, and if something terrible happens, it's our fault that God didn't save us/the project/the people. There is an underdeveloped theology of evil, and there is a misunderstanding of God's grace.

---

21 Elcoat, "Ancient Heresy."
22 Holcomb, *Know the Heretics*, 11.

Gnosticism (first and second century)

Gnosticism comes from the Greek word "to know." The Gnostics believed that salvation comes through knowledge. Gnosticism pits the spiritual realm and material realm against each other. Spirit = good. Flesh = evil. Some Gnostics emphasized the body and indulgence, and some the spirit and secret knowledge. No matter which is emphasized, dualism is a crucial feature of Gnosticism then and now.

In risk, anytime we emphasize one aspect—the body's importance or the spirit's importance—to the diminishment of the other, we are engaging in echoes of Gnosticism. Spiritualizing risk, especially out of spiritual pride, and thus not engaging in risk assessment and management is poor stewardship. On the other hand, emphasizing security practices and ignoring spiritual realities is an echo elevating the physical realm over the spiritual. We are called to steward everything in God's creation, including our physical bodies and who we are—our mind, heart, and whole being (Hebrew: *nephesh*).

> Spiritualizing risk, especially out of spiritual pride, and thus not engaging in risk assessment and management is poor stewardship.

Judaizers (first century)

This heresy is the belief that Jewish laws, like circumcision, are required for salvation. However, good deeds do not contribute to salvation (Acts 10:45; 11:2; 15:23–29; Gal 2:14). In contrast, we are saved through Christ's work on the cross and God declaring those of us who follow him to be righteous and accepted in his sight because of Christ's blood.

The idea of echoing Judaizers in risk and persecution is the attitude or belief that risking one's life or being persecuted makes one more righteous and more pleasing to God. Communities facing danger can look down on those who leave as cowardly and unworthy of God's favor. There is tremendous social pressure to do the risky, dangerous thing without considering what our Lord is inviting someone into and what obedience for that Christ-follower looks like.

Docetism (first to fourth centuries)

This heresy is from the Greek word *dokein*, which means "to seem." Docetists believed that Christ only seemed to be human. They thought Jesus was pure spirit and did not physically suffer. Docetism was an integral part of Gnosticism.

In risk, we are sliding toward echoing Docetism when we deny the physical reality of suffering and the cost of sacrificing for Christ and the need for a human (physical/logical/emotional) response to risk and persecution. The Docetistic attitude is also indicated by those who feel more spiritually virtuous by not taking care with their security profile (not doing a risk assessment and management) because "who cares what the terrorists do to us."

Recognizing our unique temptations, idols, and propensities in risk and persecution takes practice. Which idols do we tend to fall back on when we are afraid, stressed, or feel God isn't listening? How can we be vigilant against unwittingly allowing echoes of heresies to creep into our thinking?

In the first century, taking up one's cross meant being willing to face horrifying death as our Lord did. The call by Jesus means that we are willing and prepared for the most "severe social consequences, condemned as a subversive or criminal of the worst kind," or even accused of heresy by those in the religious establishment.[23] We have the strength to do this because we serve a God who is worthy of such a high price.

---

23 Penner, *In the Shadow*, 108.

Chapter 5
Anti-Fragile Faith

I have told you these things so that you will not stumble or be caught off guard or fall away.[1]
—Jesus Christ

You are not invisible to God. But you and those you are trying to reach with the gospel are also not invisible to the enemy. We can predict enemy behavior, and one way we can do so is by beginning to decipher wolf behavior and sheep vulnerability, as Jesus taught in Matthew 10. "Behold, I am sending you out as sheep in the midst of wolves, so be wise as serpents and innocent as doves." It appears wise to learn a little more from my friend, Brian Lubinski from Visible Verse, about wolf behavior and what is the probable lifespan of sheep at risk in a wolf-infested environment.

Sheep among Wolves[2]

Every time Jesus taught, he used imagery familiar to his audience. When he taught about sheep and wolves in Matthew 10:16, the hearers would have likely been picturing the small gray Arabian wolf (*Canus lupus arabs*) and Awassi sheep.

The Arabian wolf is the smallest wolf subspecies and is specially adapted to the desert. They are omnivorous (eating both plant and animal food sources), but they primarily prey on smaller mammals. They are primarily active at nighttime, and they see, smell, and hear their way under cover of darkness.[3] The Arabian wolf is known not only as a silent, single hunter that opportunistically seeks patterns of vulnerability in their potential prey, but also exploits the cover of darkness that conceals them and makes their prey vulnerable.

Arabian wolves are uncanny experts at detecting patterns of vulnerability: they simply have an extraordinary ability to detect weakness, whether in age (youth and elderly), pathology, injury, numbers, or exposure.

---

1 John 16:1.
2 Lubinski. I am grateful to Brian for his research. This entire section and any references to sheep, wolves, snakes, doves, and eagles, are from his summary, synthesis, and sources he cited unless otherwise noted.
3 Hefner and Geffen, "Group Size and Home," 611–19.

Awassi sheep are the most numerous and widespread breed of sheep in southwest Asia, the dominant species in Iraq, the most important in Syria, and the only indigenous sheep in Israel, Jordan, and Lebanon. Awassi sheep are most vulnerable when alone, unattended, eating, and especially when they are young. They have a solid flocking tendency and readily follow a leader.

These sheep are least exposed to predation by wolves when in the center of the flock—especially flocks tended by a shepherd. They are most vulnerable to predation when they are alone. Their food source is grass—they are grazers; as a result, their heads are often down. It's hard to detect a wolf in this position! However, predation (death) only occurs when there is no protective action, like a shepherd or a corral.

Right Expectations

Re-reading the teaching on persecution in the Gospels,[4] considering our own experiences, and listening to others in light of this animal biology, what are some right expectations we can have as (sheep) followers of Jesus (our Shepherd)? While this list is not exhaustive, it includes some of what we know we can expect:

1. Uncertainty: A Christ-follower moves to a dangerous area and is likely immersed in several types of uncertainty within one to two days of leaving their passport country.

2. Failure: Those looking for modern metrics of ministry success in cross-cultural kingdom endeavors will likely be disappointed. It is probable we will grow in seeing and accepting our limitations, as well as experience how little we control.

3. The Need for Restorative Soul Practices: Looking into the spiritual and physical darkness every day can be exhausting, over days, months, and years. Cultivate daily soul-restoring habits to offload the darkness and plan time for yourself to rest physically, mentally, and spiritually. Many Christ-followers use escapism (entertainment) to distract from the darkness, which does nothing to restore us. We must learn to discern what activities will help in soul restoration.

4. Treasures in the Darkness: There are treasures we experience only in the darkness (Isa 45:3). Some of these are deeply personal between us and God.

---

4 Matt 5:10–12, 10:16–39, Mark 4:17, 8:34–38, 10:39, 13:9–13, Luke 12:11–12, 51–53, 21:12–19, John 15:20–21.

5. Loneliness: Risk, danger, and persecution often feel lonely, but we must grasp the truth that we are not alone, however tenuous the thread.

6. A Change in Our Spiritual Senses: As we grow in intimacy with Christ, he often removes our familiar ways of sensing his presence and voice in our lives so that the spiritual senses, the eyes of our hearts, are sensitized to him in new ways.

7. Our Continual Need for a Savior: We all need a Savior. We want to remember to never forget our need for him and how he saved us even as we share our Savior with others.

8. Spiritual Attack: We will likely experience pressure or evil targeting the particularly vulnerable places in the soul, body, ministry, relationships, etc. One of our enemy's tactics is to attack our strengths when we are most weak and tired.

9. Accusations: Satan is the accuser of the brethren, and he will accuse you. He does this through the most unlikely and unexpected sources.

10. Discouragement from Family: The discouragement from family surprises us because it's a source of discouragement we do not expect. The Greek "cause to stumble" (*Skandalon*) means the form of worldly thinking that is discouraging. Peter rebuked Jesus in Matthew 16:23 and Mark 8:33, to which Jesus responded, "Get behind me, Satan." Peter was unwittingly being used by Satan to attempt to discourage Jesus from his calling to go to Jerusalem and die. Our families and even friends may be used to deter and dissuade us from obeying him. Now, of course, we won't say to our families, "Get behind me, Satan." This text is not prescriptive for how we are to respond. The statement by Jesus to Peter illustrates discernment of what is from God and what is not.

11. Strength in the Moment: Our Shepherd will give us just what we need to endure. It may be a picture, a verse from a song, one word, a phrase, or a short prayer. Listen carefully to what seems to be taking shape in your heart or mind over time. He knows us intimately and what we need to endure at each stage. There is a mystery in the life of the spirit, but Jesus gave us a guide—"wisdom is known by her fruits," listed in Galatians 5:22, 23.

> Listen carefully to what seems to be taking shape in your heart or mind over time.

12. Disappointing Ourselves and Others: We can expect to disappoint others. Christ gave us a formidable task, and we cannot individually do all that we wish to do. We must accept our human limitations and that we will likely disappoint others. In hostile ministry circumstances, we must assess our priorities. Values are often in tension with each other. Risk assessment and management, crisis management, dealing with trauma, language learning, and learning how to minister cross-culturally requires a certain amount of time and energy, which means we will have to say no to other good things.[5]

    Here is where our enemy wishes to distract us, using "good things" to keep us from the "excellent" things. We must take care to discern the good from the excellent. It may be helpful to orient ourselves less to what to say "no" to and more towards what to say "yes" to. We will be disappointed in our own limits and failures, and have to wrestle with ourselves, our calling, and even God (like Jacob did).

13. Uncomfortable Questions: We can expect difficult questions to arise inside of us when we face a reality that is uncertain and God doesn't make sense. The sample questions below can be categorized into at least four different areas: sacred questions, faith calling questions, philosophical (core) questions, and emotion questions (see below). The question or questions rising in our souls is very likely the journey God wants us on, and he wants us to turn to him and wait for the answer.

Figure 6: Four Categories of Questions in Risk

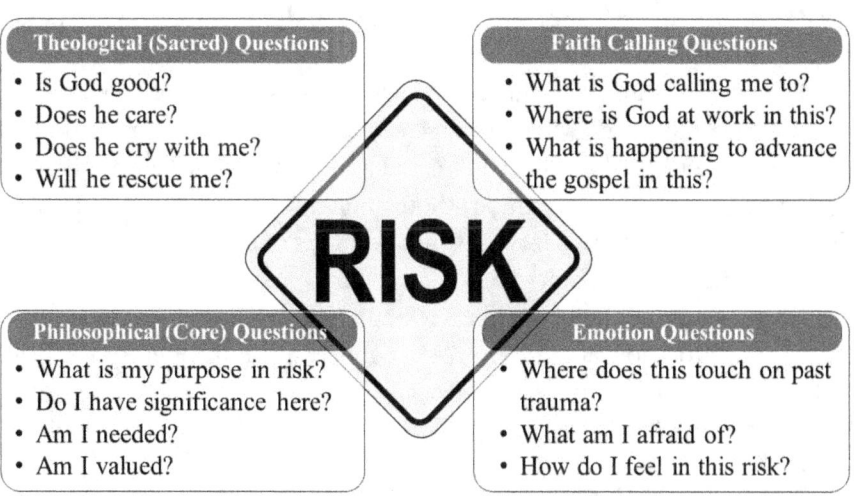

© 2022 Neal & Anna Hampton

---

5 Blincoe, *Ethnic Realities*, 193–230.

Uncertainty and Black Swans

Humans naturally crave certainty and control. Many people have very low ambiguity tolerance, and learning to be comfortable with it is a growing process. The desire for control and certainty is why it's necessary to grasp that uncertainty can never be separated from faith and risk.

"Uncertainty is a profound intellectual humility before the known unknown,"[6] Young writes in "Uncertainty in Theology." He continues, when God is silent, uncertainty often deepens. But,

> "without [some] doubt, every concept of God and every linguistic description can become an idol, [or] a projection, [or] a reduction of God to a mere item in the universe … All you can do is let go of the need for control, and TRUST. For trust in a moral and spiritual reality vastly bigger than yourself, beyond yourself, a reality capable of creation and re-creation, of blessing beyond anything we can ask or think—that's what faith is."[7]

Becoming comfortable with a certain level of uncertainty expands and strengthens trust in God because faith is the courage to live with uncertainty.[8] Of course, we can say faith in Christ is the courage to endure short-term uncertainty with the certainty of our hope in the whole future reality of Christ's kingdom. But if I believe I have absolute certainty, I probably don't need to trust in God and probably don't have much of a relationship with him. I have information about him. This describes a faith that will not work in the face of danger. Neither God nor evil can be boxed. It is one thing to have faith when you (think you) understand him, but it's quite another to have faith when you realize you don't understand him. God is mystery and there's a mystery to life in the Spirit.

Risk, by definition, is uncertain. Uncertainty is a right expectation when going into a risk where a range of persecution may happen because it's impossible to control the evil targeted at us. Learning to make decisions in situations of great uncertainty without enough information is challenging. Fear also produces uncertainty. At times, fear asks unanswerable questions—or at least questions we don't want to consider.

Even though it is highly unlikely to happen, there's a particular risk event that we need to know about it. In risk language, this type of event is labeled a "black swan risk event." A risk event is named a black swan when it has three attributes: "rarity, extreme impact, and retrospective predictability."[9]

---

6 Young, "Uncertainty in Theology."
7 Young.
8 Sacks, "Courage To Live."
9 Taleb, *Black Swan*, 17.

(1) Like a black swan, it is a rare event, and this means it is something that happens "outside the realm of regular expectations; (2) It carries an extreme impact;" and (3) despite it being a unique event, humans inevitably describe the reason "for its occurrence after the [event] making it explainable and predictable" (retrospective predictability or hindsight bias).[10] People often blame themselves for not doing enough to prevent it or engage in self-criticism. "I should have _____." Black swan risk events are so rare that for many, it's automatically an immediate crisis when they occur.

Even though risk is uncertain, Christ-followers often seem surprised when bad things happen, and they seem unaware of personally targeted malice against them. For them, the risks in their environments may be interpreted as "black swan risk events," even though they don't fit the real definition. If we genuinely want to know ourselves and what we value, not our espoused values and ethics, we must cultivate keen observance of ourselves in risk, crisis, suffering, persecution, and facing death, and anticipate personally targeted evil when risking for Christ. There are common risks faced when going into places hostile to the gospel, and these risks are *not* black swan risk events. The uncertainty of risk requires growing in risk literacy and ambiguity tolerance, all while remaining calm, listening to the Holy Spirit's leading, and working in our professional capacity in another language and culture group.

Our relationship with uncertainty affects our abilities to function well in increasing risk. "People who are nervous about uncertainty can make quick decisions because they want to get them out of the way, but they often do it without enough facts. At the other end of the spectrum are people who quite like uncertainty and weighing up options. But in an urgent situation, you don't have the time to do that."[11]

When the gun is to our head (or our loved one's head), what we were confident we were willing to die for may change. We become more sure about what is of primary importance, and it's usually way less than what we thought when we entered risk and persecution. While it's a normal aspect of humanity not to have total congruence between our espoused beliefs and our core beliefs, this is an opportunity for increasing maturity when our convictions and values are refined in extreme situations. Clarity comes in the terrifying millisecond when we see the terrorist ready to pull the trigger and fire his gun at our loved one's forehead. That moment is when we learn what issue, value, or belief is genuinely worth dying over. And we will never be the same again.

---

10 Taleb, 17.
11 Waring, "Don't Panic!"

Unsurprised by Failure

Imagine enduring all the cross-cultural adapting, personal sacrifice, hardship, and suffering, and then viewing your life, work, or project as a failure. What if, in God's economy, you didn't fail? What if you could look at your past day, month, year, or term and realize that it was not a failure, you are not a failure?

When I think of people in the Bible who faithfully emulated ministry "failure," my mind immediately goes to Jeremiah. He was called to stay in a situation where the people rejected both him and his (God's) message. Yet God's sovereign plan for the nation of Israel and Jeremiah was for him to suffer with and experience the horrific consequences of his nation's rebellion.

What can help sustain a Christ-follower when their feelings and perspective indicate failure, but the reality is different? We often send people to the field with an undetected neo-Pelagian transactional salvation and ministry philosophy. In other words, they seek divine favor by doing good works but without the monastic asceticism of the desert fathers.

When moralism (read the Bible more, pray more, etc.) is preached as the road to a mature faith, those we send to the field believe that success is defined by what they can show, not who they are as faithful, obedient Christ-followers even in apparent failure. We are who we send. So if church-as-business becomes mission-as-business, then the mission must look successful to keep the money flowing. There is no room for failure of any type in this approach.

Not only is awareness of anticipated failure not taught, we unwittingly train resiliency out of our children. Beyond just helicopter parents, there are now Zamboni[12] parents who go before their child and smooth the way so there are no difficulties. Stewarding our children before a righteous God, we must ask ourselves how we help or don't help our children become courageous in hardship and how to overcome it. What exactly are we modeling to the next generation?

Jesus teaches how failure will come two ways. He told his disciples they would fail him and abandon him, and he also told his disciples that there will not always be an apparent success in ministry. If he is telling his apostles who walked with him, how much more could this teaching be true for us?

- Matthew 10:14 "And if anyone will not receive you or listen to your words, shake off the dust from your feet when you leave that house or town."

---

12 A Zamboni machine is used for ice hockey and figure skating to make the ice smooth for the skaters.

- Mark 6:11 "And if any place will not receive you and they will not listen to you, when you leave, shake off the dust that is on your feet as a testimony against them."
- Luke 9:5 "And wherever they do not receive you, when you leave that town shake off the dust from your feet as a testimony against them."
- Luke 10:11, 12 "Even the dust of your town that clings to our feet we wipe off against you."
- John 16:32 "Behold, the hour is coming, indeed it has come, when you will be scattered, each to his own home, and will leave me alone. Yet I am not alone, for the Father is with me."
- Acts 13:51 "But they shook off the dust from their feet against them and went to Iconium."
- Acts 18:6 "And when they opposed and reviled him, he shook out his garments and said to them, 'Your blood be on your own heads! I am innocent. From now on I will go to the Gentiles.'"

In his last book before his death, Kenneth Bailey teaches about failure in *The Good Shepherd: A Thousand-Year Journey From Psalm 23 to the New Testament*. In Mark 6:6–13, Jesus instructs his disciples,

> Then he went about among the villages teaching; and he called the twelve and began to send them out, two by two, and gave them authority over the unclean spirits. And he ordered them to take nothing for their journey except a staff; no bread, no bag, no money in their belts, but to wear sandals and not to put on two tunics. And he said to them, "Where you enter a house, stay there until you leave the place. If any place will not welcome you and they refuse to hear you, as you leave, shake off the dust of the feet as a testimony against them."

Bailey summarizes the teaching of Jesus in the following three points:

1. Jesus affirms mission from below—from a state of powerlessness, not part of a victorious army, with no military force to back them up. In other words, the disciples needed the people's help, the very ones to whom they were preaching the gospel!
2. Jesus gives them a perspective on failure. We tend to define "failure" in front-line missions as planting a church but not having it last, or when people who have professed Christ at significant cost then deny him or walk away when the pressure increases. We may have no glamour stories, no stories of great numbers, no evidence of "success" available for broadcast on the big stage of a theater-like megachurch. As Jesus

said, when one of his disciples is rejected, he is rejected.[13] Yet there is this constant (felt) pressure from our sending churches to have a "great story to tell." Instead, what is a better theology of failure for the twenty-first-century disciple?

Bailey describes what Jesus said as "The Sacrament of Failure." I love that imagery—the sacrament of failure can be a holy situation. For the disciple, when a person or a people group does not receive you, when they run you out of town with barely the clothes on your back, Jesus says, "Shake the dust off your feet." This is an ancient way still used today to get rid of a relationship or task. Bailey says, "Shaking your feet or lower robes to shake off the dust stirred up by your feet means "I am finished with you and am leaving. Furthermore, as I leave, I take nothing from this house, not even its dust!" I love how kinesthetic Jesus is—as humans, we need physical ways to deal with rejection, trauma, or difficulty. Our bodies and minds need to have ways to have closure, to know something has ended or we've ended something.

3. Jesus directed them to engage in a holistic mission—proclaim, cast out, heal. Notice what Jesus did not tell his disciples. He did not send them out and tell them to stay safe. He did not tell them the object was to have so many baptisms and conversions. He did not tell them the ten commandments of ministry that his disciples must follow.

   Sometimes he may prescribe for us to suffer like our brother Jeremiah did, suffering with the Israelites even though they rejected God. Jeremiah experienced God's heart of pain when he was rejected. We aren't sacrificing our lives in dangerous places for what people think, but because of our love for Christ and his love for those who have never heard the name of Jesus and the good news of what he did. While we do need to build bridges and find ways to communicate to supporters back home, we have to tell our own soul (and ego) that our service is for the King of Kings who understands our fears, our failures, our fear of rejection, or lack of recognition, and is simply asking us to obey and be faithful, no matter what.

How can we "talk to our soul" when we feel like our sacrifices and ministry are failures? There are practical steps we can take to deal with our emotions and responses to what feels like a failure in front-line ministry:[14]

---

13 1 Sam 8:7; Luke 10:16.

14 Kiev, *Psychology of Risk*, 74–78.

1. Consider a situation that seems like a failure.
2. Write down all the facts of the situation, what happened, and what you wish was different. Acknowledge any sin over which you may clearly sense conviction from the Holy Spirit and put that in a separate column from your own human limitations and the facts.
3. Write your emotional reaction and bodily sensations you experience with this apparent situation of failure.
4. Write down what the situation means to you. What is your interpretation of it? What do you think will next happen?
5. Consider how much your perspective on the situation is a long-standing one, a point of view you developed long before the present situation occurred? (What your core beliefs are.)
6. Consider all the words of Jesus and the experience of the early church. Carry your situation as you see it into the throne room of God. Ask him what he thinks about it. Compare your situation to what Christ said would happen, and what the early church experienced.
7. What is his interpretation of the facts so that you can separate the problem (based on your perception) from his perspective?
8. Notice what the situation now looks like through the eyes of faith and obedience, hrough the perspective of Jesus rather than your perspective of ministry failure.

When we shift our frame of reference to a different perspective, a more eternal perspective, we begin to interpret the facts differently and have other bodily responses. We are freed from the chains of failure, depression, and disappointment residing in us towards ourselves, others, and God. While we may have residual disappointment and sadness, we can typically be more pragmatic about our perceived failure once we have processed it to a certain level. Resiliency more easily happens when we accept and embrace the harsh realities of life and ministry. Life may not get any easier, but by facing difficulties and failure, we become stronger; stronger in our faith, more vital in our resiliency, and more robust in moving forward in hostile, dangerous places for the sake of the gospel. We are developing anti-fragile faith.

What I am not saying is that we are to always leave difficult situations. A significant part of a theology of failure is to "shake the dust" from your feet. However, this is a descriptive text, not a prescriptive text. Plenty of times, God calls people to remain "despite lack of fruit." He asked Neal and me to be willing to stay for twenty years even if our ministry looked like

Jeremiah's. At the time, that felt like a lifetime, and I gasped at the idea of my thirties passing me by with nothing to show from my life and ministry. But that's exactly what God asked us to be willing to do back in 2004. We sat on our veranda that August afternoon in Kabul and wept as we considered what he was asking of us. We realized how much our ego had been tied into the ministry and how sinfully we cared what people back home thought. We repented and committed to obeying, one day at a time, and learned to love the people, the culture, and the place. We committed to stay for twenty years even if at the end, there was nothing really to show for it, but if that's what obedience to him was, we would do it.

The next time you describe a ministry or term as a failure, look at it through the eyes of Jesus and re-evaluate your assessment of the situation. Were you obedient? Did you try to the best of your ability to be faithful to what he wanted you to do? If you can lean in close to his heart, his response to you is a warm hug and a gentle, "Well done, my good and faithful servant. You bring me great joy."

Worst-Case Failure

Jesus prepared Peter for the absolute worst failure imaginable: total denial. In Matthew 26:33, 34, Peter exclaims with untested bravado: "Though they all fall away because of you, I will never fall away." Jesus said to him, "Truly, I tell you, this very night, before the rooster crows, you will deny me three times" (cf. Luke 22:34; John 13:36–38).

We have to know that we could be like Peter and deny Christ as we stand by the fire. I could be Peter. If you realize you are in the company of Peter and you just denied Christ when it mattered, do what he did. *Weep bitterly.* Weep until you have no more tears. Weep and mourn your failure of courage. But don't stop there.

When you are done weeping, look up. Listen for his voice. See him. He's standing by a different fire. He's standing there looking right at you, *you!*, calling your name. He made breakfast for you because he wants to sit with you on the beach and enjoy fresh bread with butter melting all over it and flame-roasted, fresh-caught fish. He wants to accept you and receive you back at his side. He wants to enjoy *you*. He wants to give you a new task to do, a new opportunity to serve him.

As you picture yourself sitting with him, look deeply into the kindest, gentlest, loving eyes you've ever seen. Decide you will never deny him again. You *will* stand firm. The next opportunity he gives you to stand as one of his followers or reject him, you've decided you won't deny him. He will provide you with the strength and courage to not deny him the next time you are pressured to do so. And then you will be again in great company, with Peter, the rock, the one who served him faithfully to his own martyrdom.

Only the Wounded Can Serve

Peter was wounded in his failure, but God used him to build his church. The suffering in risk and persecution causes wounds in us, too. In his book, *The Wounded Healer*, Henri Nouwen relates the two aspects of the person who would minister healing to others. The wounded healer is the one who not only looks after his injuries but also prepares to heal the wounds of others.

There is a particular medicine for inner healing, heart wounds, and spiritual wounds in the Old Testament, and it's called "the balm of Gilead." Balms in the ancient world and today have several uses, including preserving and healing physical wounds. *Balms can be made from tree resin and tree leaves.* In Jeremiah 8:21, 22 and 46:11, God spiritualizes the balm as the type of healing his people need. Who is the physician? What is the balm? The Israelites had turned to many other "medicines" to heal their wounds, but there was no one there who knew how to comfort and speak to them, and they had not turned to the one who could heal.

"For the wound of the daughter of my people is my heart wounded; I mourn, and dismay has taken hold of me. Is there no balm in Gilead? Is there no physician there? Why then has the health of the daughter of my people not been restored?" (Jer 8:21, 22).

While the balm of Gilead is not explicitly mentioned in the New Testament, "the leaves of the tree [of life] for the healing of the nations" are found in Revelation 22:2. There is still a spiritual balm for the wounds and traumas of today. What do the nations need healing from? We all need healing from idolatry, ethnic wars, racism, violence, sins of all types, trauma resulting from evil, and sin sickness. We all need healing with the balm from the tree of life, the balm of Gilead.

In a world defined by risk and persecution, Christ-followers are called to recognize the sufferings and trauma which impact our hearts "and make that recognition the starting point of service. [Our] service will not be received as authentic unless it comes from a heart wounded by the suffering [we speak] about" and healing from the only one who can heal us.[15]

Thorton Wilder wrote a play in 1928 to demonstrate the spiritual reality of John 5—the healing at the Pool of Bethesda. The doctor wants to get into the pool to relieve his grief and depression, but the angel will not allow him.

---

15 Nouwen, *Wounded Healer*, xvi.

The physician begs the angel: "What I might yet do in Love's service were I but freed from this bondage." The angel replies,

> Draw back, physician; this moment is not for you. Without your wound, where would your power be? It is your very remorse that makes your low voice tremble in the hearts of men. The very angels themselves cannot persuade the wretched and blundering children on earth as can one human being broken on the wheels of living. In Love's service, only the wounded soldiers can serve. Draw back.[16]

Broken on the wheels of living, our wounds are our source of healing power in a pain-filled world. A deep understanding of our pain from walking through the chaos will convert weakness to strength. Fully feeling all we feel, turning to God and offering it as a source of healing to those who also feel isolated and alone—this is the work of the wounded healer. There is loss and grief in knowing that internal woundedness in us is what provides the healing balm of Gilead that God wishes to use in us to help others heal.

I began by discussing wolves and sheep. Having the right expectations of living as sheep amidst wolves facilitates our endurance and ability to develop resilience. Knowing that uncertainty is a part of living in danger in hostile places, we will not be surprised by even black swan events. Knowing that God often uses us more in our woundedness—even when all we feel is faithful fragileness—than if we were not wounded, assists our resolve to remain spiritually steady.

Three types of faith may be observed in such situations. Fragile faith initially says, "I believe in God," but when it encounters difficulty, this faith is crushed. With resilient faith, when we encounter an obstacle, we endure through it and bounce back like a rubber band. We can keep going despite suffering and trauma. This endurance exemplifies resilient faith. But there is a faith even greater we are called to, which is anti-fragile faith. Anti-fragile faith is not broken or crushed in adversity; it does not merely endure, but when this faith encounters an obstacle, anti-fragile faith becomes something more than it was before; more robust, stronger, tougher, more powerful. The more we suffer and embrace suffering with this faith, the more anti-fragile our faith becomes. There has never been an easy time to follow Jesus, and less so in the twenty-first century. The world does not need more Christians with shallow, immature adolescent faith that "feels and looks good." Anti-fragile faith is faith that can be relied upon to demonstrate his love no matter what injustice is repeatedly done to it. This is our calling because he is worthy.

---

16 Wilder, "Angel That Troubled," 54–56.

Chapter 6
Put the Candy Jar on the Lower Shelf[1]

> *I choose the awful agony of Christ*
> *to charge my senseless sorrows with meaning*
> *and to make my pain pregnant with power.*
> *I choose you, good Jesus, you know.*
> *Count me among the victories*
> *That you have won in bitter woundedness*
> *Never number me among those alien to you.*[2]
> —Joseph Tetlow, SJ

Sometimes the pain of living through risk and persecution is so great that we may think God isn't there or he doesn't care. When we lose all sense of the reality of God's presence, it's almost easier to cope with a God who isn't there than a God who doesn't care. One of the most challenging aspects of risk and persecution is discerning reality and seeing the meaning of what we are walking through. It takes practice to figure out what's happening, what's real, what's fake, what's a rumor, what's speculation, what's a fact, which threats and information to evaluate and which to ignore, to see that God is there, God does care.

Discernment and meaning are two challenging aspects of risk and persecution, and if they were candy, how can we put them on a lower shelf where everyone can see and understand for themselves, take, and eat? Training in the discernment of reality and finding meaning is part of training for suffering, preparing people to handle it, so their faith is not shipwrecked. We have to start at the beginning of the story to do this. Because "understanding the beginning, will help prepare us for the end."[3] Isaiah 46:9–10 reveals,

> Remember the former things of old; for I am God, and there is no other; I am God, and there is none like me, declaring the end from the beginning and from ancient times things not yet done, saying, "My counsel shall stand, and I will accomplish my purpose."

---

[1] A phrase from an Indian pastor who is a shepherd of persecuted churches.
[2] Harter, "I Choose to Breathe," 5.
[3] Gruber, *End from the Beginning*, 8.

Discerning Reality at the Beginning

Genesis 1:1–3 lays the groundwork for reality and meaning.

v. 1: "*In the beginning, God created the heavens and the earth.*"

This first phrase of the Bible fills our lives and our time in history with meaning. God begins history, he is in history, and history came through him. History is not a random chain of events; therefore, what we are experiencing does not take him by surprise. In what seemed like nothing, an absence of God's presence, God was there. God's presence brings about a very different reality at God's initiation. This "in the beginning" is the foundation of our awareness of God, the world, and humanity.

v. 2a: "*The earth was without form and void, and darkness was over the surface of the deep.*"

Then we are told something astonishing. The Bible immediately contrasts God's creative, gracious, loving, and wise work with four shocking words.

- *Tohu*: Waste, emptiness, meaningless. The opposite of created, meaninglessness; desolation. It is a condition of utter confusion in which the singularity of distinct objects cannot be distinguished.

- *Bohu*: The Hebrew root is an expression of surprise, astonishment, and pain. It marks the chaotic condition as unbearable pain, full of contradiction and struggle, and excruciating pain.

- *Hosek*: It's so "much more than the absence of light. ... [It was] a darkness which can be touched."[4] Darkness, confusion; physical, psychological, morality. Throughout the Bible, darkness is often a symbol of evil, misfortune, death, and oblivion. It's used in the context of both physical darkness (Egypt) and the darkness of choosing evil; it is not seeing; it includes the condition of inner confusion when we don't know our way and we don't know ourselves.

- *Tahom*: The terror of the deep abyss; the root of this Hebrew noun is hum, murmur, roar, groan, tumult; in other words, noise that is death—this is our reality. Those who have been in war zones know the sounds, smells, and atmosphere of dying that never translates into written text.

The world God created held the four elements of chaos. These are the symbols of the uncontrollable, unimaginable horror: formless and void, darkness, water, deep. Together, *tohu-va-bohu*—formless and void—

---

4 Gruber, *End from the Beginning*, 156–57.

represent a condition not as it is but as it affects our power of perception and means a blurred and muddled, unclear, painful, confusing, and indistinct situation. In this place, there is no life, the exact opposite of "land," which represents an ordered designation. There is the threat of disintegration, of annihilation. *Tohu-va-bohu* is the place and world of death, where life is no longer possible. Chaos reigns. Disorientation confounds. We feel like we are in a swampland of our soul.

v. 2b: "*And the Spirit of God was hovering over the face of the waters.*"

Then we notice something startling. The spirit/breath/wind of God is hovering over the deep. Even the Hebrew word for "spirit" is "*ruach*," a word that cannot be said without mostly breath. Spirit, wind, and breath are symbols for what cannot be nailed down, captured, or enclosed. God will not be boxed in by our cultural or denominational theology, the right risk assessment methodology, or the best security practices.

And what is God's spirit doing? It's hovering nearby. The word used here for hovering is like a gentle eagle. The only other time in the entire Old Testament this is used is when Moses describes God's ways in Deuteronomy 32:11, "Like an eagle that stirs up its nest, That hovers over its young, He spread His wings and caught them, He carried them on His pinions" (NASB). To hover here is the strength it takes to come near without overwhelming but to be soft, a feeling of tender love, brood over, and affect. God forms all that we observe from his love with tenderness and compassion. "The God of the [Bible] is not like any gods of war, not in character [or] method."[5] The creation reflects the Creator. God's hands were soft, warm, and gentle from the beginning.[6]

"All ancient cosmogonies except Genesis portray the beginning of [creation] as warfare."[7] "The Genesis account ... [uniquely] stands as an alternative to the competing mythologies of surrounding cultures."[8] God does not create from conflict or by battling evil. He creates from love right from the beginning.

> God's world, where he is working, is reality, and things are always different where he is.

When we see that darkness was over the deep, but then at the same time, the spirit of God is over the deep, there's a word change. It's not "deep," it's "water."

---

5 Moen, "Gods of War."
6 Moen.
7 Moen.
8 Moen, "Beneath Egypt."

God's world, where he is working, *is* reality, and things are always different where he is. Or, stated differently, *the world is not the way I perceive it, but it is how God sees it.* When I'm in a situation of chaos, confusion, and terror of the world being swallowed by the deep abyss; when God doesn't seem to be there; when my logical expectation, my feelings, imagination, and intellectual understanding run dry; when despair is threatening; when it seems impossible to feel God's existence and goodness in the face of our most profound horror—I have to remember he is there, hovering close by. We can choose to continue to live in openness to God despite what all our senses and ways of knowing tell us.

v. 3: *"And God said, 'Let there be light,' and there was light."*

Into the darkness, chaos, and emptiness, God spoke. God spoke then, and he is still speaking today. "At many times and in many ways, God spoke to our fathers by the prophets, but in these last days he has spoken to us by his Son" (Heb 1:1, 2).

Aren't risk, danger, and persecution like this chaotic emptiness? These four words are astonishingly applicable to the experience of Christ-followers when we live as his witnesses in hostile places. Chaos, confusion, emptiness, pain, and struggle are looming. We receive premonitions of danger, warnings, desolation, threats upon threats, ambiguity, and great uncertainty. When we choose to do righteousness, we push back the chaos, confusion, the darkness. These verses give us four vital stabilizing forces:

- God is in history; what is happening is not a random chain of events.
- There is purpose in what I am going through in risk and persecution.
- A loving God is there in the darkness with me.
- He is constantly speaking and helping me.

> He offers us the sanctuary of his presence in the middle of the chaos, however deep and highly uncertain and horrifying it seems to be.

This place without form and void, a place where we are confronted with the unknown, the thing that we fear the most, is also the source of creativity. When life is not the way we wish it were, let us not be paralyzed by the illusions of reality created by risk. God overcame chaos then, and with and through us, he will overcome the chaos in our day. He offers us the sanctuary of his presence in the middle of the chaos, however deep and highly uncertain and horrifying it seems to be.

LogFrames and Human Responsibility

A logframe is a logical framework analysis tool directing the progress of a project. It is a useful instrument employed for planning and implementing a project, detailing individual parts of a comprehensive design, and revealing how they are related, or describing the project's flow from beginning to end. It is a table that typically shows "if/then" steps, and it is a tool that guides decision-making. The problem with logframes is that they require a detailed understanding of everything going on in the project.

When logframes are applied to situations with inherent uncertainty, they may quickly break down because there are too many exceptions outside of the boxes. Logframes are based on logic, and evil is not logical in the way we are used to thinking. If/then statements will inevitably not fit for discerning reality or meaning. The risk flow chart in chapter eleven is used in our RAM Training. As a modified logframe, it requires input and discernment through the whole process and allows for change at any point. We point out the need for discernment and listening to the Holy Spirit each step of the way. A useful logframe cannot be set up and followed blindly without further thought, reflection, and allowance for the Spirit's leading.

A fixed logframe, which has no space for the Holy Spirit, may become a crutch that leads to ignoring the human responsibility of developing individual, team, and organizational (system) discernment. We can have all the professional logical framework analysis we want, but God may still call us to do something that goes against all responsible risk analysis. We have to have discernment from the Spirit to know this. Human responsibility requires us to be involved with God at all steps of the process and not rely solely on a chart or table. Logframes, valuable tools in humanitarian project work, may be applied carefully to risk discernment but do not provide meaning in risk and persecution.

Discerning Meaning in Risk and Persecution

There's nothing worse than meaningless suffering. The essential fact of life in risk and persecution is suffering. Questions of meaning are questions of the purpose of why we are going through something. We all have an innate desire to give as much meaning as possible to our lives, to actualize as many values as possible, what Frankl calls "the will-to-meaning."[9] When we do not see and feel the meaning, frustration and despair soon set in. Finding the meaning in suffering more than anything else requires asking the right question, and finding it will justify the suffering and lead to faithful endurance for our Lord.

---

9 Frankl, *Doctor and the Soul*, 222.

The problem is that we are strongly influenced by the modern theories of finding meaning, such as the human motivation in Maslow's hierarchy of needs, Freud's view that we are motivated by sex, and Adler's view that we become our best selves when we are connected and valued members of the community. All these approaches and reasons for meaning break down entirely in extreme situations such as torture and persecution when we are not free to choose how we wish to self-actualize or when we are not needed or valued except as an object of torture.[10] Yet we must be aware of the limitations of finding meaning. It can result in "unhealthy nationalism, obsessive jealousies, ethnic hatred, or a compulsive work ethic" when taken in excess.[11]

Frankl, a Nazi concentration camp survivor, explains at least four possibilities for giving life meaning and realizing values. "[We can achieve purpose in our] lives by realizing experiential values, by experiencing the Good, the True, and the Beautiful."[12] Or we experience meaning by knowing and loving at least one other human being. We can achieve meaning through creative values by achieving tasks. Or, in situations where we are in distress, when we cannot achieve or create or experience, we achieve meaning by the way we face our distress and the unavoidable suffering brought by risk and persecution. Frankl calls this fourth way attitudinal values.[13]

> We achieve meaning by the way we face our distress and the unavoidable suffering brought by risk and persecution.

Frankl explains that meaning and fulfillment are found through attitudinal values cultivated when suffering is unavoidable and inescapable. "Lack of success does not signify lack of meaning."[14] He explains there are two time frames for attitudinal values: eternal and situational. Each risk and persecution situation asks the person in it to find the meaning for that situation without forgetting the eternal values of joining the cloud of witnesses in obedient faithfulness to Christ. In the right-now danger situation, calculated, planned sacrifice performed to bring the desired end loses ethical significance. This choice reduces the sacrifice to the cult of success, of achievement. In contrast, only when we have no choice but to suffer and know we are "running the risk of having sacrificed in vain" do

---

10 Frankl, *Man's Search for Meaning*, KL 15–33, 37–40.
11 Frankl, *Doctor and the Soul*, 105–15.
12 Frankl, xxi.
13 Frankl, 105.
14 Frankl, 107.

we have the highest ethical value in our suffering and reveal courage in our attitudes and actions. This reality imbues the sacrifice with meaning.

Genesis 1:1–3 also provides eternally significant meaning. The first phrase, "*In the beginning,*" implies a beginning, a middle, and an end. We are now in the middle and while we don't know *when* the end is (the Day is coming soon), we know *what* the end is (Christ's kingdom come in full glory). There is a meaning and purpose in our lives because there was a meaning and purpose in the beginning. Midrash Numbers Rabbah 18:22 states, "In every place, the Holy One, blessed be he, accomplishes his purpose, and he has not created one thing without purpose."[15] Our beginning, middle, and end are in his hands.

When ministering through risk and persecution, we find meaning in our association with both Jesus and the prophets. Scott Cunningham writes, "In Luke, there is a 'persecution interlock.' Jesus and the disciples are persecuted just as the prophets were before them. The prophets were persecuted for being God's messengers, just as Jesus and the disciples are. The disciples are persecuted because of Jesus, and it was because Jesus was persecuted that the disciples would be persecuted in the future."[16] We join the cloud of witnesses who suffered persecution in our suffering of persecution.

In John, association with Jesus includes:[17] rejection by his own family (John 7:1–10); being threatened with arrest (John 7:30–52); being threatened with stoning (John 8:59; 10:31); his reputation being besmirched (John 9:24–29); being slandered (John 10:19–21); being arrested, interrogated, killed (John 18:1–19:37). Unrequited love is a profound form of suffering. The love Jesus demonstrated for humanity was not just not returned—it was violently, disdainfully rejected.[18] His wounds and death give ours the meaning we can seize and hold on to.

Discerning reality and finding meaning requires naming. Naming takes discernment. Learning discernment requires both discipleship and time to become aware, understand, and discern what action to take.[19] Risks are real, constant, and in the context of ministry among hostile cultures, increasing. Naming these, understanding them, and preparing for them reduces our fear and anxiety and helps us strengthen or be more on guard in our weak points. Then we have more space in our souls to consider and reflect on God's calling, and what losses *and gains* may be ahead. We can begin to

---

15 Quoted in Gruber, *End from the Beginning*, 12.
16 Cunningham, *Through Many Tribulations*, 178.
17 Penner, *In the Shadow*, 121.
18 Tetlow, *Always Discerning*, 113.
19 Gallagher, *Teaching Discernment*, 29.

understand the meaning of what he is calling us to as we walk down the steps into the darkness of adversity. "When the wells of logical expectations, feeling, imagination, and intellectual understanding run dry, when confusion threatens to turn to despair, when it seems impossible to feel God's existence and goodness in the face of some concrete suffering, the wise and discerning Christ-follower continues to live in an openness to God."[20] Openness is a refusal to think our suffering is a waste, recognizing that everything leads to something in God's kingdom economy, not to nothing.

Openness to God and the reality he is in begins by asking the three questions of a theology of risk as summarized in the introduction: "What's our foundation?," "How is God calling me to worship him as I move into and through or retreat from risk?," and "Who is he choosing to go through this risk?" When we reflect and realize these answers, it opens a space for us to begin to see the meaning and purpose of why he is asking us to walk on that path.

Further theological reflection on our reality and meaning is an invitation to a prayerful guided reflection in which we put everything before God, asking him to reveal the meaning to us. In prayerful reflection, we wait for him to do whatever he wishes to do within us and in our situation.[21]

1. Ask for the grace to join with God's desires for your understanding of the meaning of your suffering.
2. Summarize the situation that is the focus of discernment.
3. What stands out, whether positive or negative?
4. What biblical text, parable, or metaphor comes to mind?
5. What theological theme(s) interconnects in the situation? Examples may include creation, sin, redemption, justice, ethical living, community, justice for the marginalized, or grace. How is that playing out in your situation and life?
6. Notice your internal feelings, whether positive or negative. Notice any blocks to inner freedom, any "weight" that does not seem to be from God. Confess those to God, and ask him to help you deal with any of those "unfreedoms."
7. Ask God for the grace to see his heart for you, specifically in this situation.
8. Spend as much time as possible in quiet waiting. Present to God all the complexity of the situation, and be open to hearing from him.

---

20 Rolheiser, *Shattered Lantern*, 113.
21 Liebert, *Soul of Discernment*, 107–22.

9. Savor this experience, and reflect on what images, imaginations, and Scripture passages come to mind. It might even be images of Christian saints from the past.
10. Describe this experience of reflection to someone: pastor, spouse, friend, spiritual director, and savor any new freedom, even if it is as simple as a new awareness.
11. What habits can you cultivate to support this new freedom?
12. What theological truths now express this freedom for you?
13. Name the grace God has given you in discerning the situation.

How do we know if we are on the right path to discerning reality and meaning in life-and-death situations?[22] Scripture gives us the criteria for recognizing the activity and leading of the Spirit in our lives. Jesus taught, "Every healthy tree bears good fruit, but the diseased tree bears bad fruit. A healthy tree cannot bear bad fruit, nor can a diseased tree bear good fruit … thus, you will recognize them by their fruits" (Matt 7:18, 20). He also taught, "Wisdom is justified by all her children" (Luke 7:35). The children of wisdom are purity, gentleness, open to reason, full of mercy, humility, innocence, peace, and sincere kindliness (Jas 3:13–18). We see the fruit in moral behavior, ethical decision-making, and life in the community of saints.

The wisdom of discerning reality, understanding God's purposes, and grasping the meaning for us is a wisdom that comes from reflection and time with him. It is not necessarily a wisdom we aspire to because it's a wisdom often tied to loss. It's a wisdom that makes us swallow hard and square our shoulders, and despite the metallic taste in our mouth, we recognize the honor it is to learn this wisdom first-hand, and we move forward.

Richard Wurmbrand described what helped him hold on to meaning. In his darkest days, when evil seemed ever-present, he composed a poem in his mind that thwarted the threats of the Devil:

> *Love is its justification. Love is not for the wise.*
> *Through a thousand ordeals, she will not cease to love.*
> *Though fire burns her and the waves drown her, she will kiss the hand that hurts.*
> *If she finds no answer to her questions, she is confident and waits.*
> *The sun will shine in hidden places one day, and all will be made plain.*[23]

Jesus was faithful and obedient his entire life, but he was not granted a peaceful, calm, death. He who was without sin suffered deep agony;

---

22 Dubay, *Authenticity: A Biblical Theology*, 143–59.
23 Voice of the Martyrs, *Wurmbrand: Tortured for Christ*, 145.

his cry, "*My God, my God, why have you forsaken me? Why are you so far from saving me, from the words of my groaning?*" still echoes through the centuries and includes how his disciples often feel.[24] Sometimes the meaning of our suffering is to learn what that felt like for him so he is not alone; it is to stay awake with him through the night in the garden and then to be present to him at the cross and observe his painful death; it is to offer the simple comfort of silent, mourning presence to his mother Mary, John, and the others.

Some of his followers, called to be united with him in his physical agony like this, are regarded as sheep set aside for slaughter. These "sheep" carry the aroma of death.[25] Their robes, washed in the blood, have a purpose now and in eternity. Some of us, perhaps not called to martyrdom but to suffer the pain and horror as first-hand witnesses, are called to see the sacrifice of their blood and felt abandonment and not turn our face away but tell others.[26] By doing so, we will also not escape unscathed from the suffering. Their blood may splash on us, too. Just as he suffered and shed his blood, he is worthy of all our sufferings and the shed blood of his saints.

---

24 Psalm 22:1.
25 Romans 8:36.
26 Isaiah 30:21.

Part Three
Essentials of Decision-Making in Risk

Chapter 7
Shrewd as a Serpent

> *Where God is known by faith to be the ultimate reality,*
> *the source of my ethical concern will be that God is known*
> *as the good, even at the risk that I and the world are revealed*
> *as not good, but as bad through and through.*[1]
> —Dietrich Bonhoeffer

In risk, there is sometimes less than a second to make a moral decision, so we must be absolutely clear ahead of time on the values and convictions guiding our decisions when it's not easy to ascertain good and evil. Our identities and our core values without stress are magnified under the extreme pressure of risk, and threats of persecution, violence, and danger.

Jesus taught, "Behold, I am sending you out as sheep in the midst of wolves, so be wise as serpents and innocent as doves" (Matt 10:16). What does "being shrewd and cunning as a serpent" mean? How can we be shrewd and morally good according to God's standard? Furthermore, how do we do it under the severe pressure of long-term risk, long-term torture, or the isolation of imprisonment, pain, hunger, and cold when it's hard to think clearly? First, we have to learn a little bit about snakes, again from my friend, Brian.

Snakes and Habitat Sinks[2]

Jesus liked to refer to the familiar to teach the unforgettable, so likely, he was thinking of one of the venomous snakes in Palestine. There are forty-two snake species in Israel, but only nine are venomous,[3] and one, the Palestine viper (*Daboia palaestinae*), is the national snake of Israel (2019) and the most venomous.[4] So how are snakes shrewd, and how can we humans be like them?

The Palestine vipers detect prey, friend, or foe by tasting air molecules in the back of their heads, feeling subtle vibrations through a highly sensitive inner ear, and detecting warmth through specialized holes called pit organs. Their ability to detect subtle vibrations in the ground is amazing. They have infra-red sensors in their heads that pick up thermal radiation from several

---

1 Bonhoeffer, *Ethics*, 48, kindle edition.
2 All of the following discussion on Israeli Snake Behavior is research from Brian Lubinski, Visible Verse Outdoor Ministry.
3 Haimovitch, *Field Guide to Reptiles*.
4 Segev, "Vipera Palaestinae Envenomation," 691–99. JTA, "Deadly Palestine Viper Declared Israel's National Snake."

meters away. They are capable of detecting the steps of a mouse from a distance. Their ability to "know" when they are camouflaged, concealed, or inaccessible is enough to make anyone pause and ask, "How do they know?"

Like all poisonous snakes, the viper must make split-second decisions on whether to release venom into a potential threat or use other means of protection. The decision can mean life or death for the snake and its target. They are incredibly sharp and extremely fast decision-makers. The speed between the decision to strike and the actual strike has been measured at just under three meters per second.[5]

Palestine vipers are cold-blooded (ectotherms) and receive heat from external sources. If there's no heat, they won't move. Snake activity increases during periods of higher temperatures, so when it is cold, they either seek warmth or find protection in camouflage, concealment, or inaccessibility until it warms up. These three protective measures: camouflage, concealment, and inaccessibility, are in nearly continual use, especially when pregnant, approaching the shedding of skin, or during and after feeding. A viper is also vulnerable right after releasing venom, because it takes a while to replace the venom in its body.

When a viper pursues prey, it uses camouflage, concealment, and the cover of darkness as it waits to ambush its prey. This ambush behavior is effective because of the viper's ability to see, smell, and feel its prey (vibrations and heat), in complete darkness and with a split-second strike. When sensing danger, snakes usually try to avoid contact and warn their potential foe. The Palestine viper will make an exhaling sound before they bite. Biting for defense is a last resort because their venom is their ultimate protection and source of provision. To bite is to lose their most critical source of security and provision.

Perhaps Jesus is referring to the snake's ability to make a rapid and accurate strike or hold decisions (implications for us in decision-making). The Palestine viper (like many snakes) possesses impressive capabilities for navigating in total darkness, "seeing" things through highly specialized senses used to survive in hostile environments. They "taste" air molecules with the ability to analyze and interpret the chemical complexities in the air.

We can see some immediate applications. As noted above, the viper continually employs three protective measures, camouflage, concealment, and inaccessibility. Under the principles of risk communication in chapter thirteen, cybersecurity experts teach cover, conceal, compartmentalize, and reduce. This is wisdom based on the shrewdness of snakes.

---

5 Pennington, Sawvel, and Moon, "Debunking the Viper's Strike."

Another aspect of shrewdness is discovered in the parable of the unrighteous manager. The same word for "shrewd" used in Matthew 10:16, appears again in Luke 16:8, "The master praised the unrighteous manager because he had acted shrewdly. For the children of this age are more shrewd than the children of light in dealing with their own people" (CSB). What is Jesus teaching here? Moen writes that shrewd also includes the concept of creative activity. It is brilliance manifested. The verb is often used for God's judicial and redemptive activity. Jesus is praising the man's inventiveness, not his avoidance of responsibility. He is focused on the creativity of the solution, not endorsing the ethics of the man's actions. Jesus is pointing out that people who are savvy about the world's ways often show greater imagination than those concerned about following God. He highlights our need to think outside the box when it comes to kingdom work, even while staying within the "rules" of ethical living.[6] Isaiah teaches, "Woe to those who call evil good and good evil, who put darkness for light and light for darkness, who put bitter for sweet and sweet for bitter! Woe to those who are wise in their own eyes, and shrewd in their own sight" (Isa 5:20, 21). We must be shrewd in applying worldly wisdom congruent with God's ethics and character.

When Jesus sent his followers as sheep amid wolves, everyone knew that sending a sheep out in habitats patrolled by wolves would be exceptionally dangerous. Without the wisdom of the Palestine viper, we would not have a chance. None at all. Biologists call habitats that do not offer sufficient resources to survive (food, water, shelter from predators, etc.) a "habitat sink." A habitat sink attracts animals to it but only results in animals dying from predation or starvation. Jesus was saying, "Don't get lured into habitat sinks; stay shrewd as serpents and gentle as doves. Live smart!"[7]

Kingdom Ethics

What is ethics? As a general concept, "ethics" is defined as applying the values of "good" and "evil" to a thing, person, or action. Knowing good and evil is much deeper than moralism, which is acting by a set of rules. As Christ-followers, our standard for knowing good and evil is derived from "Kingdom Ethics." Kingdom ethics are not abstract concepts of good and evil, nor are kingdom ethics "moral certainty." No universal principle of ethics works in all situations without nuance. For example, the principle "never tell a lie" carried to its extreme means I would be required to tell a murderer where someone

---

6 Moen, "Parable Ethics?"
7 Eph 4:13–15.

was hiding in my house (for them to kill).[8] In situations of uncertainty and dangerous, ethics are often situational.

Instead, kingdom ethics applies the designation of "good" or "evil" of reality from God's viewpoint on his throne to our specific life experiences.[9] Kingdom ethics and our ethical obligation find their foundation in Genesis 1–3. In the Garden of Eden, when Adam and Eve first "knew" evil, the same word for knowing is used as in the verse when Adam "knew" Eve. Kingdom ethics are relational and interconnected.

> One's claim to be ethical means nothing unless it is expressed in relationship action. This is true for relationships with other people and relationship with God. What can it possibly mean to say that I am ethically justified, ethically motivated, or ethically correct with God if I do not fulfill the obligations he asks? No matter what I say, I am not ethical because ethical affirmation requires the fulfillment of an obligation to another.[10]

Being made in both the image and likeness of God, means "[humans] are not just representatives, but representational. [We are] the visible, human, representative of the invisible, bodiless God."[11] Likeness implies humans are "an adequate and faithful representative of God on earth."[12] Childs observes, "The biblical narratives are not a collection of teachings on virtue, character, and morality. The Bible amazes us with its remarkable indifference to our conceptions of good and evil. For example, why create the tree? Rather its chief concern is not the doing of man but God. The Bible is about God's point of view, not ours."[13]

And what is God's view? To love in a costly way, as he loved, is a self-sacrificing love on behalf of others. It is costly love. There were no limits on what he did to rescue you and me, so there can be no limits on what we will do to rescue others within the context of his character.[14]

Jesus expressed his ethic of love in his summation of the Torah: "'You shall love the LORD your God with all your heart, and with all your soul, and with all your mind.' This is the great and foremost commandment. The second is like it, 'You shall love your neighbor as yourself.' On these two commandments depend the whole law and the Prophets" (Matt 22:37–40, NASB). In this

---

8 Brocker, "Bonhoeffer's Appeal for Ethical."
9 Heschel, *Prophets*, V1, 15.
10 Moen, "Personal Ethics."
11 Roskoski, "Biblical Model of Human."
12 Roskoski, "Biblical Model of Human."
13 Childs, *Biblical Theology*, 679.
14 Moen, "Kingdom Ethics."

summary of the Law, for Jesus, there was no way of loving God except through loving one's neighbor. Jesus, who claimed that the entire Torah depends upon the double love commandment (Matt 22:40), also claimed that "whatever you wish that others would do to you, do also to them, for this is the Law and the Prophets" (Matt 7:12). Love your neighbor who, like you, is created in God's image and who, like you, requires forgiveness. Likewise, love your neighbor the way you want to be loved: do unto others as you would have them do unto you. And certainly do not do what brings harm to your neighbor. According to Jesus, when we act in this way toward our fellow human beings, we also express our deep love for God.

As stated above, kingdom ethics requires seeing and knowing reality from God's point of view and then acting congruently to kingdom ethics with others, even at cost to self. When we know what to do, kingdom ethics requires the resolve to immediate, decisive response.[15] One deed of heroism can change the world.[16] "But solid food is for the mature, for those who have their powers of discernment trained by constant practice to distinguish good from evil" (Heb 5:14).

Schirrmacher describes three essential aspects of any ethical decision for the Christ-follower. These are the normative, situational, and existential aspects.

> The normative aspect's importance is expressed in God's unchanging commandments. In ethics we generally find the normative aspect in basic values. The situational aspect's importance is expressed in wisdom, which gauges situations on the basis of experience and specific situations. In ethics a so-called collision of obligations, a situational ethic, and cultural assimilation all play a role. The existential aspect's importance is expressed in the meaning of the heart and the conscience, whereby in the individual the actual decision is made on the basis of normative and situational considerations. At this point in ethics, one generally speaks about the conscience and motives.[17]

Not one of these stands alone. All three must be present in any ethical decision in the unique situation of risk.

Schirrmacher also discusses the ethical challenge when there is no clear guide in Scripture for what to do when in the risk situation biblical commands are in conflict with each other. He describes the "ranking" of ethical commands throughout Scripture. Rahab was counted righteous

---

15 Sacks, *Heal a Fractured World*, 226–37.
16 Sacks, *Covenant & Conversation*, Vayeshev, 245–52.
17 Schirrmacher, *Leadership and Ethical Responsibility*, 45–46.

when she lied to save the lives of the spies (Jas 2:25). Jesus taught in Mark 3:4 it was okay to break the Sabbath command to rest in order to save a life. When Kingdom ethics are in conflict with each other, even lying to save a life is clearly the ethical decision.[18] With this brief summary in mind, we can discuss ethical boundaries in risk and the most common ethical dilemmas in witness risk.

Piquah Nefesh and Other Unethical Things You'll Never Do

What are the boundaries within the ethics of God's kingdom? Within the biblical ethic of the command to love God with our whole being and love one's neighbor as oneself, there is the first century concept of *piquah nephesh*. This notion is the ethical guide of what to do when keeping the commandments of God conflicts with a person's physical well-being. Saving a life is *always* the ethical goal and overrules any other commandment, such as keeping the Sabbath. But three behaviors are always forbidden, leaving martyrdom as our only moral option. It is always prohibited to engage in idolatrous worship, to engage in immoral sexual behavior, and be involved in bloodshed.[19] The Sermon on the Mount given by Jesus in Matthew 5–7 encapsulates and expands the concept of *piquah nephesh* both in our inner being and how we treat others, e.g. "murder" is anger towards others; "adultery" is entertaining lust towards another.

When we are in a danger of violence, our natural human response is to have one of three responses: fight, flight, or freeze. The Bible teaches us not to choose the action of fear but to choose the action of courage when faced with one of these three options. "Freeze," which is being paralyzed by fear, as discussed in chapter three, is "melting in the face of danger." The Bible tells us not to do the action of fear even when we feel this pull to freeze, but to do an act of righteousness, which is courage. "Flight" may be Holy Spirit-led, or flight could be an abdication of responsibility to stay. In the third response, "fight," we may somehow be tempted to lash out against our circumstances.

From the concept of bloodshed in *piquah nephesh*, violence may be expanded to include violating the identity and integrity of another person.[20] However, because each person is made in the image of God and because of the ethic of love taught by Jesus, instead of fighting (meeting violence with violence), the way of non-violence is the commitment in every situation to act in a way that honors the soul of another, even the violent perpetrator.

---

18 Schirrmacher, 83–85.
19 Tilton, *Jesus' Gospel*, 49–54.
20 Palmer, *Hidden Wholeness*, 169.

Usually, however, we are not immediately forced to make such drastic ethical decisions, such as saving our life or being forced to engage in sexual immorality, idolatrous worship, and bloodshed (violence). "People resist leaping from innocence to evil, but they can be lured into it one innocuous step at a time."[21] Cognitive dissonance is the feeling of tension humans experience when we have behaved at odds with our beliefs and values. Yet when we are under severe stress and do something even slightly dissonant from our espoused beliefs, we can experience "unethical amnesia." This experience is when we have difficulty remembering our dissonant behavior, and it becomes easier to repeat it.

To help prevent this possibility, "write a [personal] list of actions you will not take, [ever]. Reread it from time to time. Writing [this list does not] shield us from temptation, [and] it doesn't guarantee [we] won't do something [we'll] regret later ... It doesn't resolve questions about lesser evils. [Our list helps us] recognize where [our] slippery slope begins."[22]

Ethics and Risk Management

Why should these two complex fields be connected? *Who we are is who we send.* The ethics of the senders will be the ethics demonstrated in the mission context. Head describes four reasons why we need to connect ethics and risk management:[23]

1. For an organization to manage its risks well, everyone who represents [it] must practice good ethics.
2. For an organization to act ethically, everyone [including the senior leadership] who represents that organization must manage risks well.
3. An organization that permits or encourages unethical actions by anyone who represents it is not practicing good risk management.
4. An organization that permits or encourages anyone who represents it to manage its risk poorly is acting unethically.[24]

"Rather than countering complex risks with an even more complex risk-management system, which comes with its blind spots" and inflexibility, equipping individuals and teams with common, ethically-informed levels of risk awareness, codes of conduct, and values-based decision-making is

---

21 Chussil, "Keep a List."
22 Chussil.
23 Head, "Why Link Risk Management."
24 Head.

shrewd practice.[25] "Just as David was able to slay Goliath with a simple sling, complex risks are best addressed with simple measures."[26]

It is clear from my 2022 informal survey of risk managers and security professionals that there is an urgent need to change how senior organizational leadership engages in this task.

> Remoteness breeds indifference. Attitudes toward risk are deeply informed by the top [leadership's] tone, tenor, and remoteness. Leaders who practice what they preach, have conviction, and lead by example are better at managing risks than those that merely pay lip service to ethics, value systems, or codes of conduct. Simplicity is key in addressing this gap. When senior leaders encourage bounded risk-taking and show that they are open to hearing bad news, they can help hone an organization's muscle memory [to respond] to emerging threats. [Moral lapses] become more likely when those executives conversely dismiss details as too "in the weeds" for their attention, show that they don't want to hear questions or bad news, or are simply impossible to ever track down in the hallways.[27]

How can we train people to be sensitive to ethical decision-making? Training and equipping teams in ethical decision-making in high-risk and persecution situations is increasingly necessary for the global culture influenced by a moral reality that says "truth (and reality!) is what I feel or say it is." We can no longer assume even Christ-followers have a solid foundation in biblical literacy to guide them if they also have no training in ethical decision-making.

However, according to Soltes, three obstacles make ethical decision-making in real life different and more complex than in the training environment:[28]

> In training, "the consequential decision is identified for participants." [Specific dilemmas written out] "vastly simplify one of the main challenges—identifying the ethical dilemma in the first place—by placing a single decision into focus."

> "Training inevitably exposes different points of view and judgments." [Although most teams] "express a desire for a diversity of opinions, in practice, those differing views are often stifled by the desire to agree or appease others." [We struggle with dissent.]

---

25 Disparte, "Simple Ethics Rules."
26 Disparte.
27 Disparte.
28 Soltes, "Why It's So Hard."

"In training ... a single decision might be given an hour of careful analysis; most actual decisions are made quickly and rely on intuition rather than careful, [detailed] reasoning. This is especially problematic for moral choices."

Time is needed for deep reflection on what is happening and evaluating the consequences of an action. It takes humility to invite and listen to diverse opinions. Practical training in ethical decision-making requires case studies that show the complexity of circumstances, pressures, and sheer level of decisions that must be made in a short period. Values matter most when living by them will not only be inconvenient or unpleasant but will also bring discomfort and even pain to the pain of death. "Ethical lapses [happen] when people take risks but do not [consider] the downside of their risky behavior."[29] What are the practical ethical standards for duty of care to guide corporate risk-management practices? Four ethical standards are legal, value-centered, moral, and spiritual aspects of duty of care. This description is by necessity a general one, since it is nuanced from culture to culture.

1. From a values perspective, some duty-of-care standards cross all cultures that govern risk assessment, management, and decision-making. In our two-day Risk Assessment and Management Training (RAM), we have consistently heard that there is a universal standard that leaders have obligations of care in risk regardless of culture. Leaders should care for their people (although this care may look different culturally!) and the lives of people should be valued. Leaders should communicate the risks, etc. Cultural elements of duty of care carry different expectations, standards, and staff-care policies in different cultures.

2. Legal requirements for duty of care in risk management vary from nation to nation. There is no one-size-fits-all because governments mandate different types and standards for duty of care in risk management. The guideline of informed consent is helpful here. NGO workers (volunteers) need to know as much about the risks as any reasonable person would want to know about a situation to make an informed decision."[30] Additionally, they need to be trained and equipped within a reasonable standard, and as mandated by one's government.

3. Moral and spiritual duty of care: Jesus made it clear (Matt 23) that the Pharisees did not care for the people and laid heavy burdens on them.

---

29 Disparte, "Simple Ethics Rules."
30 Sherry Dingman, CEO, Fang Protective Services.

His teaching was based on the Old Testament teaching (e.g. Ezek 34) on how shepherds should care for the sheep and not neglect them. Shepherding people in risk will look different in different contexts.

Duty of care does not include personal preferences when they conflict with organizational policies. One Christ-follower wanted to keep weapons in his home as part of his risk management approach as a humanitarian worker. He was firmly invited by his leader to stay on the team if he was willing to get rid of his firearms. In addition, the duty-of-care standards from one culture group should not be automatically be imposed upon another, but we may need to be influenced by what another group does. Nuance and situational discernment is required here.

Just because duty of care may not be documented does not mean there are no expectations. Just as there is no legal contract between parents and a child, there are right expectations and quality of care for what parents provide for a child. In the same way, from a corporate and community perspective, there is an understood minimum element of care that personnel expect. These are not wrong, but they need to be addressed before someone goes into danger.

Duty of Care and When Staff Refuse to Evacuate

A classic challenge in a risk situation occurs when three critical values related to ethics are in tension: risk, safety, and calling. The leadership views the risk as too high, but the field staff feels a strong calling to stay. The risk is high, so does the calling of the organization and the field staff match the risk level? To further complicate the question, what if half the team wants to leave and half want to stay? How should the decision be made in this case? Which value—risk, safety, or calling—takes precedence? Which value, which decision is correct, and which is not?

Of course, leaders do not want to stand in the way of the leading of the Lord, but they are also given the responsibility for their people in the field. These situations are complex and require careful discernment together. The answer may be simple, but not simplistic.

Ideally, this scenario is thoroughly explored with all involved before staff go to a location. Both the team and the leadership agree that when the leader decides it is time to evacuate, the staff person will follow their leader and submit to the decision. Even with this agreement in place, staff who previously verbally acquiesced may now refuse to evacuate, leaving the leaders and organization in a precarious situation. Insubordination and refusal to evacuate when instructed can also significantly impact staff in other fields and the rest of the organization.

I would strongly urge people to obey their organizational leaders, even if they feel called, and they believe the leader is wrong. "Obey your leaders and submit to them, for they are keeping watch over your souls, as those who will have to give an account. Let them do this with joy and not with groaning, for that would be of no advantage to you" (Heb 13:17).

> The Lord asks us to obey our leaders, and so even if a field member feels the leadership is wrong, there is a blessing in obedience.

Why? Responsibility for staff in dangerous situations is a heavy burden. The leader is accountable to the board's oversight and often has to respond to the national and global media. The Lord asks us to obey our leaders, and so even if a field member feels the leadership is wrong, there is a blessing in obedience.

The common reason for staff giving push-back is, "I feel the Lord is calling me to stay," even when the leadership has decided all staff need to evacuate. One response utilized by some European sending organizations to staff who refuse to leave is to ask the staff to sign a legal waiver, acknowledging the staff person is going against organizational leadership and refusing to leave when asked. The waiver will release the organization from the legal duty of care for that person and any future evacuation requests. It would also state that the staff person and their family will not hold the organization liable for any adverse outcome.[31]

In cases of disagreement like this, leadership would reevaluate their own assessments:[32]

- Have we thoroughly evaluated government recommendations?
- What is the training level of the field staff (did they receive the proper training for the situation they are in)?
- Are the field staff ready to endure the situation as we understand it?
- Have the field staff taken care of temporary guardianship of children should parents be unable to care for their minors?
- Do all stakeholders have unity on the staff staying?
- What is the strength of the staff person's calling?

---

31 Henger, "Risikomündigkeit in der Mission." Consultation with the author.
32 Henger.

Other Duty of Care Thoughts:

- Leaders don't necessarily use the government as the main criteria for go/not go
- Leaders need to be checking on current government announcements
- Leaders need to make sure the people going to the field are prepared according to best practices
- Evaluate if the people choosing to stay have resiliency
- What do local and expatriate partners on the field say?
- It's different when experienced, so refrain from passing judgment when someone changes their mind
- Let people know before they go to the field that they may die there
- Pray together to sense the direction from the Holy Spirit
- What is our organizational and personal responsibility to our local friends and partners?

Applied Ethics

Applied ethics means taking kingdom ethics and applying it to specific moral problems in risk and persecution. Five significant ethical dilemmas are commonly faced: (1) deception vs. truth-telling; (2) interrogation; (3) bribery and extortion vs. gifts; (4) paying ransoms; and (5) risking the lives of people, including children, for the sake of the gospel. (Even though interrogation falls under deception vs. truth-telling, it is treated as another category because of its complexity.)

A common assumption or bias in determining "right" or "wrong" can be to presuppose that "my" view is the correct way. If a Western Christian says their interpretation of the Bible is right, it can be alleged to be the "Christian way," also known as cultural theological imperialism.[33] Lan says, "Biblical truth cannot be prepackaged, but must be found in the actual interaction between text and context in the concrete historical situation."[34]

Deception vs. Truth-Telling

Deception and truth-telling in risk and persecution asks questions like, "Is there a fine distinction between literal honesty and honesty in spirit and intent?" or is truth-telling largely a matter of timing? "Are there times when

---

[33] Lan, "Discovering the Bible," 289–305.
[34] Lan, 289–305.

to tell the truth is to be false to the truth that is in you?"[35] What is lying? What is truth-telling? When is deception a sin? Those without power ask these questions and more when fighting for survival.

As noted previously, Christians from different theological and cultural backgrounds may formulate the question and the answer differently. When faced with the temptation to deceive hostile entities, Jesus Christ asks, "Or what can a man give in return for his soul?" (Mark 8:37). Calling lies truth and truth a lie results in losing our sense of morality. In other words, we "perjure" our own soul, Thurman says. Unwavering sincerity is living with unstoppable awareness that we live in the presence of God, always under divine scrutiny. None can fool God, and nothing is hidden.[36] Within the constant awareness of being in the presence of God, there are numerous situations where the Christ-follower has to determine how to answer questions that can compromise their security and even get them put in jail or worse. Such situations include:

- Filling out visas, forms, and visa renewal interviews
- What you tell your children
- Switching NGOs within the same city
- Proselytization accusations
- Predictable surveillance and going off-grid

Does telling a partial truth imply telling a lie? Some cultures say truth-telling is only telling the full truth, otherwise it's lying. But could there be wisdom in withholding information that is unnecessary and would only compromise safety? What if we have two reasons for being in a country, but only one we really want to share? Is that lying? What if we are answering visa forms within the spirit of the law, not the letter of the law? As Schirrmacher stated, when two Biblical values are in tension, the one that preserves and saves a life is the ethical choice. Lying may be the right choice in certain situations.

If we are accused of proselytization, first ask them to define what they mean. It's usually an easy one to truthfully deny. What if the law requires us to always carry micro-chipped identification cards with us, and we choose to go off-grid because otherwise we would compromise a meeting of Christ-followers. Is this lying about who we are and what we are doing?

What about telling our children who we are and what we are doing? Little children did not ask to be there, nor are they the ones with the specific

---

35 Thurman, *Jesus and the Disinherited*, 62.
36 Thurman, 70–71.

ministry calling. Christ seems quite clear on not causing a little one to stumble, and the burden of living in creative access places is often more than a child should have to deal with. Keep it simple.

Interrogation[37]

There are three levels of interrogation. **The difference is your level of freedom.**

1. Delay: This usually happens at a checkpoint in the initial contact with an official authority figure. It is often when a uniformed official calls you over for a little more info (stop the car). A respectful attitude and a short, legitimate statement will be critical to defray suspicion.

2. Interruption: This is when something about you is suspicious, so you are invited to come into the office for further conversation. The uniformed official requires a little more info that you have to explain, and all information has to match. At this point, there is some limit to your movement until the suspicions are allayed. You are brought in for further questioning, often fined, and then released.

3. Detention: If you handle the interruption poorly and what you say doesn't match, they will take your freedom until they are satisfied. Alternatively, you may have handled the interruption well, but you are still detained indefinitely.

There are predictable techniques used in interrogation. Just as in anything, having the right expectations for what is likely to happen, how to spot it, and how to respond accordingly is wise (shrewd) training.

1. The Christian Guilt Technique: During interrogation, Richard Wurmbrand shared a commonly used line that went this way:

   > As a Christian, you must promise to tell us the whole truth about everything. It never worked on Richard. Since anything he [said] might lead to incrimination or apostasy, he devised a plan to confuse and mislead his interrogators until they couldn't continue their investigation.[38]

2. Patience and Tricks:

   > [They] preferred a more patient approach—the prisoner must ripen first. The goal was to create enough guilt and anxiety to extract information gradually. Prisoners were rarely told why they were

---

37 Author conversation with Jim, intelligence analysis expert.
38 Martyrs, *Wurmbrand: Tortured for Christ*, 123.

arrested, which threw them into a state of self-examination and uncertainty. Endless tricks created tension, doubt, and fear in their minds. [Mock] trials were scheduled and then postponed at the last minute. Firing squads or [fake executions] were simulated. Recorded screams and random shouts played throughout the night.[39]

3. Good Cop-Bad Cop: Interrogation has a chilling effect. Interrogators know how to make you feel bad and cause you to question your own decisions. Interrogators know how to play "good cop-bad cop." It is a technique to get you to soften or slip up. If you feel like the person interrogating you has your best interests at heart, you may feel like you can begin to trust them. Intimidation morphs into mercy. Promises are made to end the suffering, but only if the prisoner admits guilt and confesses to "crimes."

4. Fake Torture of a Loved One to Induce Answers: One of the hardest things for a husband is the thought of his wife being questioned and tortured. It happened to Richard Wurmbrand.

> One evening, as he was trying to doze, the sound of a woman's sobbing voice emerged from a nearby cell. "No, no!" she pleaded. "Please don't beat me. Not again! I can't take it!" The corridor echoed with shrieks as the guards beat the woman senseless. Richard listened intently until his eyes widened in horror. It was Sabina's voice! She had been captured and brought to [jail] … Richard [later learned that] the woman's voice was not Sabina's, but only a recording played for every prisoner, each thinking the sound belonged to his wife, girlfriend, or mother.[40]

Bribery and Extortion vs. Gift-Giving[41]

My colleague, Dr. Ernest Magnes, lectures on bribery in his ethics class and was kind to share his insights with me. A bribe is anything given to a person

---

39 Voice of the Martyrs, 132.
40 Voice of the Martyrs, 134–35.
41 Manges, "Bribery." Dr. Manges gave me his lecture notes to use with his permission. He notes that in the three standard evangelical textbooks on ethics (Kaiser, McQuilken, and Davis), amounting to almost 1200 pages, only one sentence can be found that mentions bribery. Dr. Manges' work is based on his own experience and research, but also "Folded Lies: Bribery, Crusades, & Reforms" by Michael W. Reisman (New York: Free Press, 1979), for this two-fold distinction of bribes. Much of the material for this lecture is adapted from: Richard L. Langston, "A Biblical Perspective on Bribery and Extortion and Its Implications in the Philippine Context from a Missionary Viewpoint," Doctor of Missiology project (Trinity Evangelical Divinity School, Deerfield, Illinois, USA, June, 1989). And also Richard L. Langston, *Bribery and the Bible* (Singapore: Campus Crusade, 1991). I have one document in my possession of a comprehensive enculturated bribery policy by an organization serving in a closed country. For security reasons, I am unable to use it here.

or entity that encourages a person or entity to do something illegal or wrong. It is different from a gift or tip, which may express appreciation for service. Bribery is the act of paying a bribe or receiving a bribe.

Extortion is the demand by a person in authority for a bribe. Usually, the person who receives this demand is a member of the public who expects some service from the official or authority figure of the people. The official is using his position of authority to ask for money. With extortion, there is a threat, either implied or stated. The presence of a threat makes extortion closely related to robbery. To clarify, a bribe is a payment, and extortion is the demand for payment.

There are two classes of bribes: transactional bribes and variance bribes. A transactional bribe is given to a public official or someone in authority to speed up the processing of papers or encourage the official to do his duty more quickly. Laws are not usually violated with a transactional bribe, and it is typically solicited to speed up the standard transaction. In soliciting or extorting a transactional bribe, the official says, "You will get quicker and better service if you pay me." "A bribe is wrong when justice is perverted." In many places, transactional bribes are the only way to get justice that the law owes me, and is not unethical.[42]

A variance bribe is given to a public official so that he will violate the law. In paying a variance bribe, the citizen requests the official not to follow proper procedure. In asking for or extorting a variance bribe, the official says, "I will let you escape the requirements or punishment of the law."

The Bible condemns the taking of bribes. "You must not take a bribe, for a bribe blinds the clear-sighted and corrupts the words of the righteous" (HCSB) (Exod 23:8; cf. Deut 16:19). Bribery destroys a nation's stability and corrupts the hearts involved (Prov 29:4; Eccl 7:7). Conversely, those who reject bribes are promised blessings.

Discerning a bribe from a tip varies from culture to culture. One way to learn is to explain to a local friend that you want to know the local cultural context for the difference between a bribe and a gift or tip, even if they are not a Christ-follower. You can explain the ethical teachings of Jesus and ask them to help you know how to apply them in culturally appropriate ways. This is also a great way to build relational bridges with a local and have spiritual conversations!

Dr. Manges gives the following questions to help discern when to give a gift or tip and when to refrain:

---

[42] Private conversations with a pastor working in a persecuted area.

1. Does the gift support justice, or does it hurt justice?
    d. Is it hurting or taking away the rights of the innocent?
    e. Is it allowing the wicked to escape justice?
    f. Does it help the official in his duty or confuse him about his duty?
2. Does the gift hurt impartiality and promote favoritism?
    a. Does it affect the judgment of someone who should be impartial?
    b. Does the official respond with favor to you because of the gift?
    c. Does the gift result in favor to some and unfavorable treatment to others?
3. Is the official motivated by greed or dishonest gain?
    a. Does the official use any kind of extortion to ask for a gift?
    b. Does the official request for or demand a gift?
    c. What do righteous people do in this situation?

In these difficult situations, we must not let our fear control us. We may suffer for not paying a bribe, as Paul did in Acts 24:26, 27. It costs us money, time, and convenience to not pay the bribe. However, there is often no other way to get a needed service accomplished for those who have no power. To resist and refuse to pay a bribe may be a matter of life or death.

Paying Ransom

People and organizations often repeat, "We will not pay a ransom." The problem with this statement is that it leaves no room for negotiation when someone's life is at stake. If kidnappers would accept twenty dollars in exchange for your spouse's life, would you pay it? For another example, negotiations in shame and honor cultures could include digging a well that provides water for the community, enabling the kidnappers to "save face" and return the loved one.

Another ethical dilemma in the issue of paying ransoms is organizations that refuse to pay ransoms and also prohibit families from paying the ransom. There are unequal consequences for the organization and the families. An organization does not have the same relationship with the kidnapped person as the family does. If a father is kidnapped, but no ransom is paid, and he is killed, his death will have a disproportionate impact on his wife and children who have lost a loved one as opposed to an organization that has lost a staff member.

Organizations and individuals should know the laws associated with paying a ransom. For example, in the USA, it matters if the kidnappers are criminals or terrorists. But even those laws are laden with ambiguity, and if the family pays a ransom, will they be prosecuted? It is critical that sending organizations have professional organizational help to know how to navigate kidnappings, negotiations, and paying ransoms. See the Global Risk Resource List on my blog for recommended companies. Even if one's government allows for ransoms to be paid, getting the money to the criminal, terrorist, or other entity legally may be almost impossible.

Risking the Lives of Adults and Children

The morality of putting people's lives—adults and children—in dangerous situations is commonly questioned. My persecuted pastor friend related how an American institution told him they would not give any funding to him and his ministry (to the unreached). Their reason was that he was putting people in danger that resulted in the physical loss of life, and they would not have blood on their hands. This response reveals an ethic based on the concept that this life is heaven, or "this is your best life now."

This difficult question is one that each adult going into danger has to answer for themselves. A wife should not consent to a husband's calling without prayerful consideration and reflection on her own, and vice versa. Are they each willing to risk their lives for the sake of Jesus Christ, and are they called to do so in that situation? For children, the hard truth is that God gives the parents a calling, and then blesses them with children. It does not automatically follow that children have the same calling.

The job of the parents living in dangerous situations, like any parent anywhere, is to do their utmost to protect their children from harm but also obey our Lord. There are times we make decisions based on the needs of the children, and other times when we have to make sacrifices as a family. Children and spouses will suffer in risk and persecution, and this has to be wrestled with before God.

Doves and Moral Courage

Moral courage is the ability to see evil and respond to it with the right ethical response. Bonhoeffer, known for his moral courage in standing up to the Nazis in World War II, briefly describes the failure of six different ethical orientations to come to grips with the evil of Nazism.[43] These are reason, ethical fanaticism, conscience, duty to obey, freedom, and private virtue.

---

43 Bonhoeffer, *Ethics*, 80–83.

First is the person who relies on reason to help them recognize good and stand against evil, yet they find that evil will not be stopped by reason. Next is "the utter failure of all ethical fanaticism." This person believes the strength of their will and principles will succeed in opposing evil. Instead, the moral fanatic gets tangled in "non-essentials and petty details" and loses sight of the totality of evil.

Third is the person of conscience, who makes his choice with only his inner conscience. Yet Bonhoeffer describes how evil comes upon him in "countless respectable and seductive disguises so that his conscience becomes timid and unsure of itself, till in the end, he is satisfied if instead of a clear conscience, he has a salved one, and lies to his own conscience in order to avoid despair."[44]

A fourth ethical orientation that fails is the duty to obey what is commanded. The responsibility is on the one who commanded, not the one who carries out the order. In the end, he says, this person will obey the devil.

Fifth are those who guard their "freedom to choose." They will, in the end, "sacrifice a [fruitless] principle to a fruitful compromise, [or] … consent to the bad … to ward off what is worse, … [and] will no longer be able to see that precisely the worse which he is trying to avoid may still be the better."[45] And finally, Bonhoeffer says, those "who seek to escape from taking a stand publicly find a place of refuge in private virtuousness." This person obeys all Ten Commandments but remains "blind and deaf to the wrongs" committed around him or her and chooses to avoid "responsible action in the world."[46]

Bonhoeffer's prescription to avoid being crushed or co-opted by evil in situations when "all concepts are confused, distorted, and turned upside down [is to] combine simplicity with wisdom. [Simplicity] is to be single-hearted and not a [person] of a [divided] soul (Jas 1:8)."[47] He writes,

> Because the simple man knows God, because God is his, he clings to the commandments, the judgments and the mercies which come from God's mouth every day afresh. Not fettered by principles, but bound by love for God, he has been set free from the problems and conflicts of ethical decisions. They no longer oppress him. He belongs simply and solely to God and to the will of God. It is precisely because he looks only to God, without any sidelong glance at the world, that he is able to look at the reality of the world freely and without prejudice. And that is how simplicity becomes

---

44 Bonhoeffer, *Ethics*, 68.
45 Bonhoeffer Kindle edition by Fortress Press ebook, *Dietrich Bonhoeffer Works*, Volume 6. General Editor, Wayne Whitson Floyd Jr. 2005, 79-80.
46 Bonhoeffer, 80.
47 Bonhoeffer, 80.

wisdom. The wise man is the one who sees reality as it is, and who sees into the depths of things. That is why only that man is wise who sees the reality in God. To understand reality is not the same as to know about outward events. It is to perceive the essential nature of things. The best-informed man is not necessarily the wisest ... And so the wise man will seek to acquire the best possible knowledge about events, but always without becoming dependent upon this knowledge. To recognize the significance of the [facts] is wisdom.

Moral courage requires a clear ethical foundation of righteousness, purity, and singlemindedness of soul in action.

The wise man ... knows that reality is not built upon principles but that it rests upon the living and creating God ... To look in freedom at God and at reality, which rests solely upon him, this is to combine simplicity with wisdom. There is no true simplicity without wisdom, and there is no wisdom without simplicity.[48]

Moral courage requires a clear ethical foundation of righteousness, purity, and singlemindedness of soul in action. It is winsome and admirable. The second part of Matthew 10:16 has to do with the innocence of doves. My friend Brian writes,

> There are several species of doves in Israel, the Eurasian-collared dove, the Turtle Dove, and the Rock Dove. Doves exist in harmony with all other life forms. Because they feed on seeds, their life cycle does not depend on the death or displacement of other species, although their predators displace them! In general, their life strategy is in harmony with other flora and fauna in a way that embodies grace, agility, and gentleness. When in flight, they are fast and agile, and their looks are attractive; hues of blue, shades of greens and brown, colors of white and black all blending in attractive patterns.[49]

Our winsomeness in how we face evil is how we embody the teaching of Jesus to be characterized with the shrewdness of a Palestinian viper and the beautiful purity of doves.

Living inside of "God's imagination" enables us to see reality as it can become, what can be different,[50] the kingdom present, and the kingdom coming. His kingdom is not (yet) come where brutality towards Christ-followers is likely to require moral courage. Living inside God's imagination is ethical because it is concerned with bringing God's justice, kindness,

---

48 Bonhoeffer, 70–71.
49 Lubinski, "Doves."
50 Brueggeman, *Prophetic Imagination*, 39–57.

and mercy to places characterized by injustice, cruelty, and pitiless cold-heartedness. It is courage because it is the right action despite the consequences and internal fear one may have. Moral courage requires moral passion for standing against the evil and injustices of the age. What is the greatest evil? Apathy about evil—the inhumanity of humankind—is the greatest evil. Moral courage breaks through denial, numbness, and the inhumanity of cruelty towards Christ-followers and points even torturers to Christ.

In contrast, moral cowardice knows what is right but will not do it. It lets evil prevail. "It is sin to know the good and yet not do it" (Jas 4:17, CSB). Cowardice tries to justify itself before its peers. It values safety over truth and leads to violating our conscience and lying if necessary. Moral cowardice is controlled by the fear of consequences of standing for the truth and thus has misplaced priorities.

What leads to moral courage? Moral courage requires purpose of heart. "But Daniel resolved that he would not defile himself with the king's food" (Dan 1:8). Decisions to act against the status quo in brutal societies require foreheads of flint. "Do not be afraid of anyone, for I will be with you to rescue you" (Jer 1:8, CSB). "I have made your face as hard as their faces and your forehead as hard as their foreheads. I have made your forehead like a diamond, harder than flint. Don't be afraid of them or discouraged by the look on their faces" (Ezek 3:8–9, CSB). "Therefore I have set my face like a flint, and I know that I shall not be put to shame" (Isa 50:7).

I began the chapter by discussing the shrewdness of snakes, and our shrewdness is based on the kingdom ethic of the love of God. God's love is ultimately defined by the submission of God's only son to unjust, shameful torture and crucifixion. Thus, the cross of Jesus Christ is the only way for Christians to discern what Christ is demanding of us.[51] When we freely identify with him in his sufferings by voluntarily choosing to suffer for his sake, this is the "only kind of deed [that] can strike at the heart of evil and overcome it."[52] Those called to moral leadership in societies troubled by dehumanizing criminality are asked to enter into the patterns of Christ's life speaking the gospel word to people and standing up for the truth about God's love for the world. "It is doing the right thing under the tacit, steady guidance of God's Word and Spirit conjoined."[53] Lord, may we be "powered by a holy resolve that is incessantly subversive."[54] He is worthy.

---

51 Kelly and Nelson, *Cost of Moral Leadership*, 178.
52 Bonhoeffer, *Ethics*, 12.
53 Kelly and Nelson, *Cost of Moral Leadership*, 80.
54 Prayer attributed to Brueggeman.

Chapter 8
Thinking about Thinking

> *For though by this time you ought to be teachers,*
> *you need someone to teach you again the basic principles*
> *of the oracles of God. You need milk, not solid food,*
> *for everyone who lives on milk is unskilled in the word*
> *of righteousness since he is a child. But solid food is for*
> *the mature, for those who have their powers of discernment*
> *trained by constant practice to distinguish good from evil.*
> —Hebrews 5:12-14

Just as reality and perception of reality are two different things, risks and perception of risk also differ. How can we separate them? That's the focus of this chapter.

In the movie *The Matrix*, the main character, Neo, learns that there is a different reality to know about, contrary to the one he perceives (thinks) is accurate. He can choose to swallow a red pill or a blue pill. "Each pill represents [a different reality]. The red pill [is] the path to finding out the truth behind the lies, providing the opportunity to forever change [his] knowledge and perception of reality. Taking the blue pill instead, on the other hand, is to choose a life of ignorance, refusing to shatter the illusion [he was] living in."[1]

While we can't just take the red pill as he did, we can learn to examine our thinking, how we see and interpret the world, and how we discern what is real from the fog of war in risks. Why do we want to do that? For two primary reasons: (1) if we keep asking the same questions, we will get the same answers. And the converse is also true: if we are looking for a specific answer, we will frame our questions without realizing it to get that answer; (2) because reality is where God is, and he is continually working to make order out of chaos. He hasn't changed. He often uses risk and persecution to reveal where he is at work or shift our attention to a new focus.

Previously, in *Facing Danger*, I discussed the value of understanding stewardship and discernment in risk, hearing God's voice and the Spirit's leading in the risk moment,[2] and critical aspects of risk decision-making (*Facing Danger* chapter twelve). I've discussed how the Sixteen Risk Myths[3]

---

1 Weston, "Matrix's Red Pill."
2 Hampton, *Facing Danger*.
3 Hampton, Chapter 10. *Facing Danger* 1st ed has 12 Risk Myths. There are 16 Risk Myths in *Facing Danger* 2nd Ed (Est. 2024).

reveal some of the things we tell ourselves that get in the way of our thinking. They are repeated so frequently we think they are facts and continually repeat them to ourselves, deluding ourselves into thinking that we are actively reasoning.

This chapter builds on these previous discussions by examining additional elements impacting witness risk perception and decision-making. We want to ask ourselves how we approach thinking about risk and how our biases, dangerous attitudes, perceptions of risk based on emotions, and experiences inform our current perception of risk. God gave us minds to think and make reasoned judgments, so we want to learn the critical factors that impact decision-making in situations where the stakes are immense, uncertainties are overwhelming, time is of the essence, and stressors are severe.

Ways of Approaching Risk[4]

Too often, we are unwittingly influenced by Plato and Aristotle. The assumption is that knowledge is the highest virtue, and emotions are considered impediments to rational thinking. The Stoics took Platonic and Aristotelian thought even further—the emotions are unreasonable, unnatural, and the source of evil. The highest good is to be free of emotions, suppress them, and control emotions by reason. This aim defines morality, what is labeled good, and ethical behavior. The extent to which we are influenced uncritically by these views will influence our approach to risk assessment.

The traditional view that risk assessment is purely scientific (empirical-logical) is inadequate. Psychologists researching risk identify three main ways we humans approach risk: experientially (more emotional, intuitive), analytically (logical), and politically (power). Slovic writes, "Danger is real, but risk is socially constructed. Risk assessment is *inherently subjective* and represents a blending of science and judgment with important psychological, social, cultural, [spiritual], and political factors" (emphasis mine).[5]

Risk as Politics, Feelings, and Analysis

In witness risk, confronting risk as politics is probably the least common scenario. Most sending organizations know that risk analysis needs to occur, so I'll briefly discuss this approach and move on to the other two. How might risks as politics be demonstrated in a sending organization?

---

4 Slovic, Finucane, Peters, MacGregor, "Risk as Analysis," 21–36, in *Perception of Risk*. Slovic cites numerous empirical studies that demonstrate the statements in this section.
5 Slovic, "Trust, Emotion, Sex, Politics."

Confronting risk as politics means defining risk as an exercise in power. I wonder if it's a combination of spiritual pressure and church metrics of success. This combination demands that risks be ignored and not thoroughly evaluated and mitigated. For example, churches, organizations, and individuals deny risk exists in dangerous endeavors in the 10/40 window by saying, "We are called to go and die." With this mindset, evaluating or acknowledging risk is an irrelevant topic of discussion because it "reveals fear or a lack of faith." In this way, the leadership uses religion to determine risk, and they frame the question so that they get the answer they want: there is no risk—or it's not true faith to evaluate it.

However, most people and organizations are engaging in risk assessment and management and crisis management preparedness. Yet it's much more common to make the mistake of engaging in risk assessment as a purely logical endeavor. Risk is approached logically with two goals: usefulness and protection at all costs. Yet, scientific research has known for decades and shown in numerous studies that humans *predominantly* use the affective (emotional), intuitive approach to risk analysis even when they *think* they are entirely logical.[6]

Below I present a summary (edited for simplicity) of the overwhelming, validated research that we humans know and make decisions using interplay between our emotions and logic-analysis. As far back as 1994, the two primary modes of thinking in risk were identified, and the following table compares them.

Experiential (Holistic) System	Analytic (Logical) System
Affective (emotions): pleasure/pain oriented	Logical: reason oriented (what is sensible)
Feeling and sensing connections	Logical connections
Behavior is mediated by "vibes" from experience (intuition)	Behavior is mediated by conscious appraisal of events
Reality described in concrete images, metaphors, and narratives	Reality described in abstract symbols, words, and numbers
More rapid processing: oriented toward immediate action	Slower processing: oriented toward delayed action
Self-evidently valid: experiencing is believing	Requires justification via logic and evidence

Table 4: Two Modes of Thinking[7]

---

6 Slovic, Finucane, Peters, MacGregor, "Risk as Analysis," 21–36.
7 Epstein, "Integration of the Cognitive," 709–24.

Experiential, intuitive feelings refer to the fast, instinctive, intuitive reaction to danger. Most risk analysis is done quickly and automatically in the "experiential mode" of thinking. Although "fear certainly plays a role in risk as feelings,"[8] researchers also identify the role of affect (emotions) in how we analyze risk. Termed the "affect heuristic," this perception describes how we consciously or unconsciously identify "goodness" or "badness" experienced as a feeling, and then demarcate a negative or positive quality about a risk.[9]

Our feelings about a risk play a role in how we interpret the reality around us. We see reality in the experiential way of knowing in "images, metaphors, and narratives to which affective feelings have become attached."[10] However, relying only on our affective interpretations of reality would be a mistake. In the twenty-first century, our emotions are manipulated by social media and by expert fear-mongers (politicians, propaganda, extremists, media, etc.). We are also vulnerable to our human drives and needs.

Because risk as feelings can cause us to weigh the risks we fear the most as higher than likely, we must employ "risk as analysis to give us a perspective on the likelihood of [the risk, which calms us]."[11] Risk analysis is critically vital. Risk as analysis means a "deliberative, analytical system that functions [through] established rules of logic and evidence (e.g. probability theory)."[12]

In a volatile, uncertain, complex, and dangerous world, we make decisions very quickly, most often with our affect and emotions. However, the experiential and analytical mode of thinking is constantly interacting. Researchers have concluded that describing these two approaches to risk is more helpful as "The dance of affect and reason. Affect is essential to rational action"[13]

We've seen that when a Christ-follower has succumbed to compassion fatigue or has numbed out due to all the trauma, they often do not make effective decisions on the rational side. We need *both* the emotional and analytical sides of ourselves in risk. "Emotions can be reasonable just as reason can be emotional. There is no need to suppress the emotional roots of one's life to save the integrity of one's principles."[14] Being made in God's image means we reflect both his heart and his mind in ours. This reality implies using our hearts and minds in our risk approach.

> Emotions can be reasonable just as reason can be emotional.

---

8 Slovic, Finucane, Peters, MacGregor, "Risk as Analysis," 21–22.
9 Västfjäll, Peters, and Slovic, *Perception of Risk*, 109.
10 Slovic, Finucane, Peters, MacGregor, 28.
11 Slovic, Finucane, Peters, MacGregor, 35.
12 Slovic, Finucane, Peters, MacGregor, 28.
13 Slovic, Finucane, Peters, MacGregor, "Risk as Analysis," 24.
14 Heschel, *Prophets*, Vol. 2, 36.

Perception of Risk[15]

The perception of risk "refers to (1) a person's subjective judgment or appraisal of risk"[16] (feeling), and (2) how people frame the risk. Because fear comes from perception and judgments about a situation, fear adds to the dissonance between perception (how things appear to us) and reality.[17]

How people perceive risk has been extensively researched[18] and these discoveries helpful to know for witness risk include:

- People in positive moods tend to evaluate risk more favorably than participants in a negative mood.
- People incorrectly attribute their incidental attitudes as a reaction to the risk.
- Even sunny vs. cloudy weather can remind people to influence their judgments of well-being in light of the risk they are facing.
- The ease with which people recall or think about a significant tragedy, environmental event, or terrorist event elicits negative feelings, and this influences how people think about and view their future possibilities (Negative feelings = more pessimism = fewer possibilities).
- How risk is framed influences how risk is perceived as more or less dangerous.
- In general, men tend to perceive risk as lower than women do; this is not related to rationality and education as traditionally believed.
- White males tend to rate risks lower than all other groups (women, minorities).
- Several studies have demonstrated the following racial perceptions of risk:
  » Non-white males and females are more similar in their perceptions of risk than are white males and females.
  » White males are different in their perceptions and attitudes toward risk. Gender and, to a lesser extent, race remains a robust predictor of risk perception.

---

15 Finucane, Slovic, Mertz, Flynn, and Satterfield, *Feeling of Risk*, 125–40.
16 Society for Risk Analysis, "Risk Analysis: Fundamental Principles," 4.
17 Mermelstein, "Constructing Fear and Pride," 449–83.
18 Risk perception studies commonly focus on people's perception of the risks related to dangers of handguns, nuclear power plants, second-hand cigarette smoke, multiple sexual partners, and street drugs.

Factors that influence a person's risk perception include worldview, trust, the tension between control and vulnerability, feelings of benefit, and the ability to influence the decision about the risk (sense of power). "Differences in risk perception originate not just because of substantive differences in power to control the risk but also because people with less power over risks feel more likely to be at risk and feel the risk to be inequitably distributed."[19] No matter their education level, women will almost always feel more vulnerable due to rape used as a weapon of persecution and war.

People from different cultures, ethnicities, and generations have different views. Mercer's research revealed that the cross-cultural Christ-follower deals with at least three distinct cultural perceptions and understandings of risk. The first perception understands risk from the person's home culture perspective, and the second is the perception and understanding of risk from the host culture the Christ-follower is living in. The third cultural understanding of risk is somewhere between their home and host cultures. A person from the United Kingdom will face different challenges and cultural assumptions living in Uganda than a Ugandan Christian. The perceptions of risk and perceived need for security are motivated by other fears and understanding of risk.[20]

The conclusion by researchers is to integrate a variety of inputs by including a spectrum of people from different backgrounds in the risk discussion. Research and experience shows this increases the likelihood of arriving at the best risk decision for all involved.

While there is little peer-reviewed research on the role of worldview, religious conviction, and risk, it's apparent that ideas, ideals, and principles hold key positions impacting perceptions of and responses to risks.[21] It's normal human nature to use the simplest possible perception to see the world. In terms of witness risk, it is always best to have all team members identify what risks they are concerned about and work together to rate the risks as a team or community.[22] As we listen compassionately to each other and feel understood, trust in the team and leadership increases. Giving input on risk in respectful dialogue does not cost money, only time and energy, and the benefits far exceed the energy required.

It's helpful to explore all aspects of a risk people may have concern about. For example, if the concern is about being imprisoned, the conflicting value is that they want to continue sharing the gospel. To manage this fear, instead

---

19 Breakwell, *Psychology of Risk*, KL 1975.
20 Mercer, "Risk and Security."
21 Assmuth and Finkel, "Choices and Rationalities," 42.
22 See the RAM Action Guide in *Facing Danger* or my website. I explain how to do risk assessment there.

of ignoring the fear of imprisonment, take time to mentally explore how to manage and survive imprisonment, including how one would continue to share the gospel. This practice leads to feeling less vulnerable in some regard and feeling more equipped to be resilient and demonstrate endurance. There is also a greater sense of control in that the Christ-follower is not taken (as much) by surprise. Working through risk assessment and mitigation with a team or community of believers increases trust with each other and with leadership. Furthermore, integrating conflicting values with integrity increases resilience.

Psychology of risk researchers have also spent a great deal of time looking at how people perceive risks and benefits. Typically,[23]

1. If the *benefit of the risk is high*, they feel good about it and thus perceive *the risk as low*.
2. If information about the risk says the *risk is low*, they feel positive and *infer the benefit is high*.
3. If the information about the risk says the benefit is low, people have a negative feeling and *infer a high risk*.
4. If the *information about the risk says the risk is high*, people feel pessimistic about the risk and *infer the benefit to be low*.

However, witness risk is unique: Christ-followers often perceive (and assess!) the risk as high; they have a negative feeling (negative affect) about it but feel called into it. The affect (emotion) does not necessarily deter them from moving into the risk.[24] What propels Christ-followers forward in these circumstances are their strong belief and personal conviction, and commitment to Jesus Christ. It's also been shown that "presenting the same information about risk in different ways alters people's perspectives and actions."[25] We want to use thoughtful care in how we present risks!

Thinking across Cultures

To the Western mind, using care in how we present risk makes sense. How do we know reality (and truth)? This question is what the field of epistemology is all about. But to the Western Christian mind, the "correct" answer seems to lie exclusively in a logical deduction from observation and re-integration of theology into an analytical framework for analysis. I would point out that much of the research I've cited is based on data gathered from focus

---

23 Assmuth and Finkel, "Choices and Rationalities."
24 Assmuth and Finkel, "Choices and Rationalities."
25 Tversky and Kahneman, "Framing of Decisions," 458.

groups who are "Western, educated, industrialized, rich, and democratic."[26] This distinction doesn't mean the data is wrong, but it does not reflect multiple ways of knowing and making decisions.

We also want heightened sensitivity to the diversity of thinking from different cultures. The Western mind and the Eastern mind think differently.[27] As the world has become global, it seems wise to work together within Christ's global family to think together about how we discern reality in risk and value each other's unique contributions as complementary, rather than seeking to elevate one way over another. Nisbett contrasts Westerners to Asians, the Greeks to Confucians in his book, *The Geography of Thought: How Asians and Westerners Think Differently … and Why*. He describes the following preferences and tendencies:

- The Western mind prefers to think in concepts and categories; Asians attend to objects in their broad context.[28]
- Westerners use formal logic in problem-solving; Asians look at a host of factors that operate with one another in no simple, deterministic way.[29]
- "Westerners believe they can know the rules governing objects and, therefore, control the object's behavior."[30]
- Westerners seek to control the environment; Asians seek self-control.[31]
- Westerners emphasize individual personal agency; Asians emphasize collective community.[32]
- Westerners are concerned with finding the truth; Asians are more concerned with finding a way to live in the world.[33]
- Westerners prefer to live by abstract principles. "Asians live in an interdependent world in which the self is part of a larger whole";[34] "Westerners … view events in a cause-and-effect model, [and] this is goal-oriented reasoning."[35] The Eastern view is that "everything in the

---

26 Robson, "How East and West."
27 This would be an area for further research. One classic work is Boman's 1960 work *Hebrew Thought Compared to the Greek*.
28 Nisbett, *Geography of Thought*, xvi.
29 Nisbett, xvi.
30 Nisbett, xvii.
31 Nisbett, 6.
32 Nisbett, 6.
33 Nisbett, 15–19.
34 Nisbett, 77.
35 Nisbett, 129.

universe is somehow related to everything else,"[36] and "It's [impossible] to understand the pieces without considering the whole."[37]

While Nisbett elaborates on many more differences, I think you get the idea. The way we in the West approach "how to know" compared to Asians and others is very different. By inviting different approaches to problems and even risk assessment, we may collectively have better, more creative ways to manage challenges together and model the unity of Christ's family to those watching and also find out we aren't as different as we might at first think.

Crisis vs. Non-Crisis Cultures

Because risk means a situation of potential crisis is looming, and persecution implies the crisis has arrived, learning how crisis cultures are oriented compared to non-crisis cultures is beneficial. Lingenfelter explains this idea in his book, *Ministering Cross-Culturally*.[38]

> Crisis orientation anticipates crisis, emphasizes planning for a crisis, seeks quick resolution to avoid ambiguity, repeatedly follows a single, authoritative, preplanned procedure, and seeks expert advice. Non-crisis orientation downplays the possibility of crisis, focuses on actual experience, avoids taking action [by delaying] decisions, seeks ad hoc solutions from multiple available options, [and] distrusts expert advice.[39]

How both risk and crisis are managed differs depending on the orientation. It would be a mistake to judge conflict on an international team in a risk situation as a spiritual issue without considering the cultural dimension summarized above and described in more detail in Lingenfelter's book. If some people think in ways different from us, we must learn to see the world the way they do. We can learn another culture's crisis management style and learn from those different from us. Our goal is to cultivate the unity of the body of Christ even in our approach to risk, which requires us to think of others better than ourselves.

Dread Fear

Dread fear is a critical aspect of how people perceive risk. For laypeople, "feelings of dread [are] the major determiner of ... perception and acceptance of risk for a wide range of hazards."[40] A risk that is perceived as a dread

---

36 Nisbett, 129.
37 Nisbett, 129.
38 Lingenfelter and Mayers, *Ministering Cross-Culturally*, 53–65.
39 Lingenfelter and Mayers, See the summary of the chart on page 58.
40 Slovic, Finucane, Peters, MacGregor, *Feeling as Risk*, 25.

risk will be assessed as more likely to occur.[41] While the studies that led to this statement were not conducted with the values of witness risk, let's be humble enough to accept that even as Christ-followers, we are not immune to allowing our dread fear to "color" our risk analysis and risk tolerance.

When I first went to Afghanistan, I would have said the object of my dread fear was rape or mobs. I found over the years that the object of my dread fear changed. Let's have grace for people to help them learn where they are now with their dread fear and give them space to change as they grow in their walk with Christ. I suggest sending organizations guide their staff in an exercise to identify their dread fear. It means reflecting on what is the thing that you're most afraid of. An exercise like this must be led very sensitively and gently, as one's dread fear may be highly personal, which automatically brings up feelings of shame. Most likely people don't need to share their dread fears, especially in an organizational situation. But it is wise for each person to take time to identify and sit with it with the Lord and perhaps a wise veteran who has faced danger. Recognizing one's dread fear doesn't mean just naming it; and it means exploring every facet of what that experience would be and the impact on the Christ-follower. How do they imagine themselves responding? This practice is an exercise in endurance and resiliency training.

Biases in Witness Risk[42]

Decision-making in high-risk environments is challenging. Biases in ourselves and others can prejudice decision-making. Not everyone experiences biases in the same way or extent, but even a minor bias can distort critical thinking and effective decision-making. Biases are not necessarily wrong or harmful. Typically humans make decisions very fast, using what can be termed "mental shortcuts." Our biases are these shortcuts to decision-making so that we are not overwhelmed by all the decisions we need to make every day. These biases fall into the "risk as emotion" category discussed above.[43] The other primary way humans make decisions is "risk as analysis," which takes time and effort to think through logically. We want to heighten awareness of both approaches to risk decision-making.

We need to become consciously aware of the specific biases to identify them in ourselves and others as we respond to danger and risk. Our decision-making principles can and are being affected by our subconscious biases. Identification is the first step in preventing irrational judgment. Researchers have identified over one hundred fifty biases humans can have. Neal and

---

41 Slovic, Fischhoff, Lichtenstein, *Perception of Risk*, 152.
42 Hampton and Hampton, "RAM: A Workshop."
43 Kahneman, *Thinking Fast and Slow*.

I have noticed the following common biases that influence communities engaged in witness risk decision-making. These biases show up in the perception of risk (causes and consequences), probabilities estimation, and information evaluation.[44]

1. Confirmation Bias: People don't like to change their opinions. Looking at a risk situation in a new way might mean reconsidering one's long-held beliefs. Doing so is hard and uncomfortable, and it is far easier and more comfortable to resist or ignore new information that threatens those beliefs. This tendency is referred to as confirmation bias.

2. Hindsight Bias: Hindsight bias is a bias of memory. We look back and tell ourselves we could have done better than the leader, or the leader looks back and tells herself what she should have seen and done. There is a place for critical reflection (see chapter fifteen on a system risk audit), but hindsight bias is not critical reflection or a proper risk audit. Hindsight bias inherently focuses on the decision made, not the decision-making process used at the time as well as the factors that were involved in making the decision, usually under extreme stress, with very little time, and almost always without enough accurate information.

We encourage leaders to avoid hindsight bias by writing down their decisions even during the pressure of risk and crisis and why they made the decision. We often forget all the factors that were impacting us at the time. This practice helps us have more grace towards ourselves when engaging in appropriate critical reflection later on.

3. Anecdotal Bias: This bias is when the risk situation increases to a level which activates an individuals' anxiety. Situational anxiety intensifies or decreases based on their perception of the risk. This impairs decision-making. "In particular ... anxiety drives decision-makers to more heavily emphasize subjective, anecdotal information in their decision-making, at the expense of more factual statistical information."[45] This habit results in a less-than-optimal decision.

4. Predictability Bias: It is much easier to recall something horrific, catastrophic, or terrifying. Those events stay with us, even if we did not experience them. People assume the probability is higher that an event will happen if they can remember an instance of it happening. This explains why many assess terrorist attacks as having a high probability, and a much lower probability is attributed to car accidents even though statistically, these assessments should be reversed.

---

44 Vinney, "What is Cognitive Bias?"
45 Yang, Saini, and Freling, "How Anxiety Leads," 1789.

5. Anchoring Bias: Anchoring bias causes a person to be excessively influenced by the first information about risk. This bias can cause tunnel vision and an unwillingness to evaluate additional information accurately.

6. Halo Effect: People with certain personalities can cause us to feel good about their decision-making abilities and have a disproportionate influence on risk management efforts. We may not realize that we are led by our positive impression of someone or their winsome presentation rather than rational realities.

7. Loss-Aversion Bias: We attach more value to something once we have invested in it. This investment may relate to time spent developing something, emotional energy expended toward it, or financial resources paid. We may become too attached to these things to willingly consider abandoning them, even when it is clear that the danger associated with continuing is high.

8. Authority Bias: Favoring the risk perspective of leaders over the valuable input of other team members can impair good risk management. Although there are essential roles for leaders in risk (covered in the leadership section), relevant input must be appraised from all sources, regardless of rank.

9. Optimism Bias: "The optimism bias is a cognitive bias that causes people to assume they are less likely to experience a negative event than other people are. The 'that will never happen to me' attitude"[46] is related to the dangerous attitude of denial discussed below. This cognitive approach underestimates the negative consequences and over-estimates the positive results. It leads to "a false sense of security because 'this could never happen to us,' or an inflated sense of preparedness, essentially that 'we have got this under our control.'"[47]

10. Action Bias: Some people react negatively when faced with the ambiguity of risk environments. They would favor doing something—anything—over taking time to assess risks thoroughly. They may be prone to take action regardless of whether it is a good idea or not.

11. Bandwagon Bias: When we first look at what everyone else is doing in response to a risk scenario and then follow suit, we are experiencing bandwagon bias. Everyone begins doing the same thing. This practice can be effective if it is the right choice, but it could also be a poor decision to join in what everyone else is doing.

---

46 Gloeckner, "Optimism Bias."
47 Gloeckner.

In one case, a civil war broke out in the country's extreme south. A critically necessary community project was doing significant work eight hours north of the airport and the fighting. The airport was the only means to get out of the country, and the war threatened its closing. All the NGOs were evacuating their staff from the south. Bandwagon bias in this situation resulted in all agencies from the north and south pulling out all expatriate staff, resulting in the community project being severely limited in its response as well as significant disruption to the lives of families.

Meanwhile, there was no violence anywhere near the community project. While seeking wisdom from diverse sources is crucial, groupthink and bandwagon bias seem to have been the main criteria in risk decision-making in that situation. If leaders of that organization had included both demographic and geographic proximity in their overall risk assessment, their stewardship of the project and staff likely would have been different.

Uncover Biases in Witness Risk

How can we uncover our biases? It starts by assuming bias! We all have some biases that are influencing us. The goal is not necessarily to get rid of them but to become aware of them. There is no such thing as total objectivity.

> If leaders of that organization had included both demographic and geographic proximity in their overall risk assessment, their stewardship of the project and staff likely would have been different.

- We can help uncover biases by making risk decisions "in the community," even if that means with others through a virtual connection. It helps to cultivate the habit of listening to, reading, or watching people who have different perspectives from us.

- Ask yourself, "What makes me think they are wrong or right?" and "What makes me frustrated with them?" It's crucial not to make the mistake of relying on your current Google feed.

- Algorithmically, we will only see what interests us or confirms our bias. When doing internet research, make a point to look at the opposite point of view to "mess up" the algorithm that will otherwise only send you what you want to hear (confirmation bias).[48]

- Ask yourself and ask someone from another culture, "What is a common bias for people like me?" (e.g. my personality, nationality, gender),

---

48 See the video: "The Social Dilemma."

"What is a common bias of our team?," and "What is a common bias in our organization or community?"

- What concerns often come to my mind? For example, am I constantly feeling pressured by what I think my supporters want to hear, what my leader wants, or my perceived expectations from my organization?
- Spend time becoming aware of what you label "good" and "bad." From another perspective, these could seem the opposite. Why do I call something good—what assumptions are behind that valuation, and the same for "bad."
- Practice mock scenarios (role-play) with your team to see how each person would make the decision, and then discuss your differences.
- In what ways do people (myself included) make decisions when lacking information? What type of information am I looking for? (The answer may partially reveal my bias.)
- Read this book to learn more about biases: *The Undoing Project* by Michael Lewis.

Personal growth means increased awareness of our biases. We can never fully get rid of them, but awareness and understanding them help us evaluate our decision-making and adjust when necessary. Challenge your instincts, embrace a willingness to welcome new information, and grow in your willingness to speak up when you see biases in others, especially those in risk.

Diminish Groupthink

A mob is an extreme (and violent) example of groupthink. People can also practice groupthink in a sophisticated manner. The following discussion on groupthink has been modified from De-Risk Management group.[49] Groupthink is "when a group of well-intentioned, intelligent, experienced people come together and collectively make bad decisions. ... When people come together and discuss things in groups, they are immediately subject to social pressures. Most of these pressures we don't even realize affect us, but they do. One of these social pressures is the pressure to conform, fit in, and go along with everyone else."[50]

When Christ-followers get together, they may over-spiritualize because it is uncomfortable to share what we think about things out of fear of being labeled as "fearful" or "not having faith." Things do not get discussed, and everyone goes along with the most decisive leader or idea put forth.

---

49 Baxter, "What Is Groupthink?"
50 Baxter.

As a result, groups tend not to discuss ideas as thoroughly as they should for fear of upsetting those around them or out of fear of what others will think of them. Groups like this take more risks or implement more risky behaviors than they would do individually. There is also pressure on groups to seek unanimous agreement even in the face of contrary facts pointing to another conclusion.

Because of the lack of awareness of the dynamics of groupthink, and the strong possibility of mistaking group unity as unity of the Holy Spirit, resulting in a false sense of spiritual security, it is important enough to include the entire description of groupthink based on the psychological definition. Awareness is always the first step in making a better decision.

Psychologists now think eight symptoms define groupthink. Sometimes they are worded differently, depending on which study you look at, but essentially include:

1. Interpersonal Pressure: In groups, we feel enormous pressure to reach an agreement with the other members of the group. Even if we don't fully agree, we are more likely to just "fit in with the crowd." Another type of pressure is direct pressure. In these cases, group members keep quiet so that they aren't branded "disloyal."

2. Self-Censorship: The desire for group cohesiveness is so strong that people will often keep their personal opinions to themselves. In such situations, people ignore warnings that might challenge the group's assumptions by self-censorship of ideas that deviate from the apparent group consensus.

3. Mind Guards: Similar to the self-censorship symptom. A mind guard is someone who omits information. They leave it out if they think it will jeopardize what is a strong social desire to keep a cohesive group.

4. The Illusion of Unanimity: If everyone is too afraid to voice their opinions, then it creates the illusion of a group consensus. If it seems that everyone is in agreement, this makes it even harder to disagree with the group. In organizations which value the unity of the Holy Spirit, this would be a major mistake to interpret unanimity as unity of the Holy Spirit.

5. The Illusion of Invulnerability: If no one is objecting, complaining, or criticizing the group leader or decision-makers, then it can seem like everything is going well. This, in turn, can breed over-confidence, creating excessive optimism that encourages risk-taking.

6. The Illusion of the Morality of the Group: The desire to see the group succeed can be so strong that it even overrides an individual's sense of right and wrong. An unquestioned belief in the morality of the group

can cause members to ignore the consequences of moral dilemmas and their actions.

7. Biased Perceptions of the Outgroup: A tightly cohesive group can, in time, come to stereotype and discriminate against the "others" that are not involved in the group. The result is that "outsiders" are devalued and considered not as proper, [as spiritual,] or as [strategic] as the ingroup. This is sometimes referred to as negative cohesion.

8. A Defective Decision-Making Process: More often than not, groupthink situations result in the deciding on and execution of wrong, improper, or poor decisions. All of the above symptoms compound together to shut out or omit alternative and what could be—better decisions.[51]

In witness-risk, typical consequences of groupthink include:

- Failure to examine risks
- Poor information research
- Inability to work out risk contingency plans

One way to diminish the impact of groupthink is to invite discussion from the group, with the leader reserving their opinions until the very end of the discussion. Designate someone to contribute opposing viewpoints and challenge each assertion purposefully. Additionally, we can diminish groupthink when we: "Bring in external experts to challenge the group thinking, set up multiple groups to work on the same issue, appoint a 'devil's advocate' for key meetings to test conclusions, [and ask leaders to] deliberately avoid expressing opinions before key meetings/projects."[52]

Dangerous Attitudes[53]

Studies show that our minds most often prevent us from risk mitigation. During times of high risk, it is common for things to get in the way of our cognitive functioning.

Here are some common dangerous risk attitudes:

1. Defiance: While some degree of boldness is a positive mental resource for persevering through risk, defiance can hinder our ability to respond appropriately. Defiance causes a person to focus on winning instead of continuing.

---

51 Baxter, "What Is Group Think?"
52 Baxter.
53 Hampton and Hampton, RAM.

2. Resignation: This dangerous attitude can sometimes look like fatalism. We are on unstable ground when we feel like there is nothing we can do to cope with dangerous situations.

3. Compulsivity: Compulsive people manage risk through action. The problem is that it is not a well-intentioned activity. Driving forward without evaluating the road ahead can be hazardous indeed.

4. Comparison: It is sometimes tempting to look at what others are doing when we are confused. That is not a completely flawed approach, but it has limits and falls far short of mitigating through one's own careful discernment and analysis. "So if everyone jumped off a bridge…."

5. Denial: Believing that we are somehow immune from being impacted by danger causes us to avoid dealing with it in the first place. To effectively manage risk, one must first acknowledge exposure to the threat.

Identifying which one or two dangerous attitudes we are prone to enables us to recognize what's happening the next time we face a risk situation. Instead of just letting it happen, make a plan to mitigate your natural tendency of personal biases and dangerous attitudes.

Mental Mistakes People Make[54]

"People think, therefore, they err. All humans err; it is the burden of being human."[55] Just like we all have biases, so we each have certain mental mistakes we are prone to. To improve our critical thinking requires learning to identify the most common mental errors we tend to make. Knowing these tendencies, we can devise strategies to "catch ourselves" making errors and improve our analysis. The following are just some of the many mental errors identified by Hall and Cintrenbaum in their chapter "Critical Thinking" which are pertinent in witness risk:

1. Mirror Imaging: This error fills gaps in one's knowledge by assuming someone would act in a certain way because that is how you would act under similar circumstances. It means only looking at the situation from your perspective (a kind of cultural arrogance) and not from another perspective. In this instance, understanding the differences in motivation between honor and shame cultures, fear and power cultures, and truth and guilt cultures will help.

---
54 Hall and Cintrenbaum, *Intelligence Analysis*, 93–120.
55 Hall and Cintrenbaum, 93.

2. Assumptions: When there is a gap between what is known and unknown, people assume what will happen. Of course, we have to make *some* assumptions because there will always be an information gap, and decisions must be made, sometimes exceptionally rapidly. However, knowing that we make assumptions and then to some level base our planning and mitigation on these assumptions, we can take several steps to make the best possible assumptions and check for poor ones. First, become aware that we make assumptions, and identify what they are as we make them. Then, constantly pay attention to how valid those assumptions are as events unfold. As risk increases, constantly re-assess the risk and the mitigation procedures in place. Invite a person who always asks difficult, uncomfortable questions, even if they feel slightly threatening to the leader's ego, to ask difficult questions and check what critical thinking is happening.

3. Circular Reasoning: This error is the use of reason where the conclusion is based on the premise. The conclusion should follow the premise but not be the same as the premise. An example is "The Taliban are evil and the source of the suicide bombings because they follow Sharia law, and therefore, the Taliban are responsible for the suicide bombings."

4. Hasty Generalization and Oversimplification: These failures happen when we stereotype a group or individual. We do not have enough evidence to make the conclusion, but we do anyway, basing it on simplistic generalizations. We must look for the evidence to warrant the conclusion. In risk, it is extremely common to make the error of oversimplification. Simplistic answers are when we give easy answers to complex issues and problems. The reality in risk is almost always much more complex and nuanced than we realize.

5. A False Dilemma: This fallacy occurs when only two possible options are given, but almost always other options are available that have not been considered. Much of gospel risk has a middle ground between the extreme options available. "There is no situation involving human beings in which simple yes or no, black or white, or unequivocal positions or slants exist."[56] Complexity is always involved when people are involved.

6. Historical Comparison: Comparing two situations is useful as long as you are careful not to draw faulty conclusions. There may be similarities in some respects, but it is dangerous to ignore the differences and assume there will be similar outcomes.

---

56 Hall and Cintrenbaum, *Intelligence Analysis*, 105.

How can we help ourselves avoid some of these common mental errors? One simple step we can take to reduce our propensity to committing a mental error is taking time to reflect on the list of mental errors and considering which one we are likely to make. Second, we can invite input and critique from trusted others on our logic pattern in the decision-making. Thirdly, we have to cultivate an attitude that we could be wrong. A willingness to admit mistakes in thinking will help us become more open to the possibility that we have not been as brilliant as we'd like to think we are. Thinking about our thinking takes time, a willingness to be honest with ourselves, lay our egos aside, and avoid minimizing the effect of our mental errors on the decision and the people impacted by it.

Here is a list of questions we can ask ourselves to check how we are doing:

- Have I neglected to find the right expertise to help with my particular problem or challenge?
- Have I failed to ask for support from other [people] in my situation? Ask for support from local people from various socio-economic levels, those who are Christ-followers, and those who are not Christ-followers but are not against me (people of peace).
- Have I stated my limitations and risk tolerance correctly?
- Have I, in the interest of saving time, oversimplified the situation?
- Have I presented poor assumptions or [not acknowledged my] assumptions behind my thinking at all?
- Have I engaged in mirror imaging and therefore neglected to identify the [likely strategy the adversary may use or what my vulnerabilities are from their perspective]?
- Have I seized upon expert opinion … and … failed to explore alternatives [from the locals' perspective?]
- Have I used faulty cause and effect logic in exploring anomalies in relationship to baselines?[57] (See discussion on baselines in chapter ten.)

Taking time to reflect on the information coming in and how we are thinking through it is essential, even when time is limited. As risk increases, the situation often changes rapidly. It is critical to take time to reflect and observe what is happening from a distance, even as you continue to gather facts and evidence for those facts. It's also vital to reflect on your thinking and cultivate curiosity about your own biases, attitudes, and tolerance levels

---

57 Hall and Cintrenbaum, 107.

for various risks. We also want to consider what is happening spiritually and physically around us, the possible meaning underlying the current events, and possible ideas about the cause and effect of what has already happened.

Things are never simple, so typically, there are multiple causes for any one event, but one thing will usually stand out. Take time to look at the major and minor details in the flow of events. Notice the complexity and interconnectedness of the causes and effects, relationships, variables, and the windows of strategic opportunity presenting themselves within the risk. Doing this prayerfully may reveal insight into what God is doing and what can happen that was not visible before.

Chapter 9
Witness Risk Axioms

Most kingdom workers address risk tactically when they should embrace it devotionally.
—Neal Hampton

As Neal and I have trained, consulted, and answered questions about witness risk globally, we heard ourselves repeatedly making the same statements about risk—so we began writing them down. We realized there are risk axioms—things that are true about witness risk and shared by everyone from every culture. I've reduced them to just these seven and tried to summarize each one.

- Noun: ax.i.om/æk.si.əm: A statement or proposition that is regarded as being established, accepted, or self-evidently true.
- Example: "the axiom that supply equals demand."
- Synonyms: accepted truth; general truth; dictum; truism; principle.
- Risk Axiom: A statement or assertion of judgment about witness risk. These risk axioms are short statements that are memorable, useful for equipping Christ-followers, and short enough to come to mind when needed.

Risk Axiom #1: Risk Is Situational

A theology of suffering and a theology of risk are not the same. Risk and suffering ask different questions, thereby requiring different answers. Responding to risk questions with suffering answers is unhelpful. Too often, the answer given is "Risk is right" or "You aren't risking." Both of these over-spiritualized answers have been addressed in *Facing Danger*. The tension between these two theologies in daily life is one we have to work out in tandem with the Holy Spirit's leading.

The nature of the risk problem is unique.[1] It is urgent. A person asking a question about risk is not asking a question of intellect or a hypothetical question. A risk question is not the result of a thirst for knowledge that can be answered only through deductive or inductive reasoning. A person asking about risk is facing a problem in a specific situation involving their whole selves and people who are dear to them.[2]

---
1 Heschel, *Who is Man?*, 1–10.
2 Tierney, *Social Roots of Risk*, 52–56.

> A person asking about risk is facing a problem in a specific situation involving their whole selves and people who are dear to them.

Many questions call for an answer, but a problem in risk specifically calls for a solution. A risk problem exists because it has grown out of a real risk situation. Facing risk means facing a specific threat to the well-being of people, projects, or efforts. Complex risk questions rarely have simple answers. Often, taking a step back to evaluate the question we are asking will enlighten us to any assumptions we might be making. Common risk questions and problems include:

- How do I know whether to move into danger or stay in a safe place?
- How do I know when I have enough information about the risk?
- How do I know how to make the best decision in risk?
- When is too much risk being experienced?
- What is God calling me to in risk?
- How does God feel about the risks I am taking for him?
- I'm afraid—am I lacking faith?
- What do I tell my family back home? (or, What do I say to my children here in risk with me?)
- Am I called to move into greater danger with my children?
- What if my children are murdered because of my choice to follow Christ?
- What is the meaning and purpose of this risk?
- I never understood that when I risked coming _____ (here), it would mean _____ (this).

Two sources of understanding risk are in constant tension: conceptual thinking and situational thinking. Conceptual thinking deals with broad concepts through philosophical and theological analysis; it involves thinking about concepts and the phenomenon of risk based on conjecture rather than thinking about risk through experiential knowledge or concerned involvement (deep inner empathy). Conceptual analysis is practical when dealing with intellectual questions. But this is where it falls short in helping Christ-followers think through risk. To predominantly utilize conceptual thinking when evaluating risk is not engaging in the problem. Often, conceptual thinking spiritualizes risk at an inappropriate moment or as a tool to manipulate.

Situational thinking about risk involves thinking through concerned involvement. It is thinking about the risk through specific concerns and assessing and managing specific risks for specific situations.

However, those engaging in *only* situational thinking are wise to maintain perspective by remembering teaching about the future such as Daniel 4:34–35:

> For his dominion is an everlasting dominion and his kingdom endures from generation to generation; all the inhabitants of the earth are accounted as nothing, and he does according to his will among the host of heaven and among the inhabitants of the earth, and none can stay his hand or say to him "What have you done?"

God is in control. Eventually, there will be no risk when his dominion is over all kingdoms. The Bible must be relevant for today's problems, and this requires careful thinking and feeling through what he has called us to do. Becoming aware of the risk problem and equipped to answer it situationally and conceptually as appropriate is critical. Through his voice and his word, the Holy Spirit can answer our toughest questions in risk if we are willing to take the time to stop and listen.

#2: Safety Is Not a Feeling

We felt unsafe under the Taliban (in 2000) and didn't realize they protected us in reality. Once Kabul was liberated by coalition forces in early 2002, and we returned as a family, we felt the freedom on the streets and thus felt safe. We had no idea we were in grave danger. Just a few months later, in November 2002, we experienced a massive armed robbery when ten armed men entered our home one evening during the month of Ramadan. They had murdered folks in the previous two homes they robbed that day. Neal was almost killed. It shook the expatriate community and resulted in the American Embassy and US Ambassador following up with us a couple of times (the ambassador even enjoyed an early Christmas meal with us!). We increased the height of our walls and added concertina wire and glass shards to the tops of our walls.

But I knew concertina wire and glass shards would not stop robbers or a mob—those barriers are easily overcome but would at least slow someone down if they attempted it again. One day I was returning by foot to my Kabul home, and just as I reached my gate, an American, CIA-looking guy stopped his steel-plated, bullet-proof SUV and opened his dark-tinted window to ask me if I felt safe. I took a breath to decide if I should be brutally honest and replied, "You can't see them, but we have angels standing guard on the tops of our walls and at our gates and doors." Unsurprisingly, he didn't ask any more questions.

Neal and I were impacted differently and recovered in different ways from the trauma of the robbery. But the main lesson is that *safety is not a feeling*! Bad things happen, and they happen to good people. Equating comfort with safety is a fatal flaw and gets people killed.[3] Situational awareness is essential and is discussed in greater detail in the next chapter. But it asks questions like:

- What is the police force like?
- Are they getting paid enough to make righteous decisions, or is the economy so bad that they are easily bribed?
- Who is truly in charge around here?
- What percentage of the neighborhood or city is supporting those in charge and how many soldiers are employed by them? Who is their enemy and how strong is that strong man?
- Who is the strongest "strong man" in the neighborhood, suburb, or city?
- Which shopkeepers and neighborhoods would help shelter me?
- Where are safe places to run to?
- Which ethnic group is most hospitable and open to a person like me?
- Where is the best place to hide if gunfire and bombs go off? (Constant situational scanning with an exit strategy without looking like you are hyper-vigilant.)
- How far have evil people been known to infiltrate? (One Afghan colleague told me the line around my suburb where I should not cross, where even he would not go. We often had parts of the city "off-limits" to us, and it was the Afghans telling us these things.)
- Where do I situate myself in a room? I want to see who comes in, but I also want to be able to get out easily and not be surprised from behind. (Back to a wall but not a corner.)
- Where can I keep my communication devices handy? (Both our handheld VHF radios were on the fireplace mantle when the robbers entered. I quickly grabbed my cell phone and hid it under my armpit. Neal's cell phone was next to his radio in the living room.)

There are subtle cues we likely won't be able to pick up on no matter our linguistic abilities, cultural competence, and even our training in situational awareness, simply because we are still outsiders. For example, one time I was

---

3 Quesenberry, *Spotting Danger Before*, xxvii.

walking in the Kart-e-Char bazaar. It used to have the best second-hand shoe shops, and we liked the atmosphere because few foreigners shopped there. I went with two other women, one brand new to the country. As we walked, she said, "That shopkeeper back there just leaned over and spoke to me in English and told me we shouldn't be here right now. Is that normal?"

I had been enjoying the bustle of the Afghan bazaar and taking my time looking at the items in the shops. But my adrenaline immediately shot into high gear as I focused on a potential kidnap threat. To my surprise, my instinct was not to go inside a shop for refuge but to move us three women to the middle of the street where we could easily be seen and get my husband on speakerphone so he could hear what was happening. I looked frantically around for an old Hazara man wearing glasses and driving a taxi to take us home.

The majority of Afghan drivers don't wear glasses, which means somewhat haphazard driving experiences! Hazaras are a friendly cultural group, and an old Hazara man wearing glasses would be the safest driver to get us out of there. I spotted the type of driver I was looking for and we hustled into his taxi and told him to drive fast. I breathed a sigh of relief when we were three kilometers away from the area but asked Neal to stay on the phone with me until both women were dropped off and I was safely home. Despite having lived in Afghan culture for such a long time, I simply didn't know the cultural cues when there was an elevated threat of some type, whatever it was.

Heaven is the only truly safe place where evil will not be able to touch us. Until then, it's wise to be as aware as possible and not let our guards down. 1 Corinthians 16:13, "Stay alert, stand firm in the faith, show courage, be strong" (NET). Ephesians 6:18, "Keep alert with all perseverance." 1 Peter 5:8, "Be sober-minded; be watchful. Your adversary the devil prowls around like a roaring lion, seeking someone to devour."

#3: Severity Is as Severity Is Felt

While it is true that safety is not the same as our feelings about a risk environment, emotions must be taken into account when weighing risk's impact on ourselves and others. It is essential to measure two key aspects when assessing the severity of witness risk. First, evaluate how severely a risk event would impact those in at least six groups of relationships: my relationship with myself, family, team, community, partners, and organization/NGO/company. Second, evaluate the likelihood that a risk event would have a severe impact. Probability refers to how likely it is that something will happen, and severity refers to how much of an impact an event would have.

Each person will feel the impact of severity differently. Emotions are directly tied into an interpretation of severity—is this a risk event that touches prior trauma in the individual, team, or community? Or is the potential severity of the risk event touching a fear within the person? Do not discount emotions as unreasonable or a sign of weakness.

#4 Emotions Can Be Reasonable, Just as Reason Can Be Emotional[4]

We reflect God's image in our emotions and rational thought. Proclaiming "I am willing to die for Christ" or "I've counted the cost" are emotional statements based on deep conviction of thought. These emotional statements are based on the reasonable facts of what Christ has done for each of us.

In terms of risk analysis, paying attention to emotions is imperative. "If you do not account for your emotions in risk, then your risk assessment will be faulty."[5] "[Risk] analysis of [the perceived threats and the resulting] decision-making that fails to consider the [emotion] attached to a [threat] or the [individual's] emotional state ... is inevitably flawed."[6]

In the risk event, emotions may be confusing, but research on risk helps shed light on the various emotional events that may be occurring simultaneously. (1) We experience daily emotions based on our physical status. How our day is going if we are in a good relationship with those closest to us, our food intake, the amount of sleep we've had, etc.; (2) then there are emotions attached to the perceived hazard based on what we've heard or seen about it; (3) at the same time, we may have feelings attached to our reaction to the perceived hazard, like feeling guilt over our fear; (4) it's also possible to experience emotions from past trauma, triggered by the current risk or persecution we are dealing with; (5) finally, because living in risk and persecution opens up the possibility for spiritual transformation, we may also be experiencing emotions related to how we feel about God and how we think he feels towards us. Identifying and untangling these interrelated emotions helps us know at least we aren't going crazy!

If you do not account for your emotions in risk, then your risk assessment will be faulty.

---

4 Heschel, *Prophets*, V2, 36.
5 Hampton, *Facing Danger*, 149.
6 Breakwell, *Psychology of Risk*, 122.

Risk is an invitation to examine:

1. Our misconceptions of being human (What is man?—a question of ontology)
2. Who God is and what he is like? (a question of metaphysics)
3. What we should do in risk? (a question of ethics)
4. How do we know? (a question requiring a new epistemology because it requires a deeper and higher pneumatology—study of the Holy Spirit) The Spirit speaks, and he is not always predictable and often works outside our "cultural theology box."

#5 Risk Is Opportunity

Witness risk is defined as "the potential for loss and gain when following Christ." While we risk much in going to dangerous places to share the gospel with unreached, unevangelized people, we also experience incredible opportunities. The time of risk is a time of "liminality." Liminality is "a threshold experience. It is composed of any or a combination of danger, marginality, disorientation, or ordeal and tends to create a space that is neither here nor there, a transitional stage between what was and what is to come. … It is experienced as a place of discomfort and agitation that requires us to endure and push into what is to come."[7]

In terms of risk, it seems we live in the condition of liminality because we simply don't know if the risk we fear will materialize, so we are constantly "living on the edge." We want to evaluate the opportunity that risk brings by evaluating opportunity on several levels to understand what God might be up to in risk, and what is truly at stake. "Shrewd thinking" means we look at what is happening in risk from as many different perspectives as possible, considering all aspects of being human, of God's personal and corporate strategic plan, and his leading in the cosmic battle we are engaging in with him.

A careful evaluation of opportunity in risk may reveal the spiritual reality of what God is doing and what our enemy is trying to conceal. There are at least three types of opportunities to look for in risk:

Salvation Opportunities

What opportunities exist to push his kingdom forward in proclaiming the gospel or modeling the peaceful behavior of a dove or sheep in risk? Recognizing this opportunity could mean our project changes focus, strategy, or geographic area to be more kingdom strategic. What open doors exist—which peoples are hungry to hear more and which are not receiving me well?

---
7 Frost and Hirsch, *Faith of Leap*, 19.

Where is he leading me to interact with the leaders in my community to point them to Christ? This hostile person persecuting me could be the next "Saul" amongst these people whom God wishes to redeem and call to him. What is my role in this situation?

Community Opportunities

What opportunities exist to glorify God through the Christian community involved in the risk? How might my team have a unique opportunity to put his love on display? (John 13:34, 35). Where might we need to engage in a different project work to help people? Is there another physical need they have that this risk threat is the source of a new opportunity for me to change my/our work focus?

Personal Sanctification Opportunities

Living through risk and persecution provides an amazing opportunity for personal spiritual transformation. What opportunities are there for me to have increased self-awareness of what is happening in my heart toward God as I move through risk? What emotions do I need to process, either those triggered by past hurts or in my fears about the risk I am in? What aspect of God am I having a hard time trusting right now?

Risk is an honor to steward in our hearts, lives, and ministry. When we take the time to remember what we've faced, when we reflect on the risks we took, the experience of risk continues to give opportunities long after the threat has passed as we share the stories of what God did and how he worked. We can continue to learn from our experiences in risk and teach them to the next generation (Ps 78:6).

#6 Risk Can Be an Offering of Worship

The central tenet of Leviticus 19 is to worship God only, not any idols or replacements of God or a false god of our making. But there were also offerings to be given, offerings representing a heart overflowing with love for the Lord. Worship, sacrifices, and offerings, including the libation (drink) offering, must be made with a whole heart that loves God and obeys Him.

Psalm 51:17, "The sacrifices of God are a broken spirit; a broken and contrite heart, O God, you will not despise." Psalm 40:6, 8, "In sacrifice and offering you have not delighted; but you have given me an open ear. Burnt offering and sin offering you have not required ... I delight to do your will, O my God; your law is within my heart." God sees acceptable worship as a humble, contrite heart, obedient to his word and spirit." Romans 12:1, "I appeal to you, therefore, brothers, by the mercies of God, to present your bodies as a living sacrifice, holy and acceptable to God, which is your spiritual worship."

Worship involves the whole being—attitudes and action. Therefore, unacceptable worship would be any effort that fails in one of these areas—attitude or action. Paul describes his future suffering in these terms: "*For I am already being poured out as a drink offering, and the time of my departure has come*" (2 Tim 4:6). Paul sees his life and coming death as like the drink offering, which was a supplemental offering as an act of worship in contrast to the required sacrifices (see Num 15:1–10).[8] In this way, Paul links his death to Christ's voluntary sacrificial death.

We cultivate risk as worship when we offer our discomfort and even sacrifices to Christ and obey him, however he leads. Risk is worship when we choose self-sacrifice to help another. Risk becomes worship when we are able to work through conflict with others even under great distress and tribulation. Risk as worship means that we are doing our best to walk in unity and forgiveness with others and that our inner heart dialogue is a posture of grace and forgiveness to God, others, and ourselves.

Risking our lives for Christ can be a beautiful, worshipful experience. We see our shortcomings so well in risk, but we also see God's grace poured out on us and others through the experience. As we generously offer our whole being for his use to love others, no matter the risk of suffering, he is glorified and that is worship!

#7 Reduce Uncertainty with Subjective Probability

"If the outcome of a decision in question is highly uncertain and has significant consequences, then measurements that reduce uncertainty about it have a high value."[9] Hubbard demonstrates when assessing the intangibles in (business) risk that we can effectively reduce the uncertainty (which increases our clarity) by utilizing subjective probability. When we are in a risk situation, trying to assess risks, we can make educated guesses (subjective probability analyses) about what we think won't happen and is unlikely to happen. Doing this reduces the number of items we are uncertain about and helps us determine what to focus on. Hubbard suggests that the framework for reducing uncertainty best utilizes Applied Information Economics (AIE) to measure the uncertainty. The general framework is as follows:

1. Define the decision.
2. Determine what you know now.

---

8 Louw and Nida, *Greek-English Lexicon*, 53.27 σπένδω.
9 Hubbard, *How to Measure Anything*, 9.

3. Evaluate if you need additional information (if none, go to step 5).
4. Measure where information value is high (return to steps 2 and 3 until a further measurement is not needed or time runs out).
5. Make a decision and act on it (return to step 1 and repeat as each action creates new decisions and as new information comes in).

Reducing uncertainty using this method minimizes distraction from risk threats that aren't real (what we fear instead of actual situational reality). For example, one Sunday during our years of living in Turkey, I was apprehensive about the active ISIS threat against our international church (they had surveilled the actual building and issued a reasonably specific threat to attack us). Neal and I utilized the AIE adjusted for witness risk and had a conversation where we applied the four aspects of risk analysis (frequency, severity, geographic proximity, and demographic proximity). We reduced our uncertainty by talking through what we subjectively guessed would most likely happen and not happen.

In our discussion, we reviewed the current ISIS threat in our neighborhood, city, country, and region, as well as the police presence, the location of the church, and the risk mitigation that had been put in place. We also discussed the longevity of the risk threat: it had been about six months since the police had revealed the threat to our church leaders. While new threats and new "chatter" were continually coming in, in reality, the threat level had not increased or changed much (nothing new had been added to the constantly repeated verbal threat of "we will kill the infidels and anyone who converts." We also reviewed the current political climate, and through a subjective analysis of all that data, we decided all the signs pointed to there being more certainty there would not be an attack. We reduced our uncertainty by subjective probability. There has been no attack and no increased threat of an attack for over a year, which means that the threat most likely can be considered inactive, although the risk mitigation procedures are still in place as a deterrent. (The severity of the attack would be high, so this measure is appropriate.)

There is no hard and fast rule on this risk axiom and how to use it, and one's gut about the situation is very important. I will stress that Neal taking the time to talk me through this was vital for me to work through my emotions and reduce my fear level so that I could interact calmly with my teenagers that Sunday morning and go to church. By thinking through the subjective probabilities, you will have more clarity on what specific threats you may be facing. Ironically, scientific research by Douglas Hubbard gives us the certainty that we can reduce our uncertainty by subjective probabilities.

Chapter 10
Becoming Shrewd as a Serpent

You can never fight what you can't see coming.[1]
—Gary Quesenberry

Embedded within the church's assignment in the world are a defenselessness and vulnerability. Remaining hospitable to others and welcoming them, even hostile actors, constantly exposes Christ-followers to potential harm. From a security standpoint, vulnerabilities are resources to be protected. Security aims to defend, protect, surveil, lock down, and scrutinize people. Yet, often stewardship of vulnerabilities means opening ourselves to harm, and even death. There is a constant tension between determining openness and welcoming while learning how to assess and minimize potential violence so that we can live another day to serve Christ and share the good news.

> The human violence we abhor and fear the most, that which we call "random" and "senseless," is neither. It always has purpose and meaning … As long as we label it "senseless," we'll not make sense of it. … Violence [has] detectable patterns and warning signs. … [Yet] we want to believe that human violence is somehow beyond our understanding because as long as it remains a mystery, we have no duty to avoid it, explore it, or anticipate it. We need feel no responsibility for failing to read signals if there are none to read. … The truth is that every thought is preceded by perception, every impulse is preceded by thought, every action is preceded by an impulse, and man is not so private a being that his behavior is unseen, his patterns undetectable.[2]

"Violence is rarely random."[3]

According to Becker, even the way people conceal their evil intentions is predictable once you know the patterns to look for. Quesenberry adds, "Just as violence and evil start in the mind, real security starts in our minds. The ability to logically process what's going on around you and spot danger before it has a chance to materialize … allows you time to plan and act well before anyone else even knows what's going on."[4]

---

1 Quesenberry, *Spotting Danger Before*, xxiii.
2 Becker, *Gift of Fear*, 15, 16.
3 Federal Bureau of Investigation, "Making Prevention a Reality," 25 and Becker, 15.
4 Quesenberry, *Spotting Danger Before*, 39.

The Art and Phases of Situational Awareness

> Becoming "shrewd as a serpent" includes learning the art of situational awareness.

Fear and paranoia are counterproductive to mature courage and resiliency.[5] However, the need for preparedness and becoming "shrewd as a serpent" includes learning the art of situational awareness. "Recognizing a threat early and taking measures to avoid it … is more of a mindset than a hard skill."[6] It means knowing as much as possible about the particular place you are in, a heightened awareness of what specifically to look for in terms of threats, and how to respond to them. It's the cultivated ability and learned skills to spot danger to protect yourself and those close to you. It requires becoming observant and aware, and developing the habit of consistently being mindful of what is going on around you. The three phases of situational awareness are "(1) understand the threat; (2) build your situational awareness; and (3) develop personal defenses."[7] "It involves equal measures of comprehension, planning, and intuition. … It's a mental game and requires focus as well as critical thinking."[8] There are two ways to approach situational awareness: to exploit to our advantage or to deny and ignore. One leads to courageous witness and the other to needless loss and potentially death.

Situational awareness works both ways. There are at least two types of unknowns: what is unknown to the Christ-follower about what hostile entities may do, but also what is unknown to hostile actors who cannot necessarily predict what a Christ-follower will do. When ten armed men attacked our home, there was one point when the barrels of two guns were touching Neal's temples, and I recognized he was about to be murdered. At the same time, the hesitation of the robbers to pull the trigger registered in the back of my mind as proof that we were not responding predictably to the robbers, based on how locals would likely have responded (we found out later the robbers had killed Afghans in two previous homes that day). As foreigners, we were unpredictable to them in their situational awareness.

We can exploit vulnerabilities like this to our advantage in witness risk.[9] History is filled with violence begetting violence. Acting reflexively with the

---

5 Stratfor, *How to Look*, 14.
6 Stratfor, 15.
7 Quesenberry, *Spotting Danger Before*, xxvii.
8 Quesenberry, 39.
9 Treverton, Jones, Boraz, Lipscy, "Toward a Theory," 25.

firmness of conviction characterized by kindness and love when faced with violence is generally unpredictable to those hostile to the gospel. When we do not respond with violence, we take advantage of their vulnerability and presumption. This response testifies to Christ and his love for them. "Acting reflexively" does require a level of training, preparation, and imagination to practice how we will react in hostile situations since those situations often happen when we least expect it.

Imagination is similar to "visualization." It is a skill to creatively imagine or visualize how we would react in certain situations. If the situation does occur, we reflexively act quicker and more innovatively as if we had practiced. For example, when I would take a taxi in Kabul, I'd visualize how I would respond if my taxi was suddenly caught in a mob. How would I scan the environment and react? If I've practiced scenarios in my mind, I have several ideas on how to exit the situation. (I often stuffed a blue burqa in the grocery sack I carried to the shops during the last couple years I spent in Afghanistan. Doing so enabled me to blend better if I felt the need.) This kind of thinking is not paranoid and can save our lives.[10]

Yet, Christ-followers sent out to share the good news about Jesus don't tend to think about this. All too often, we think, "It won't happen here," or "It can't happen to me," or "It hasn't happened for forty years." As Christ-followers, we actively cultivate attitudes towards others that think the best of them. Of course, we can't build relationships very effectively with people if we are suspicious of them or think they will harm us. But we are taught by Jesus to be as shrewd as serpents, and John 2:24 states, "But Jesus did not entrust himself to them."

"Apathy, denial, and complacency [in hostility] are deadly."[11] "[Those] with a complacent or apathetic mindset will be taken completely by surprise and could freeze up in shock and denial" as in a newly recognized and unforeseen situational reality, making it unlikely they will be able to react, resist, or flee appropriately.[12] Situational awareness is a critical skill and could save lives. There is no easy answer, but we can and should cultivate wise situational awareness (i.e., "relaxed awareness"[13]) while at the same time seeing others from Christ's perspective. Stewardship of ourselves and our resources implies we do all we can to stay and live in the place he has called us to. It won't hurt to develop skills that you never use!

---

10 Personal correspondence with Randy McAlister, Behavioral Threat Assessment expert, Captain, Police Department in a suburb in Minnesota.
11 Stratfor, "How to Look," 15.
12 Stratfor, 16.
13 Stratfor, 16.

Learning the local language and gaining cultural competencies that most Christ-followers develop in dangerous areas dramatically enhances situational awareness. These skills should not be underestimated but are assumed and incorporated into "Context" in the next chapter. While learning the practical aspects of situational awareness is best done in person through one of the security specialty training companies that offer it in your country or nearby, this chapter will outline some of the key skills that enhance shrewdness and potentially save lives. Please do not assume reading this chapter is all you need in the area of situational awareness. In-person training from experts is best. Many security training companies will consider training people from majority-world countries at a reduced cost, so ask!

Determining a Baseline

To detect when something has changed within your environment, you have to know what is "normal" for the time, culture, and location in which you are living. This is called having a baseline. Depending upon the volatility of where you are, the baseline can change rapidly, or evolve over months. The baseline is the natural, normal, predictable state and patterns of movements, interactions, emotional temperature, and mindset of the people around you.[14] When you know the baseline, it becomes easier to spot the anomaly. An anomaly is anything that is outside of the baseline. If there are three anomalies, it's not coincidental and usually requires a response, a decision of some type. Sometimes one change from the baseline requires rapid decision-making.[15]

Baseline + Anomalies → Decision

For example, one day in 2006 in Kabul, over forty-five minutes away from my home on the extreme opposite side of Kabul City, the brakes on a US military vehicle failed. Regretfully, civilians were killed even as the driver tried to stop by hitting parked vehicles. Because we had a habit of constantly monitoring information coming in, we were aware of changes in the baseline and listened to reports of the movement of the mob. We were ready, even though less than one hour had passed since the initial report of brakes failing, for the mob of enraged Afghans that marched across the city and down my street, yelling "Death to the infidels." Baselines can change rapidly.

---

14 Department of the Army Headquarters, *Advanced Situational Awareness*, 1-3 to 1-5.
15 The USA Army *Advanced Situational Awareness*, 4-1, teaches the OODA loop. Observe, Orient, Decide, and Act. This practice incorporates what psychologists have been saying for a long time about heuristics and decision-making under pressure. Ignatian spirituality teaches Observe, Awareness, Action, a similar concept but for different purposes. Both can be combined by the global worker facing potential, violence, danger and risk, because together they are a holistic, discerning, and wise decision-making response. However, the Holy Spirit may lead contrary to what security and military professionals would suggest, because he bids us come and die as we follow Christ. Luke 9:23–26.

A common mistake made by expatriates overseas who work in a compound is to hide behind the compound walls. In case after case, pre-attack surveillance starts just outside the walls of the compound/facility. If you don't get outside the walls, personally know the street vendors, know the "life tempo" at different times of the day, and know and scan surveillance points, you're setting yourself up for disaster. While in some situations it's too dangerous to spend much time outside the walls, one should always know what's going on, and what is normal outside the walls.[16]

In witness-risk, often the Christ-follower is ministering cross-culturally, not in their home environment. Another aspect of a baseline is how you, the outsider, impact the baseline. How do people usually treat outsiders, and how are they treating you, the Christ-follower? What is your impact on their baseline and how they are treated? There are subtle cues to pay attention to here, and each cultural situation is unique.

Since dangerous situations often have "normal" baseline levels of hostile threats against Christ-followers, this level of hostility is a critical baseline to pay attention to. Remain curious about the environment you are in and don't assume anything. Have the tempo and emotional level of the threats changed? How do they see you? What is their perception of who you are? Do they see you as posing a threat to them, or a risk to their family member? Do you appear like an easy, naïve, culturally unaware, and weak target for them?

Suppose you have only been in the location for a short time, and likely have only a few close local friends. In that case, there is very little for locals to lose if they attack you for any reason, whether petty crime or overt hostility, because you are known to be Christ-follower. In the case of Graham Staines, having the children with him was likely a bonus in the eyes of the mob—they knew (if they thought about it in their rage) that if they killed children, it would likely cause fear enough in other foreigners and to make them leave (they hoped).

Baselines can also be very simple. How people walk, when they walk, and where they walk give normal/not normal indicators. Learning to blend into the baseline is critical for safety in dangerous situations. This practice is called "gray man" or "gray woman," and is defined by blending with the locals in how you look and how you act. For example, my local friend, Parwana,[17] wanted me to visit her in her newly built, two-room home. It was in a location where

---

16 McAlister, Private conversations with the author, 2022.
17 Not her real name. She later became a refugee with her family and registered with the UN in Turkey. I lost track of her after that.

foreigners never went. We agreed that to lower the risk level for her and me, she would need to select my outfit and teach me how to walk and carry my purse like a local woman. If I appeared like a local, there would be no apparent anomalies to her neighbors. After explaining our plan, securing permission from my team leader and security officer, and agreeing to check-in before and after the visit, Parwana selected my outfit and jewelry out of my closet and then made me practice walking like a local. After she was satisfied with my efforts, she gave me further instructions on following her like a local, and then we set out. It was a huge success! I had great fun visiting her and accepting her hospitality, but I also knew I had not increased her risk and had "passed" as a local since her neighbors never asked about who I was. I fit into her "baseline" of normal and learned culturally valuable information.

The Five Senses of Observation[18]

Situational awareness means using everything at our disposal to have increased awareness of what is going on around us. The five senses of our body are critical tools to help us, and we can learn a great deal about the environment using all our senses. Sight, sounds, touch, smell, and taste are the five senses that our body uses to alert us to what is going on around us.

"The body cannot respond to a threat until directed by the brain, and the brain does not initiate action until the senses react to some external stimuli."[19] Our senses help us decide on what action to take.

We use all of our senses for observation. Observation is a process involving three essentials: awareness, understanding, and action. Awareness means being conscious and alert to one's environment. Understanding the environment is both interpretation and evaluation and is significantly enhanced by cultural knowledge and experience. Taking action means knowing how to respond. Learning to cultivate our skills of both observation and listening is particularly critical.

Hearing and listening are not the same. Hearing is what our ears detect, and listening is attaching interpretation and meaning to sound. Effective, active listening requires energy and is a learnable skill. In terms of listening in risk or increasing danger, pay attention to the following:

1. Actively listen while others speak. Demonstrate interest in what is being said. Maintain eye contact when culturally appropriate and acknowledge understanding. (In some cultures, maintaining eye contact is aggressive or improper.)

---

18 Department of the Army Headquarters, *Advanced Situational Awareness*, 3-1 to 3-25.
19 Department of the Army Headquarters, 3-19.

2. "Effective listeners listen to the words and focus on the message."[20] Sometimes delivery is less important because the information must be shared quickly.
3. "Focus on the person's central idea."
4. "Try to organize what you hear [and remember it.]"[21]
5. Do not get hooked or overstimulated emotionally by what you hear. Stay calm (keep your emotions under control) and communicate compassion through response and tone.
6. "Most people talk at 120 words a minute. The speed of thought is about 500 words a minute."[22] Use the time in between to observe non-verbal cues, anticipate the main point, and weigh the evidence for potential danger.

Cooper's Color Code: Levels of Awareness

There are five different levels of situational awareness that impact our capacity to react. "These five levels give us an overview of situational awareness and the psychological states associated with each level."[23] The five levels were created by Jeff Cooper, a US Marine Corps Lieutenant Colonel. These colors are used in police, military, and civilian applications. The following version is from Gary Quesenberry:[24]

1. "Condition White: In this condition, a person is entirely relaxed and unaware of what's going on around them. In [most] cases, condition white is reserved for when you are asleep or when you find yourself in an environment you assume to be completely free of threats, like your own home."[25] Or, you may be daydreaming, walking with your head and eyes down, and those looking for an easy target will spot you. "If you are ever attacked while in condition white, the chances of escape are diminished because your attacker caught you off guard. Your actions at this point will be completely reactionary."[26]

---

20 Department of the Army Headquarters, *Advanced Situational Awareness*, 3-19.
21 Department of the Army Headquarters, 3-19.
22 Department of the Army Headquarters, 3-19.
23 Quesenberry, *Spotting Danger Before*, 43.
24 Quesenberry, 43-45.
25 Quesenberry, 43.
26 Quesenberry, 43.

2. "Condition Yellow: This is a state of relaxed awareness [and alertness.] You appear to those around you to be entirely comfortable in your environment while paying close attention to the sights and sounds surrounding you. This condition of awareness does not constitute a state of paranoia or hypervigilance. Instead, you've simply upped your attentiveness to a level that would prevent you from being taken off guard."[27] Your head is up, and your eyes open. "Condition yellow is where you begin taking a mental inventory of your surroundings; you'll gauge your environment based on a preconceived baseline of behavior and … look for people or actions that rise above that baseline."[28] This level of awareness is the ideal state to be in because it is not healthy to be in a long-term condition of hypervigilance (Condition Red).

"Condition Orange: At this stage, you have identified something perceived as a potential threat, and you've narrowed your attention to that specific person or area. The transition from condition yellow to orange is subtle and happens several times a day without you even knowing it. Think about driving [your car.] … When you're driving, you're maintaining a consistent condition-yellow awareness (hopefully). Suddenly the car in front of you arouses your suspicion;"[29] it looks like the driver is texting while driving and is beginning to swerve or not maintain a consistent speed. "You instantly notice this behavior and shift your level of awareness to orange to accommodate [a potential problem.] This is also the stage where you begin to put together spontaneous plans. Once the perceived threat has passed, it's easy to transition from condition orange to yellow."[30]

3. "Condition Red: This is where you find yourself right before you act on your plans. … You spotted a perceived threat and began the planning stages for an appropriate reaction. In condition red, the threat has materialized, and it's time to put those plans into action. The heart rate elevates, and the fight, flight, or freeze responses are triggered. Your body prepares itself for confrontation, and the adrenaline starts pumping into your system."[31] You are experiencing a state of hypervigilance. "Condition red is where your level of training has a

---

27 Quesenberry, *Spotting Danger Before*, 43.
28 Quesenberry, 43.
29 Quesenberry, 43.
30 Quesenberry, 44.
31 Quesenberry, 44.

significant impact on how the situation resolves." It's an appropriate stage for a crisis and emergency, but staying at this level of stress and adrenaline long-term can lead to mental and physical burnout.[32]

4. "Condition Black:[33] Condition black is much like condition white in that you do not want to find yourself there when the fight starts. Condition black is characterized by an excessively elevated heart rate (above 175 beats per minute) and a complete loss of cognitive ability."[34] The person has "been exposed to a stressful event and [experienced] a catastrophic breakdown of mental and physical [ability]."[35] It may be "due to the lack of training necessary to properly deal with an active, violent threat. A person in condition black lacks the power to process the information being taken in effectively and becomes utterly useless in response."[36]

Behavioral Assessment, Behavioral Threat Assessment, and the Rule of Three

"A threat is an expression of intention to inflict injury or damage."[37] Threat assessment is a fact-based process that incorporates multiple sources of information and practical experience to determine if a threat is likely to materialize. It focuses on a person's thinking and behavior patterns and results in assessing and mitigating the threat. There are anonymous threats and direct threats. Direct and specific threats should be evaluated; it's important to remember that "some persons who make threats ultimately pose a threat; some persons who pose a threat never make a threat, [and] many persons who make threats do not pose a threat."[38]

However, when a person close to you makes a direct threat, the likelihood of them acting on the threat dramatically increases. This is described as the "Intimacy Effect." It should be taken very seriously and immediately mitigated. Direct, anonymous threats are rarely acted upon, and thus we should not overreact. Leaked threats, and communications of intent to harm shared with a third party, are much more concerning. When threats are not anonymous, they are usually more severe.

---

32 Stratfor, *How to Look*, 16.
33 Not originally part of Coopers Color code. According to the Army, this was developed by the Marine Corps.
34 Quesenberry, *Spotting Danger Before*, 44.
35 Department of the Army Headquarters, *Advanced Situational Awareness*, 4–11.
36 Quesenberry, *Spotting Danger Before*, 44.
37 Federal Bureau of Investigation, *Making Prevention a Reality*, 15.
38 Federal Bureau of Investigation, 15.

Consider also the difference between behavioral assessment and behavioral threat assessment in the security field (e.g. police, military). Both kinds are relevant to gospel workers facing danger. The difference is the length of time to be situationally aware of behaviors and verbal threats before the attack. Behavioral threat assessment generally refers to concerning behaviors and threats which are days, weeks, or months before the attack. But they all signal a movement toward violence in the future.

Behavioral assessment is relatively contemporaneous (minutes) to the attack itself. Behavioral assessment (learning normal baselines, recognizing anomalies from baseline, etc.) means, for example, if I go into a busy market in the morning, but there are no children present (an anomaly), an attack could be imminent. Or, in one case, a guest went for a walk in Kabul city up on TV Mountain, a place usually busy with people enjoying the walking paths (baseline), but he was enjoying the fact there was no one around (an anomaly). He topped the hill and noticed children scampering away (another anomaly). The kidnappers were already parked, blocking the path (a danger sign), waiting for him to descend.

Whomever the person of concern is, the one who has caught your attention, there are predictable patterns of behavior to take note of. Key danger signs to observe include:[39]

- Hidden hands: hidden hands could "be concealing intent to harm."[40]
- "Inexplicable presence: does the person"[41] of concern have a reason for being where they are? Are they acting according to baseline behavior for that situation?
- Target glancing: Someone targeting you likes to watch but avoids eye contact. They repeatedly look at their target and then away.[42]
- "Sudden change of movement: You feel you are being followed. [If you] suddenly change your direction"[43] of movement, watch for people or cars around you and note if they change their direction. You might be their target.
- Inappropriate clothing for the temperature or season: Someone overdressed for the temperature or location may be concealing something.

---

39 Quesenberry, *Spotting Danger Before*, 72.
40 Quesenberry, 58, 72.
41 Quesenberry, 58, 72.
42 Quesenberry, 58, 72.
43 Quesenberry, 58, 72.

- Seeking a position of advantage: Someone seeking to harm may back you into a corner or block an exit.
- "Impeding your movement: If someone inexplicably blocks your movement [in a specific direction, you are likely being funneled] into a position of disadvantage."[44]
- "Unsolicited attempts at conversation: ... Attempts at small talk are often the ... last move before the attack. If someone you are unfamiliar with approaches you and makes unsolicited ... small talk, take a very close look at your situation [and respond accordingly, especially if you are at a disadvantage.]"[45]
- Physiological signs of danger include heavier than usual breathing, appearing tense, pupil dilation, and excessive sweating. Likely, avoidance and escape are the two best options for your safety.

Quesenberry notes that these are common denominators from those seeking to harm regardless of cultural differences. Both research and experts on assessing violence say that once someone exhibits at least three abnormal behaviors (the "Rule of Three"), it's beyond coincidence and wise to take immediate action.

Means, Intent, Opportunity

In times of duress, such as a situation moving from the color "Orange" to the color "Red," it's crucial to know when to act. There are three critical questions about means, intent, and opportunity.

1. Means: Does the person perceived as a threat have the means to hurt you?
2. Intent: Has the person articulated a direct threat to harm you?
3. Opportunity: Do they have a direct and immediate opportunity to do you the harm they've threatened?

Typically, we have four options for response in such scenarios. Avoid, escape, de-escalate, and confront.[46] Avoiding is the safest option for survival, but that is not always possible, especially in the case of witness risk and persecution. In de-escalating and confronting, we choose to interact with someone we've identified as intending to do us harm. This engagement takes courage, calmness, and confidence. We want to humanize ourselves and build a relational bridge to the other person. For example, talking about our

---

44 Quesenberry, 58, 59.
45 Quesenberry, 59, 72.
46 Quesenberry, 77.

families and something fun about us in a way that the other person can relate to is "humanizing" ourselves, making it harder for them to harm us.

Actor Mapping

"Actor mapping is an exercise to identify all the key individuals, stakeholders, or other organizations that will have an affect [on your team or organization's functioning]."[47] During the actor mapping process, consider that the "declared interests of an individual or group may be very different from their actual interests."[48] Once the key actors are identified, examine how they may be interconnected and influence relations with one another, and determine which actors are allies and which are opposing the other. From a security standpoint, "actors" in any place of ministry can qualify as an adversary, a neutral, or a friend.[49] Actors can be individuals, groups of individuals acting together, paramilitary or military forces, communities, or a country's government.

Threats against Christ-followers continue to escalate and evolve. It is increasingly common for complex or hybrid threats from entities to join forces together. For example, criminal gangs may join with jihadists under the banner of a politically disenfranchised group to kidnap a foreigner and split any ransom paid. While these are challenging threats to pay attention to, part of situational awareness is to map who the "actors" are in the local environment.

Who are potential "actors" who may threaten or target a Christ-follower, whether expatriate or local? The list to consider includes:[50]

- Government leaders, department heads, government security officials
- Opposition figures, groups, or key supporters
- Insurgents (organized opposition groups desiring to overthrow the existing government)
- Guerrillas, transnational or subnational political movements
- Terrorists, a terrorist organization
- Drug and human traffickers, other criminal organizations (gangs, drug cartels, hackers)

---

47 Cornerstone OnDemand Foundation, "Actor Mapping and Context."
48 Cornerstone OnDemand Foundation.
49 Department of the Army Headquarters, *Advanced Situational Awareness*, 10-2.
50 This list is compiled from the Department of the Army Headquarters, *Advanced Situational Awareness*, 10-1 to 10-10 and Cornerstone OnDemand Foundation, "Actor Mapping and Context Analysis."

- Media
- Jihadists
- Tribal groups
- Offended relatives
- Bandits
- Insider threat actors
- Donors
- UN agencies
- Community leaders
- Other NGOs, both national and international
- Shopkeepers, businesses
- Beneficiary groups
- Host communities
- Employees: office staff, drivers, guards
- Other? There may be an actor not on this list who is present in your situation.

Once you've identified all the potential actors in your situation, you want to do two things with the list. First, try to think through what might motivate them to act. For example, suppose it's a political group. In that case, their motivation might stem from a religious or non-religious ideology different from the ruling party, desire to resist a foreign power, nationalistic purity, revolutionary groups wanting to overthrow the current power, or other political, religious, or ethnic/social ideologies. Secondly, organize the list into four helpful categories: supportive [+], neutral but tending to be supportive [+/-], neutral but tending toward hostile [-/+], and hostile [-]. The objective is to move people toward [+] or [+/-], especially those who are [-/+] and [-]. Consider ways to build relationships with those actors who tend toward the hostile categories and strengthen relationships with those who are neutral and tend toward positive.

In what ways can we, as Christ-followers, find common ground as humans to build bridges with potential adversaries in such situations? There are numerous creative ways to approach this task. For example, as NGO workers, when medical care is given to anyone in need, such as saving someone's wife and newborn during birth, it often will do more than any other good deed.

In one Central Asian country, a project focuses on resourcing any special needs or disabled person, from baby to adult, from any group. This project has built many bridges into a broad spectrum of socio-economic and religious groups and continues to provide (visa) stability to those involved in the project. Sometimes, someone who appears to be an adversary will quietly protect Christ-followers simply because of their compassionate work.

Terrorist Planning Cycle[51]

In chapter two, I described the global reality of increased terrorist attacks against Christ-followers in the twenty-first century. There are predictable phases of how terrorists plan and execute an attack. The phases may be organized into six, seven, or eight phases. "The terrorist attack planning cycle is not a static, linear process but rather could begin in any of the several stages with variances in details, sequence, and timing."[52] The goal is to identify, mitigate, and disrupt this cycle.

Surveillance is a significant aspect of these phases. "Almost any criminal [or violent] act, from a [petty crime like] purse-snatching to a terrorist bombing, involves some level of pre-operational surveillance,"[53] even if a very short length of time of surveillance. This fact is the one common denominator of all threats. A simple acronym can help attune our observation skills to notice if we are being surveilled. TEDD stands for Time, Environment, Distance, and Demeanor. "A person who sees someone repeatedly over Time in different Environments, over Distance, or who displays [unusual] Demeanor can assume [they are] under surveillance."[54] "Demeanor" means behavior or clothing out of place for the baseline in that situation.

There are eight stages in the terrorist attack cycle.[55] These are:

Phase 1—Target Selection: Who are relatively easy targets to obtain the objective? What is the value of the target? Will it generate the level of fear and paralysis desired? Is the target easy enough to make an attack successful?

Phase 2—Initial Surveillance: Surveillance of the target. Collecting data on movements and routines, or if a place, building layout.

---

51 Stratfor Global Information Services, *Terrorist Attack Cycle*.
52 NCTC, DHS, FBI, "First Responder's Toolbox."
53 Stratfor, *How to Look*, 17.
54 Stratfor, 17–18.
55 NCTC, DHS, FBI, "First Responder's Toolbox." See also the Counterterrorism Guide.

Phase 3—Final Target Selection: Confirmation this target provides enough opportunity to attack.

Phase 4—Pre-Attack Increased Surveillance: Refinement of details on the person or entity. Includes learning the physical layout of the building or compound; patterns of leaving, travel, and movement; security measures in place; and rotation of guards.

Phase 5—Planning: Plans have to be formulated on how to get to the attack site and identify the most opportune time to implement the attack. All the details necessary to implement the plan must be worked out.

Phase 6—Rehearsal: Practicing how to get people and weapons to the attack site.

Phase 7—Execution (the attack): Once the adversary has deployed for the attack, it's almost impossible to stop. It's commonly thought an attack will not happen at the same place again, but history has revealed otherwise. An attack could happen in the same place again in the future, but it could be planned for immediately after first responders are there so that a second wave of terror is unleashed. This tactic was not uncommon in Afghanistan.

Phase 8—Escape and Exploitation: Often adversaries want to escape unless it's a suicide bomber. They will typically claim the attack within hours to three days of the attack (exploitation). Attacks against Christ-followers are often further exploited in the media to spread fear and terror, demonstrate their power, and prevent more people from following Christ. The video of the beheading of the twenty-one Coptic Christ-followers is one such example. In this case, as is often true, media exploitation backfired by terrorists because it demonstrated the strength of faith and encouraged believers!

There are many more aspects of situational awareness. My hope is that all Christ-followers in dangerous areas will see that it is not that difficult to learn to be more observant, spot trouble, and prayerfully (quickly!) discern how to respond—whether to avoid, escape, de-escalate, or confront.

The books cited within this chapter are excellent resources for further information, especially Gavin de Becker's book, *The Gift of Fear* and Gary Quesenberry's book, *Spotting Danger Before It Spots You*. Quesenberry concludes his book by summarizing the six main habits of spotting trouble: (1) Scan the area; (2) identify exits and escape routes; (3) pay attention to your gut feeling; (4) monitor the baseline for changes and anomalies; (5) use what-if scenarios to rehearse the four reaction options: avoid, escape, de-escalate, and confront; and (6) keep a positive mental attitude.

Devil's Playground

Revelation 2:13 describes Pergamum as the place of "Satan's throne." Throne implies authority and control. Perhaps it's similar to how this phrase is used in specific places at specific times as "Satan's playground." Sometimes certain cities or areas are known colloquially as "the devil's playground" or "the devil's sandbox." These are places where he seems to "play," and do what he wants. The Apostle Paul teaches in Ephesians 6 that our spiritual enemy is powerful, organized, and wicked. Spiritual awareness is a necessity, not only for survival but also for resiliency.

Because situational awareness means paying attention to what is going on around you in time and space and understanding the meaning and direction of what is happening, we can begin to form a picture of the spiritual realities in spiritual observation. In member care, as we listen carefully to what evil is being experienced and described, what is revealed is not just the current physical, situational awareness but also spiritual situational awareness.

Some cautions about this practice: We are not looking for a demon behind every inference, but we are using wise discernment and sensitivity to discern spiritual realities. It also does not mean that we can avoid doing practical situational awareness as summarized in this chapter and from situational awareness training from security professionals. These are responsible training and habits to implement in high-risk and danger situations, and both types are part of a holistic situational awareness response to gospel witness.

> There are four main skills of spiritual situational awareness: awareness, observation, action, and meaning.

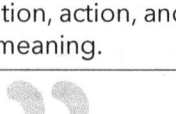

Awareness, observation, action, and meaning, are the four main skills of spiritual situational awareness. Becoming spiritually aware includes awareness of what the Holy Spirit is doing, where we sense "the wind is blowing." But it is also an awareness of the evil that may be occurring, demonic elements being experienced, and the timing of when traumas occur. It includes observation and learning about the region's history, wars of the past and present, and what conflicts pervade the region. What are the major national sins? Spiritual awareness requires familiarity with the culture and history of the place. These elements impact the Christ-follower and should be processed with a mature spiritual mentor.

Action means listening to the Holy Spirit to hear what needs to be done. What did he lead us to do, and what is he asking us to do next? We cannot respond to everything, but what darkness is he calling us to bring his light into? And finally, what is the meaning personal to us, to the people, the time, and the place? We are there for a reason, so we must determine his purposes, and in that, we will find the meaning. These skills require mentorship to learn and gain confidence in, and there are very few skilled spiritual-culture mentors. Try to find someone who will listen reflectively without trying to give you all the answers.

In their quest to share the gospel, some may say, "It's too much! I don't want to have to think about these things. I'm called to share the good news of Christ!" To which I respond, "Yes, and to do that, we need to be alive, and that requires responsible stewardship and learning to be as shrewd as a snake and as innocent as a dove." "A living dog is better than a dead lion" (Eccl 9:4). He is worthy for us to learn to become situationally aware *and* share the gospel.

Chapter 11
Information and Death-Threat Analysis

We will never be accidentally excellent at managing risk.[1]

The situations of perilousness that are the focus of this book require analysis of a lot of information, sometimes conflicting information. Knowing how to gather good information, evaluate it, make the decision, and then take action are parts of information analysis and are the focus of the following two chapters. "Good information" must also be defined. Here, we define it as information that is meaningful, valuable, useful, and relevant.[2] In the RAM flow chart below, the steps of risk assessment and management (the focus of *Facing Danger: A Guide through Risk*) shows the loop of information gathering and assessment. The loop of information is the "Find Instruments to Assess Risk and Assess the Costs and Benefits of those Instruments. How to follow that loop is the focus of this chapter.

Figure 7: RAM Flow Chart

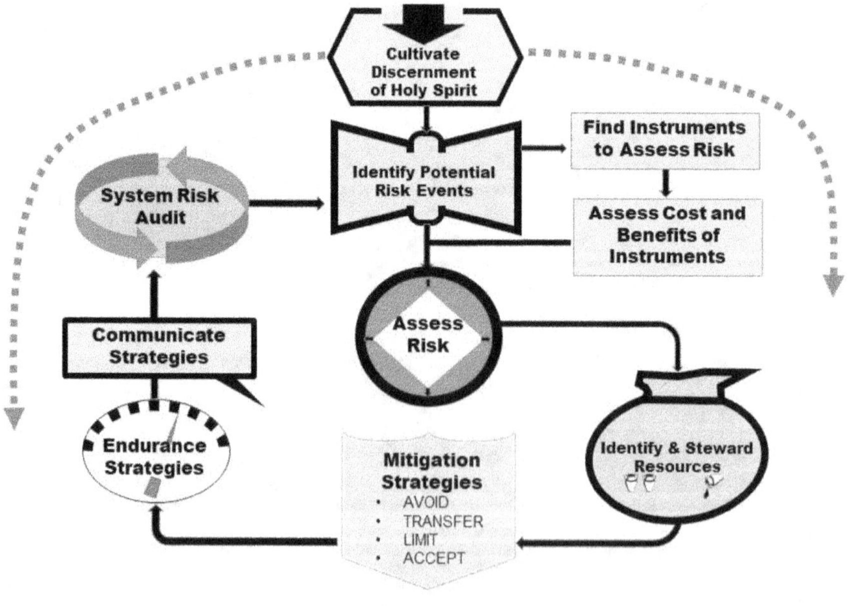

© 2022 Neal & Anna Hampton

---

1 Saying of risk management professionals. I do not know who coined this phrase.
2 Nash, "Differences Between Data."

Information Analysis vs. Intelligence

Information is different from intelligence. "In and of itself, it is rare that action can or should be taken on raw, unevaluated information on its own. At some point, context must be provided; corroboration must be supplied; value must be added to this raw information. The major component of the process that turns raw information is analysis; the product is intelligence," then we can make an informed decision.[3] Intelligence, for our purposes, may be defined as the "product" resulting from information analysis. This process is the collecting, evaluating, and interpreting all available data and information concerning the likelihood of the risk materializing or of the means, intent, and opportunity of a hostile entity carrying out its threat. To simplify it even further, **Information + Evaluation = Intelligence.**

We can visualize the steps of this process like this:

Figure 8: Aspects of Risk Decision-Making Process

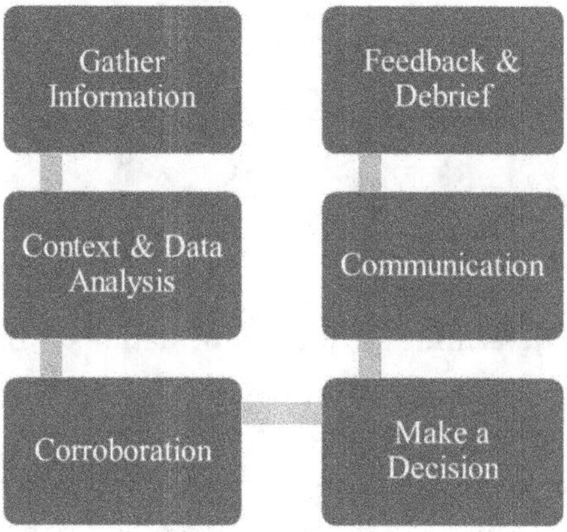

```
Gather Information        Feedback & Debrief

Context & Data Analysis   Communication

Corroboration             Make a Decision
```

© 2022 Neal & Anna Hampton

Range of Information

Increasing risk environments often require knowing how to sort through a wide range of information, yet there is always the nagging feeling that enough of the "right" data isn't available. There are at least seven types of information, and learning to recognize which category specific data falls into will help to simplify analysis. Otherwise, it's just a lot of "white noise."[4] White noise in risk is a combination of an overload of uncorroborated and

---

3 Palmieri, "Information vs. Intelligence."
4 Palmieri, "Information vs. Intelligence."

unevaluated information and data along with unevaluated verbal threats and dangers. This flood of information can be so overwhelming that we require help in organizing and naming what is happening. Figure 9 shows the types of information typically available to us:

Figure 9: Types of Information

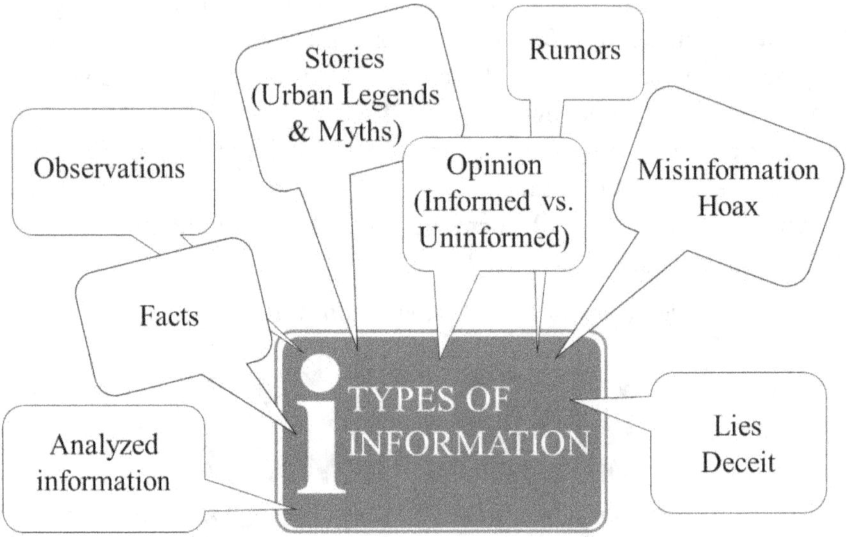

- Stories (Urban Legends & Myths)
- Rumors
- Observations
- Opinion (Informed vs. Uninformed)
- Misinformation Hoax
- Facts
- TYPES OF INFORMATION
- Lies Deceit
- Analyzed information

© 2022 Neal & Anna Hampton

How can we determine which information is helpful? Evaluating the source of information and asking critical questions about it assists in separating the valuable from the distracting.

First, we must evaluate the source of information. Who gave the information? How credible are they? What would be the motivation behind the information being framed the way it is? How recently has the source of data been in the actual risk situation? A local person living in the situation may be more credible than a professional security analyst living seven thousand miles away. An eyewitness observing the situation may be more credible than the organizational security officer using Google Earth. However, an organizational security officer may also provide contextual analysis since they see it from a macro, outsider view. Both types of information sources are valuable, and both should be evaluated as to how much "weight" their information and analysis should have in the final decision.

Each type of information requires consideration to ensure it is not misinformation, lies, rumor, or story (urban legend). This consideration likely involves insider help (from a local person) to figure out or find and verify the facts that reveal the lie. "The possibility of deception should not be rejected until it is disproved or, at least, until a systematic search for evidence has been made and none has been found."[5]

Rumors are unconfirmed information that sound true but are unsubstantiated, so attempts should be made to trace them to the source. They tend to spread quickly and elevate fear levels drastically. Often, the content of the rumor does not occur. If there are no credible facts behind the rumor, this information should be discarded as not factual. However, the rumor should not be ignored entirely. Rumors that ramp up in emotional and violent intensity reveal a change in "temperature," and fuel some potential violence. Rumors tend to diminish over time.

One of the most challenging types of information to analyze is informed versus uninformed opinion. Opinions can be true or false. In an artificially created reality, an opinion can sound like a well-informed, logical deduction of facts, but it may be designed to sound entirely credible for the purpose of misleading or distorting reality. After someone has given information, it is always good to ask what it is based on, and if it is their opinion. What biases might they have to form that opinion?

As noted in chapter seven, facts are not necessarily truth. Both observations and facts are based on perspective, and what someone observes from one viewpoint could be different from a different angle. Humility in speech is conducive to the analysis here: "What I saw, from my perspective, was _____." This approach leaves room for another person to give their input for a more holistic picture. When multiple different entities (with different motivations) state the same facts, those may likely be the facts of what happened.

Sometimes, we have to account for already analyzed information, for example, data from a government to its citizens. Often, the pronouncement is the same each time, so it's easy to ignore it. Don't do this. What should not be overlooked in government announcements are the slight wording changes. The nuances in these word changes reveal policy changes. For example, in many high-risk locations, it is common for an embassy announcement to encourage its citizens to leave the country. We usually had someone check the wording change from one announcement to another and compare these types to other embassy announcements. How much "weight" these announcements and wording changes mean for witness risk decisions must then be determined.

---

[5] Heuer, *Psychology of Intelligence Analysis*, xxiii.

Two other significant factors that influence information credibility are money and power. Analyzing information requires following the money trail or the force behind the information dissemination and benefitting the entity communicating the information. What individual, organization, or government stands to benefit from the data being believed? Who is funding it?

Predicting the Chance of Rain

One of the most common mistakes made in risk analysis is comparing data sets that are not comparable. One example is, "We have a better chance of being hit by a bus in downtown Chicago than being killed by a terrorist in Kabul." It's incorrect to compare the risk of one Westerner in Chicago, a city of 2.6 million, versus a Westerner who is one of 400 in Kabul, where terrorists were targeting foreigners. The two data sets of traffic accident rates in an international city compared to terrorist attacks against Christian expatriates are incomparable. The terrorist attack is not as statistically predictable as the traffic accident rate. It's essential to ascertain if there are statistical associations between Data Set A and Data Set B. When we throw numbers around and make statements like the one above, we can sound wise and brave, but we are unintelligently correlating incomparable data sets.

Another mistake we make with data sets is looking for the data we need to confirm our bias on anything. In the age of information, we have witnessed an explosion of access to a wide range of information, opinions, and data. We will usually find what we look for, which will lead us in the wrong decision.

Gerd Gigerenzer, psychologist, author, and risk researcher, gives a simple example of how we are all confused by probabilities.

> Do you know what it means when the weather report announces a 30 percent chance of rain tomorrow? 30 percent of what? I live in Berlin. Most Berliners believe that it will rain tomorrow 30 percent of the time for seven to eight hours. Others think it will rain in 30 percent of the region, most likely not where they live. New Yorkers believe that it will rain on 30 percent of the days for this announcement; ... that is, there will most likely be no rain tomorrow.[6]

He advises, "Always ask for the reference class: In this case, it's the percent of what?" In his chapter titled "Are People Stupid?" he explains that "we teach our children the mathematics [and sciences] of certainty, such as geometry and trigonometry [and biology,] but not the mathematics of uncertainty, statistical thinking, ... [and] not the psychology that shapes their fears and desires."[7]

---

6 Gigerenzer, *Risk Savvy*, 2–5.
7 Gigerenzer, 14.

No matter our education level, we are all prone to make mistakes in understanding data sets and making predictions. We will make mistakes, and this is human. No matter how good our technology and data are, risk is uncertain and evil is not predictable. The point we need to realize is that we need to examine the data sets we are using to make predictions and take care to not utilize data sets that are not comparable. I cannot emphasize this enough, especially when lives are at stake.

> Risk is uncertain and evil is not predictable.

Context Is King

Context is paying attention to the circumstances of the situation and applying meaning to them. Context includes the objects, people (relationships of people in the context), language, location, environment, culture (customs, norms, etiquette),[8] and what is occurring in that specific situation at that time in history. It includes our risk-aversion level particular to that situation, the current threat level, socialization, cultural awareness, and so much more. Context is complex and infinite but limited by one's perspective and words.

We use words to describe the context, and words have limitations of meaning by their nature. The more we understand the culture, the deeper we know the context. "The misinterpretation of a particular word or phrase is not unusual, but rather, it's the norm. All words significantly underspecify their interpretation."[9] This fact is complicated by international teams using a common language to communicate with each other when words need to be defined even further. For example, what units are being used to describe the context, i.e., imperial or metric?

In the previous chapter, I introduced actor mapping. In context, we evaluate all the "actors" in a situation. We ask similar questions of the "actors" as we did previously about the information. Who is involved in creating the information? What are their motivations? By whom are they threatened?

Understanding the context requires defining words so that all team members have a similar frame of reference for understanding. Doing so aids in decision-making and buy-in by all members.

Death-Threat Assessment

"But Saul, still breathing threats and murder against the disciples of the Lord" (Acts 9:1a). Luke's word choice here means that Saul was committed with his

---
8 Devlon, "Confronting Context Effects."
9 Devlon, "Confronting Context Effects."

whole being in his threats against Christ-followers. The intentionality behind the threat was credible, confirmed, and genuine. Saul had followed through on his threats, and many were in jail in Jerusalem. In light of Stephen's recent murder, Saul's threats of murder were credible, and in a new development, Saul was now on his way to Damascus to do more evil.

> [Although] all threats are not created equal, they must be taken seriously and thoroughly evaluated. Content (i.e. the words or deeds used), context (i.e. what happens before, during, and after a threat is made), and circumstances (i.e. surrounding facts, such as a method of delivery, the relationship between threatener and target, or type of target) must all be thoroughly assessed to determine what level of concern is appropriate when a threat is made.[10]

The general threat assessment process is (1) evaluate what the threat is; (2) rate the likelihood of it happening; and (3) identify the impact of the danger on resources to steward vulnerabilities. The previous chapter addressed behavioral threat assessment. There, threat assessment is defined as a fact-based process that incorporates multiple sources of information and practical experience to determine if a threat is likely to materialize. There are many threats against a Christ-follower, but death threats in witness risk must be assessed uniquely.

Anonymous vs. Direct Death Threats

There are two main types of death threats: anonymously issued threats and threats from identifiable sources. All communicated threats should be initially taken seriously. Four tasks should immediately take place: (1) determine the credibility of the threat; (2) ascertain the probability of violence; (3) mitigate the threat by swiftly protecting the targeted individual or organization; (4) continue to investigate the threat and work to build bridges of peace to the entity (if known).[11]

Whether the threat is issued anonymously or by a known entity, the input should be gathered from various sources, including local police, trusted locals, people with significant cultural astuteness, local pastors and leaders, etc. Significant questions to ask include:

- "How was the communication delivered?"
- "How many communications have been received and by whom?"
- "During what time frame?"[12]

---

10 Federal Bureau of Investigation, *Making Prevention a Reality*, 15.
11 Simons and Tunkel, *International Handbook of Threat*, 235–56.
12 Simons and Tunkel, 241.

- Is this an isolated, one-time threat or a series of threats issued through various means?
- Is there a potential relationship between the issuer of the threat and the intended target?
- Does the danger indicate a time frame?
- Are there any apparent means and opportunity for the issuer to carry out the threat?
- What is the motive of the threat?
- Who is targeted by the threat?
- What steps did they take to anonymize the threat?
- About the intended target: What information is there about conflicts or past witnessing conversations that the intended target had in the local culture?
- If the target is an organization or company, what are their relationships with employees and families, business suppliers, and government ministers?

These questions are not exhaustive, but they give some idea of the thoroughness of evaluation that death threats need. Highly localized, place-specific, and person-specific threats are highly likely to be valid, and local context relationships are valuable interpreters to validate the death threat.

Intimacy Effect

Evaluation of the threat includes evaluating whether the author of the threat: (1) justifies the threat with moral righteousness as a cause for action; (2) reveals contempt towards the target; (3) has the means to act on the threat; (4) displays acceptance of the consequences if they act on the threat; (5) includes a "no other alternative" aspect to the threat; (6) lists the name of the target explicitly; and (7) has a relationship with the target (intimacy effect). The closer the relationship, the more valid the threat.[13] A threat from someone relationally close requires immediate action of protection. These and other factors indicate credibility and a higher likelihood of the threat materializing.

When evaluating threats from a government, Helene Fischer of Open Doors asks the following questions: "Do they have the means (people) to hinder your work? Are there laws on the books forbidding gospel work? Do they have access to you?"[14] The current volatility of the community should be assessed. Historical summaries of various people groups are not

---

13 Calhoun and Weston, *Perspectives on Threat Management*, 258–67.
14 Workshop presentation by Helene Fischer at RHP 2022, Athens, Greece.

always accurate for the present situation, so a Christ-follower working cross-culturally should evaluate the historical context in light of the present-day situation. For example, demographic and anthropological research completed hundreds of years prior on various people groups in India described which groups had a history of violence and were listed as reasonable. To this day, certain groups are known as "headhunters," though they have been completely transformed in the present day. Savvy culture advisors should double-check assumptions.

Evaluate the source of a threat issued by a people group by asking the questions listed above but also: How strategic would it be to kill you? How militant are they? Do they have the means and opportunity to do so in this context?

Threat levels are based on the degree to which combinations of these factors are present:[15]

- Existence: A [hostile person or] group is able to gain access to a given locality.
- Capability: The capability of a [hostile person or] group to carry out an attack has been assessed or demonstrated.
- Intent: Evidence of [hostile] activity, including stated or assessed intention to conduct [the action.]
- History: Demonstrated [hostile] activity in the past.
- Targeting: Current credible information or activity exists that indicates preparations for specific [hostile] operations—intelligence collection by a suspect group, preparation of destructive devices, other actions.
- Security environment: Indicates if and how the political and security posture of the threatened [person or community] affects the capability of [hostile] elements to carry out their intentions. Address whether the [government, community, or family] is concerned with terrorism and whether it has taken proactive countermeasures to deal with such a threat.[16]

For example, a couple serving in a militant Muslim nation had an active, credible death threat against them. They came to us after speaking to their organization, people on the ground, and professional security analysts. They still didn't know how to evaluate the threat and decide if they should return to the situation. They were still unsure of what to do, as each entity had its own opinion which conflicted with the other.

---

15 Leson, "Assessing and Managing," 13
16 Leson, 14.

Neal and I started with the risk assessment grid. We walked them through how to evaluate the likelihood of this threat based on each of the grid elements: severity, frequency, geographic proximity, and demographic proximity. After graphing, we then had them list all the sources of information they had about this threat. We evaluated each source based on who they were, their motivation, how recent their knowledge about the current threat was, and the emotional "temperature" of the people in that city. The couple included their government's embassy analysis, professional security input, locals on the ground, organizational input, views on the threat, local media, etc.

> We evaluated each source based on who they were, their motivation, how recent their knowledge about the current threat was, and the emotional "temperature" of the people in that city.

After we went through each of these sources of information, they could see that they needed newer information from local people from a range of socio-economic positions, locals from the majority religion, and those who were Christ-followers to give them input. Based on the risk assessment, we could be reasonably confident that the embassy and security professionals would be unlikely to change their feedback on their input. After working through that information, we asked what their adult child felt about returning, knowing this was an active death threat from an entity that had the means, intent, and opportunity to kill them. They laid it all out before the Holy Spirit, asking for confirmation on their return with all of that analysis. They and their adult child felt a peace and calmness about returning that they had not felt before, knowing they had thoroughly assessed everything and accepted the risk. The entity never followed through with the threat. The couple is still alive and serving in the same location years later. Going through all the analysis described above did not take more than an hour and a half, and it calmed them both down and gave them clarity on their calling.

"Situations requiring threat [assessment and] management are usually marked by great volatility, stress, and extreme sensitivity to changes and new developments. These situations require attention, flexibility, and quick responses."[17] The higher the risk, the more explosive the mix. Ananias was wisely risk-averse as he protested the Lord's assignment to visit Saul immediately. Ananias did not know the Lord was working in Saul's life simultaneously. Yet he was obedient despite the threat's validity, and history was changed.

---

17 Calhoun and Weston, *Perspectives on Threat Management*, 262.

Chapter 12
Risk Decision-Making

Everything is a risk. Not doing anything is a risk. It's up to you.[1]

Decision-making in extreme insecurity is inherently challenging because of the ambiguity of the situation. We think we are making decisions using deliberate, logical reasoning, setting our emotions and biases aside. We believe that "objectivity" exists and that we have it. In reality, we are partially ignorant and rely much more on intuition and emotions than we realize.[2] Numerous aspects influence the risk decision: our fear level and emotional state, the urgency of threats, biases, risk framing, the needs of the people, the value and reliability of whatever information is available, concern for the safety of personnel, the calling of the individual and the organization, the values, mission, and goals of the team or organization, spiritual discernment, etc. All decisions run the risk of the wrong decision being made. Clear thinking and awareness of the aspects of decision-making analysis provide guidance (but not the answer)!

Inferences and Errors

First, it's critical to accept the reality that in situations of chaos like risk and persecution, there is a high likelihood of making errors in judgment. Our cognitive rationality and experience in employing all aspects of knowing are finite. Stress is high. Unconscious, subconscious, and conscious forces are influencing us, some of which are not totally under our control. We can be entirely faithful to following God, but we may make a poor risk decision due to bad judgment, lack of training, lack of experience, lack of information, or some other factor. The goal is to be faithful in obeying God. In risk decision-making, we can only do our best with who we are at that time and stage of personal differentiation, maturity, and awareness.

Because we have limited information and decisions must be made quickly, one tool we use is inference. We employ both conscious inference and unconscious inference. The conscious inference is a well-informed guess based on observation. The phrase "read between the lines," refers to inference. Based on the information available through observation and logical reasoning, we guess or infer or extrapolate what we think will happen. Quite a bit of validated, peer-reviewed research on how people think and

---
1 Renita, "Accountable for Risks."
2 Refer to chapter 10 of *Facing Danger* and chapter 7 in *Facing Fear*.

make judgments reveals that "Every intelligent system makes good errors; otherwise it would not be intelligent ... Going beyond the information given by making inferences will produce [some] errors, and not risking errors would destroy intelligence."[3]

The unconscious inference is what happens under stress when our field of vision narrows (a physiological response), and the brain

> weave[s] together data from the senses using prior knowledge about the world ... these unconscious perceptual inferences are strong enough to act upon, but unlike other intuitive judgments they are not flexible. ... They are triggered by external stimuli in an automatic way. An automatic process cannot be changed by insight or information external to the process. Even now, when we understand how the intuitive perception works, we cannot change what we see.[4]

In a sense, an error may be finding the correct answer to the wrong question. In witness risk, a common mistake is to evaluate risk performance after the fact on logical criteria that do not account for all the stressors, fears, and inferences surrounding the specific risk situation. We always encourage leaders to write down their decisions as they make them under such severe pressure because humans naturally tend to forget and then engage in hindsight bias of what they think they should have or could have done when it simply wasn't possible.

Stakeholders and Who Makes the Decision

There are at least five levels of stakeholders to consider in risk decision-making. First, we reflect on the options available to us depending on the decision and its effects on us. Which decision are we called to make right now in line with our calling? Second, what is the impact of the decision on our children? Then we consider the effect of our decision on both expatriates and locals. We must also evaluate how our decision will impact our leadership and their capacity to manage the situation. Next, we need to assess the impact on financial partners who may be asked to help mitigate the cost of our decision. A wise, well-thought-out decision equips our leaders with the confidence they need should the fall-out of the decision result in media attention or even questioning by the board.

When I asked Mary Ho, the International Executive Leader of All Nations, Inc., to explain the circumstances surrounding John Chau's decision to go to a dangerous unreached people group, she articulately explained

---

[3] Gigerenzer, *Rationality for Mortals*, 66.
[4] Gigerenzer, *Gut Feelings*, 44.

the comprehensive training he received in the critical areas necessary. He engaged in responsible, holistic training with multiple confirmations of his calling and full legal permission of all required entities. However, this still leads to the thorny question of who makes the decision? In John's case, the decision led to his martyrdom.

The answer to the question, "Who makes the decision?" is not always straightforward, although sometimes it may be. First, ideally, everyone involved in the risk is also involved in assessing the risk to some degree. It is ideal to have consensus decision-making when risk assessment and management plans are created before the risk increases. Once the situation moves to an actual crisis, leadership must be more directive because of the speed required for decisions. However, extreme risk and crisis decisions should be based on a long history of consensus input and decision-making prior to the crisis.

> Neal and I recommend the principle that risk decisions are made at the lowest level possible.

In general, Neal and I recommend the principle that risk decisions are made at the lowest level possible. In practical decision-making, those who are the ones living in the risk situation make the final decision. As risks increase, the situation is "heating up," situational leadership may require senior leadership to become more directive and make decisions, even when not on site. Organizations must consider who holds decision-making authority in times of high risk. One specific, extreme situation requiring discussion before staff move to the field relates to evacuation. It should be agreed by both field and system leadership that the team or organizational leadership will decide when to require the individual/team to evacuate. Field staff should be given the freedom to decide to self-evacuate at any time until the leadership determines that it is necessary to evacuate. At that point, field staff do not have the freedom to choose to stay. (See the section on when staff refuse to evacuate in chapter 7 on ethics.)

A significant aspect I urge team and organizational leaders to keep aware of is when compassionate leadership requires the leader to make the decision for the field staff to leave the risk situation. Sometimes the most compassionate thing a leader can do is decide for a subordinate who is incapable of making that decision for themselves.

Risk Detachment and Emotional Events

Because emotions drive how a person approaches challenges, problem-solving, [and decision-making,] emotional control is critical to developing and sustaining resilience and psychological health. ... One's ability to approach life's challenges in a positive, optimistic way and to demonstrate self-control, stamina, and good character in choices and actions [are essential to long-term success.][5]

When making a decision, we are wise to first evaluate ourselves according to the acronym HALT. How might experiencing Hunger, Anger, Loneliness, or Tiredness be impacting our decision? Often the world looks better after a good night's sleep or a nap. Sometimes in risk, we are not eating enough calories to fuel our bodies because we are so stressed. If possible, at least drink water, but it is wise to eat protein to stabilize the body's chemistry. Eating may be a both a spiritual discipline *and* endurance strategy, as keeping up our physical strength means we have an easier time keeping our emotions in check.

> How might experiencing Hunger, Anger, Loneliness, or Tiredness be impacting our decision?

This point leads us to risk detachment. First of all, detachment is *not* "not caring." It's caring, but with freedom from disordered fears and loves, including freedom from the desire to control what cannot be controlled. Risk detachment is knowing we've done all we can to assess and mitigate the risks, make wise decisions, and steward well all entrusted to us according to our calling. Risk detachment is trusting all that happens to God. An appropriate level of risk detachment allows for more flexibility and agility with the Holy Spirit's leading within uncertain and chaotic situations. Appropriate risk detachment helps us make better risk decisions because we are not fixated on any one outcome. As we work to cultivate risk detachment in decision-making, increasing awareness of what influences our feelings about risk helps us mitigate the emotional impact on the decision-making process and likely make better decisions.

---

5 Department of the Army Headquarters, *Advanced Situational Awareness*, A-7.

Intuition

In decision-making (synonymous with "making a judgment"[6]), we often think we are making a logical-rational decision, but in reality, intuition is often what we subconsciously rely on. Intuition, also termed "gut feeling," or in risk research, "heuristics" are all synonyms for our brains' speedy cognitive process, especially when under threat. "Intuition is our brain's way of bypassing the sometimes slow and cumbersome logical thinking process."[7] The Latin root of intuition, *tuere*, means "to guard, to protect."[8] Intuition is a bodily response different from spiritual discernment, although the Holy Spirit also inhabits intuition.

Extensive research has shown that "intuition is a cognitive process, and when we feel threatened, this cognitive process moves faster than we can control or perceive. We often second guess gut feelings because we put more trust in a logical step-by-step approach to thinking. Some of the signals our brain sends us to warn of danger (see chapter three), we disregard as trivial and unimportant because we cannot connect the dots between what we see and the threat. We owe it to ourselves to pay closer attention to gut feelings."[9] Gigerenzer defines intuition as:

> A judgment that appears quickly in consciousness, whose underlying reasons we are not fully aware of, yet is strong enough to act upon. Having a gut feeling means that one feels what one should do, without being able to explain why. ... An intuition is neither caprice nor a sixth sense but a form of unconscious intelligence. ... Don't ask for reasons if someone with a good track record has a bad gut feeling.[10]

Another influential book that addresses intuition is *Thinking, Fast and Slow* by Daniel Kahneman. He discusses how our brains think fast and slow, and we use both from the time we awaken until we go to sleep. Kahneman also discusses how we could "be blind to the obvious and blind

---

6   Cokely, "Skilled Decision Theory," 476–504. "Historically, researchers have distinguished between judgments (e.g. estimates) and decisions (e.g. choices), based on traditions from the 1940s (e.g. decision researchers followed conventions in economics and statistics, while judgment researchers followed conventions in perception). Here, and for general purposes, the terms judgment and decision-making are roughly synonymous (e.g. a decision is a judgment about what to do; Baron, 2008). Thus, general decision-making skill refers to stable differences in judgment and decision-making quality exhibited across diverse and wide-ranging domains (e.g. health, wealth, and happiness)" 476–77.
7   Quesenberry, *Spotting Danger Before*, 69.
8   Becker, *Gift of Fear*, 28.
9   Quesenberry, 66.
10 Gigerenzer, *Risk Savvy*, 107.

to our blindness."[11] One of the most significant conclusions of the research on thinking is that we are far more emotional and intuitive than we realize, even when we believe we are using logical inferences and thinking logically, rationally, and objectively. In the pressures of risk and persecution, we will make better decisions if we view intuition as an asset, not a detractor, and listen well to what is happening inside us.

Risk Savvy Decision-Making

Making risk-savvy decisions is an art and a science. In times of pressure and urgent concern for personnel safety, it is tempting to make reactive, emotional decisions when information is limited. At these times, it is crucial to keep the long-term vision of the ministry in mind.[12] Ideally, risk decisions will be in-line with the "personal calling of personnel rooted in the organization's mission, values, and goals."[13] In chapter eight, I discussed biases that impact how we think. Of the biases described there, the three that most impact risk decision-making are optimistic bias, hindsight bias, and confirmation bias. How risks are framed dramatically impacts the decision which will be made.

Making risk-savvy decisions is an art and a science.

"I" vs. the Group

In many cultures, decision-making often occurs in a group, not as individuals. "We are, therefore, I am."[14] For example, Robert Blincoe, in his masterful treatise on a Missiology for Workers, wrote, "The concept of 'I' hardly exists in the context of a tribal culture's value system: 'We' (the tribe) predominates. Individuals define themselves entirely in terms of their tribe. They are first a member of this or that tribe, then a Muslim, a Yezidi, or a Christian."[15]

Cultures approach decision-making differently between two extremes of consensus (input from all) and hierarchical (top-down). For example, Meyer discusses the espoused values of Americans (egalitarian democracy where all participate) to everyday reality (hierarchical, top-down decision-making). According to Myer, "Germans consider American companies hierarchical because of their approach to decision-making. German culture places a

---

11 Kahneman, *Thinking Fast and Slow*, 24.
12 Brawner, "Decision Making."
13 Brawner.
14 A saying community cultures have to describe their identity and decision-making process; also quoted in Blincoe, *Ethnic Realities*, 201.
15 Blincoe, 201.

higher value on building consensus as part of the decision-making process, while in the USA, decision-making is largely invested in the individual."[16] As risk increases, decision-making does need to become more directive, which will feel more hierarchical. We need to build trust, relationships, and communication across cultures, but be prepared for a different leadership style in times of increased risk and crisis on international teams. The better we know ourselves, the more we'll be able to understand our own biases and cultural tendencies.

Algorithms vs. Discernment

We can get enamored with software programs, statistics, probabilities, and any tool that feels like it is helping us manage the uncertainty of risk. Gigerenzer summarized, "The danger is that by extending probability to everything, it is easy to be seduced into thinking that one tool—calculating probabilities—is sufficient for dealing with all kinds of uncertainty."[17] Consequently, we forget some helpful thinking tools already discussed, such as inference, intuition, information analysis, emotions, and logical thinking.

Wise decision-making includes the awareness of all these factors and discernment of God's leading. "For it has seemed good to the Holy Spirit and to us to lay on you no greater burden than these requirements" (Acts 15:28). The church leaders in Jerusalem owned their decision without diminishing God's role in it. That's what distinguishes differentiated and courageous Christian leadership from cowardly Christian leadership. Mature Christian leaders stand with God; they don't hide behind him.

Practice under Pressure

> Dr. Sara Waring at the University of Liverpool [...] researches decision-making in critical and major incidents, such as terrorist attacks and natural disasters. Waring stresses that one of the most important things that makes someone good at making decisions in circumstances where they have very little information and very little time, is practice. "The more experienced you get at making decisions, the quicker you get at making them," she says. Experience equips you to fill in the gaps at the start of an incident when information is lacking, and also to [sort] important information when it comes flooding in later on.[18]

---

16 Meyer, *Culture Map*, 144.
17 Gigerenzer, *Risk Savvy*, 26.
18 Pires, "Don't Panic!"

"Our relationship with uncertainty affects our abilities."[19] There are at least two ways people respond to uncertainty. Those who have low ambiguity tolerance have higher anxiety or nervousness about making decisions, and may make them too quickly (before more reliable information comes in) to get the decision out of the way. "[Others] quite like uncertainty and weighing up options. But in an urgent situation, you don't have time for that."[20]

Categories Influencing Decision Analysis

Decision-making in witness risk and times of uncertainty includes awareness and analysis in the following categories:

1. Spiritual Analysis
   a. What does the Holy Spirit seem to be leading me, my family, and my team to do? Staying in and moving towards more risk or leaving? (Evaluate the seven ways the Holy Spirit often leads to risk.[21])
   b. The inner self in relation to God: am I moving toward God or away from him? What seems to be my core question of God in this risk situation?
   c. The inner self in relation to others and self: Am I increasing in faith, love, and hope?
   d. In what ways do I/we see the heavenly realm participating in this risk situation? (i.e. demonic opposition?)

2. Emotional/Psychological/Intuition
   a. What are my strong emotions in this risk situation, and what about the risk is impacting me the most?
   b. What is the level of fear and anger team members are experiencing? (Fear often dampens risk mitigation and anger often causes us to think we have more control.)
   c. How am I behaving in comparison to predicted behavior in risk?
   d. Which of the eleven biases (chapter 8) are influencing my decision-making?
   e. How is confirmation bias informing the decision-making?
   f. What does my "gut" or intuition tell me about this situation? Where am I "sensing" this decision in my body?

---

19 Pires, "Don't Panic!"
20 Pires, "Don't Panic!"
21 Hampton, *Facing Danger*, chapter 5. These include Christian and secular security consultants, the expat and local community, biological and spiritual family, the Bible, the Holy Spirit, dreams and visions, leaders, and authorities.

3. Stewardship and Information Analysis
   a. Do I have enough and the right kind of information to decide?
   b. Have I done enough evaluation of the data and my staff/families?
   c. What have I identified that I cannot know or will remain uncertain?
   d. Based on my information, what and how am I being called to steward?
   e. What does stewarding the information look like in this risk situation?
   f. Who should give input on the decision, who makes the decision, and who can veto the decision? Who needs to be informed about the decision?
4. Risk Framing/Benefits and Losses:
   a. Using the analysis questions above, what are the potential values of losses and gains?
   b. How is the risk being framed from a crisis perspective or non-crisis perspective?
   c. If time allows, have we invited all stakeholders in the group to help make the decision? Have we accounted for Groupthink (chapter eight) so that the leader is not only hearing what people think they want to hear?

Hopefully, since chapter 8, I've demonstrated the complexity of factors influencing our decision-making. Making the best decision in risk and persecution under severe pressure is challenging. Knowing that humans are somewhat predictable in risk helps us become more self-aware of how we are reacting. We can then use this awareness to ask ourselves honest questions in the risk situation and potentially make a better, more effective decision.

It's deeply encouraging to know that not only can we grow in discernment, wise decision-making, and risk savviness, but we also have the Holy Spirit's help. Openness to the Spirit's leading fosters generosity and creativity in the sacred moment of risk and persecution. Tetlow writes, "The Spirit of Christ can call for a revision of any decision, which reminds us of a fundamental truth: When we decide that we have discerned what God wants to be done and choose to do it, we have not reached certainty. We have reached hope-filled enactment."[22] Once the decision is made, we move forward with confidence. The next step is risk communication, aspects of which are discussed next.

---

22 Tetlow, *Making Choices in Christ*, 106.

Chapter 13
Risk Communication and Trust

Beware of posing as a profound person;
God became a Baby.[1]

One of the critical pieces lacking in dangerous situations is enough of the correct information. In abundance are rumors, false information, threats, chaos, and fear. We de-escalate ourselves and others by how we choose to handle risk communication. Risk communication includes both soft skills and the use of technology.

Witness risk communication is sharing information at different levels of transparency to the various stakeholders to inform others what the actual assessed risks are and what risk mitigation will be implemented. "It is multi-directional and includes formal and informal messages and purposeful and unintentional ones."[2] Likely any risk message competes with multiple other conflicting statements, views, and unofficial sources.[3] It involves sharing what is happening (as appropriate) with others so they can pray intelligently and specifically. It also identifies the hardware necessary to maintain communication in deteriorating situations.

Witness risk addresses two levels of risk communication: (1) the practical and (2) the actual practice and characteristics of effective risk communication at all levels within the team and organization. It also includes information management, which answers the question, "Who gets what information?" The graphic below demonstrates the aspects of risk communication that all require trust: risk perception, risk communication, information management, leadership communication, information analysis, and decision-making.

---

[1] Chambers, *My Utmost for His*, 377–78.
[2] Society for Risk Analysis, "Risk Analysis: Fundamental Principles."
[3] Society for Risk Analysis.

Figure 10: Aspects of Trust

© 2022 Neal & Anna Hampton

Trust

A generational shift in risk communication has noticeably occurred on a global scale in the twenty-first century. There have been three significant changes to influence risk communication: (1) "experts and authorities are less trusted, and issue of real or perceived trust is now central to health communications and risk communications";[4] (2) many people's primary sources of information are online open-source information sites and social networks; and (3) "the way the media works has changed to embrace 24-hour journalism; the reduction in resources and 'beat experts' to follow health news; the increase of citizenship journalism and social media, and the rise of opinion versus the well-sourced and referenced new stories of the past."[5]

What impacts whether the risk communication is a success or a failure? Three critical aspects determine success: risk perception and framing of the same risk within the team (unity on what the risks are and an agreed-upon risk management plan); the trustworthiness of the information; and "buy-in" regarding the reliability of the leader giving the communication.

How we frame something dictates what we see and don't see.

---
4 Gamhewage, "Introduction to Risk Communication."
5 Gamhewage.

Framing is critical. How we frame something dictates what we see and don't see. Frames dictate our view of reality.[6] Facts logically laid out are not enough. The perception of the risk communicator (often the leader) and the information is critical. A major frameshift is happening, particularly in the USA, but it may have ripple effects elsewhere. Seel writes in his book, *The New Copernicans*:

> Since the American evangelical church is heavily committed to rational left-brain Enlightenment ways of thinking and the apologetic approach that reinforces it, the church and its leaders are crippled in their ability to see the frameshift occurring. The American evangelical church has an underdeveloped poetic imagination. Imagination is sometimes viewed with outright suspicion, and the imagination is viewed as subjective and therefore intrinsically relativistic. This is not only bad theology but bad neuroscience. Our bias toward rational left-brained Enlightenment thinking makes it very hard for the evangelical church to communicate effectively to a cultural frameshift.[7]

Are the risk communicator and organization trustworthy? Perception, beliefs, biases, and trust are intertwined. Personal experience informs perceptions of trust. Trust will carry a team through a difficult situation even more than interpersonal skills. The most productive teams are the most trusting people because trust is essential in human relationships. "In low trust groups, interpersonal relationships interfere with and distort perceptions of the problem. In contrast, in high trust groups, there is less socially-generated uncertainty and problems are solved more creatively and efficiently."[8]

Risk communicators have to know who should say what to whom, how uncertainties are addressed, and how to interpret and explain probabilities that have been assessed.[9]

Building Trust as the Risk Communicator

1. Expertise: You know what you are talking about and admit when you don't (demonstration of humility). You interact (not necessarily in person) with the experts and give well-reasoned answers when you differ from expert input. The experts you interact with include those from multiple backgrounds, including security experts, people on the ground both local and foreign, organizational strategists, organizational leadership.

---

6 Seel, *New Copernicans*, 7.
7 Seel, 7.
8 Asherman, Bing, and Laroche, "Building Trust Across Cultural," 7.
9 Society for Risk Analysis, "Core Subjects of Risk," 3.

2. Identification: You verbally connect the values and purpose of why you are there as you share the risk information. Frame the mitigation plans within the bigger picture of the vision and purpose of your ministry.

3. Goodwill: Your tone and selection of words demonstrate your care for the people involved and impacted by the risk. You know and address the concerns of the individuals, and you express gratitude for them.

4. Neutral framing of risk information is not possible.[10] But acknowledging your perceptions and understandings about the information as you share it will go far in building trust with your teams or those impacted by the danger.

5. Avoid acronyms and difficult-to-understand numbers and words. Explain simply so that people do not feel stupid. Risk analysis and security terminology can be intimidating, and data sets are hard to understand. Explain probabilities and numbers, recognizing that even the smartest people get this information wrong. Be sensitive to sports analogies and idioms that are difficult to translate or hard to understand for those from other cultures and use simpler English.

6. The frequency of communication should increase as the situation changes/deteriorates.

7. The risk communicator shares the plan of action with sufficient details and transparency, scaled to the audience. For example, a parent back home will receive a different level of detail than a team member in the risk situation.

8. Send out information that was communicated verbally to the team in writing if possible.

9. Explain why decisions were made and clarify how consensus was arrived at or if the leader made the decision.

10. Be inspirational in your phrasing: "Hold on." "Hold firm."

11. Don't overuse technology. Ask yourself, "Is it essential to send this email, or will this message be more effectively shared via phone, video, or in-person?"

---

10   Peters, Hibbard, Slovic, Dieckmann, "Numeracy Skill," 351.

Developing a Risk Communication Strategy

In her article regarding the need for effective risk communication, Lisa Ellis states:

> While every situation is different and needs a different response depending on the specific circumstances, there are five common elements Viswanath identifies that can serve as a good starting point for developing any applied risk communication plan.
>
> 1. Prepare for the crisis and be ready for it ahead of time, regardless of what type of crisis it is or whom it will affect. Planning for various scenarios can help you be ready to act when needed.
>
> 2. It's essential to know your audience and understand who they are, what they care about, and their situation. "For instance, you can't talk about evacuating if people don't have the means to access a car. You have to be sensitive to the conditions under which the information you share can be acted upon," Viswanath says.
>
> 3. Sometimes saying less is more. "Being measured in one's communication of risk, especially in times of uncertainty, is especially critical," he points out. [Prepare the team that guidelines or recommendations may change.]
>
> 4. Be open about what you know and also what you don't know. Telling people that you are still waiting to find out more and will share the latest findings as they become available is [essential] to maintain your credibility over the long term.
>
> 5. It's important to practice and learn from experience. Every situation will be different, so take the time to debrief after a crisis and assess what you did well and what areas you may be able to strengthen in the future.[11]

Cross-Cultural Communication

"Cultural patterns of behavior and belief frequently impact our perceptions (what we see), cognitions (what we think), and actions (what we do)."[12] There are three influential studies on communication significant for our focus which I will summarize starting at the macro-level. Roland Muller described human culture (and how we share the gospel) into three broad categories in terms of shame and honor, fear and power, and truth and guilt perspectives.[13] Hofstede's six dimensions of culture give insight

---

11 Ellis, "Need for Effective Risk."
12 Meyer, *Culture Map*, 13.
13 Muller, *Honor and Shame*.

into how people approach other people and life. The dimensions are: (1) the power distance index; (2) individualism vs. collectivism; (3) masculinity vs. femininity; (4) Uncertainty Avoidance Index; (5) long-term orientation vs. short-term normative orientation; and (6) indulgence vs. restraint.[14] These sources are helpful, especially when comparing several nations that represent the cultures of members of a team. However, Meyer nuances communication in her book based on an eight-scale model:[15]

- Communicating: low-context vs. high-context
- Evaluating: direct negative feedback vs. indirect negative feedback
- Persuading: principles-first vs. applications-first
- Leading: egalitarian vs. hierarchical
- Deciding: consensual vs. top-down
- Trusting: task-based vs. relationship-based
- Disagreeing: confrontational vs. avoiding confrontation
- Scheduling: linear-time vs. flexible time

Cross-cultural communication is nuanced in terms of how meetings are conducted, what listening looks like, expectations of presentation, leadership styles, language and style of management communication, conflict and disagreement style, trust, and many other elements that influence how messages are given and how they are received.[16] For example, some cultures want the communicator to share the news immediately and get to the main point or application. Other cultures cannot hear a message unless it is framed with the context of the speaker, the message, and the context of the application. In all cultures, the pace of speaking is nuanced. On an international team, Asians will often wait to be invited to speak. If the Westerner never pauses long enough to leave space or ask the Asian counterpart to speak, the Asian voice will not be heard.[17]

> If the Westerner never pauses long enough to leave space or ask the Asian counterpart to speak, the Asian voice will not be heard.

---

14 Hofstede n.d., "Culture Compass: Compare Countries." He has a tool on his website to compare 2 or 3 countries on any of the six dimensions.

15 Meyer, *Culture Map*, 15.

16 Lewis, *Cross-Cultural Communication*, vii–xix.

17 Meyer, *Culture Map*, 4–7.

A significant aspect of cross-cultural communication is how the culture approaches trust in a relationship and how trust is built. Americans begin at a place of trust until proven otherwise, but many other cultures are the opposite: no trust until relationships are formed. This approach requires more time to build the relationship before getting down to business.

In times of risk and danger, it's critical for trust to already be present to communicate effectively under pressure. Scheduling time for team building and emotional bonding in times of low risk will aid in building trust to draw on in times of danger.

One effective way to build trust is to have the team discuss what trust looks like on their team for them in that situation. This exercise will help all entities understand the other culture more quickly and easily and know what to do to build trust. Then trust can be monitored as they give each other permission to ask, "How am I doing in building trust?"

Four Principles of Secure Communication[18]

The four principles are cover, conceal, compartmentalize, and reduce. These will be summarized, but contact a security professional or cybersecurity expert for further information.

- Cover: All practices and technologies you use should first work to enable you to blend in with others and not draw attention to yourself.

- Conceal: Even if you blend in with others, you should assume that at some point, you will come under the scrutiny of some type, whether by the government or hostile actors. Use encryption to protect sensitive communications and documents. Do not make it easy to see your private, sensitive information.

- Compartmentalize: In case your digital devices or information falls into the hands of adversaries, keep your most sensitive information separate from non-sensitive information. This practice reduces the consequences of a breach.

- Reduce: If your most sensitive accounts and information are vulnerable to being compromised, periodically remove sensitive conversations and files from your data stores and applications. Reduce the possibility that hostile actors obtain a whole year's worth of data.

---

18 Corey K., Version 1.1, June 2020 Anonymous Collaborative Christian Cybersecurity Group.

PACE (Practical Hardware Communication Plan)

PACE is an acronym for a methodology used to build a resilient communication plan.[19] "The PACE acronym stands for primary, alternate, contingency, and emergency." The PACE approach establishes four methods of communication between you and your team. The genius of PACE is its resiliency—when one communication channel fails, you have three others to try.

1. "Primary: The routine and most effective method of communication.
2. "Alternate: Another [standard method] of passing a message with minimal to no other impact.
3. "Contingency: This method will [typically] not be as convenient or efficient as the first two methods but capable of passing [info] when necessary.
4. "Emergency: This is a method of last resort that [is more challenging to use and may be slower.]"[20]

An example of a resilient communication plan that follows PACE principles would be:

1. Primary: Smartphone—the Apple iPhone is preferred over Android (as of this writing).
2. Alternate: Basic phone (less trackable).
3. Contingency: Satellite phone or Satellite tracker/messenger (It's not uncommon for phone systems to crash in situations of chaos due to overwhelmed communication towers. A satellite tracker/messenger is a much less expensive way to stay connected when necessary.)
4. Emergency: VHF radio (if all communication in the country is jammed) or trusted people within the local population to help pass messages. It's wise to have a non-technological communication backup plan.

Cybersecurity

In witness-risk, we want to protect our digital information and how information is shared via phone, VHF radio, computer, and any other means. Stewardship of data and the communication of data is critical and may save lives. There are cybersecurity best practices and resources available for Christ-followers. For security reasons, nothing more is discussed here. Contact a cybersecurity expert to learn what available tools and best practices are tailored to the Christ-follower based on the assessed threat level.

---

19 Miller, "Think Like a Green."
20 Miller.

Information (Mis)Management

Risk communication implies decisions have to be made concerning what information is shared and with whom. This practice is termed "information management." *Authority* means, "Who has the authority to have the information?" and "What are they allowed to do with the information?" First, what not to do:

1. Pseudo-Courageous Risk Profile: This mindset is a particularly immature approach to information management—that since all the information is out there, we can say whatever we want. "It's all known," "I get a threat a day," implying information management is cowardly. It assumes, "I'm courageous because I don't care who hears." This attitude does not display stewardship of calling or stewardship of communications. Courage is not defined by not caring who knows what. Not caring about information management does not consider the different risk profiles of servants within Christ's body and what he has called *them* to.

2. Risk Obtuseness: Refusing to become risk communication savvy is obtuse. Obtuseness is defined as the quality of being stupid and slow to understand or unwilling to try to understand.[21] A persecuted pastor told me, "I've asked the pastors from our supporting churches in the USA at least half a dozen times to get on a secure communication app—they keep sending me (non-encrypted) emails."[22]

3. Picture Data Sharing: The metadata in photos reveals time, location, and date. Posting photos on social media may compromise entire projects and people, both local and expatriate, unless the metadata is stripped.

4. Rumor Sharing: Christ-followers (including Christian politicians and famous preachers) are often naïve and gullible about internet information. There are unverified stories (rumors) and false information (purposely created to look real). Verify, verify, verify, VERIFY. Double-check sources. Know who you are getting information from and what their biases and motivations are.

5. Social Media, Digital Footprint, Online Presence, and Naïveté: Groups hostile to the gospel and Christ-followers are often extremely technologically proficient. They know how to mine social media to find social connections, and they can tune into Western church

---

21 *Cambridge Dictionary*, "Obtuseness."
22 Signal is the most secure communication app available to civilians 2022.

services and watch the "Short-term missions reports." Anyone using social media should be trained not to reveal information they would *not* want hostile groups to know (locations, names, events, relational connections, organizations, sending entities, financial partners, political affiliations, political views, etc.).

It would be implausible for a modern, technologically connected person to have no online presence (besides, it is not a wise concealment approach). It is better to curate your online profile congruent with who you are and what you say you are doing. In other words, it should reflect the legitimacy of your life.

6. Pooled Ignorance: The virtual expatriate communities within countries are often sources of pooled, ignorant information. These communities may be giving advice that could get you killed. For example, in one country, kidnappings were severely high.

   An expatriate passing herself off as a security expert was giving mixed advice in a Facebook expatriate community on what to do if kidnapped. While there was some good advice, mixed in was the following *terrible advice* which did not humanize the person at risk:

   - "Change all your contacts [in your phone] to something impersonal. Mom and Dad should be Bob and Sally. Sister should be Judy. But if you have a 'trusted' PNH or hitman—he is now 'Dad.'"
   - "Clear your contacts frequently. If you call your mom 4x per day—you won't want kidnappers to see that."
   - "Put together a plan in case you get kidnapped. If anyone calls my sister to tell them I was abducted, she knows to say to them, "that b*#%h—keep her!" and hang up. Then call my "Dad" (see above) and give him the location of my Life 360 [a tracking app]."

7. Many Code Words Are Known: Many sending organizations use common phrases on their websites as if they conceal information that is already very clearly known to hostile entities. Terms like "SE Asia" are already well known to the Indian government. It's dangerous to list all the short-term trips to SE Asia, and the hostile government can cross-check that with incoming flight information. It also endangers the lives of locals on the ground who receive short-term teams. There are many such other phrases and "code words." Governments are smart enough to figure all these out. It is better to share generally without revealing enough to connect specific information to you or those in your community.

8. Be found guilty for the right thing, not for concealing in silly ways. Being as cunning as a serpent means caring about what words are used in communication. One global worker's monthly newsletters talked about "lifting" to "dad." Too many Christ-followers think they are cunning when using words like the following:

"Great seeing you at R**S. Would you pr@yerfully consider filling this role in 2022? As I remembered you to Father today, the Rushing Wind put a thought in my heart that you would be the best person for this task to reach Mulim in your area. I am yarping fervently for Mulim to Father. Please yarp and see what Father would say to this Wind-driven petition. Thankful for your mini$try!"

People who still send messages like the above are more often trying to virtue signal gospel hardship for attention rather than trying to secure their communication.[23] These words fool no one. Governments have people and software that catch these silly derivations of keywords. Hostile governments are not dumb. They have profiles of what "undercover" Christ-followers are doing. They already assume we pray. A Christ-follower should be known as someone who prays, reads their Bible, loves Jesus, and follows his teachings.

There are two key questions: (1) What do you want to be found guilty for? I want to be found guilty of being a Christ-follower who prays, reads her Bible, and talks about who she loves the most. I want to be like Daniel and found guilty of predictably doing what a Christ-follower does, spending daily time praying to him; and (2) How can I *not* publicly draw unwanted attention from the government to myself, yet continue in the tasks God has called me to?

While we need to assume that governments know what we are doing, we can conduct ourselves so that we do not publicly embarrass the government or "force" them to act.

Specifically, avoid using words that can be mistaken as proselytizing. Most Christ-followers associate proselytism with the abuse of people's freedom and the distortion of the gospel of grace using coercion, deception, manipulation, and exploitation. Many actors like governments, media, and religious leaders suspect all Christian faith-based organizations are involved in proselytization, yet they define it differently. We need to be

---

[23] Personal correspondence with Scott Brawner, March 12, 2022.

sensitively engaged and scrupulously ethical in our behavior and words.[24] Being cunning is knowing definitions of words and the implications of those definitions and words.

Information Management: Guidelines

1. Confirm reports before sharing, or at least qualify that you are sharing unconfirmed information.
2. Verify the source of information.
3. Share the source of information.
4. Examine the motives of the source who supplied the information.
5. Evaluate: Is the information credible?
6. Calmly share the information. Don't panic.
7. Did I mention *evaluate and confirm*? Do not engage in rumor sharing except possibly to acknowledge what the rumors are and the scale/rate of intensity if that is relevant.

Communication When Danger Is Increasing or in an Ongoing Crisis

Signal groups (encrypted communication apps) are often formed for information sharing and networking. There are guidelines for effective communication in these high-pressure situations when security is degrading rapidly.

1. Introduce yourself: Provide your name, which entity you are with, and who in the network knows you.
2. Express compassionate empathy briefly (not always, but doing so may be appropriate if someone just shared something very tragic).
3. Get to the point.
4. If you create a group chat, immediately introduce every number/member included so that everyone knows who is there.
5. Concisely state the need with relevant details.
6. Thank people regularly for their help.

Additional Aspects of Risk Communication When Risk Is Increasing

1. People who took the time to give advice and analysis want follow-up information and should also be told the final result. Anyone who invests energy is invested and should be told what happens. When you are asking them to care, they usually do care.

---

24 Galpin, *Undivided Witness: Jesus Followers*, 84.

2. Encourage those in trauma and crisis to keep working for survival. People need to be encouraged to run the race until there is no more hope.
3. No promises of certainty should ever be made in circumstances where extremists are operating. The only guarantee that can be kept is "I am here with you through it all, whatever happens."
4. Moral courage and clarity when your back is to the wall and you have everything to lose is painful but righteousness. Stay the course.
5. Extremists are masters at fearmongering. They know precisely how to make people afraid. Stay calm and keep working on the situation. Clear thinking is needed.
6. It's irresponsible not to eat and drink, and it would be best to keep taking fluids as you work on the problem.
7. Effective communication takes time and energy.

"To communicate risk effectively, we need to understand who the target audiences are and the challenges they are likely to face in assessing the risk and acting on it."[25] This understanding takes critical contextualization under tremendous pressure.[26] How we do that as Christ-followers, the words we choose to describe a dangerous situation, the tone of voice, and the type of demeanor, communicate to what degree we trust in a powerful yet loving God. An impactful and effective risk communicator knows how to frame even the worst news in a way that inspires vigilant purpose, unity of spirit, and righteous action for the sake of his name without demeaning the group. A single, well-spoken message given with conviction may promote courage transcending what any single individual could do. At the same time, a well-delivered message may invite non-believers to say, "I want what they have: hope for the future, joy in a relationship with God and neighbors, a new center in life that is infectious."[27] Developing excellence in risk communication is a worthy aim because he is worthy.

> Moral courage and clarity when your back is to the wall and you have everything to lose is painful but righteousness.

---

25 Ellis, "The Need for Effective."
26 Waldorf, *Undivided Witness*, 156.
27 Waldorf, 157.

Chapter 14
Embracing Grief and Loss

*I will build an altar from the broken
fragments of my heart.*[1]

Those who experience persecution know suffering and loss. There is also a particular type of suffering and loss in risk. Both engender grief since both involve loss. Humans tend to compare suffering and minimize it when it "seems" less than someone else's. It's easy to spiritualize, ignore, dismiss, and think it's irrelevant. Yet pain is a gift, a sign that we are alive. Only the dead feel no pain. Those who have the "leprosy of the soul" have become too calloused to love and have lost the ability to feel anything.[2]

However, we all experience the pain of suffering at different levels of intensity. The maxim "suffering is as suffering is felt" reminds us to accept these differences in felt grief. It is normal to suffer much loss in risk and persecution, yet it's also easy to treat grief the same as suffering—we minimize the loss and ignore, suppress, or deny grief. Not grieving is all too often spiritualized. Although grief can be set aside for a while, grief suppressed will eventually leak out in all sorts of ways. Ultimately, it must be walked through somehow (Heb 12:12; Isa 35:3, 4).

In risk and persecution, there's plenty of grief and loss to embrace while sharing with people who have never heard the joy that Christ came to reconcile us to him. We should expect grief when we choose to risk our lives for Christ and to be persecuted. Grief is the cost of commitment.[3] Grief shapes us if we let it.[4] Grief is normal. "Grief is not a disorder, a disease, or a sign of weakness. It is an emotional, physical, and spiritual necessity, the price you pay for love. The only cure for grief is to grieve."[5]

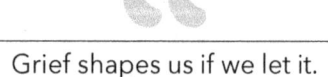
Grief shapes us if we let it.

A few principles about loss cross all cultures: loss is cumulative. It adds up. Loss is not abstract. It is an experience we like to avoid. There are many little losses and also significant losses. No two losses are ever the same.

---

1 Wolfe, *Making Loss Matter*, 1.
2 Sittser, *Grace Disguised*, 49.
3 Parkes, *Bereavement Studies of Grief*, 5–6.
4 Wolfe, *Making Loss Matter*, 1–22.
5 Attributed to Dr. Rabbi Earl Grollman, although I could not find it in his published books.

Each loss is unique and inflicts its unique pain. I think of the 10-year-old boy who still felt the loss of having to sell a beloved toy when his family sold everything before they moved overseas and how disappointed he was that a girl bought his toy, not another boy. It sounded silly to him, but in the safe place Neal and I created for him to share, he could still name this loss and disappointment a few years later. Loss is a normal part of life. "It is how we respond to loss that matters. [Our] response will largely determine the quality, the direction, and the impact of our lives."[6]

We can artificially divide loss into two categories: catastrophic loss (irreversible loss) and natural loss that is generally reversible (or can be restored in some way). Some will say even "reversible" loss is catastrophic. Nothing is ever the same again. Sometimes our loss involves death. I lived under the threat of kidnapping and death for years on end. Preparing to live and preparing to die are the same thing. Living within the reality of our mortality refines our priorities and values. Contemplating our death is not about being ready to die, it is about being prepared to live fully.[7] However, there are many other losses for those who go through danger and suffering besides death. Naming the suffering and loss is yet another exercise in naming to tame, as in discernment. When we become aware of our loss and suffering, we name them, and then we can bring them to our Father as an act of both worship and also identification with him.

The Suffering of Risk and Persecution

Living in a situation where threats are constantly issued, risks are regularly assessed, and persecution is real results in a kind of suffering. The suffering is a constant grieving of the loss of normal, loss of a known reality to a situation of great uncertainty. There is a sense of lostness-in-the-world, a lack of uncertainty about when it will end. Managing this kind of uncertainty requires awareness and action by entering into grieving these losses. The suffering of risk is difficult to explain. It is deeply personal and unique to each person. But like anything, by not naming the loss and suffering of risk and persecution, they gain greater power to intimidate and paralyze. They keep us from acting in faith and allowing ourselves to be transformed into his likeness through the difficulties. Failing to acknowledge the loss and suffering of risk also keeps us from fully realizing what God is up to and why he's allowing the suffering of risk into our lives. What are some things suffered and lost in risk and persecution?

---

6 Sittser, *Grace Disguised*, 16.
7 Inge, *Tour of Bones*, 10.

- Being called irresponsible—slandered at worse, misunderstood at least, even by family
- Sicknesses we wouldn't normally experience back home
- Physical ailments from the sheer stress of living in constant threats of kidnapping and murder take their toll. For us, it took months to recover even after debriefings.
- Depression
- Isolation and loneliness
- Constant loss of friends coming and going
- Loss of familiar coping mechanisms—things like being unable to take public walks due to security reasons
- Death of loved ones, or those in the community
- Physical loss of home, property
- Loss of ignorance—seeing death and blood, traumatic pictures that stay in your mind
- Loss of dreams, of what could have been
- Fears of all kinds assailing us
- Living under constant threat and with constant fear
- Rage and hate fill our hearts which must be processed and forgiveness extended to those who caused so much pain
- The anger of injustice and feeling of powerlessness
- Ambiguous loss existing in between things we cannot name
- Immense stress from being in leadership during high risk. Being a country director of a large international team meant responsibility for their physical lives, the project work, getting permissions from government officials, overseeing all facets of security, and member care to make sure people were doing well.
- Attacked, slandered, and criticized severely by other global workers and Christ-followers
- Loss of future
- Loss of community
- Loss of family relationships. After being away for years, the children grow up and are not close to extended family.

- Loss of indifference to evil. Indifference is not the quality of *not* caring, but not caring enough. Christ-followers care so deeply they cannot look away from all those still lost and bound by chains of separation from God and often living in oppressive circumstances. There can be occasionally a wistful longing to live life without the first-hand knowledge of the evil that people suffer around the world.
- As the years have passed, it slowly became clear to us the impact of living in constant danger. We've changed, our values changed. We no longer fit "at home." We see the problem of the world and the church differently from our passport culture. This change is also a kind of suffering of risk that we didn't know would happen.

Part of the calling to the suffering of risk and persecution is that you didn't know to expect certain aspects of it, you didn't know it was part of the deal when you signed up, and it's hard to believe (especially if you are a Westerner) that there are people out there who want to kill you. This realization is quite shocking and hard to grasp, even when we've prepared for it and publicly vowed that we are ready to die for Christ. The suffering of risk and persecution is painful, personal, and a privilege.

The suffering of risk and persecution is painful, personal, and a privilege.

It requires perseverance marked with a firm commitment to continually turn toward, not away from God in our pain; to name our fears, distresses, and sacred questions we have of God; to cry and grieve and fight for joy with everything we have. This assurance is not some glib emotion, but a deep sense of purpose and acceptance that he will be with us no matter what. The suffering of risk is what clarifies our understanding of God. As we experience the real God, not our false image of him, we begin to shed our false selves and experience our true selves. Sometimes, only the suffering of risk and persecution is what can do this.

There is one grief that most of us do not feel as deeply as Christ did. This is one of the easiest to ignore and look away from, even when we have given our lives to serve him full-time. We do not grieve enough about those who reject us because they are rejecting him. People are watching, even when those same people are rejecting the good news of Jesus Christ. Instead of grief, we take it personally and our egos are damaged. May we be motivated to cultivate hearts of grief for the lost and those rejecting him. This grief mirrors God's heart and deepens our spiritual transformation. Decide to let nothing be wasted, even our grief. Since the moment of risk is by definition a moment of liminality, the suffering we experience in danger and trauma is also the moment of the potentially deep, sacred transformation of our most inner selves to more clearly reflect the God whose image we bear.

Enduring Courage in Deep Grief

To love, lose, and begin again or just to keep going ... this perseverance takes courage and resiliency and the help of God.[8] "Deep sorrow is good for the soul [if we allow it to] make us more alive to the present moment."[9] One can be high functioning in deep grief. Deep grief can be mistaken psychologically for depression and can feel in the body just like fear.[10] C. S. Lewis wrote, "No one ever told me that grief felt so like fear. I am not afraid, but the sensation is like being afraid. The same fluttering in the stomach, the same restlessness, the yawning. I keep on swallowing. At other times it feels like being mildly drunk or concussed."[11] Lewis's experience reflects a physical aspect of grief. Grief is carried in the body, and all of us carry it differently.

The Hebrew word for grief can be translated as physical illness. Variations include: growing weak, falling sick, being ill, tired, and the misery of suffering. When deep grief has lifted, we do have more energy. This reality implies that we need to allot physical and time margin in our lives to allow ourselves to grieve. If we are living in risk and persecution, we also need to allow a margin for these aspects of living and their impacts on us which require energy and time.

Fears feed grief. There is fear of the future, fear of loss, fear of fear, fear of being alone, fear of the risk, fear of making a mistake that will cost someone else's life, and fear of failing God, myself, and others. This fear leads to grief. We are free to choose, to choose courage to face the grief, even when overwhelmed by things that make one afraid, like grief. We feel grieved by the lostness of innocence of a former reality of life. Grieved that people back home can never understand what we've gone through, and we are alone, possibly forgotten, certainly not understood. Home is not the same nor is it where we are now. There is no more home. There is no return to what was before. In the darkness where we cannot see the light at the end, how do we combat this tidal wave of fears, loss, and grief overwhelming us and deepening our grief? Discerning reality includes being able to see and name the treasures of walking in the valley of grief. "There are things that can only be seen with eyes that have cried."[12]

---

8 Brener, *Mourning & Mitzvah*, xxiii.
9 Sittser, *Grace Disguised*, 69.
10 Lloyd, "No One Shall Make," 358–64.
11 Lewis, *Grief Observed*, 1.
12 Christopher Munzihirwa, Archbishop of Bukavu.

Those who walk in the valley of deep grief know the treasures of walking with him in the darkness. There are many treasures in this valley. One treasure we find is that these fears are normal, our griefs are normal, and we are normal. Another treasure is that when we run to him we find he is not standing next to us, nor in front, nor behind, but holding us and holding a bottle to collect our tears. How close to us does he have to be to do that? As he collects our tears and we look up, we see he is crying too. "You keep track of all my sorrows. You have collected all my tears in your bottle. You have recorded each one in your book" (Ps 56:8, NLT). "Keeping our tears in a bottle" is an idiom meaning he knows all our griefs and keeps a list of them.

Another treasure of the valley of grief is "If we face loss squarely and respond to it wisely, we will become healthier people ... we will find our souls healed, as they can only be healed through suffering."[13] We must turn towards the pain and fully feel it in all its relentlessness. It requires us to enter the darkness and bewilderment of whatever the grief and loss are. Sittser wrote, "Darkness ... invaded my soul, but ... so did light."[14] Both contribute to our transformation.

Courage in deep grief is learning to lament. We are lamenting the unwanted transition from one reality to another.[15] In the Psalms, we see lament as complaint, lament as resistance and justice, and lament as newness and hope.[16] Biblical lament is not a whining or angry venting, but a structured language of complaint, protest, and appeal directed to God. The Psalms reveal the entire range of emotions, with the lament Psalms often demonstrating lament moving into praise and hope. Courage is running to him every time grief threatens to overwhelm us, and learning to recognize the loss or fear that triggers the grief. Courage requires taking time and energy to grieve until we no longer feel the need to grieve. The time frame and the process of grieving are different for every individual.

Show Self-Compassion

There is a little exercise we can do to show ourselves compassion in our grief. Sit and relax, and feel your breathing, in, and out. Feel your grief. The grief could be fear, anger, sorrow, or pain. As you breathe, whatever you become aware of is what you want to speak to, and offer yourself self-compassion in your grief. Continue to also breathe deeply in, and out. Speak to your grief:

---

13 Sittser, *Grace Disguised*, 16.
14 Sittser, 40.
15 Brener, *Mourning & Mitzvah*, 14–15.
16 Cathi, "Lament and Hope."

"I know you are there, my grief (or pain, or anger)." Breathe in and out. "I will take care of you. I know you are there my grief, I will take care of you." What words of compassion would you like to offer yourself? Invite God into your grief. Picture him sitting with you. He is also grieving. Breathe in and out. What does God say to you in your grief?

Grief Process

In the process of grief, it is helpful to identify what it means to fully face and walk through grief. The path of grief is not linear. Five stages are shown in the figure below. It is more like an oscillating process, going from one stage to another and back again. One drawback of the drawing and "stages" is that it may be seen as a prescription of what one has to go through. Instead, the process should be thought of as a general description. Each person grieves uniquely, even though it appears very similar to these stages.[17] It's okay not to process grief until we are ready to do so; we can acknowledge grief but then put it in our back pocket until we are ready.

Figure 11: The Grief Process

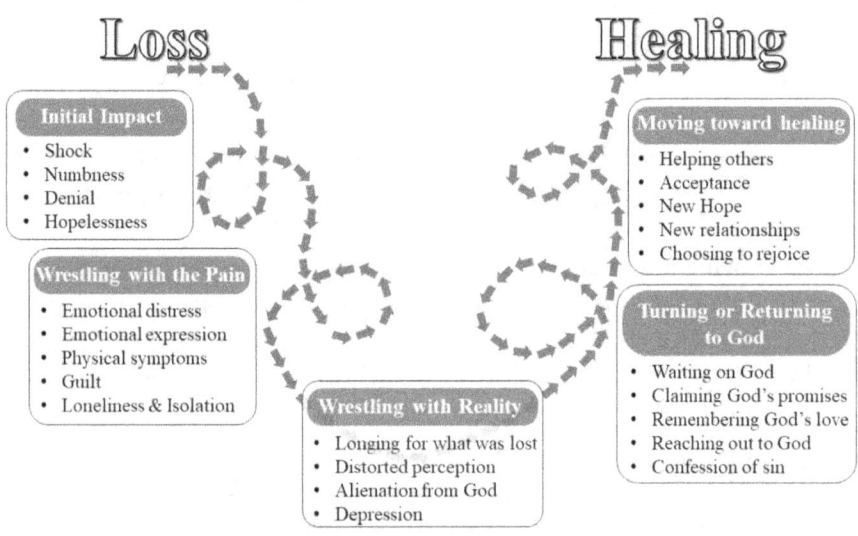

© 2016 International Training Partners. Used with permission.

Processing grief takes time and energy. The following steps are adapted from the book by Lauren Wells, *Unstacking Your Grief Tower*. Three steps help us to enter into the process. The first is to list all the losses we can think of in a specific time frame. Third culture kids (TCKs) may focus on their entire childhood, while adults could choose the last month to six months to

---

[17] Kessler, *Finding Meaning*, 1.

the past term. Often grief is associated with death, but we grieve many types of losses, including:

- Material: Loss of a physical object or familiar surroundings
- Relationship: Loss of the emotional and physical presence of a significant person
- Functional: Loss of the physical ability to do certain tasks
- Role: Loss of a specific social role or status
- Systemic: Losses in the family or organizational life (e.g. changes in traditions, familiar structures, financial benefits, ministry focus)
- Psychological: Loss of hopes, dreams, sense of safety, security, or esteem.[18]

As you list the losses, record everything which comes to mind related to that loss, including sights, sounds, smells, and colors. Once you have listed all the losses, organize them by date and construct a plan for processing each one. Record the emotions which come to mind with each loss. Make sure to include both positive and negative emotions. As you work through the remaining steps, add more emotions to the list as they come to mind. Second, write out your timeline. It can be written in a creative way or as a simple list. Third, circle the hardest losses, the biggest griefs. Fourth, look at your list and ask yourself what you notice. What relational patterns and connections are there? Fifth, ask yourself questions about the losses. Wells gives nine questions to consider. You don't necessarily have to ask these for every loss, but take time to reflect and use these as tools to help you process.

1. What emotions did I feel in that season or situation?
2. What hidden losses accompanied that grief, or what made it feel so hard?
3. How did it feel in my body?
4. What coping skills did I use to get through that season or event?
5. How has it influenced my thought processes going forward?
6. How has it influenced my actions going forward?
7. What do I want to take from the experience, and what do I leave behind?
8. If I haven't talked about this aloud yet, who is one safe person I can tell?
9. Do I need help to move forward healthily?

---

18 Carr, Appendix A, "Crisis Response Packet."

People grieve differently. Consider what works for you, whether journaling, taking walks in nature, using art to create a representation of the loss or grief, talking with someone, work, exercise, or some helpful combination. Allow yourself whatever time is needed until the grief feels like it can take a rest.[19]

"the path of grief"[20]

a never-ending path in a wilderness world
of shortcuts hotkeys fast food and fiber-optic speed

walking the path of grief cannot be hurried

the only way out of grief is through it
each grief has its limits
those who say one year is enough
do not understand

there are always new paths to walk in grief
different stages
new levels of depth

but the smellsightsoundfeeling is always the same

naming grief is a learned skill
honed over decades of walking its path

if naming is taming,
the wild animal is quiet
… only for awhile

naming shadows
lightens them
the path called "Dark Scary Confusing"
diffuses from black to gray

perhaps i can begin to see my never-ending tears where they fall

Gated Grief

Sometimes loss and grief open a hole in our hearts that never fills and never goes away; it integrates into our souls. We can choose to allow this hole to callous over, or we can let ourselves feel the grief of what should

---

19 Wells, *Unstacking Your Grief Tower*, 38, 58, 66.
20 Hampton, "Grief," first published on my blog, *Behind the Veil*.

have been, what God's intentions were, but never was, never will be, and must be mourned the rest of our lives to keep our hearts soft. While the grief diminishes in intensity, it will never end.[21] The grief is freshly triggered by certain things: a scene in a movie, a story, a picture.

Levenson talked about this type of grief when she began to work out the unprocessed grief of an emotionally absent father. He was one of the American GI's tasked with liberating the living skeleton survivors from Nazi concentration camps. He never talked about the horrors he saw and experienced. She understood his inability to speak about his trauma, which impacted her, and resulted in his inability to be emotionally present to her. She had grief she had to walk through to heal from her father. She termed it "gated grief," trauma inflicted on the next generation when the earlier generation didn't deal with their trauma and grief.[22]

We live in an age of trauma. Peer into the darkness of our lives or our neighbors' lives, and we see trauma. Risk and persecution mean accepting that trauma will enter our lives, as it did for Neal and me in Afghanistan. Trauma is around us everywhere we see a refugee. Never before have there been 100 million refugees at one time like today. As of 2022, there are tens of millions of internally displaced people. There is a lot of trauma to resolve.

My father was a war refugee when Hitler and Stalin carved up Poland; his family was caught on the Russian side of Poland. It didn't matter which side you ended up on—both were bad. People like his family were sent to Siberian gulags by the Russians. On the other side, they could have suffered the fate of what Hitler did to five million Poles. If you go to Dachau and look at the suitcases displayed, you'll see our family name scrawled across one of the ones towards the front. My father survived a harrowing escape from the Russian side—then, he survived refugee camps on the German side of Poland, where he was beaten up regularly. He survived all the transition stress of coming to the USA, and he likely never resolved all his trauma.

PTSD is a relatively new concept, but it's likely he had it. He never spoke German again once he left there. He learned English, got a university degree, and made a success of his life, marrying and raising four kids.

He was a Christian man. He read his Bible every day. He loved the Lord. But, he was emotionally unavailable to me. I regret the hole left in my life and heart from his absence. Perhaps if he had worked more to resolve the pain of his early traumas, he may have been different. I've had to resolve that pain in my life, and I've had to do a lot of forgiveness work. When he died in 2021, there were no tears left.

---

21 Kessler, *Finding Meaning*, 2.
22 Levinson, *Gated Grief*, 173–74, 192–94, 224–28.

Trauma not resolved in one generation will have to be resolved in the next, or it carries on. Trauma always has grief mixed in, but not all suffering is traumatic.[23] Trauma can be resolved, but grief may never fully be resolved. Risk and suffering carry their traumas that must be addressed so they are not passed on to the next generation as gated grief. There is a world out there that needs us Christ-followers to be salt and light and bring the healing balm of Gilead to deep pain and overwhelming grief.

The Sixth Stage of Grief

Meaning is the sixth stage of grief. Through meaning, we find there is more than pain in grief. It's easier to grieve when we can see the meaning of our suffering and loss than when it feels meaningless and hopeless. Meaning, like grief, takes many shapes.[24] For example, meaning may be found in gratitude for what was and now is lost; awareness of the value of life, of the simple things of life; gratefulness for freedom to move in a new direction; the grief that the loved one is gone and we suffer so they don't; new rituals which commemorate the loss; healing of relationships as a result of the loss; and so many more possibilities. It takes time to find meaning in suffering, especially when we do not ask for the suffering.

Kessler writes, "I've often been asked, 'Where am I trying to find meaning? The death? The loss? The event? ... Or am I trying to find meaning in my own life after the loss?' My answer is yes, yes, yes, and yes."[25] We can find meaning in one or all of those, leading us to more profound questions and answers.[26]

It's critical to discern what risks God is calling us into. That's why the discernment discussion came earlier. Foolish courage and foolish risk lead to unnecessary loss, grief, and suffering. "Suffering for Christ is not self-inflicted suffering."[27] We do not seek suffering and persecution; we pursue Christ. What he wills, we accept joyfully. Therefore, we must have as much clarity as possible in understanding what it means to be as shrewd as a snake but not to sin, so we don't have to experience self-inflicted suffering. "We need the wisdom to know what to do, where to stand, and what not to do so that when suffering and loss come, it is for the sake of Christ and not because of one's foolishness."[28]

---

23 Kessler, *Finding Meaning*, 14.
24 Kessler, 3.
25 Kessler, 5.
26 Kessler, 5.
27 Ton, *Suffering, Martyrdom, and Rewards*, 424.
28 Penner, *In the Shadow*, 100.

There is no magic answer to grief and loss. Nothing, not even time will make the pain disappear entirely. But loss is transformed if it is met with faith. Faith in our Savior is our tool to make sense of loss, because Jesus knows grief.

> He was despised and rejected by men, a man of sorrows and acquainted with grief, and as one from whom men hide their faces, he was despised, and we esteemed him not. Surely he has borne our griefs and carried our sorrows; yet we esteemed him stricken, smitten by God, and afflicted.

When Isaiah 53:3, 4 says he was a man of sorrows, it means he knows the intense emotional pain of suffering. When the English text says he was "acquainted" with grief, that word does not encapsulate the depth of his knowledge. This knowledge is the knowledge that comes from the senses. It is a deep familiarity with grief, up close and personal. It's someone who has explored its depths of intensity. He supports us in our grief—we are not alone in enduring it. The Bible gives us many pictures of a God who hears the cries of men, women, and children.

- Genesis 21:17: He hears the wailing cry of a woman and the quiet cry of a boy and answers
- 1 Samuel 1:10: He hears the silent shaking cry of a woman and provides in her crisis
- Psalm 18:6: He hears my voice and my cry
- Psalm 31:22: He hears my cry and takes care of my enemies
- Psalm 56:8, 9: He keeps a record of what I cry over and heals them in Heaven
- Isaiah 25:8: He will wipe the tears from our faces
- Luke 19:41: He wept over the people (the city of Jerusalem)
- John 11:34, 35: He weeps over the separation of death and the pain of loss
- John 20:11–15: The women wept, but the angel gave a different perspective!
- Revelation 7:17: He will wipe the tears from our eyes
- Revelation 21:4, 5: He will show me how he was with me in my tears; He remembers each grief

Often when we live in places of extreme hostility to the Christ-follower, evil happens to us when we didn't expect it. It's unjust, and it's painful. It may impact us physically, mentally, and emotionally for the rest of our lives.

We don't have to understand why something happened to cause significant loss to find meaning. Even painful memories will begin to heal when we can find the meaning.

Experiencing and witnessing grief and loss in risk and persecution can enlarge our souls if we allow it by fully embracing them and letting ourselves grow. How can we live in loss and enlarge our souls? It depends on what choices we make in response to the loss—we need to recognize the graces we are given in our loss and grief, as well as the transformation we experience within the loss.

> Even painful memories will begin to heal when we can find the meaning.

If we make a place for our grief, our grief will change. The loss won't be returned, and we may still be in sorrow and lament, but our world becomes bigger, healing becomes possible, and we will see life with more clarity and uncluttered values.[29] Deep grief means deep love, and we offer our grief to him because we love him and know he loves us.

We can also choose to shrink from grief and decide not to experience it. In a sense, grief can be optional.[30] If we choose this route, we will never share deep love with other humans and God, and we will never grow.

It's possible that one meaning for our grief when we are persecuted for his sake is to identify with him in his sufferings (Col 1:24). Our grief reflects the heart of a grieving Christ; our pain-bearing is helping him bear his pain, so he is not alone, just as he helps us bear our pain. Entering Gethsemane with him means we will experience our own Gethsemane of aloneness, emptiness, and submission to God's will for us. "The stronger the faith, the more savagely Satan will storm its fortress through whatever means,"[31] including suffering, grief, and loss. When we acknowledge our losses in grief as we serve him in risk and persecution and offer them up as sacrifices of worship on the altars of our hearts, we find a new integration of the sorrows into our hearts and an unexplainable, unexpected peace and comfort. Grieving can bring the strength of soul[32] which helps us bear up and endure resiliently as we suffer for him. He is worthy.

---

29 Brener, *Mourning & Mitzvah*, 175–86.
30 Kessler, *Finding Meaning*, 9.
31 Lewis, *Grief Observed*, KL 136.
32 Parkes, *Bereavement Studies*, 10–13.

Chapter 15
Standing in the Tragic Gap

When you pray, meet us in the room of God's throne where
we can have communion, Fatima says.[1]

Standing in the tragic gap means standing firmly, purposefully, and strategically in the place where physical endurance is required to persevere in a spiritual battle. Parker Palmer describes the tragic gap as: "The capacity to 'stand in the tragic gap' [requires the ability to stand in the tension] between corrosive cynicism and irrelevant idealism, between what is and could be. We need the inner strength to hold both the reality and our hope at the same time."[2]

Wherever evil threatens and Christ is not known, in that sense we are standing in the tragic gap and enduring whatever hell throws at us because we know there is a better reality—his kingdom come. In the tragic gap, standing with endurance is challenging, and even more so when there is complete disregard for human life, and there is no end in sight, when brutal violence is the norm, our senses are constantly assaulted, and all signs indicate it will worsen, yet he is calling us to remain and move farther into it.

Courage is expressed through endurance while facing the fear of death for the sake of the gospel.[3] Yet there's more to courage in endurance. "It is more difficult for the soul to endure fear when there is no other possibility of resistance than endurance."[4] While I address hope in chapter nineteen, this chapter addresses bold endurance practices to help us courageously remain in the places of increasing risk and persecution. Practical theology of endurance teaches us to integrate holistic theology with the best security practices, habits of endurance, ritualized resiliency, validated psychological research, neurobiology, and most importantly, thoughtful self-reflection.

Endurance and resiliency go hand-in-hand. One can endure without thriving, without resilience, and without demonstrating the fruits of the Spirit. Resilience, the ability to recover from adversity, can enable Christ-like endurance if we let it. Discipling Christ-followers means helping others discover how to endure and persevere through various levels and types of hostility and persecution. In risk, endurance includes training and preparation for martyrdom.

---

1 Open Doors, September 29, 2021.
2 Palmer, "Tragic Gap."
3 Qiaoying, "Aquinas' Transformation," 471.
4 Qiaoying, 480.

Going to dangerous places with a plan for endurance and resiliency is much better than going with no plan. Firmness of spirit does not "just happen," and evil doesn't wait for us to be ready. Taking time to develop patterns of endurance and resilience for persecution and martyrdom offers a good return on investment (ROI). We typically think of ROI in terms of finances. However, getting and maintaining a Western Christ-follower in dangerous countries often costs a lot more than a local Christ-follower ministering in the same place. Either way, in light of current statistics, only 3–5 percent of all global workers go to reach the unreached, unengaged people groups where Christ's name has yet to be proclaimed. From a financial and resourcing perspective, there is a good kingdom ROI from discipling Christ-followers for endurance through persecution even to death, so they endure resiliently in these hard places and continue in faithful gospel witness.

Infused vs. Acquired Courage for Endurance

Endurance implies a duration of time, a feeling of present danger when one is facing a stronger entity. Endurance is an inward act of the soul, but it is also an outward action. "The strength of the soul in enduring or resisting evil is essential to the virtue of courage."[5] Two types of courage help us endure: infused courage and acquired courage.[6] As discussed in chapter three, God infuses courage into us. When we are willing and open to his activity in our life, he gives us the strength to be bold and courageous in action and in heart. Acquired courage is what we do to strengthen ourselves to endure and act boldly for Christ, especially at a high cost to ourselves.

> Endurance is an inward act of the soul, but it is also an outward action.

An example of working to acquire courage for endurance is related to the story of Richard Wurmbrand.

> Richard had prepared his mind and body for interrogation, torture, and malnourishment. On the day of his kidnapping, he was in perfect condition to endure beatings, verbal harassment, and the brutal conditions of his cell. Richard had spent years studying how other Christians endured intense suffering. "In being tortured by them, we learned to love them," Richard later claimed. "The gates of heaven are not closed for the communists. Neither is the light quenched for them."[7]

---

5 Qiaoying, "Aquinas' Transformation," 480.
6 Qiaoying, 480.
7 Voice of the Martyrs, *Wurmbrand: Tortured for Christ*, 122–23, 149.

Another significant factor helping to infuse courage is cultivating a perspective of transcendent reality. When we recognize and submit to God and transcendent values (things which are higher and much bigger than me),[8] it infuses our behavior and goals with transcendent purpose and leads to real action. When we cultivate constant awareness of ultimate reality, we are infusing ourselves with the tools of courage as we work towards that reality: self-denial, self-correction, choices, and behaviors that reveal a person of courage.

Stress Inoculation

Just as vaccines build up our body's defenses against disease, stress inoculation builds our mental defenses against severe stress. Stress inoculation training (SIT) is a crucial component of resiliency in dangerous situations. SIT has been recognized as valuable training for soldiers and even civilians in many spheres of life. Research on SIT reveals that "education, skill training, and exposure to relevant stressors are important components for preparing individuals to perform well under stress."[9]

Stress inoculation training helps people know how to respond to unaccustomed levels of stress and stress resolution, so they know how they react and prepare better for real-life endurance. For Christ-followers going into dangerous situations, stress inoculation training is a simulated exercise that helps trainees experience distress similar to the pressure in a dangerous context. Trainees recognize their "strengths and learn new skills that focus on developing more adaptive ways to think about and respond to these stressors."[10] Trainees also experience the effect of stress resolution.

Security trainers providing the stress simulation observe each trainee's reactions to stress. How is the trainee holding themselves during and after the simulation? How did they react physically, verbally, and mentally? Did they respond appropriately or poorly? Were they able to handle the pressure? If the trainee responded with learned helplessness, regressive behaviors, or could not separate reality from the simulation, additional training is required. People who have had stress inoculation training are much better equipped and confident, because they know what to expect in stressful situations and how to respond under extreme physical and mental stress. Stress inoculation training is directly connected to posttraumatic growth, discussed in chapter nineteen. SIT should be a standard duty-of-care training required for anyone going to the types of situations and places referenced in this book.

---

8 Cloud, *Integrity*, 244–48.
9 Robson and Manacailli, *Enhancing Performance Under Stress*, 12.
10 Porter, "What Is Stress Inoculation?"

Ritualized Endurance and Resiliency

Ritual means "a way of doing something in which the same actions are done in the same way every time."[11] We can ritualize our endurance habits, which leads to resiliency. "Resilience is the mental, physical, emotional, [spiritual], and behavioral ability to cope with adversity, adapt to change, and recover, learn, and grow from setbacks. A resilient and fit person is better able to leverage intellectual and emotional skills and behaviors that promote enhanced performance and optimize long-term health."[12] It's significant to note that resiliency is not a trait, but the behaviors and mindsets that lead to resilience can be cultivated over time and fostered through practice.[13]

Six areas associated with resilience include self-awareness, self-regulation, optimism, mental agility, strength of character, and relational connection to others.[14] But we also learn endurance by habits of ritualized resilience whenever we feel the powerlessness and chaos created in violent situations. Ritualized means an act or words done regularly, often without even thinking about it. These habits infuse every aspect of our day and all parts of our being. Endurance leads to resiliency, and resiliency leads to endurance. It's a positive growth cycle. The following eight resiliency habits many have described as helpful for endurance.

Food and Water

While our spiritual resources are significant, we should not underestimate the critical value of sleep and drinking adequate water to improve our outlook and ability to endure. Because the stress and pressure of risk and persecution are so severe, cultivating habits of resiliency includes daily habits of drinking and eating, even when we do not feel hungry or thirsty. At the least, performing these tasks forces us to stop and tend to our bodies. Even a one-minute break may be enough to re-orient ourselves and persevere for another hour or day.

Personal Agency

An essential aspect of resilience is resisting a fatalistic attitude in situations of powerlessness. It takes courage to face reality, name it, and then accept what we can control and live in peace with what we can't, even as we deeply grieve and move forward. We always have choices to control our own inner

---

11 *Cambridge Dictionary*, "Ritual."
12 Department of the Army Headquarters, *Advanced Situational Awareness*, 2–3.
13 Elverson, *Building Resilience*, 2–4.
14 Department of the Army Headquarters, *Advanced Situational Awareness*, 2–4.

life minimally. Personal agency, the ability to exercise control over tasks and attitudes in which we hold the outcome, resists giving up. Resilient people do not deny the reality of their lack of power but they take responsibility for what they can and let go of what they cannot.[15] In this way, they stay grounded in reality, survive the chaos, and grow through it.

Reflection on Thinking

Endurance requires mental abilities to analyze and reflect wisely on what is happening. This reflection takes time. We always make time for what's important to us, and reflection is a path to wisdom. Mental agility to manage biases, fear, and data requires embracing uncertainty, knowing your dread fear, getting help to analyze the data, and looking for more straightforward solutions rather than complex ones.[16] Resilient people continually reframe and re-orient their perspectives to look at adverse situations realistically and maintain optimism in the middle of challenges. They avoid the victim mentality and self-pity.

Tragic Humor

One of the most significant indicators of resilience is the ability to laugh. "Tragic humor" (dark humor) makes fun of things we don't usually laugh about. Laughing at things like death, terrorism, disease, depression, and disaster makes them less scary. Tragic humor is a survival technique. Laughter keeps us from drowning in the seriousness and tragedy and is a means of resistance against chaos and evil. "Laughter interrupts the system and state of oppression and creatively attests to hope, resistance, and protest as an invaluable means of ethical and theological resistance."[17] This type of humor is our way to survive and push back against the people and structures who seek to oppress us in the global genocide against Christ-followers. Tragic laughter teaches us that the line between tragedy and comedy is really quite thin.[18]

Find Meaning

It is a cultivated skill to find meaning, hold on to that meaning, and mine its depths for ourselves and for those around us. Our discernment is helped by strong values based on a firm foundation rooted in Scripture. These values infuse a chaotic environment with meaning because they offer ways to interpret and shape events. None of us are immune to despair or the pain of

---

15 Elverson, *Building Resilience*, 5.
16 Gigerenzer, *Risk Savvy*, 17–42.
17 Bussie, *Laughter of the Oppressed*, 103–7.
18 Claassens, "Tragic Laughter," 143–55.

significant loss. Meaning is often found in the tension between the ultimate vision of Christ's kingdom and the importance of courage for the next moment to do an act of justice, mercy, or kindness. Meaning, like courage, is both great and small, seen and unseen.

But what happens if we cannot find the meaning in the risk, suffering, and persecution we are walking in? Resilient, enduring, anti-fragile faith assumes there is meaning in our suffering even when we can't tell what it is. It is faith that won't stop, even when it seems like God isn't there, and he has abandoned us. It assumes that one day we will know the meaning. And this belief on its own imbues our suffering with purpose and meaning.

> Resilient, enduring, anti-fragile faith assumes there is meaning in our suffering even when we can't tell what it is.

Creativity

Creativity is called for in endurance and resilience. Ritualized ingenuity is the ability to make do with whatever is at hand. It includes creative ways to soothe and calm ourselves and show compassion to ourselves, our neighbors, and God. It is physical ingenuity and spiritual, mental, and emotionally creative ways to unite our minds, emotions, and bodies. There are ways to systematize soul awareness in the chaos of risk and persecution, even if we are in a jail cell with little apparent resources at our disposal.

Empathy with God

Showing compassion toward God is a strange thought. But when we reflect on God's heart in the situations of risk and persecution, violence and evil, we begin to enter into his grief, longing, anger over injustice, and lovingkindness. Showing compassion towards God turns our disappointment, maybe even our anger towards him, into standing with him. Standing with God results in both acquired courage and infused courage.

Speaking to Our Soul

We can develop internal resilient rituals to help us stay centered on Christ no matter our circumstances. These are cultivated habits of the mind, of "speaking to our soul" as David did, encouraging ourselves to faithful endurance. Speaking to our soul like David did means we must memorize Scripture regularly and hide God's word in our heart. This is possibly the most important resiliency habit to help us endure.

In the areas described related to developing resiliency, which ones does it seem the Holy Spirit is pointing you to cultivate specifically for yourself? What would you add to this list?

Relationships and Endurance

When we allow fear to turn us to God and others, it leads to greater faith, hope, and love. But if we allow our fear to turn us away from him and others, it's hard not to feel alone and powerless. Thinking we are alone (isolation) and that the situation is so bad that there's nothing we can do (resignation) are the two things that diminish endurance and resiliency and lead to poor decision-making. We want to equip people with the ability to discern God's presence, grow in awareness of his speaking to us, and see the value of developing meaningful relationships. Endurance happens more easily when we have a community of others around us who become like family. We must have significant connections with others to help us cultivate wise endurance and creative resiliency. Resiliency grows even more potent when we develop trusting relationships with people from the host culture, not just our own culture group.

Ordered fear of the Lord, based on kingdom ethics, means we will put our life at risk for another and be grateful that we have the honor of the opportunity. When someone from within the community is martyred, it impacts us differently. It re-orders our priorities. Life is not the same anymore, and our values, priorities, and purpose are refined and simplified. Secondly, it makes endurance easier in some ways and harder in others. Endurance becomes more challenging because we want to be with the loved one yet paradoxically easier because our priorities are refined, and we become more focused.

In general, experience reveals that living for Christ is more challenging than dying for him. How do we know if this is true? Those martyred can't tell us about their endurance versus martyrdom experience, and we have no martyr autobiographies. Reading martyrdom stories from the past two thousand years of Christian history, I suspect martyrs may say that death came quickly, even under torture, because of the grace Christ promised to give his disciple at that moment. With extensive reflection upon endurance and martyrdom and my own experience of long endurance over the years in a severe threat environment, my hypothesis (and that's all any of us can have) is that long endurance, with joy and resiliency, is more demanding than martyrdom, especially when there is no end in sight.

Another impact of martyrdom on those of us who remain alive is the veneer, the curtain between God and us becomes thinner. "*They go from strength to strength; each one appears before God in Zion*" (Ps 84:7). The Hebrew word for "appears" means to see God. Seeing, in Hebrew, is connected to knowing experientially. We are fully known, and we increasingly know him. As the veneer between God and us thins, endurance becomes easier. This happens primarily through suffering.

Endurance under Torture

Richard Wurmbrand was so severely tortured at one point that he began to have hallucinations. He describes them and then explains his strategy to fight them off. He had pleasant hallucinations of banquets of food, walls filled with books, and faces listening to him speak and then applauding. But he had darker hallucinations, gruesome acts of violence and gore, sexual fantasies and erotic dreams, women trying to seduce him, and more. His solitude, coupled with uncontrolled symptoms of tuberculosis, increased his sexual appetite. "The more he sought to remove them, the more perverse the visions became. Richard almost began to feel that he deserved the torture. Frustrated and plagued with guilt, he cried to God for relief."[19]

With God's help, "Richard developed a strategy for shaking off the hallucinations. He [thought] of them as hostile intruders—temptations, not sins. Instead of blaming himself for his visions, he weaponized himself with cool reason."[20] Throughout being beaten, drugged, and deprived of sleep, he forgot the three hundred poems he wrote while imprisoned. Later, they returned to his mind, and he wrote them down. "Day after day, he enslaved his hallucinations by bringing them into intellectual submission. He refused to allow sinful thoughts to dominate his cell and rested wholeheartedly on God's promise, '*No weapon formed against you will succeed, and you will refute any accusation*' (Isa 54:17)."[21]

Torture is difficult. There are many techniques used to try to break a Christ-follower, and torture has been even more refined since the time of the Romans. Historically, torture works to pressure Christians to forsake Christ. The church has often been unmerciful to those who do not do well under torture but want to return to Christ.[22] A simplistic response to the complexity of torture from those who have never endured torture for the sake of the gospel is unhelpful here. Torture, like kidnapping, is a choiceless, unrelenting event that has no discernable end until we return safely to our loved ones, or are martyred.[23]

---

19 Voice of the Martyrs, *Wurmbrand: Tortured for Christ*, 174.
20 Voice of the Martyrs, 174.
21 Voice of the Martyrs, 174–75.
22 Sittser, *Resilient Faith*, 101, 160.
23 Korkie, *558 Days*, 19.

ISIS martyred twenty-one Christian Copts on a Libyan beach in 2015. One of their spiritual fathers related, "Every Christian must have a cross—a real one and a symbolic one, and both must be present. Every Christian must live the life of Jesus anew."[24] When we suffer torture and martyrdom for the sake of Christ, we are living and dying as an example of this reality.

Christ asks us to trust him to give us strength in the moment. We can trust that he holds us—our whole being—in his hand and will not let go.

> When they deliver you over, do not be anxious how you are to speak or what you are to say, for what you are to say will be given to you in that hour. For it is not you who speak, but the Spirit of your Father speaking through you ... You will be hated by all for my name's sake. But the one who endures to the end will be saved. (Matt 10:19–20, 22)

Courageously Remaining

What is courageously remaining? In his chapter "Wise Endurance," Tim O'Brien, an American soldier in the Vietnam War, wonders about proper, wise courage in endurance.[25] "Courage is nothing to laugh at, not if it is proper courage and exercised by [people] who know what they do is proper. Proper courage is wise courage. It's acting wisely when fear would have a [person] act otherwise. It is the endurance of the soul despite fear—wisely."[26]

He continues, "It is easy to say that courage of conviction is wise courage, but what if our convictions are wrong? We can think we have the right convictions and demonstrate apparent courage in endurance, but it could be well-disguised cowardice. We cannot deem every kind of endurance as courageous."[27] Foolish endurance reveals itself in pride and a type of moral certainty that does not reveal deepening fruit of the Holy Spirit in ones life; it is a type of endurance that harms others and one's soul.

More than the fear of death, navigating through the absurd combination of certainty and uncertainty of a nightmare world in which the most basic sense of physical space cannot be relied on, we "must know what we do is courageous, that what we are doing is right. That kind of knowledge is wisdom and nothing else."[28] Wise endurance accepts our less-than-perfect heroic limits and accepts that some acts will be cowardly. Resilient courage includes when we are disappointed in ourselves but resolving to do better next time, and then doing better next time.

---

24 Mosebach, *21: A Journey*, 130.
25 O'Brien, *If I Die*, 133–47.
26 O'Brien, 136.
27 O'Brien, 138.
28 O'Brien, *If I Die*, 140.

Living in risk and persecution is a marathon, not a sprint, and enduring well through months and years of uncertainty and threats of violence requires purposeful attention, focus, and increasing awareness. Taking up our cross is costly. We'll feel like we never know enough or have enough information or resources. Evil will relentlessly come at us, shaking the ground under our feet and attempting to make us fall. Stubbornly standing in the gap in righteousness and justice requires strength we don't have but must pray for, care about, and cultivate with God's help and the help of others. "Let your hand be ready to help me" (Ps 119:173). He will infuse us with courage and help us stand with grace and poise under the worst circumstances. He is worthy.

Part Four
Leadership

Chapter 16
Systems and the Liminal Moment

Nothing changes until blood is shed.[1]

In February 2022, I informally surveyed the Risk Management Network members, asking, "What are the most urgent challenges/weaknesses related to risk and security that need to be addressed by your organization?" Here is a compilation of their responses:

1. Awareness of risk issues and buy-in at all levels. All staff need to assess risk.
2. Unity on teams when divergent opinions on risk exist.
3. Lack of current risk assessment/contingency plans in all fields. Lack of follow-up security training for those on the field.
4. Because our workers serve in their home countries/cultures, long-term threats or danger potentially becomes "white noise or a constant static hum that is ignored." Organized crime or ongoing war in a remote part of the country is very present, and some of our team members are not vigilant to keep up their situational awareness.
5. How to get people on board with thinking through risk and actively putting mitigation measures into practice. The climate (political, environmental, etc.) has changed since they were last overseas and they cannot assume it is the same as it was when they lived abroad previously.
6. Developing a theology of risk or risk "appetite" document.
7. Keeping current and reviewing security training. Having our programs follow and maintain what is actually in their security plan.

Organizations and teams that go to higher-risk places are impacted greatly. What is often unrecognized by staff who do not go to high-risk areas is that all people associated with the organization must implement appropriate security habits, not only those living in the higher-risk environment. This reality touches on the tension between the individual and the organization. Does the organization exist to facilitate the individual's ministry, or is the individual joining the organization to carry out the organization's mission?

---

[1] A common saying among security practitioners who clearly see threats and risks developing, yet who have a difficult time convincing decision-makers to take action.

The difficulty is that the individual fieldworker often believes the organization is the tool to facilitate the individual, so any "talk of restricting what I want to do because of people in other locations is absurd."[2] It's a tension that must be navigated for the security of the staff in the high-risk areas and the locals in relationship with those staff. In this case, it is necessary to create an organizational culture centered on what it looks like to love one's neighbor in the context of long-term organizational and individual ministry.

> All people associated with the organization must implement appropriate security habits, not only those living in the higher-risk environment.

The organization will experience the pain of change as all parts of the system have to adjust to what is necessary, particularly in terms of vocabulary and communication, social media/online presence, digital security, raising finances, marketing, the reputation of the organization, relationships with partners, required training and preparation, steps to risk assessment and management, crisis management preparation, fear management, and more. Yet, many individuals within the system are unaware that they are risk illiterate or may have some literacy but are not risk savvy. At times the entire senior leadership of a sending organization is risk illiterate, even when the organization is regularly sending people to dangerous areas. Risk management may be seen as an irritating appendage attached to the organization's side by a couple of loose, rusty screws. It's seen more as a specialty and an irritant than a valuable asset and incentive for gaining system-wide skills.

We must ask then, what does a risk-savvy organization look like? Perhaps we should start with risk literacy. What does a risk-literate organization look like? What level of security and theology of risk training do people within the organization have, and how much is being implemented? Is the risk management plan being followed? Are people reviewing it regularly? What is necessary to develop a risk-savvy culture where everyone at every level of the organization takes responsibility for managing risk rather than merely deferring to the security director? The security director of a sending organization is often a male with prior police, government, or military expertise. How can we cultivate an atmosphere where men and women with no professional security experience recognize their part and do not just leave it to the security professionals? It's a continuum of growth and

---

2 Author's private email discussion with Al Williams, SIL.

increasing discernment as we learn practical theology of risk individually and organizationally. People need teaching and training to understand how to connect risk assessment with front-line missions and to engage in risk assessment and mitigation procedures mandated by the organization.

Organizational leaders help increase staff buy-in and trust by acknowledging the price being paid, naming potential fears, empathizing with the impact on staff of what is asked of them, and directing them back to the overall vision. When leaders do this, people are more likely to accept new procedural and training requirements cheerfully. Jesus taught, "You shall love your neighbor as yourself" (Mark 12:31). When people realize that growing in risk literacy is one way of loving your neighbor, and as the entire system begins to implement risk literate procedures, hopefully, everyone will start to understand what their responsibility is and engage in the strategies for systemic risk mitigation.[3] What are the consequences of ongoing risk illiteracy? "For the simple are killed by their turning away, and the complacency of fools destroys them." (Prov 1:32). We must all be responsible for engaging in risk analysis as part of our devotion to Christ and loving others.

Yet there are different risk tolerance levels in the global church. In a Missio Nexus 2022 risk-in-missions survey of 230+ North American mission leaders, field workers, and church mission staff, the question was asked, "How much risk is enough?"

- Three percent will send and support staff in countries that are generally welcoming to Westerners, and that accept missionary visa.
- Nine percent will send and support in any country at any time, no matter the threat.
- Eleven percent will send and support staff in countries that are gospel resistant, but only if the country has received approval by the state department for US citizens to travel or live there.
- Twenty percent will send and support staff in countries that do not accept missionary visas but instead require another platform for entry.
- Fifty-four percent will send and support staff in countries regardless of threat level, provided that there are options for relocation or evacuation if the threat to staff increases to an unsafe level.
- Three percent no response.[4]

---

3 Buechner, *Listening to Your Life*, July 27.
4 Missio Nexus, "Global Missions and Risk."

Risk Literacy and Risk Savviness

The survey answers above reveal a general approach of risk aversion. There's a difference between how a person thinks they *should* respond to risk and how they actually do. We usually fall somewhere on a scale of risk-averse and risk-tolerant. One question that would be informative is to consider how our risk tolerance to witness risks as described in chapter two changes as our attachment-to-God deepens over time of walking with him.

We could be averse to some risks but tolerant of others as individuals, teams, or organizations, and perhaps this difference is impacted by the spiritual maturity of the team and organization. Entities of every size ought to determine their risk attitudes in general and towards specific, high-impact risks.

Figure 12 shows the scale of risk attitudes from opposed to risk savviness.

Figure 12: Risk Attitude Scale

| Opposed | Annoyed | Naïve | Illiterate | Aversion | Obtuse | Tolerant | Literate | Savvy |

◄──────────────── Risk Attitude ────────────────►

© 2022 Neal & Anna Hampton

Merriam Webster defines the following terms:

- Opposed: unfavorable towards; contrary to
- Annoyed: the feeling of being slightly angry
- Naïve: deficient in worldly wisdom or informed judgment
- Illiterate: showing a remarkable lack of acquaintance with the fundamentals of a particular field of knowledge
- Aversion: tendency to avoid
- Obtuse: the quality of being slow to understand; unwilling to try to understand
- Tolerant: marked by forbearance or endurance
- Literate: educated, having knowledge or competence
- Savvy: having or showing perception, comprehension, or shrewdness, especially in practical matters; practical know-how

With this range of attitudes within a system, even a vast system, it seems prudent to develop a risk-literate culture. We *develop* risk literacy before *becoming* risk savvy, so what is risk literacy? A researched-based definition is: "Risk literacy refers to one's practical ability to evaluate and understand risk in the service of skilled and informed decision-making."[5] I would suggest that for witness risk, risk literacy is the basic knowledge required to assess various witness risks and mitigate them based on a mature discernment of Holy Spirit-led stewardship.

> Risk literacy is the basic knowledge required to assess various witness risks and mitigate them based on a mature discernment of Holy Spirit-led stewardship.

"In many ways, our ability to understand risk depends on external factors like" how risk is framed and communicated as well as our risk perception. "In other ways, risk literacy depends on specific skills and abilities."[6] These include understanding probabilities, risk-savvy decision-making, knowing how to do risk assessment and management, having an articulated theology of risk, and additional skills addressed in this book. Risk literacy includes skilled and informed decision-making, which incorporates awareness of the types of thinking and their impact on our risk perception discussed in previous chapters. "Risk literacy promotes skilled and informed decision-making by helping people understand and evaluate risk and reward [with Christo-centric ethics.]"[7] The following sections in this chapter address developing a risk-savvy culture in all types and sizes of systems.

A brief note on systems: in this chapter, I use "system" interchangeably with "organization." Systems are entities like a family, the postal system, a government, a team, a church, or an organization. A system can be any size, but systems thinking is a prerequisite to organizational resiliency in chaos and for agility in risk and persecution.

When risk is high and persecution is likely, a crisis will probably occur. Supplying all participants within the system with the necessary knowledge and training to perform well when a crisis comes is part of creating a resilient system.[8]

Systems Thinking and Agile Cultures

A system is a collection of connected parts that create a new whole that can do things that the individual parts could not do alone. System science investigates how systems connect and disconnect. Science mostly focuses on breaking things down into smaller and smaller categories until it can understand all the bits. Systems thinking, or "systems wisdom," is a

---

5 Allen, "What Is Risk Literacy."
6 Allen.
7 Allen.
8 Mercer, "Crisis Leadership Lessons."

fundamentally different way of viewing life, studying how systems connect and disconnect, including living systems. "Peter Senge and his book *The Fifth Discipline* is the best-known systems thinker in the field of organizational development."[9] Systems wisdom steps back to see the bigger picture and how the parts and whole work together. It helps explain much about the world that mainstream science cannot. Systems can be obvious or simple, complicated, chaotic, or complex. Even chaotic ones can have predictability.[10]

> Systems thinking involves an enhanced ability to hold the one and the many in one's mind at the same time and to perceive the interrelatedness. This capacity requires a level of comfort with not knowing, with uncertainty as opposed to certainty. Pressure, anxiety, and fear do not go well with systems thinking. They dumb down this ability to perceive interrelatedness, and to attend to one's more subtle sense perceptions.[11]

"Systems thinking is a way to look holistically at how distinct components are related and how, when combined, they create a particular outcome. Systems thinking helps people make sense of complex phenomena."[12]

There are three general ways to apply systems thinking.[13] First is looking at how people and policies interact within the system—what are the subtle feedback loops and unintended consequences of policies. This could mean creating a way to gather staff input without fear of consequences if they speak directly. The second area is the mental models—assumptions, biases, and faulty reasoning. Frequently asking "why" without feeling threatened helps reveal blind spots and assumptions in the risk assessment. It also provides clarity and uncovers biased thinking. What risks and crisis events are not an issue for your particular system? How do people within the system respond to pushback?[14] And thirdly, systems thinking allows for the ability to make decisions at the lowest possible level, rather than a decision that is best for the global system. This practice increases the speed of decisions, raises morale, and results in better-quality decisions.

To practically apply systems thinking in risk and persecution, it is first vital to anticipate the often competing values that impact decision-making under severe pressure with little time to reflect and evaluate. Systems thinking and prioritizing competing values are core skills necessary to create an agile culture resilient to hazardous and volatile situations. Organizations

---

9 Systems Thinking Marin, "What Is Systems Thinking?"
10 MacGill, *From Violence to Love.*
11 Systems Thinking Marin, "What Is Systems Thinking?"
12 Murphy, "What Is Systems Thinking?"
13 Large Scale Scrum-LESS, "Systems Thinking."
14 Mercer, "Crisis Leadership."

may want to diagnose their organizational culture by evaluating themselves as described by the competing values framework.[15]

Another practical application of systems thinking means not micromanaging teams from the sending headquarters on the other side of the world, whether in terms of benchmarks or thresholds for departure or return. For example, one organization required the banks to be open before staff returned. Twenty years later, the banks still have not opened, and the team has not returned. The organizational mitigation allowed for no creativity in how money was carried into the country and set a non-negotiable benchmark for return. Even though the team felt called to return to that place, they were not allowed to. The result was that those field staff did not fully disclose information in their next place of service or creatively concealed reality so as not to be required to leave by the headquarters on the other side of the world. Systems thinking would ask hard questions about this mitigation requirement and ask questions like,

- Whose voices were heard in the agenda-setting?
- Why was having banks opened set as a standard of normalization?
- Who made this decision, and did they consult with people on the ground before making the decision?
- Did the decision-makers consider their own risk biases?
- What other factors, if any, were considered about what "normal" life is like there?
- What if the banks never open?

A systems approach empowers people to speak up and give input into how their portion of the system is affected and "is a way to check that we analyze the answers to these questions."[16] Systems thinking recognizes the limitations inherent within the system and creates a culture of openness to discuss those. It is a wise practice to make mental health discussions part of the normal conversation within a system and to ensure that any feedback surveys post-trip or post-term include logistics and feedback on mental health and psychological experience.[17] If Peter Scazzero's book, *Emotionally Healthy Spirituality: It's impossible to be spiritually mature while remaining emotionally immature*, were applied to systems thinking, what would be the spiritual and emotional maturity of the systems we are in? We are limited by our sins, shortcomings, self-reflection, and level of differentiation.

---

15 Cameron and McQuinn, *Diagnosing and Changing*, 31–59.
16 Murphy, "What Is Systems Thinking?"
17 Lewis, Ferragamo, Yarker, Donaldson-Feilder, "Keeping International Business Travelers."

RMT before CMT in VUCA

These acronyms mean Risk Management Team (RMT) Before a Crisis Management Team (CMT) in a Volatile, Uncertain, Complex, and Ambiguous situation (VUCA). What is a VUCA environment? In a world of globalization, digitization, terrorism, technological advances, and mass migration (refugee movements), the VUCA environment is subject to quick, constant change and countless interactions that are challenging to predict.

Volatility means instability. It means things are changing faster than we can respond. It requires accelerated decision-making. Leaders may feel overwhelmed, stressed, anxious, and unprepared to lead effectively. Uncertainty implies the inability to predict what is happening now and what will happen next. There is the nagging feeling of lack of information to make the best-informed decision. There's a lot of "noise," not enough time, and the inability to see how things are related. Complex environments often have competing values, interrelated issues, too little time to reflect and see the macro picture, and the temptation to mitigate symptoms but not the actual problem. Ambiguity means struggling to clarify the meaning of events and their impact. It is a situation with a high risk of misinterpreting events; it is a confusing reality, making it hard to see the cause-effect relationships within the environment.

In a VUCA situation, several of the people you want to have on the CMT first form the RMT before any crisis. They engage in risk assessment and management and monitor the situation in a risk environment. The core of the RMT becomes the CMT once a crisis of any type occurs. Ninety percent of crisis response occurs before the crisis.[18] At that point, the team or organizational crisis management plan is implemented. There is no time lag between when the situation occurs, and the CMT meets to begin working as a team even as applicable additions/subtractions of team personnel are made to the CMT. Judicious consideration must be applied to deciding which staff members transition from the RMT to the CMT. It is beneficial to have CMT members who are fully aware of the actors involved, have situational awareness, and can immediately engage in mitigating risks while managing the crisis. Reaction time is a significant factor in influencing the positive outcome of risk events. A quick response in a crisis limits the negative impact of the crisis and capitalizes on the potential of eternal gain which may result from the crisis.

---

18 Mercer, "Crisis Leadership."

Still, two problems commonly occur when all of the people on the RMT become the CMT.[19] The personality that does well on an RMT may not automatically do well on the CMT, but the reverse is also true. People who perform very well in a security assessment and contingency planning role may not have the emotional stamina or ability to function under significant stress in dealing with a crisis resolution process. Conversely, those who reliably function in managing a crisis on the CMT sometimes perform poorly in an RMT role. Team collaboration, analysis, planning, and advising may not be strong values or talents they possess.

A second concern involves handling of risk management duties if the RMT become the CMT. In situations where a crisis occurs, those in leadership and risk management roles understandably focus on the problem. If other risks are not monitored, however, another situation could develop that is worse than the initial one. In some situations, a crisis event may require a manageable degree of attention and resourcing. It would be ideal if the CMT could continue to monitor new risks and threats while also managing the crisis; however, this is frequently more than they can handle (especially in long-term and consuming crises like kidnapping events). In most true crises, this ongoing risk management is beyond the capability of those participating in a CMT. Having to manage all the tasks of the RMT and CMT could be too distracting to address either one well. The organization will have to quickly bring additional help to the RMT side as the CMT handles the current crisis.

Organizations need to be savvy in assessing the skills, talents, and abilities of staff that can be available for an RMT or CMT and provide appropriate training to a broader range of staff than those who might currently be in those roles, so that additional people are prepared to take up those roles when needed. As mentioned in chapter seven, the RMT and CMT ideally are comprised of men and women with the right personalities for these tasks. Better risk and crisis management occur when we include various voices from different cultural backgrounds.

An RMT's purpose is to do a systematic risk assessment and mitigation process. Risk management is both preventative and reactive, but it's better to prevent a crisis than to manage one. To summarize, this process begins with addressing a risk event itself, then considering what might cause that event to occur (consider all causes, asking three deep questions for each cause). It is followed by assessing all potential consequences (positive and negative) if the event occurred. After that, comprehensive risk management strategies are

---

19 Private correspondence and conversations with the author. Al Williams, SIL, contributed heavily to the discussion on topics within this chapter and on the Systems Risk Audit.

formed and implemented. The RMT develops strategies to manage multiple risk events. Individual and organizational risk perception impacts risk agility and decision-making at any stage within this process.

Short-term solutions must be rejected if they do not support the long-term goal. There are several approaches an RMT will want to keep in mind regarding their role and decision-making. First, risk flexibility means using one technique for various risk events and discarding it when it no longer has significant value. Risk mitigation adjusts flexibly as risk assessment changes.

Second, increased vigilance is beneficial for mitigating many of the risks. Perhaps a specific risk mitigation technique performed daily reminds one to remain attentive to the variety of threats in that environment (an evening check-in, for example). In that environment, a basic rule is not to relax or become numb to the appropriate level of vigilance; all team members require alertness and continual situational awareness.

Third, risk mitigation options should never be viewed as an "either/or" dilemma. Instead, redundancy in risk management is desirable. A simple example: "Would I rather have the lock on my gate or on the front door?" I'd rather buy two locks (which we did). It may be unacceptable to consider one risk mitigation technique as the only dependable one.

Fourth, mitigation efforts that are too costly with only minimal benefit should be abandoned. Costs of mitigation are not just financial, and "cost" includes stewardship of all aspects of risk. If the risk mitigation technique requires excessive energy, annoying personal interruption, expensive infrastructure, cumbersome processes, etc., and the benefit is proportionally nil, it is wise to discontinue the practice. Again, this practice speaks to the risk flexibility above.

Finally, in high-risk, complex environments, risk agility is critical. Risk mitigation should be scalable to the dynamic risk environment, referred to as risk agility. A community's mitigation approaches are boosted with staff buy-in. Buy-in is not the same as agreement but is more reflective of general confidence in decision-making. When buy-in does not exist, the associated group accountability may deteriorate, or worse—some may opt to undermine the mitigation efforts.

In a deteriorating situation, when what we are concerned about (risk) happens (crisis), and the CMT moves into action, it feels like everything that can go wrong usually does, and unforeseen adverse

> In high-risk, complex environments, risk agility is critical.

events occur. Crisis preparation allows for adaptable procedures and plans as the crisis unfolds.

What about the culture of the system in a VUCA environment? VUCA environments require leaders to put people first. The soft skills of leadership are primary.[20] Six key competencies characterize any risk savvy system, and these attitudes and skills should be developed throughout the organization and team.[21]

1. A Learning System: Organizational cultures that cultivate learning are more likely to avoid blind spots that make them vulnerable. Learning happens through reflecting on experiences, reading, and being open to pollination by ideas different from the tradition.

2. Alignment: People understanding the system's mission, vision, and goals when there are deep connections across all system levels. Making meaningful relationships takes time to develop trust, and trust is created differently in different cultures, as discussed previously.

3. Agility and Redundancy: Handling change in an uncertain environment and risk requires responding to the unique opportunities in danger. However, people and systems can only handle so much uncertainty and transition. This is a crucial area for leadership to pay attention to, especially in risk environments. Agility should be considered in at least three areas: context-setting agility is being able to scan the environment, frame the initiatives needed, and clarify desired outcomes. Redundancy of options means having an agile response when one option becomes unavailable.

4. Adaptability: Being adaptable, flexible, and learning over time, is easier for some than others. Becoming adaptable requires a cyclical habit of reflection and action, followed by review that provides the necessary perspective to adjust and change to better adapt the next time. Organizational and individual ritualized resilience habits and increasing self-awareness and self-management skills are critical to developing adaptability.

5. Clarity: Being able to see through the confusion and provide the vision that inspires everyone is a significant individual task, not just a leadership task. Reminding ourselves of our calling and how God has led in the past helps provide clarity in the confusion.

---

20 Rohei, "Leadership Competencies that Matter."
21 Lewis and Bywater, "Leadership."

6. Integration and Connectedness: Embracing diverse perspectives and bridging differences allows for creative innovation. It uses the knowledge and experience of everyone to create something more significant.

Risk Vulnerability: Fighter Jets and Rocks

A friend of mine shared about the research he did as a young college intern working for the US Air Force before he became a global worker and then a member care specialist.[22] One of the projects he worked on was researching why the F-4 Phantom fighter jet and AC-130 Gunship were vulnerable to ground fire during the Vietnam War. The high number of F-4 losses during the war was alarming to the US Air Force. A cartoon in his office showed a Vietcong soldier throwing a rock at an F-4 and bringing down a jet (valued at approximately $15 million in today's estimation).

He explained, "No aircraft is perfect in design nor free from operational malfunctions or pilot error … and placed in a war theater, the added vulnerability from receiving live-fire makes it all the more susceptible to loss of aircraft." A detailed questionnaire was developed to assess which parts of the airplane were most vulnerable to certain types of hits and which parts could take a hit, but the aircraft could still survive and return to base.

As a result, a number of mitigation strategies were employed to reduce airplane vulnerabilities. A senior engineer wrote a paper to the Pentagon proposing to reroute important hydraulic and utility lines to avoid confluence of the lines. In other words, critical systems that had been bundled together in one spot were separated and rerouted in a way that did not impact the center of gravity of the airplane (which could negatively impact the agility, flight, and performance) and thereby improving survivability. Redundancy was built in wherever possible. Some systems were determined to require armor plating to defend against shrapnel.[23] Aircraft combat survivability is a well-developed discipline within the US military establishment.[24]

There are at least two organizationally significant applications: (1) your survivability is directly established by a clear, sober, and honest knowledge of your vulnerabilities; and (2) knowing your vulnerabilities and making modifications based on facts and not feelings is the key to survival.

---

22 Friend with 47 years of cross-cultural experience.
23 Friend with 47 years of cross-cultural experience.
24 Ball, *Fundamentals of Aircraft Combat*, xxviii.

Survivability is measured by probability, but inherent in probability is some level of uncertainty and unpredictability.[25] Many variables influence whether people survive ministering in hostile situations. In witness risk, survivability is defined as more than just physically surviving through some danger, but also the ability to remain functional in all areas and continue on mission. In terms of witness risk, vulnerability is how susceptible to a threat or a harm such that a person or project is hindered or unable to minister effectively or in an extreme case, cannot recover.

Both individuals and the system as a whole have vulnerabilities. One case study exemplifies how a Christian sending organization's goals in a region were not met. The organization placed a high value on maintaining a presence in an established location. The team was operating in a severe high-risk environment with extremely dangerous stressors. The team leader had no secure communication device or code word or phrase to communicate an emergency, and a hostile government monitored all cell phone communication. Because of his gospel witness, the worst kind of threats were issued to him about his wife and children, and he knew similar violence had occurred to a local whose body was found in the nearby river.

Due to their vulnerability and the extreme threats, he chose to self-evacuate his family and the other two units on the team. His organization responded over email that he had failed his assignment and then terminated him without warning via email. They never met with him face-to-face from the period of his evacuation to his termination and did not engage in relational resolution. They viewed the gospel worker's decision to self-evacuate not just as a lapse in judgment but as a mistake worthy of ending their service.

Institutional responses to risk challenges that punish people for making risk assessment decisions on the ground create a system culture where people become afraid to speak up, thereby increasing the danger and potential for the unnecessary loss of life. Organizational feedback on risk would help the system become aware of potential systemic errors that may lead to individual, team, and corporate failures.

System Risk Audit

A system risk audit (also known as an "after action report") enables the organization to analyze how well risk assessment and management were implemented to assess survivability and vulnerability within witness risk. This tool is different from a post-crisis evaluation, although a post-crisis tool that already exists within an organization could be adapted for a system risk audit as well. The primary point is to not miss an opportunity to improve

---

25 Ball, xxviii.

organizational preparedness and resiliency by implementing a system risk audit, not just a post-crisis audit. A system risk audit is initiated when the risk has passed (or greatly diminished).

"A feedback loop exists where a situation is sensed (input), and a response is initiated (output), changing the situation, so there is now a new situation to sense and make sense of."[26] A system-wide risk audit is the feedback loop examining how well the risk assessment and management (RAM) plan went, what failures occurred in the plan, and what changes should be made.[27] The audit should explore the entire process from pre-field training and preparation to end-of-risk experience (whatever the determined "endpoint" is).

A risk audit is a step-by-step approach for identifying all the strengths of what went right as well as possible failures or lack of planning in the risk assessment and management process. Failures are any errors, especially ones that negatively affect the team. The audit examines the consequences of those failures. It prioritizes them according to the intensity of negative impact on the system's people, project, and purpose, and how frequently errors occur. A risk audit has to account for the workplace, security, and child-safety standards and the legal ramifications if organizational guidelines are not followed.

The purpose of the risk audit is to take actions to eliminate or reduce blind spots, starting with the highest-priority ones. It is essential to document current knowledge and activities about the failures and risks of continued failure for use in continuous improvement. A risk management plan includes the risk audit as part of the overall plan. The audit should occur at a reasonable time when staff are no longer at risk or in crisis and have the emotional, physical, and mental capacity to engage meaningfully in the system-wide audit.

Several cautions about a system risk audit: (1) it cannot be overemphasized that a system-wide risk audit is not a staff debriefing; (2) it is not an evaluation of how well personnel did in the risk or crisis; and (3) an audit is particularly susceptible to hindsight bias (the conviction that one should have known or performed better. A risk audit requires humility to honestly evaluate what went well, what didn't, and how plans can be improved for future risk scenarios. "What cannot be talked about cannot be put to rest."[28] The following is a list of questions to consider, adapt, and add to for implementing a system risk audit that is helpful for each context.

---

26 MacGill, *From Violence to Love*.
27 ASQ, "Failure Mode and Effects."
28 Levinson, *Gated Grief*, 2.

System Risk Audit Questions

- Were our people prepared well enough?
- What additional training do they need?
- What went well?
- What organizational vulnerabilities or blind spots do we have? (Ask your field people and make sure to include the spouses, using an anonymous survey tool.)
- Do we follow our written, published policies, or are they in reality "suggestions and optional?"
- How well did organizational departments work together? What needs to be celebrated? What needs to improve?
- Do we have folks ready to deploy or sufficiently tapped into a network of people who can provide trauma debriefing/Critical Incident Stress Debriefing (CISD)?
- What was the impact of stress on the system?
- How much risk were/are we willing to accept?
- How did we incorporate input from locals who are part of the project/church plant into the decision-making process?
- How was social media handled with our team on the ground (including teenagers on the team), across the organization, and with our partners back home?
- What else needs to change?
- Who on the team is doing damage during increasing stress and risk and may need to be invited to move on from our organization?
- What do our people tell their supporters about leaving the field?
- How do we help the spiritual and cognitive dissonance with our people who announced that they were ready to die for Christ, but when it came time to decide to stay or go, they chose to go?
- How do we help them prepare their narrative for their sending partners?
- How do perceptional aspects, like fear or prejudice influence risk judgments and decisions on our team/organization?
- Assessment Analysis: How well is the risk assessment working? What have the consequences of our actions and policies been?
- Was the level of risk assessment and staff oversight appropriate?

- Were staff equipped to make their own decisions?
- What were the failures in communication? Were leaders out of the country and out of contact at inopportune times?
- When staff cannot self-evacuate and need leadership to step in and tell them to evacuate, what is the stress point?
- How might we do better? What should we try to do next, and for how long?
- Who needs follow-up, recognition, and thanking?
- When should we stop inviting input and instead commit to policy?
- How did this risk event/experience impact our organizational mission/values/project?
- How does the project strategy or focus need to change?
- What spiritual lessons have we learned?
- What else needs to be asked?

Systems that engage in the "business as usual" approach are so focused on the task that they often do not recognize the changing risk or increasing threats. This attitude is thinking short-term instead of prioritizing a long-range goal or vision. For example, Christ did not heal all but walked away from a threatening crowd. He had a long-term vision that balanced his tasks with the threat level.

Duty-of-care issues multiply in complexity during evacuation from a risk environment. Additional factors to account for require thoughtful, careful discussion. Here are some of the complex questions:

- If people are told that they can leave when they do not feel comfortable, how is the commitment and responsibility to the team and project accounted for?
- What about the perceived opinion of host-country friends and colleagues about people evacuating?
- If more experienced team members leave, what is the impact on less-experienced team members carrying on the project?
- How do we manage conflicting understanding of acceptable risk—those willing to die when staying?
- Leadership in-country and organizational leadership outside of the country: What if the critical security person in the host country has a conflict with the executive director and then quits?

- What about the planning and preparation of local staff? How are we helping them prepare for the threat?
- How well are we listening to and acting on the opinion and advice of local staff and trusted locals?
- How much dependence should we have on secular security reports?
- What level of connectedness and participation should we have with other leaders' commitment to our projects when risk increases?

There are at least five reasons why organizations do not engage in assessing what went wrong and how they can improve: (1) it's hard to admit failure; (2) the organization does not have a learning culture; (3) the organizational leaders are led more by their egos and less by their identity as a servant of Christ; (4) lack of knowledge and training; (5) prioritizing other values over risk assessment and management.

> With courage comes the essential virtue of doing the right thing at the right place at the right time. When we live with courage, we also recognize failure [including failure of courage] and admit it. And when we embrace our failures, we put all things good and bad on the table, and we take lessons from the experiences, receive knowledge, and turn it into wisdom. If we don't address our failures, fear sets in for the next time, and the issue rears its ugly head [repeatedly]. You have courage when you care about the outcomes that impact others, not just yourself.[29]

In God's sovereignty, he sometimes provides what is needed in times of crisis despite our lack of planning and preparedness. Things worked out. But there is a myth repeated within the global church that the Bible does not teach. "God's work done in God's way never lacks God's resources." God is well able to provide, and sometimes he does, but not always according to the extent we wish for and think we need. And what happens when our lived experience doesn't match this simplistic, trite myth? Dependence only upon an act of God without taking responsibility to use our minds and the best systems thinking in practical ways to improve our risk approach and crisis response is poor stewardship of the resources entrusted to us. Organizational stewardship includes a thorough system risk audit done with transparency and integrity.

Capitalize on the Liminal Moment

Liminality is a threshold experience. It is "composed of danger, marginality, disorientation, or ordeal and tends to create a space neither here nor there, a transitional stage between what was and what is to come. [It is] a place of

---

29 Ruebusch, "Virtue of Courage."

discomfort and agitation [and] requires us to endure and push into what is to come."[30] When we are in spiritually extreme and urgent situations, we are in the liminal moment.[31]

In terms of thinking organizationally, we see from Israel's history that they were not at their best when they perceived that things were going well. Usually, that's when the prophets were sent to tell them they were sinning and not engaging in righteousness and justice towards the marginalized, the voiceless, and the oppressed. When stability and security were threatened, they turned to God for help and experienced new aspects of his character.

An international SOS research paper revealed the predominant fear in 2022 is the perception that risks are increasing globally, and fears of terrorism dominate travel concerns globally.[32] The perception of the growing dangers of terrorism, disease, and civil unrest are real fears. If threats are increasing in equal and potentially more significant measures, this reality simultaneously implies increased opportunities for kingdom advancement. When people become disoriented about reality, religion, and the nature of God and evil, the liminal moment is when Christ-followers can more easily communicate Christ's love to them.

Rev. Dr. Johnson Asare from Northern Ghana, a man who has taken many risks as a businessman, pastor, Muslim-turned-Christ-follower, and community leader, stated, "It is risky not to take risks. Everything is a risk; not doing anything is a risk. It's up to you."[33] He knows what he is talking about. But risks should be taken with thoughtful care and purpose, not for one's ego, organizational growth, reputation, fundraising, marketing, or competition. As my friend Al says, choose "eyes wide open" risk management, assess the foreseeable risks, and choose wisely which to accept and which to avoid.[34]

The moment of liminality is what developed the people of Israel as a nation, and it is the same for organizations. Our faithfulness is stretched and developed when as a system of any size, we are urgently challenged to respond to desperate situations. This response requires godly, compassionate, and strategic leadership. The impact of poor leaders results in disillusionment, disheartening, and diminishing followers, which weakens courageous responses in others. Next, we turn to the ten mistakes leaders should avoid.

---

30 Frost and Hirsch, *Faith of Leap*, 19.
31 Frost and Hirsch, 47.
32 International SOS, "Travel Risks & Reality."
33 Renita, "Accountable for Risks."
34 Private conversations with Al Williams, SIL.

Chapter 17
Ten Mistakes Leaders Make

> *We don't learn from experience,*
> *we learn by reflecting on experience.*
> —Tod Bolsinger[1]

It is difficult to overemphasize the importance of a leader's impact on the wellbeing, effectiveness, and resilience of communities who are facing risk-induced fear and anxiety. I have observed terrified teams without direction or resolve become motivated and equipped because of the skillful engagement of a risk-savvy leader. Sadly, I have also witnessed the reverse effect: demoralization and increased fear resulting from a leader's inability to adapt well to danger.

Leading teams well in high-risk environments is critically important, but so challenging. Leaders will likely make mistakes—failures are inevitable when learning to navigate unfamiliar territory. It is important to learn from these errors, admit weaknesses, acknowledge how they have impacted others, and gain new skills.

In this chapter, I describe ten common mistakes that leaders make when leading teams in dangerous places.

"When a person travels a few years with an organization, or with a partnership, or any other kind of working association, he leaves a 'wake' behind in these two areas, task and relationship: what did he accomplish and how did he deal with people?"[2]

Not Changing Leadership Style

In my first book, I defined the necessity for organizational leaders to change their leadership style as risk levels increase in their operational environment. A failure to make the adjustment from a participatory to a directive leadership style is one of the common mistakes I observe leaders make.

As I have consulted with team leaders experiencing obstacles transitioning to a more directive leadership posture, I've noticed similarities in what they have identified as challenging. Many of these difficulties can be effectively addressed during seasons of low risk, making the shift much more adaptable when threats require it.

---

1 Bolsinger, *Canoeing the Mountains*, 22.
2 Cloud, *Integrity*, 17.

The most crucial groundwork a leader can invest in is trust-building. Directive leadership can feel controlling and callous to team members. When situations require a leader to be more authoritative, it is essential to have high levels of trust to draw upon.

> The most crucial groundwork a leader can invest in is trust-building.

Communicating ahead of time that risk decision-making will be directive is also helpful, particularly for leaders and organizations accustomed to consensus or participatory decision-making practices. Defining a change in leadership style in organizational security documents and contingency plans is one way to convey a reasonable expectation of this shift to team members.

Leaders should also remember that a directive leadership posture does not mean input is unwelcome, nor does it require a leader to be indifferent toward team members. On the contrary, skilled leaders will communicate security decisions with a willingness to incorporate new ideas and an understanding of how security procedures are impacting the staff.

Carrying the Load of Direct Risk Management

Risk management is laborious, and it requires an elevated attention to detail and a concentrated focus. When a leader neglects to distribute that responsibility, she often pays a high personal and professional price. Many of the routine administrative duties suffer along with demanding security management responsibilities when leaders hold tightly to both assignments.

It is wise to have skilled security personnel tasked with assessing and managing risk, particularly in environments where risks are high. Although it may be practical for those responsibilities to be managed by just one skilled person, it is often advantageous to have a team of people engaged in the various functions of thorough risk management. These functions often include communications, security consulting, personnel care, contingency development and implementation, threat assessment, tracking, and intelligence processing.

It is important, of course, that a leader remain aware and engaged in the endeavors of the risk management team. Regular briefings and opportunities for leaders to give input must be integrated into the composition of the risk management team. However, it would be a mistake for the leader to also hold a leadership position on the risk management team.

Not Adequately Investing in Preparation

Most ministry teams are staffed with highly motivated and remarkably competent people. It takes strength, purpose, and the ability to accept the calling to be a witness, especially across cultures. However, those essential skills and enthusiasm do little to prepare staff for issues related to security. When a leader neglects to sensitize his team to risks or fails to develop their competencies to manage threats well, he may potentially be placing them in danger.

Sometimes leaders rely upon team members' qualities of adaptability and self-learning to handle risk sufficiently. However, these cultural adaptation traits do not automatically transfer to the world of risk and persecution. In fact, it is unusual for personnel to perform higher than the level for which they have been equipped to manage risk and crisis, and those skills are rarely obtained in the heat of the moment.

Leaders must prioritize risk management for staff operating in elevated risk environments as well as in regions assessed as having relatively minimal risk. In the workshops that Neal and I facilitate globally, we often gather participants from many diverse locations, fields of service, and vocations. One of the exercises we task participants with involves creating mitigation strategies for preventing and managing car accidents. We are encouraged by how often people comment about the benefits of investing in this preparation activity. A leader will never regret investing in the critical work of security preparation.

Allowing Toxic Team Members to Remain on the Team

Operating in a team of people committed to being a witness for Jesus Christ is no guarantee that the community will not include challenging people. (A cursory study of Paul's epistles will reveal that it has always been so.) We are all under construction, and no one behaves rightly all the time. When friction occurs among team members, the Bible provides us with useful tools for forbearing and forgiving one another. It even points us to our example in this endeavor: Jesus himself.

Sometimes though, team members seem to create an extraordinarily high quantity of interpersonal problems. They drain the team of relational energy and frequently express criticism and contempt for others. These types of destructive personnel have sometimes been described as *toxic*. It can be difficult to define the threshold that is crossed when a *challenging* team member becomes a *toxic* one, but one thing is certain—a team leader must protect the team from toxicity.

Jeff Haden, an editor for INC., explained some important facts related to toxic staff. "Adding a superstar to a team," he said, "boosts employee morale by sixteen percent." Recruiting high-performing people to join the team seems to be a useful strategy to employ. Who doesn't want to boost team morale? However, he also added, "removing a toxic employee from a team boosts employee morale by sixty-one percent."[3]

Toxic staff significantly decreases a team's performance under normal circumstances, but the negative impact is profoundly more critical when facing dangerous threats. A toxic person will undermine leadership, create confusion, and cause additional anxiety for a team already wrestling with the challenge of managing a hazardous environment. If there is an unwillingness to incorporate change, address toxicity early and remove toxic team members.

Ineffective Communication

As I've already addressed in this book, fear is heightened by uncertainty. Risk is inherently unclear and causes those impacted by risk to seek clarity and trustworthy sources of information. Leadership often increases ambiguity instead of providing the clarity team members require.

Leaders engage in ineffective communication when they choose words laden with obscurity while describing threats, contingencies, or vulnerabilities impacting the team. A leader must refine her speech to include instructive language whenever possible.

Instead of addressing risk by stating, "We are going to wait and see what happens," or "We're trying to figure out the situation," it is better to say things like, "We will monitor this [*specific trend*] for [*a specific period*] and do [*this specific action*] when [*a benchmark occurs*]." Although a leader may seldom be able to provide answers to every risk question, she can use words that help the team know specifically how risk is being managed.

The confusion of dangerous environments may cause a leader to decrease communication with the team. The thought process is often, "If I cannot determine what is happening or I have no significant information to add, why should I waste time communicating?" Although the impulse to reduce communication is understandable, it has a negative impact on the team and considerably reduces their resilience.

---

3 Haden, "The 5 New Habits."

Holding Too Many Meetings

While it is essential for leaders to increase communication during seasons of increasing danger, that does not necessarily mean leaders should hold more meetings with their team. Expedient communication methods (such as text messaging or email) are often more helpful and better received by team members.

Many team members indicate that security meetings feel "inefficient" or like a "waste of time." This perception is especially true on teams where meetings are typically considered occasions for idea generation and problem-solving. The pragmatic provision of security procedures and clear updates regarding risk assessments can feel restrictive to team members accustomed to exercises in consensus building. Increase communication during higher levels of risk, but hold fewer meetings, not more.

Continuing at a Pre-Risk Pace

Any leader who assumes the productivity output from normal periods of operation can continue during times of elevated risk is flirting with exhausting the team's reserves. Properly assessing and managing risk takes energy and resources. Sound stewardship principles are required to manage those resources well.

It is reasonable for a leader to depend upon a higher-than-normal level of output following a risk event. Margins created for situations like that as well as the focus and adrenaline that normally accompany crisis can assist teams while they manage their response. However, leaders can tend to inaccurately evaluate a team's ability to return to normal levels of stress after the event.

The illustration below demonstrates how the normalization period does not necessarily mean a return to normal stress levels after the intensity of a risk event has subsided. Instead, a "new normal" sets in. Teams who operate in environments that experience multiple risk events run the risk of unknowingly elevating the overall stress levels, leaving team members vulnerable.[4] The following graphic shows the normalization of escalating stress, leading potentially to burnout.

---

4 Gardner, "Escalating Stress Events."

Figure 13: Impact of Stress[5]

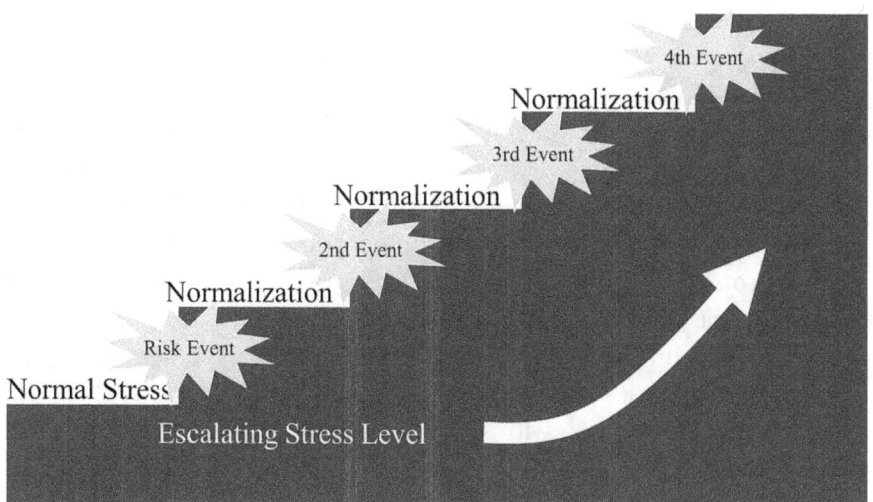

Team leaders play an essential role in setting the pace for their team. When a leader demonstrates a high value for rest and implementing restorative practices, team members are empowered to engage in their own self-care and workload moderation. Leaders who do this well will lead healthier teams that are better prepared to manage the next crisis when it comes.

Neglecting to Emphasize Worship

Risk is a meaningful opportunity for worship. We risk because our Savior is worthy, and we sacrifice because Jesus modeled for us a life of sacrifice. Leaders who point their teams toward worship encourage team members toward spiritual inspiration and a more meaningful connection to their service.

> We risk because our Savior is worthy, and we sacrifice because Jesus modeled for us a life of sacrifice.

Leaders who minimize the suffering associated with potential loss or compare one person's loss to another apparently superior sacrifice create obstacles to worship. Ignoring or diminishing pain does not help someone overcome it as much as giving it meaning and purpose empowers a person to endure it.

---

5 Used with permission from Dr. Laura Mae Gardner.

Weak Personnel Selection Practices

The standards utilized by organizations to select personnel are many and varied. Some teams follow a laborious and detailed candidacy with many steps and requirements. In contrast, others appear to follow no clear methodology whatsoever—members somehow migrate into the community via undetermined means. However, regardless of the structure (or lack thereof), leaders regularly fail to address risk in the selection process.

Not addressing the possibility of coping with risk and persecution may wrongly convey that there is only negligible danger encountered while working in the team's cultural context. Additionally, new staff may assume that the team is unprepared or ill-equipped to manage risk (something that significantly decreases their risk endurance). The most vulnerable team members (those unfamiliar with the risk realities of their environment) often arrive with unrealistic expectations about environmental challenges and are untrained in dealing with them.

Feeling apprehensive about discussing risk with potential staff is understandable. Hudson Taylor wrote about his reluctance to do so from China in the second half of the nineteenth century: "I feared that in the midst of the dangers, difficulties, and trials which would necessarily be connected with such a work, some who were comparatively inexperienced Christians might break down and bitterly reproach me for having encouraged them to undertake an enterprise for which they were unequal."[6]

Like Taylor generations ago, leaders must overcome their fear of tackling risk and danger issues during the initial phase of accepting new team members. In the process of addressing risk, leaders should keep in mind that the most crucial factor in selecting staff is not whether potential team members are aware and equipped but that God has called them. A leader is not selecting the most competent team member but should recognize God's selection.

Trusting In, Clinging To, and Relying Upon Things Other than God

A leader's most vital resource to steward risk and persecution well comes from God himself. Trusting in his promise to be with us always (Matt 28:20), clinging to the help he gives (Isa 41:10), and relying upon the Holy Spirit's comfort and intercession (Rom 8:26) are assurances a leader can count upon. Investing in risk management best practices is essential, but an over-focus on those tools can often remove God from his place as a leader's chief source of confidence.

---

6 Taylor, *Perspectives of the World*, 319.

Our fixation on collecting newer and better risk management tools and resources may even be rooted in a cultural myth that Edwin Friedman describes in his book *A Failure of Nerve*. He illustrates this self-limiting belief in this way: "The great myth of our data-gathering era … has two sides, 'If only we knew enough, we could do (or fix) anything' and its obverse, 'If we failed, it is because we did not use the right method.'"[7]

No amount of security information, risk response, or specialty training can safeguard teams working in high-risk places. Wrongly fixating on those, might woo a leader into a weak witnessing paradigm, where dependence is on personal skills, assumptions, and intelligence rather than our Savior.

---

7 Friedman, *Failure of Nerve*, 143.

Chapter 18
It's Time to Member Care Job's Wife

And I will give you shepherds after my own heart, who will feed you with knowledge and understanding.[1]
—God

What would you say if a woman came to you and told you her husband has a life-threatening and potentially contagious disease? His disease instills deep fear in others, so he quarantines away from society, and she risks her own life by caring for him. Does this story sound strangely familiar in the era of COVID-19?

What if she continued to tell you that all her adult children (her primary life's work) were recently killed in a freak accident, and all their wealth was destroyed the same day? She is now penniless, childless, and alone, trying to survive economic hardship without her husband. Applying responsible member care principles to her:

- How would you respond in a pastoral way to her?
- How would you express empathy to her?
- How would you grieve with her? Would you show her the grief curve?
- Would you administer the CernySmith Stress Assessment (CSA)?
- Would you give her a "Critical Incident Stress Debrief"?
- Is there a verse that comes to mind that you think would "fix" her?
- Would you tell her she is sinning by saying she'd prefer death?
- Would you suggest some marriage counseling to her?
- The American Bible Society Trauma Healing Institute puts out a little booklet on healing from trauma wounds. How would you provide spiritual or psychological first aid to her?

Job's wife is *always* used as an example of how to not go through suffering.[2] However, the Bible never condemns her, but Christians, preachers, and even member care professionals often seem to. I've never heard a single positive sermon on Job's wife in over five decades of going to church.

---

1 Jer 3:15.

2 I purposely use the superlative "always." In over fifty-three years of going to church, I've never heard her used as a good example.

- The global church holds her up as an example of a woman without faith.
- She is scorned in all the artists' renderings.
- She is called "Devil's Assistant." (Augustine)
- She is called "Satan's tool." (John Calvin)
- "Satan spared her precisely to use her against Job." (Thomas Aquinas and John Chrystosome)

A simple search on Google reveals Christian pop culture stating she was "angry, bitter, and wrong," "She got off easy," or "Let's not be like her."

Why did they all say this?

Because it looks like she told her husband to curse God and die. Her character has been evaluated, unjustly marginalized, and condemned as a failure by one statement she made during the deepest pain of her life.

Authenticity in Suffering

In all the loss of friends we faced in Afghanistan—over twenty foreigners martyred in about six years—in the extensive pain and loss I've experienced over the last two decades, and through the continual grief that seems never-ending, I've spent the last ten years meditating specifically on Job's wife. I'm beginning to believe that she sets a good example of authenticity in suffering.

What if we examine her through the pastoral care lens of needing both grief counseling and a Critical Incident Stress Debriefing (CISD)? Would any of us feel differently about her?

Let's first examine the background of her story before discussing what she said. She and her husband were apparently at the empty-nester stage of life. They could sit back and enjoy their older age because their children were now adults. They held the highest of all honors in a shame and honor culture. They were like royalty. Her husband was "the greatest of all the men in the East" (Job 1:3) which meant he held the highest respect of all peoples. Thus she also commanded a sizeable amount of respect. She was the "First Lady" of the greatest, wealthiest, most respected known man.[3]

People listened to her, people wanted her wisdom and her favor. She was never lacking friends. She had reached the pinnacle of what was possible for a woman of her day. She had it all: wonderful adult children who we can presume were on their way to providing grandchildren and a fabulous godly husband who was the wealthiest in all the land.

---

3 Scholtz, "I Had Heard," 819–39.

But on one horrible day, she and Job lost all their wealth. Simultaneously, all but one of their staff, managers, and servants were murdered. These were people she knew and loved and whose well-being was tied to hers. They were a significant part of her community. Job and his wife didn't only go bankrupt and lose part of their community. The unthinkable happened on that same tragic day—all ten of their adult children were killed by a storm.

How would you respond if you lost all your children in one day? Can you imagine the funeral of ten adult children? She and her husband began grieving unimaginable grief, the kind that a parent never totally recovers from. When a child dies before the parent, the parent is left with a haunting image of what that child would look like on each birthday, each holiday, and how that child would be in each year of adulthood. On one day, she and Job had to begin accepting that they would never see their daughters marry, they would never hold grandchildren in their arms.

Wealth is one thing—it can be replaced. But a child? It's too unfathomable to imagine the pain of losing all her children in one day. In all that catastrophic loss, she and her husband did not sin or complain.

But it got worse.

Her beloved husband was stricken with a disease with no known cure that made him unclean. Ancient law required him to go and live where the lepers lived, where he could scrape his skin with broken pottery.

For all practical daily life, she lost the last person she loved, who loved her. She lost her protector and provider. His was a living death, from which recovery was most likely impossible. Not only that, but in a shame and honor culture, all who once courted her favor now viewed her with guilt by association. Job must have done something wrong, some sin, implicating her.

They lost not just wealth, not just children, not just the joy and intimacy of married life together, but all social standing, their reputation, and what's more, they bore the public shame of what was interpreted as religious hypocrisy due to all the disaster that had befallen him. Their losses went far beyond death and were unending. Life had become a horror show and hope had died. Furthermore, in the Ancient Near East (ANE), a woman's ability to earn a living was practically non-existent, so she had no way or at most limited (righteous) methods of providing for herself.

Where's the compassion for this woman? Where's the pastoral heart reaching out to care for this woman, grieve with her, listen to her anger at God, at her husband, at life and death? I've listened to member care leaders use Job's wife as an example of how not to respond to one suffering (i.e. Job), as if SHE weren't suffering. I'm aghast at the callousness of those who so glibly condemn her without a thought to her pain and loss. She watched her beloved suffer, and her heart cried out, "God, let him die." It's too awful. Anyone who has seen a loved one live or die through the horror of radiation and chemotherapy understands this request. Seeing your loved one in physical distress and pain is unbearable.

She didn't spiritualize, and she didn't pretend to be happy. The Bible records an authentic, pain-filled response. She spoke what was in her heart-filled-with-pain, and she told Job either to "curse God and die" or to "bless God and die." Which did she say? In Hebrew, there is only one word for bless "*barak*", but the two Hebrew words for curse were used by Job in 3:1.[4]

In verse 2:5, Satan uses the Hebrew word "*barak*" but there's a "not" right in front of it. He literally says in Hebrew that Job "won't bless you face to face." But he speaks with an idiomatic manner here, meaning that "Job will curse you face to face." Job himself in chapter 3 uses the two different Hebrew words for "curse," one stronger than the other, as he wishes the day of his birth cursed. So how can we translate this difficult phrase correctly? Did she tell Job to "bless God" or to "curse God and die"? And why is it interpreted as a "curse" when she speaks?

Translators assume that because of Job's response to her, she used the idiom to mean "curse." The rabbis didn't believe she said "bless God" in light of all the pain she had gone through, so even though she uses *barak*, the Hebrew word "bless," they interpreted her words to Job as the same idiom as Satan—"curse God." In only a few other places in the Bible, does the clear context and usage of this word carry the idiomatic meaning of cursing God.

So the weight of scholarly opinion of both the rabbis and church interpreters seems to side with the idiomatic usage of the word to bless, *barak*, in Job's wife's situation as "curse God and die." Let's assume she said that. What if she did speak, momentarily like a foolish woman, forgetting who she was—a daughter of the King—and said, "curse God and die"? What if she said that? If we are really honest, haven't we all had those moments when life is raw and we cry out from the depths of our hearts?

We should not condemn those whom God has not condemned. Her husband Job also didn't condemn her. His response to her implied that "she is not herself a foolish woman but is speaking as if she were; he implies that she has spoken, under momentary stress, as one of a class to

> We should not condemn those whom God has not condemned.

---
4 Jastrow, *Dictionary of the Targumim*, 296.

which she did not belong."[5] He merely reminded her of who she was, and to remember the perspective of who God is. I wonder if he was responding not just to her words as much as her pain of following God and wanting to die when things get hard. In her one statement to Job, we hear her "sacred questions" of God: "How can God let this evil happen to us? How can I serve Him still? Why does He ask this of me? Why does he ask this of you? Why, God?" These are not dissimilar to our questions in risk or suffering.

The final chapter of Job and the Bible's teaching in Leviticus (and Mal 2:2) on blessing and cursing reveal that cursing God is a sin. "Whoever curses his God shall bear his sin. Whoever blasphemes the name of the LORD shall surely be put to death" (Lev 24:15, 16).

In Job 42:7, 8, the Lord spoke directly to Job's friends:

> My anger burns against you and against your two friends, for you have not spoken of me what is right, as my servant Job has. Now, therefore, take seven bulls and seven rams and go to my servant Job and offer up a burnt offering for yourselves. And my servant Job shall pray for you, for I will accept his prayer not to deal with you according to your folly. For you have not spoken of me what is right, as my servant Job has.

Where's Job's wife in that text? God was not angry with her. He did not condemn her and did not command Job to make sacrifices to atone for her speech like he did for the three friends.

The last thing we learn in the book of Job is that he was healed of disease, his fortunes were restored to him double, and he had seven more sons and three more daughters. However, the text does not mention Job's wife again, so the simple reading of Scripture suggests we can reasonably presume God blessed her physically with the ability to have another ten children with Job. He blessed her even more greatly.

Her statement to her husband is from a woman wanting her husband released from the pain. All Job did was reframe her understanding of how we are to view the good and the hard and the pains of life and what it means to serve God. The Ancient Near East held the view that when good things happened to you, the gods or God was favoring you. When a bad thing happened to you, the gods were angry at you and you had sinned. Job was telling her that the prevailing cultural view was wrong. We accept all things—good and bad—from God, a God who loves us, and whom we serve faithfully, no matter what happens. Ambiguity in how God works is a fact of existence.[6] God gave Job the grace in all his physical, emotional, and

---

5 Clines, *Word Biblical Commentary Job*, 53.
6 Wolde, *Mr. and Mrs. Job*, 23–24.

spiritual pain to still encourage his wife to persevere in faithfulness to God, despite the lack of simple explanations at the end.

Yet something else significant happened when she challenged his view of God. Before all the loss, Job had a simplistically pious view of God. He had certainty about who God is and what life is about. He was asking no questions. After she challenged him, his "box" began to open, and he began to consider God differently. His certainty was replaced by uncertainty as his view of God expanded.[7] This shift becomes the theme for the rest of the book.

Who cared for Job in his sickness? There was no hospital kitchen. We can reasonably assume that Job's wife, in her pain and deepest grief, helped keep him alive by cooking for her husband (something she didn't have to do before all her servants were killed). She probably brought him food, then went back to lay on her bed all alone in a home now empty of family and friends, and cry herself to exhausted sleep, night after night, as she fought the battle to keep on trusting God in her deepest pain when all of life had just become a living nightmare.

People glibly scoff so easily about the offensiveness of Job's breath on his wife, but anyone who has been around sickness, decay, and death knows it is odorous and difficult. Anyone who has experienced profound loss like hers knows it's common to wish to die and no longer keep living, breathing, and eating. I'm sure food tasted like sawdust to her. Her eyes, swollen with unending tears, were consumed by the sight of endless horror.

I wonder what stage of grief she and Job were in, their normal human response, and how they tried to help each other in their distress. When looking at the grief curve, it seems like she is in the place of "Wrestling with Reality."

This stage is characterized by:

- Longing for what was lost
- Distorted perception
- Alienation from God
- Depression
- Wavering

---

7 Wolde, 25–26.

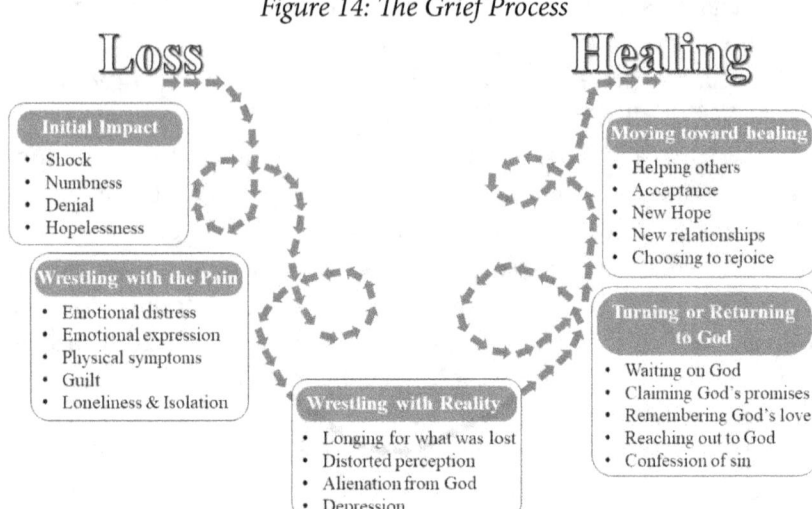

Figure 14: The Grief Process

© 2016 International Training Partners

We can guess she is likely feeling aspects from the initial impact of shock, numbness, and hopelessness. She is wrestling with the pain because she is in emotional distress and extremely isolated.

Not one of her friends would be able to understand the depths of pain and grief she was in at the time. Yet, she seems held to a higher standard than Job, who curses what God has done. What did Job do to help his wife before moving further into wrestling with reality?

A short while after she makes this statement to her husband, in chapter 3, Job uses graphic, vulgar language and curses the night his father impregnated his mother; he laments the day he was born and the day he sucked milk from his mother's breasts. Job 3:12: "Why did the knees receive me or why the breasts that I should nurse?" he asks. To modern readers, where birth and death occur in sterile environments, this question smacks of vulgarity, yet Job is often held up as an example for us, while his wife is not.

God condemns neither as sinning in their grief, and Job had no step of repentance despite all these things he said. Day after day, Job's wife watched her husband being spiritually disappointed and discouraged by "friends." Yet their own faith deepened as God took Job to a new level of understanding of his humanity and God's sovereign power.

What kept him from abandoning God at the lowest time of his life, when there seemed to be no more future and his hope had died? Job is an example of applied attachment theory. His attachment to God survived the ruin of his tidy system of beliefs and enabled him to endure and provide the meaning for his pain.[8] The change in Job's understanding of God and humanity led him to believe in God, to develop a faith in God not based on anything other than personal choice. He had no cause to expect his life to end better, and God had everything taken away, yet Job still chose to trust God and believe that God still chose him, even though it didn't feel like it. This is anti-fragile faith, a faith worth striving for.

The authenticity of Job's wife teaches us about processing pain and trauma. It would seem that those of us in member care would do well to consider how we would provide trauma counseling to someone like Job's wife instead of criticizing her and using her as an example of how not to respond. We fail in our role as shepherds when the weak are not strengthened, the sick and injured are forgotten, the strays are neglected and abandoned, no one is searching for the lost, and people like Job's wife are treated with harshness by the ones who should minister gentle lovingkindness (Ezek 34:4).[9] When it appears we do not care for Job's wife, how can we care for others who have gone through similar trauma?

By repeating this libelous interpretation of Job's wife, we are perpetuating the idea that we cannot be honest and authentic about our feelings in the face of horror, pain, and grief. It perpetuates the idea that the sacred questions we ask of God when suffering (i.e. "Why" and "Who are you, God? Do you care?") are not acceptable. *For at least 1800 years, the church has failed to care for Job's wife.*

She provides a healing example to many who feel empty and unable to give the "glorious Christian victorious response" so often pressured to show in the midst of pain. In contrast, not only are these questions acceptable, they are *necessary* for faith to become worth anything.

As for Job's wife, no, she wasn't a tool used by Satan to discourage Job. She was simply a normal woman with a normal human response to deep pain, and she stayed faithful. Job was a good friend, a good husband to her, and recognized her pain and gave her the little comfort he could out of his own pain and confusion about who God is to help her stay the course,[10] even as he began asking questions.[11] Next time Job's wife is slandered, speak up and demonstrate empathy for someone we likely will meet in heaven.

---

8 Greenburg, *Book of Job*.
9 "The weak you have not strengthened, the sick you have not healed, the injured you have not bound up, the strayed you have not brought back, the lost you have not sought, and with force and harshness you have ruled them."
10 Hampton, "Authenticity in Suffering." First published in *Behind the Veil*, and edited for this publication.
11 Hampton.

Choose to see her faithfulness to God and her husband.
Choose to see why the Bible includes her story.
Choose to see that she is honest in her pain.
Choose to see yourself in her story.
Choose to see *her*.

Five Critical Principles of Member Care

1. Allow Authenticity: It's tempting to label anyone who has suffered for Christ as a hero or heroine, but such labeling creates a gap between Christ-follower and encourager. This gap is challenging to bridge in meaningful ways. It's almost impossible to deeply encourage someone if we hold them up as a hero, a person without struggles and weaknesses. It does not allow for authenticity. Raw pain demands raw authenticity from the sufferer and the listener to be able to be processed. Pain is painful.

2. Listening Hospitality: Become a person whose very presence feels like a space of warm acceptance. Acceptance of the person in pain is a critical aspect of deep listening. Condemnation and judgment inhibit true listening and prevent ministering to someone in raw pain. Open, active listening without shock or awe of the person and what they've gone through is required.

3. Create Sacred Spaces:[12] Job gave his wife a sacred space to voice her fear honestly and in doing so, both became more human for each other and before God. A sacred space is a space where we can process what is going on between God and me, and I won't be judged by the person listening.

4. Name Strength in the Person and Powerlessness in the Situation: Help the person in pain see their strength, generosity, gratitude, and what they had no control over in the situation. Sometimes we need help to "see the reality." Just like the Psalmist in Psalm 56, we recognize our God-given strength only when we experience the powerlessness of fearful and dangerous circumstances. In these situations, when we can no longer trust ourselves or rely on another, all that is left is God. He is the only one we can trust and rely only upon. All we have is God's strength and power to act. There is healing in naming and being reminded of these things.

---

12 Myers, "Introduction: Fear and Faith," 8–12.

5. Honor Righteous Courage: Honoring righteous courage is pointing out when a person has continued to fight through their fears and obey God with love and gentleness, even in violent situations. It includes naming when someone has grown in maturity in their response to adverse conditions and when they have demonstrated more mature courage. When we grow in our "courage muscle," a wise mentor will see, name, and commend us. Culturally, courage is honored and valued in different ways, and knowing your flock means knowing how to honor and value their courage specifically.

Your Calling and the Balm of Gilead

What would it be like to sit with Job's wife and cry with her? What kind of person could "member care" Job's wife? Would she feel safe sharing her heart with you? Or do you have all the answers she "needs"? How would she member care you when she and Job were on the other side of all this suffering? What would she say to you in your pain?

Listening, seeing, waiting, patience, and being a safe presence to people who have suffered trauma in risk and persecution are skills to develop and a heart to grow towards. There are two ways to become this type of person: enduring personal pain or entering into others' pain (empathy). Either way, the path is pain, and pain is painful, and it will leave its mark on us. If you are called to help people who have experienced extensive suffering in risk and persecution, know this about your calling:

The path is pain, and pain is painful.

> Your calling is going to crush you. If you're called to mend the brokenhearted, you [will] wrestle with broken-heartedness. If you're called to prophesy, you [will struggle] to control your mouth. If you're called to [laying on of] hands, you will battle spiritual viruses. If you are called to preach and teach the gospel, you will be sifted for the wisdom that anoints your message. If you are called to empower, your self-esteem will be attacked. Your successes will be hard-fought. Your calling will come with cups, thorns, and sifting necessary for your mantle to be authentic, humble, and powerful. Your crushing won't be easy because your assignment is not easy. ... Your oil is not cheap.[13]

---

13 Weaver, Faithhill Church USA.

We are uncomfortable with our powerlessness to fix, repair, and make right. Authenticity cannot be copied, only learned. The times of desolation, loss, shaking foundations, unmanageable pain, and deep grief are when God is creating the healing balm of Gilead in us for ourselves and to be able to share with others. He is worthy of our pain.

Part Five
Contagious Courage

Chapter 19
Hope Like a Sewer Rat[1] and PTSJ[2]

> *Hope lingers in the shadows of our darkest times.*
> *Hope is precisely what we have when we have nothing.*
> —Betty Walthour Skinner[3]

A sewer, where human refuse flows, is typically underground. It is a place where all the senses are assaulted—a smelly darkness of never-ending thoroughfares full of what we don't want to see and walk through. Living in such a place may be a metaphor for walking through tribulations of the kinds described in this book. No one wishes for the physical, mental, and spiritual pain of crisis and persecution. It's hard to have hope when we are in the middle of living through unending trials. How is it possible to have hope in such a situation? I again asked my friend, Brian, to help me learn more about sewer rats to share with you. Perhaps learning about the life of a sewer rat will shed some light.

The Sewer Rat[4]

"The sewer rat is officially referred to as the brown rat, *Rattus norvegicus*, and is also known as the common rat, street rat, [wharf] rat, Hanover rat, Norway rat, Norwegian rat, and Parisian rat."[5] These names are associated with people's experience of them, thus, sewer rat stems from their common presence in sewers. The brown rat, believed to have originated in and around China,[6] began spreading in the early eighteenth century—carried along on trading and passenger ships—and is now on every continent except Antarctica.[7] This fact alone communicates the first astonishing trait of the sewer rat: it possesses an almost supernatural level of adaptability. How in the world does it achieve this skill?

---

1 Seida, *My Broken Voice*, 26.
2 RAM Training, 2019, Mosbach, Germany. A German brother attending our RAM Training used this phrase, and it made a deep impression on me. With a twinkle in his eye, he defined PTSJ for me. We all too often talk about the trauma and all the pain, but we can be defined by joy in Christ, rather than by trauma.
3 Crenshaw and Snapp, *Hidden Life Awakened*, 181.
4 Lubinski, "Sewer Rat." As a professional biologist and founder of Visible Verse, Brian provided research summaries for animal research for this book.
5 Cornish, *Standard Library of Natural*, 159.
6 Cornish, 159.
7 Musser, *Mammal Species*, 894–1531. "Brown Rat."

The brown rat is an omnivore, with a diet consisting of:

> plant material such as grains, seeds, nuts, and fruits, supplemented with mice, young rabbits, birds and their eggs, fish, [and] invertebrates such as insects. This rodent is also known to hunt larger animals, including poultry and young lambs. The animal [can] consume substances such as soap, paper, and beeswax. In addition, this rat may also use carrion on occasion.[8]

Talk about flexibility! This ability to feed on such a wide range of food items many other animals could not survive on contributes to its ability to survive and thrive in sewerage.

As evidenced by their feeding behavior and the fact that the brown rat, like numerous rat species, flourish in city environments, and the brown rat is a generalist when it comes to habitat and feeding.[9] This trait is significant because animals, like people, that hold tightly to a narrow range of acceptable conditions for thriving are quickly reduced to surviving at best when conditions fall outside of their limited range of conditions. Being a generalist allows for a wide variety of acceptable foods and a wide variety of acceptable habitat conditions that still support flourishing. The same is true for people. Those who learn to be content in any and every situation[10] seem to do better than those who quickly become disgruntled.

Parts of the sewer system serve as rat highways, and other parts as feeding, breeding, and sleeping grounds. Davis found that the home range of sewer rats "may consist of a very narrow strip connecting a feeding and a [harbor] area."[11] "Although they [could] not state their conclusions in terms of area, Davis et al. state that rats live for a long time within a limited area, the overall diameter of which seldom exceeds [thirty to forty-five meters.]"[12] How is this translated into "hope like a sewer rat"? Generalists can thrive by taking the conditions presented to them and optimizing their use of those conditions rather than seeking different conditions that may or may not exist within the range of possible travel.

The brown rat has poor eyesight but incredibly sensitive whiskers, a highly developed sense of taste, and a hypersensitive nose. The latter is surprising given it lives a large part of its life within proximity to odors we consider extremely offensive! However, almost every animal has its limits, and

---

8   "Brown Rat."
9   Schein, *American Journal of Tropical*, 1117–30.
10 Phil 4:11–13.
11 Davis, "Studies on Home Range," 222.
12 Davis, "Characteristics of Rat Populations," 391.

the brown rat is no different. There is no doubt that the brown rat has cognitive abilities most people would like to not attribute to this rodent! Rats remember areas of danger, memorize the smell and taste of rodenticides (i.e. poisons), and can be trained to come by name or a particular sound. Many wrongly disregard the amazing ability of the brown rat to exist within the world's sewer systems by believing it simply lacks the cognitive development to "know" better. Research on the rat's senses and memory has long ago dispelled this common myth: rats engage the world around them with a developed memory and senses. They exist in this putrid environment, fully capable of discriminating the full range of odors, textures, and tastes, yet thrive.

> Apparently, "hope like a sewer rat" includes self-care.

One last thought about the sewer rat: they clean themselves often![13] They self-clean and engage, often, in social grooming, similar to monkeys. It's reasonable to expect an animal that thrives in sewers to not care about its cleanliness, but this could not be further from the truth. Apparently, "hope like a sewer rat" includes self-care.

To hope like a sewer rat is distasteful imagery. No one will ever try to sell a statue of a rat as a symbol of hope. It's not beautiful. But hope in the sewer of living is not delicate. It fights and scratches and never gives up. Hope survives the darkest areas where Satan's playground is, where living is raw on the razor-sharp edge of life and death. Hope is where we keep watch with Jesus in the darkness, waiting for the next bad thing to happen. He was waiting in sorrow for his betrayal and crucifixion, and he asks us to stay awake and wait with him. Once he was taken away and crucified, their hope died. As far as they knew, "Saturday" was the rest of their lives for them.

A paradox is a situation that exhibits contradictory aspects.[14] Paradoxically, just as the sewer is a place where certain species like rats thrive, it's possible to have hope like a sewer rat that we can thrive through such a situation. It's a constant choice. A choice to courageously embrace grief and mature hope or fixate on the darkness and lose focus.

Discerning Shadows

Hope in the darkness requires us to learn something about the shadows of darkness. There are two types of shadows mentioned in the Psalms. "He who dwells in the shelter of the Most High will abide in the shadow of the

---

13 *Social Behavior.*
14 *American Heritage Dictionary.*

Almighty" (Ps 91:1). And "Even though I walk through the valley of the shadow of death, I will fear no evil" (Ps 23:4). Since shadows look and feel the same, it takes spiritual discernment to see whose shadow we are taking refuge in!

It's an unlikely source of comfort, a shadow. Shadows have no substance, so why should we abide (dwell, remain) in a place of no substance unless there's something more to it? Shadows are the dark areas when an object blocks the light. We see an obscure outline of the object in the shape of a shadow in the dim grayness. Since the darkness of shadows look the same, it requires using our senses to discern the nature of the object casting the shadow. What is it? Coming close to the objects casting their shadows arouses different feelings and thoughts within us. Our discernment of the object reveals what we should continue to do, come closer or move away.

I think the Psalmist is teaching us that abiding in the shadow of the Almighty means we are remaining so close to him that he protects us. Even God's shadow is stronger than evil. Similarly, to be near a shadow of evil is to be near the evil itself. When the shadows of evil touch us, something lacking substance is touching us. Walking through the valley of darkness and suffering, the shadows of death likely will obscure our path. But while we may feel the experience of fear, we will not be paralyzed (choose the action of fear) by the shadows of death threatening us. We will keep walking. Perhaps this is why the Bible repeatedly tells us God is our hiding place. He is so strong and so powerful that even his shadow is a place of protection and security (e.g. Zeph 2:3; Pss 17:8; 27:5; 31:20; Col 3:3). When we look for his shadow when we feel afraid and go there, that's choosing to act courageously.

Fear and Hope

Fear and hope are inversely related to each other. *We choose one or the other, but we cannot choose both simultaneously. There is no option not to choose. Either way, we are choosing.* Hope, in turn, arouses a bodily (neurological) response from within us that differs from fear. Like fear, hope orders our responses to our circumstances. Both fear and hope are anticipatory—we are anticipating something which could happen in the future.

> Like fear, hope has an object: what we focus on is what captures our attention.

It is significant that in the Septuagint (the Greek translation of the Hebrew Old Testament), "hope" is primarily translated with the good in view, while the opposite notion "fear" or "dread" is translated literally as the "hope of evil."[15] Like fear, hope has an object: what we focus on is what captures our attention.

Similar to courage, there are two primary cultural influences on our view of hope that decrease resilience if we do not evaluate our thinking: the classical Greek view and the pagan view. The Greek idea of hope is an uncertain hope with no sure future foundation. It's wishful thinking and hoping for the best—hoping that the gods won't be against us. Greek ideas are based on paganism. Paganism views hope as luck or karma which results in pessimism (which expects the worst) or optimism (which assumes the best). "Knock on wood," "good luck," and even "enshalla" imply we rely on the capriciousness of the gods, fate, or whatever Allah wills today. We have no control over anything and must simply hope for the best. Hope without God is sheer fantasy.

Biblical hope is not anything like these cultural views. Hope is not a wish, nor is it a good feeling. Hope has to do with the future. Since we cannot know the end, biblical hope is grounded in a belief that there is a God, he knows the future, can affect the outcome on our behalf, and cares for us personally.

Viktor Frankl, a concentration camp survivor, wrote:

> The indefiniteness of the hopelessness of [the concentration camp] never ending led to the sensation of futurelessness. Life was without a future, and it existed only in the past. But [humans] cannot exist without a fixed point in the future. "Normal" is living today with an eye to the future. All of life is connected. Our immune systems are affected by either our courage and will to live or our weariness of life, disillusionment, and despair. Those who subscribed to hope and directed their minds to a future goal, restored their courage and had the will to go on.[16]

"Though he slays me, I will hope in him" (Job 13:15). The Hebrew word for hope in this verse is *"yahal."* *Yahal* also is often used synonymously with waiting, hoping, delay, trust, and expectation. It is also connected with the work of suffering through the pain, and is used for the waiting, pain, and work of being in labor, with the positive expectation of the hope of a baby! Sometimes dangerous circumstances are definitely painful, but we hope and wait for God to work. "This *yahal* 'hope' is not a pacifying wish of the imagination which drowns out troubles, nor is it uncertain (as in the Greek concept), but rather *yahal* 'hope' is the solid ground of expectation for the righteous. As such, it is directed towards God."[17]

---

15 Oswalt, *TWOT*, 101 (entry 233 חָטַב *bāṭaḥ*).
16 Frankl, *Doctor and the Soul*, 98–101.
17 Gilchrist, *TWOT*, 374 (entry 859 לחַי *yāḥal*).

The Hebrew idea of hope, the same idea as expectant, patient waiting, is not focused on *our* solutions, but on God. Significantly, our focus on God is in him, not on what he might do or not do. That's why *yahal* is closely connected to *batah* "to trust." If faith is perseverance, it requires patience, expectant waiting, and trust. Micah 7:7 vows, "But as for me, I will look to the LORD; I will wait for the God of my salvation; my God will hear me." That's hope.

In biblical thought, *trust is neither a set of beliefs nor an emotion.* The fundamental meaning of the verb *batah* (trust) is "firmness or solidity. In Hebrew, *batah* expresses that sense of well-being and security which results from having something or someone in whom to place confidence."[18] Trust in God is a sure foundation because we can rely on him. Our emotions about him, ourselves, and the situation may fluctuate, but he remains the same. We base our hope in him because we trust him. Paul says our hope is eternal life with God, based on his promises of long ago (Titus 1:1, 2). Trust is based on God, not our expectations of how he will act. If we base our faith on what he does or doesn't do now, it's a conditional faith, and we may be disappointed in God and lose hope.

So really, what the Bible is telling us is that biblical hope looks behaviorally like waiting, listening, and trusting him to keep his promises. It fixes on a point in the future, the time when he will bring justice, he will judge, he will make all things right, he will wipe the tears from our eyes. Hope waits expectantly. "This is why the Hebraic idea of waiting carries a sense of expectant anticipation, not stagnant reclining. To wait for [him] is to sit on the edge of the chair, leaning forward, straining to catch even the tiniest whisper. It is an attitude of immediacy, a trust that the turning point will suddenly arrive."[19]

The Cycle of Hope and the Cycle of Despair

There is a temptation to lose hope in the darkness of the valley of suffering. We have two paths we can choose to take. One leads to despair, and the other to maturing hope. We can move in a different direction at any point in time on these two cycles—we always have a choice (that's hopeful to know!). The cycles begin the same way: we experience a disappointment, discover an unmet expectation, a loss, or something we have been focused on that didn't work out.

We begin moving down the cycle of despair when we begin to complain. Complaining, when unchecked, leads to cynicism, the attitude that nothing

---

[18] Oswalt, *TWOT*, 101 (entry 233 בָּטַח *bāṭaḥ*).
[19] Moen, "Hidden Hope."

will ever change, and it will always be a certain way. Cynicism gives way to apathy, which is easier than cynicism because it's less painful not to care. The longer we allow the attitude of not caring to invade our soul, the more apathy we feel, and our hearts become calloused. A calloused heart can't feel, doesn't care, and "knows" it is powerless to change anything. Finally, we feel full-blown despair.

There is no end to the uncertainty, chaos, and pain in the darkness of despair. There is no answer to our question of "how long will this last?" All we hear is the echo of our own voice ricocheting off the canyon walls. We feel a sense of worthlessness and begin to believe no one will miss us if we cease to exist. If this is what life is, death is preferable. Despair overwhelms us and restricts our vision so that all we can see are our problems, and there seems to be no way out.

Even mature disciples are not immune to despair when facing unending adversity. The Apostle Paul experienced despair (2 Cor 1:8). He learned how to get out of despair and by 2 Corinthians 4:8, 9, when he had faced adversity again, he was able to apply what he learned and not enter the cycle of despair. He indicated what happened in 2 Corinthians 1:9, when he realized the object of his trust was in himself, and he switched the foundation for his trust and hope to the resurrection power that raised Christ from the dead. In essence, Paul got "historical" (Christ's death and resurrection) to get a grip on his future (the hope we have). This foundation is what spoke to his present.

Figure 15: Cycle of Despair

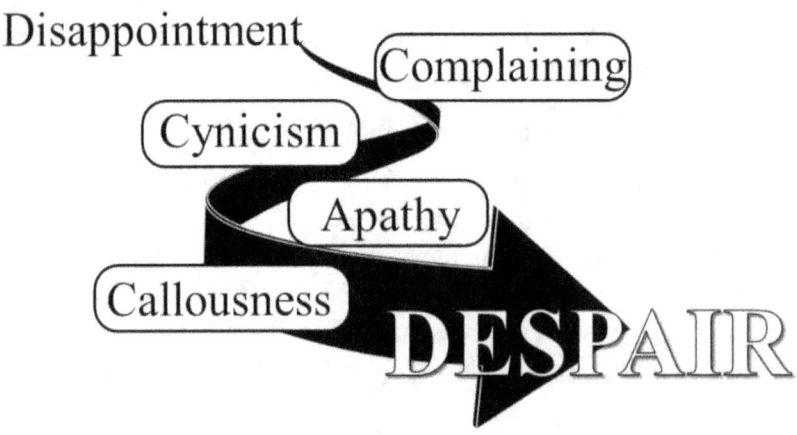

© 2022 Neal & Anna Hampton

It takes more energy and intentionality to choose the cycle of hope than the cycle of despair. I don't know why, but it's easier to believe the lies.

In this cycle, when we are faced with a disappointment or loss, we choose to train our eyes to see all that is still good and what we can be thankful for. Gratitude leads to increased trust because we trust God's provision even when it is different from our expectations. We assume the best of God, and that God is assuming the best for us. *Trusting* (the verb) begets *trust* (the noun). In the biblical mindset, we do in order to become. Trusting leads to a soft heart towards God. Then we notice subtle ways he is working and providing, and our confidence, wonder, and awe toward him increase. This confidence engenders more hopefulness and trust in him. The cycle of gratitude, trust, soft orientation towards God, and hope continues. Because this cycle also leads to greater attachment to God, our hope and courage deepen and mature, and we continue to move, speak, and act with courage.

Figure 16: Cycle of Hope

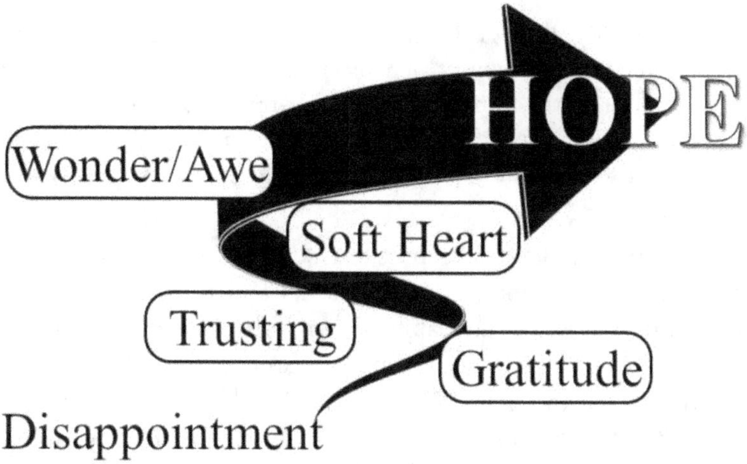

© 2022 Neal & Anna Hampton

Post-Traumatic Stress Joy (PTSJ)

Assessing the survivability and vulnerability of expensive airplanes requires extensive resources to improve technology to withstand the battlefield. Governments spend vast amounts of money to make "aircraft survivable and rapidly repairable"[20] for return to service. Airplane "battle damage" has a formal definition: "Combat damage includes all damages and malfunctions caused by munitions or their effects whether from enemy fire, friendly fire, or self-inflicted."[21]

---

20 Jerome, "Fixed-Wing Aircraft Combat Survivability."
21 Jerome.

Similarly, in witness-risk, we may experience trauma from the enemy, other Christ-followers, as well as our own sin and possible past trauma. Risk and persecution imply the likelihood of some level of trauma that requires a response from us. Several factors influence how resilient we are in the face of trauma and our recovery time. An underdeveloped theology of evil dramatically impacts our resiliency. The reality is that there are people who wish to inflict harm on Christ's disciples because they hate him.

One option available to the Christ-follower is growth after trauma, termed post-traumatic stress growth (PTSG). Earlier, in chapter 15, I discussed the importance of stress inoculation training (SIT). Having had stress inoculation training enhances the likelihood of experiencing post-traumatic stress growth. SIT equips individuals with coping skills to better manage stress. This ability leads to wise endurance and thriving, even after adversity.

> Post traumatic growth is defined as 'a positive change as a result of experiencing a traumatic event.' Whereas resilience refers to characteristics acquired prior to the traumatic event, post-traumatic growth has been described as going beyond resilience by transforming and building upon the experience to create a positive outlook. This growth process often takes time.[22]

Research reveals those who pursue God for who he is and not for the benefits (what he does for us or gives to us) and who also engage with a spiritual community, cultivate habits of spiritual practices, and are disposed towards forgiveness, experience less post-traumatic stress (PTS) and greater post-traumatic stress growth (PTSG) than those who do not engage with these habits.[23] Neuroscientist Andrew Newberg states that "Faith is the single most important element to mental health and thriving."[24] Weak faith results in greater suffering and distress than cultivated resilient faith.[25]

We see this growth in stress resiliency demonstrated in Psalm 62. In verse 2b, the Psalmist writes, "I shall not be greatly shaken." But by verse 6b, something has changed internally for him, and he writes, "I shall not be shaken." The Hebrew root of "greatly" in verse 2b refers to ten thousand-fold, or so many it's uncountable. Because he next refers to enemies, the Psalmist seems to be referring to dread, fear, horror, and terror. He will not allow himself to be overcome by fear so much that he is shaken physiologically, mentally, and spiritually.

---

22 Kay, "Stress Inoculation Training."
23 Schaefer, Blazer, and Koenig, "Religious and Spiritual Factors," 507–24.
24 Newberg and Waldman, *How God Changes*, 164.
25 Newberg and Waldman, 151.

There is movement throughout the Psalm, as the psalmist talks to his soul, names his reality, tells himself how he will respond, and who God is in the situation. Then he tells "the people" (his community) how to respond when the enemy seems overwhelming, and then provides a transcendent perspective of who we are and who God is. David names the strength but also the powerlessness humans have in circumstances we have no control over. He concludes by talking to God again and naming his character and how he acts toward his people. This Psalm is an excellent example of stress resiliency and growth.

So what is PTSJ? We know that mental health and growth occur when our mind and spirit are integrated and there is coherence between the spiritual and the physical aspects of our lives. Evil and trauma, if left unchecked, lead to disconnection, disintegration, and greater chaos, both of society and within the human brain.[26] Processing our fears and traumas grounded in a solid foundation of identification with Christ (meaning), and attachment to God and his love for us, leads to greater integration and likelihood of PTSG.

I've discussed post-traumatic stress growth, based on scientific research. Admittedly, Post-Traumatic Stress Joy (PTSJ) does not come from scientific, peer-reviewed literature but from a more ancient document. In Acts 5:41, Peter and John were beaten, imprisoned, interrogated, and released, and Luke relates, "Then they left the presence of the council, rejoicing that they were counted worthy to suffer dishonor for the name." It seems a bit sick to be rejoicing over torture—at least from a worldly wisdom perspective.

How come the disciples rejoiced when tortured? They weren't happy about pain for pain's sake, or for heavenly reward. They were honored to share in suffering for Christ's sake. As witnesses to his crucifixion, death, and resurrection, we proclaim that he is worthy when we are persecuted because of choosing to follow him. They felt their pain of persecution was a privilege because of a person.

Do we agree and say with James, "count it all joy" (rejoice) when you have to endure trials and temptations? The wounds we sustain in witness risk are the points of growth, and growth can lead to joy if we allow it. No matter what, we have a chance to choose rejoicing in suffering with him. That's the experience of post-traumatic stress joy. What are we doing to cultivate this possibility?

---

26 Thompson, *Anatomy of the Soul*, 178.

Spiritual Demoralization

Demoralization is not the same as depression or PTSD. "Demoralization always involves distress."[27] What leads to confusion is that it's usually not just one significant traumatic event but an interconnected series of events over time that lead to this state. Signs of demoralization include hopelessness, grief, loss of meaning, lack of purpose in life, helplessness, feelings of failure, lack of energy and motivation, feelings of aloneness, feelings similar to burnout, depletion, aloneness, shame over inability to get moving, or feeling the demand has exceeded the supply.

A psychiatric definition of demoralization is: "Demoralization is the state of mind of a person deprived of spirit or courage, disheartened, bewildered, and thrown into disorder or confusion … Demoralization always takes place within the context of a past, present, anticipated, or imagined stressful situation."[28]

Besides the psychological impact of demoralization, there is also a spiritual dimension. As mentioned in chapter two, the Hebrew word, *hatat* has "four ranges of meanings … : (1) literal breaking, (2) abstract destruction, (3) demoralization, and (4) terror."[29] Spiritual demoralization occurs from a number of experiences of both God and others. It could be a great deal of loss of relationships either through death or brokenness. It could come from deep disappointment after years of investing of our lives, or it could come from a long season of pouring out our all for Christ and fulfilling our calling while nothing seems to be going right. Spiritual demoralization includes a profound sense of aloneness in our valley of grief, loss, demoralization, and less energy and enthusiasm than normal. It seems like every attempt at following God results in loss, grief, stress, or closed doors. It does not necessarily mean that one is questioning God, but it can include that.

In this state, we are especially vulnerable to the deepest suffering which comes when we give into the temptation to listen to lies which tell us that God has left us, or is not paying attention, and has forsaken us. We are tempted to live as if we need to manage life (and ministry) without him—a terrifying prospect. There's a sinking feeling that goes to bed with us and wakes up with us, whispering, "I'm all alone." It feels God has failed us, and seemingly refused to answer or act, even though seven years have gone by with us begging him on our knees. We've been waiting, faithful, righteous, sacrificial. Is he impotent or unwilling to act? A vacation, a sabbatical, more Bible reading—none of these will "fix" the problem.

---

27 de Figueiredo, "Distress, Demoralization and Psychopathology."
28 de Figueiredo.
29 Bowling, *TWOT*, 336 (entry חָתַת *ḥātat*).

God says something very interesting in Joshua 1. In Joshua 1:5, God tells Joshua "I will be with you. I will not leave you or forsake you." He exhorts Joshua to be strong and courageous (do the action of strong, do the action of courageous), then ends that part of his exhortation in Joshua 1:9 with "Do not be frightened, and do not be dismayed, for the LORD your God is with you." Despite all the success God told him he'd have, the Lord knew Joshua's human tendency to fear, to think and feel that God had left him, to even be demoralized when things weren't happening the way they "should" be, and God wasn't working the way people and Joshua expect him to. Despite all that, the Lord God tells him to live in reality: "I will be with you, I will not leave you, I will not forsake you. Keep obeying me, keep doing the actions of strong and courageous. I will be with you." God is inviting us to a daily, middle-class kind of heroism no matter what we feel.[30]

One last thing about Joshua 1:9, that little phrase, "for the Lord your God is with you wherever you go." There's no verb "is" in the Hebrew text. It's a statement of fact. Perhaps a better way to hear it is, "for your-Lord-God-with-you wherever you go." Nothing can change that he is with us, not even spiritual demoralization.

So, what will lead us out of spiritual demoralization? The first step is changing our expectations that "healing" means we are going back to who we were. Instead, who we were before the series of events, losses, traumas that led to spiritual demoralization is not who we will still be on the journey out. The adventure of faith is who we are becoming as we follow him and know him more fully. This journey leads us to the pinnacle day in human history when spiritual demoralization overcame Christ's followers and all seemed lost.

Holy-Saturday-Suffering and Hope Probabilities

The day hope seemed irrevocably dead, Holy Saturday, displayed a specific type of suffering, a Holy-Saturday-suffering. It is the place of chaos in-between, the place where nothing makes sense. It's the time between death and resurrected life, a time of remaining, barely surviving, and wordlessness.[31] It is a time when we are living in unending violence, threats, torture, and the hellish uncertainty when it seems God has gone silent. It is a time when we feel abandoned by God and share in the feeling of being forsaken by a Holy loving Father, just as Christ felt forsaken on the cross.[32] Even hope like

---

30 Gallagher, *Overcoming Spiritual Discouragement*, 75.
31 Rambo, *Spirit and Trauma*, 45–80.
32 Rambo, 50.

a sewer rat seems of little help to ease the pain of Holy-Saturday-suffering. At least rats can go above ground into the light, but Christ-followers tortured in shipping containers in the desert have no way to get out.

How do we cultivate mature hope to keep our faith from shipwreck? The answer is another question: "What do we speak to our soul?" Even the feeling of abandonment by God provides meaning for Holy-Saturday-suffering, because we are sharing in Christ's feeling of abandonment. This day may be what gives us the most hope. When love seemed dead on Holy Saturday, the reality was that he was still there. Nothing, not even the day hope seemed dead, really separates us from a loving God.

As the remnant of the redeemed waging spiritual war, the reality is that Christ is sending us out as sheep among wolves, and a cunning enemy will attack. If risk is an exercise in probabilities, so is hope. Risk is looking at the probabilities of evil, and hope is looking at the probabilities of good. But it's more than good. It's hoping in the high likelihood that the origin of good—the Creator God of the Hebrew Bible—exists, that he cares, and that he is present with us in the darkness of our suffering.

Hope like a sewer rat, mature hope, is hoping when our lives are broken on the wheels of living, when we don't think we can bear one more loss or one more grief; when we feel abandoned, orphaned, forgotten, isolated because no one understands, no one seems to care, and tomorrow looks likely to bring only more bad news; when the pillars of our life are shaking, and we didn't know the cost of our call to follow Jesus would be this much and we're wondering for the first time if all the pain was worth it; when we've wept and mourned but we must go on with eyes swollen by tears; in these times, it takes courage to persevere in hope. We will have to fight and claw for this type of hope. The shadows of evil will throw the gates of hell at us and try to convince us the object of our hope doesn't exist, that nothing will ever change, and that we will die forgotten. Our hope isn't low on the risk-probability scale, however. The probability of our hope is worth gambling our lives on. Hope has a name, and his name is Jesus.

Chapter 20
Mature Courage and Spiritual Nobility

Lord, mother boldness and audacious courage in me that I may abandon myself with openness and enthusiasm to share generously in your sufferings with my heart, mind, and body.
—Anna Hampton

On Afghan holidays, it seemed the whole neighborhood where I lived in Kabul would dress in their finery and walk as families to visit friends and neighbors. Occasionally you'd spot the elegantly robed patriarch of the family, perhaps a clan elder, moving slowly and smoothly down the street. You could always identify him by his clothing and movement. Holding his head high, his long white beard flowing down the front, he usually wore a multi-color khalat robe and held a smoothly sanded wooden walking stick. With a specially decorated, extra-large keffiyeh wrapped around his head, he effortlessly moved down the street, smiling as the children scampered around him. He was the picture of nobility.

Spiritual Nobility

Nobility is more than what we wear and how we walk, however. Nobility implies kinship. Just as an earthly class of nobility is people born into a unique family, those born again into Christ's family are sons and daughters of the high king. Unlike temporal nobility, however, spiritual nobility in Christ's family is not limited by ethnicity—anyone can be spiritually noble at any age, from any ethnic group. The noble class is usually characterized as people with high moral character and a decorous manner of behaving. "Decorous" is an umbrella word that includes the following qualities: civility, graciousness, politeness, dignity, grace, discretion, appropriateness, fitness, rightness, honor, seemliness, attentiveness, carefulness, character, goodness, honesty, integrity, morality, righteousness, uprightness, and virtuousness.

Litvin describes qualities of spiritual nobility. Through a Christo-centric lens, what might that look like? These people authentically admit that life often feels more like a battleground than a praise service. Spiritually noble people enter into risk and persecution with a reasonable dose of ordered fear but an even larger dose of ordered love, which outweighs the fear for their own safety. A spiritually noble person requires courage and skill, for we risk our very lives for Christ's sake. Spiritually noble people know the secret of fulfillment: it is in serving and suffering for him in the spiritual battle that we feel most alive, most aware, and often, most fulfilled. Spiritually noble people are constantly learning about themselves and God in the places where life is on "the edge"—the place where we experience the truth that we are more than we think we are, when we can do more than we realize, and have more strength and capabilities because of Christ's power within us.

When we live in the place where we are battling for the souls of men and women, we meet God in new ways. It requires bravery to struggle with God like Jacob did and to face who we are and who we are not, to see who he is from who we thought he was. It is "a willingness to find God in all places and meet him fully, allowing him to penetrate the deepest recesses of who I am and dispel my false self. Spiritual nobility knows that we exercise faith when we are at the limits of faith."[1] We learn trust in his protection when facing our deepest fears. Spiritual nobility is choosing to see from the perspective of God's throne room, to see through the eyes of the Trinity the world in all its misery, happiness, evil, and goodness, to see and not remain indifferent.

Mature Courage

What is mature courage? As I have walked a long, reflective journey to try to discover mature courage, I considered myself cowardly in some areas of my life early on. I've come to realize several truths about the journey to mature courage. The journey to mature courage in risk and persecution requires us to continually name and face our fears and let Christ reorder them, so we fear rightly, from the right motive, in the right way, at the right time. The journey requires us to cultivate a *holy awareness of God's leading and trust in him no matter what happens.*[2] Mature courage is knowing which risks, battles, and

> Courage is a thousand small decisions and occasionally one big one.

conflicts to avoid and which to enter into, *and to train for them*. Courage is a thousand small decisions and occasionally one big one. We rarely get to see the legacy of all of our small decisions of courageous endurance on our families, our communities, and even nations ... but God sees.

Mature courage is knowing God is still on his throne no matter what. Nothing can move him from his throne. And from his throne, he looks at each of us with eyes of grace, love, and longing. As he did on the cross,

---

1 Litvin, *Spiritual Warrior*.
2 Spencer, "To Fear and Not," 229–49.

he still thirsts for us to have faith in him. Spiritual nobility goes hand-in-hand with growing, maturing courage. Mature courage is characterized by several cultivated habits and directions of the heart.

A person of mature courage knows how and when to be dangerous to evil

The focus is not on becoming less afraid but, more often, choosing bravery. The snake from the garden still comes in to twist, lie, and attack. Retreating behind higher walls is not the answer. For the Christ-follower, the world is not safe and never will be. With the strength of Christ's Spirit within us, with his power, we face our fears, then we face evil and do not shrink back. When we confront evil face to face with the love of Christ, the power of evil is disarmed and diminished. And the more we do this, the more we grow, and the more Christ's kingdom comes in its fullness.

A person of mature courage is becoming[3]

The Hebrew language "sees" the world in terms of actions rather than time. In Hebrew, there are two primary verb tenses; complete actions, and incomplete actions. Actions are either finished or not finished. Choices are open to us until the moment of our last breath—we are never finished, complete, until then. Being human is formed *in us* by the history of our choices throughout our lifetime. When we choose to obey God's instructions, our actions produce resemblance to him, transforming us until we are conformed to his image. What is his image? God is *what* he does. Even his name is a verb. He says, "*I AM WHO I AM*" (Exod 3:14). Later, in Exodus 34:6, 7, he describes the qualities of his actions toward his people: compassion, graciousness, slow to anger, forgiving, lovingkindness, mercy, and faithfulness to all generations (all qualities of spiritual nobility). So how do you and I become human? It's more than his breath in us. We become human by doing what God does. Obedience continually adjusts our lives to God's ways, heart, and character over time. At the end of our life, we will be the accumulation of our choices, either more human or less human, either more like God or less like him.

A person of mature courage smells a certain way

As we become more and more like him, Christ-followers develop a particular fragrance, even in persecution. In Daniel 3:23, 24, Shadrach, Meshach, and Abednego were thrown into the fire by King Nebuchadnezzar. When he saw that they didn't burn, and a fourth person was in there with them, he ordered

---

3 Moen, "Incomplete Life."

them to come out. He saw their bodies had not burned in the fire, not a single hair was singed, and their clothes were unharmed, "and no smell of fire had come upon them." In other words, they did not smell like smoke.

How can we be people who are changed by his presence in our sufferings but not smell like the bitter, acrid smoke of whatever we walk through and instead have the fragrance of Christ? Through his power, this is possible.

> But thanks be to God, who in Christ ... through us spreads the fragrance of the knowledge of him everywhere, for we are the aroma of Christ to God among those who are being saved and among those who are perishing, to one a fragrance of death to death, to the other a fragrance from life to life. (2 Cor 2:14–16)

A person of mature courage is historical

In Hebrews 12:1, the writer states, "Therefore, since we are surrounded by so great a cloud of witnesses." Who are these *nephos martys* (cloud of witnesses)? Hebrews 11 lists noteworthy members of the great cloud of witnesses. This "cloud" includes those in Hebrews 11 and all those faithful to Christ in history. These witnesses surround us. The Greek word for "surrounding" is in the present tense. They are surrounding us now; we are part of the same group wherever we are. As we are alive in Christ, so are they. Who are some of the people in the group? By reading the lives of the saints who have gone before, we familiarize ourselves with "the people in the cloud" and how they endured. Their example instructs us on the way of suffering through persecution.

Remembering history calls to mind the truth that most of the witnesses "died in faith, not having received the things promised, but having seen them and greeted them from afar, and having acknowledged that they were strangers and exiles on the earth" (Heb 11:13). Some of them did experience some justice on earth, but the last five verses of Hebrews 11 are often ignored.

> Some were tortured, refusing to accept release so that they might rise again to a better life. Others suffered mocking and flogging, and even chains and imprisonment. They were stoned, they were sawn in two, they were killed with the sword. They went about in skins of sheep and goats, destitute, afflicted, mistreated—of whom the world was not worthy—wandering about in deserts and mountains, and in dens and caves of the earth. And all these, though commended through their faith, did not receive what was promised, since God had provided something better for us.

A person of mature courage is "sticky"[4]

There's a specific verb used in the Hebrew Bible: the "sticky" verb. God is never the subject of this verb; only we are.[5] Joshua 22:5 teaches,

> Only be very careful to observe the commandment and the law that Moses the servant of the LORD commanded you, to love the LORD your God, and to walk in all his ways and to keep his commandments and to cling to him and to serve him with all your heart and with all your soul.

Davaq is a verb of deliberate clinging, it's about stickiness. *Davaq* is for sticking together wet clods of dirt (Job 38:38). We, the subject of this verb, stick ourselves to God. It is a willful, considered attachment to God. People with *davaq* commitment to Christ's calling in their lives are not making choices based on emotional overload but on stubbornly sticking to God, no matter what (c.f., Deut 10:20; 11:22; 13:4; 30:20; Josh 22:5, 8).

A person of mature courage has guts

Our task demands guts: endurance, courage, fear management, and proclaiming Christ wisely and boldly. Not giving up looks like putting one foot in front of the other, one foot at a time, minute by minute, hour by hour, day by day. It's guts; it's having a forehead like flint.

In the game of baseball, batting .300 means you fail seven out of ten times to hit the ball. Batting .300 is legendary, it's Hall of Fame material. In other words, those who fail repeatedly end up in the Hall of Fame because they never gave up.

Vital Spirituality for Persecution[6]

Jesus told us that the good news sparks divisions (Luke 12:49–53). "Indeed, all who desire to live a godly life in Christ Jesus will be persecuted" (2 Tim 3:12) and "For to this you have been called, because Christ also suffered for you, leaving you an example, so that you might follow in his steps" (1 Pet 2:21). A spirituality for persecution must be robust enough to withstand the toughest environments, and it will include at least the following elements:

1. An expectation persecution. We are reminded that persecution is inevitable. Jesus did not use "if" when he told us what to expect in Matthew 10, Mark 10, Luke 21, and John 16. Following Christ is costly, demanding, and requires endurance, but he is worthy of whatever

---

4 Moen, "Adhesive Qualities."
5 Kalland, *TWOT*, 177, 178 (entry 398 דָּבַק).
6 Brackley, *Call to Discernment*, 18.

it takes. If we experience no opposition, we should be concerned. "Woe to you, when all people speak well of you, for so their fathers did to the false prophets" (Luke 6:26).

2. Training for persecution. "For which of you, desiring to build a tower, does not first sit down and count the cost, whether he has enough to complete it?" (Luke 14:28). A spirituality wise and robust enough for persecution trains for it. "He trains my hand for battle" (c.f. 2 Sam 22:35; Pss 18:34; 144:1). Training includes knowing our strengths and our weaknesses.

In Luke 6:40, we learn that "A disciple is not above his teacher, but everyone when he is fully trained will be like his teacher." Training in shrewdness comes from watching the shrewdness of Jesus in the Gospels. There were times he did not answer questions but acted. At other times, he responded with an evasive answer. Still others, he responded to a question with a question. Sometimes, he remained silent, as before Pilate. He avoided mobs, and escaped when they surrounded him. He carefully chose his journey, sometimes through dangerous country and other times around. Jesus was deliberate about when he exposed himself to danger and when he did not.

3. Not underestimating our need for God's power. We cultivate an attitude of rest on God's power, even in our weakness, because that keeps us stabilized. Paul wrote, "[May you be] strengthened with all power, according to his glorious might" (Col 1:11). Only divine power, mighty power, the power that hovered like an eagle over the abyss and created the world, only this power can sustain you and me through whatever is ahead. Why divine power? "*So that you may have great endurance and patience, and giving joyful thanks to the Father*" (Col 1:11-12, NIV). A spirituality rugged enough for persecution has the power of Christ to help us in our weaknesses when we experience insults, hardships, persecutions, and calamities. When we are weak, then we are strong (2 Cor 12:10). We underestimate this power, thinking that it is a small thing, but we are not fighting a small battle. It takes omnipotent divine power to sustain Christ-followers through times of testing.

4. Consolation produced by being persecuted for Christ's sake. Consolation is a combination of inner freedom, calmness of soul, clarity of our calling and responsibility, spiritual tranquility in one's heart, and the supernatural peace that descends and pervades us even when we are afraid, so that we can go forward into danger with

peaceful firmness of mind, heart, and soul, no matter what happens. When we know we have been called to the persecution and willingly suffer it, peace reigns more easily in our hearts because we have remained true to our calling and ethics (Rom 5:3, 4; 1 Thess 1:4).

5. A maturing sense of the presence of God. "There must be a matured and maturing sense of Presence [of God]. This sense of Presence must be a reality at the personal level as well as on the social, naturalistic, and cosmic levels ... Thus, we shall look out upon life with quiet eyes and work on our tasks with the conviction and detachment of Eternity."[7] We must become aware of the sense of God's presence, and this awareness takes faith when we cannot sense him in the normal or usual ways. The tendency for the less mature is to go into faith crisis and believe he is not there. But there is another way, and that is to begin to look with the spiritual eyes of the heart (Eph 1:18).

> There must be a matured and maturing sense of Presence [of God].

6. Time spent with Jesus. We are called to boldness and contagious courage. Fear and courage are both contagious, and in the presence of wise endurance, courage inspires others to even more courage. What inspires boldness? There are no shortcuts or three simple steps. It's time spent with Jesus. "Now when they saw the boldness of Peter and John and perceived that they were uneducated, common men, they were astonished. And they recognized that they had been with Jesus." (Acts 4:13)

7. Cultivating forgiveness and unconditional love for our enemies. Loving our enemies only happens when we understand that we have the same capacity for evil as they do. Once that happens, we are freed to love them with our minds and in our hearts. Forgiving those who harm us or our loved ones does not condone or imply complacency with horror.[8] Forgiveness is a gift we give ourselves to release the other from the debt they owe us. Forgiveness for persecution is not easy, but it is simple. It takes time and is not necessarily done quickly.

8. Creativity and shrewdness. In Acts, we see how the early church responded to persecution. "Paul denounced, threatened, cajoled,

---

7 Thurman, *Deep Is the Hunger*, 138.
8 Schweitzer, "A Lesson on Courage," 759–74.

fled, cleverly pitted Pharisees against Sadducees, and appealed to the emperor. We may need to use novel forms of communication, improvisation, drama, humor, or even creative trickery."[9]

9. A communal spirit and increasing unity of the body. A spirituality of persecution is a communal spirituality that enables us to support one another when in trials and tribulations.

Walking with a Knife in Your Heart

What does it mean to walk with a knife in your heart? The mother of our Lord is an example of this. Michelangelo depicted Mary and the crucified Jesus in a statue, the Pieta, located in St. Peter's Basilica in Rome. He carved the Pieta out of one piece of Carrara marble over two years. Mary is embracing the dead, crucified body of her son. We see Jesus, draped across her lap and supported with her right hand. Significantly, Michelangelo showed her left hand upheld in an open posture, extending towards heaven. She says to God, "You did this to me and my son, and you may do more. I receive whatever you will for my life, all my suffering and joy with an open heart."

Like Mary, we as Christ-followers are called to walk with a knife in our hearts. The calling means holding space for the paradox of grief and suffering at the same time as hope and joy, based on the confidence we have in Christ. One day he will make all things right and just. "My soul dissolves because of grief; Renew and strengthen me according to the promises of Your word" (Ps 119:28, AMP).

Who will be the martyrs of the twenty-first century, and who will be their persecutors? Those ministering in dangerous areas and suffering persecution are at the forefront of the battle, pushing into evil and darkness and bringing Christ's love. Let's go forward, eyes open, constantly alert, facing our fears, creatively thinking, with clarity concerning our goals, accepting the price to be paid, using winsome words, and training ourselves to know how to stand in the gap, how to stand firm, and be ready to die well for Christ. Evil won't wait. The people who've never heard his name are dying and can't wait. Jesus called us to be loving, vulnerable, and like little children, like lambs sent to wolves. The power of Christ in us is far more potent than whatever powerful reality we see. Let us step with the solid footing of love so that we leave a trail worth following.[10] Let's cultivate a burning heart and a fire in our bellies, and a passion for seeing Christ lived in us. Why? *Because he is worthy.*

---

9   Brackley, *Call to Discernment*, 190.
10 Erickson, "Salt and Light."

Zimbabwe Pastor's Prayer, Martyred[11]

I'm a part of the fellowship of the unashamed.
The die has been cast.
I have stepped over the line.
The decision has been made.
I'm a disciple of His and I won't look back, let up, slow down, back away, or be still.
My past is redeemed.
My present makes sense.
My future is secure.
I'm done and finished with low living, sight walking, small planning, smooth knees, colorless dreams, tamed visions, mundane talking, cheap living, and dwarfed goals.

I no longer need preeminence, prosperity, position, promotions, plaudits, or popularity.
I don't have to be right, or first, or top, or recognized, or praised, or rewarded.
I live by faith, lean on His presence, walk by patience, lift by prayer, and labor by Holy Spirit power.
My face is set.
My gait is fast.
My goal is heaven.
My road may be narrow, my way rough, my companions few, but my guide is reliable and my mission is clear.

I will not be bought, compromised, detoured, lured away, turned back, deluded, or delayed.
I will not flinch in the face of sacrifice or hesitate in the presence of the adversary.
I will not negotiate at the table of the enemy, ponder at the pool of popularity, or meander in the maze of mediocrity.
I won't give up, shut up, or let up until I have stayed up, stored up, prayed up, paid up, and preached up for the cause of Christ.

I am a disciple of Jesus.
I must give until I drop, preach until all know, and work until He comes.
And when He does come for His own, He'll have no problems recognizing me.
My color will be clear!

---

11 Found among his papers in Zimbabwe after he was martyred for his Christian faith. It is the moving testimony of a martyr. This vibrant declaration was contributed by Dr. Nina Gunter who got it from veteran missionary Louise Robinson Chapman (Africa: 1920–1940). One side note is that today this commitment statement regretfully circulates among websites with the byline "Author unknown."

Appendix A
Thresholds for Departure/ Benchmarks for Return

By Scott Brawner[1]

One of the biggest challenges to ministry is dealing with threats. Sometimes the most stressful situations arise not from facing an external threat but from making the decision to stay or go. During these times relationships are often tested. Trust between field workers and their leaders may well be lost if stay/go decision-making is handled poorly. But the reality is, that this stress often does not end with the decision to leave; decision-making in the return process can be just as stressful. In some cases, field personnel have resigned from their original sending organization and returned to a mission field either with another mission agency or on their own because of disagreement over the departure and return process. In other circumstances, it has taken years for senior leaders to repair damage and regain the trust lost with field workers over these stressful decisions.

The process field workers and leaders use to develop their thresholds (or tripwires) for departure should also be used to develop their benchmarks for return. Some individuals with a higher risk tolerance might find living with a few of these thresholds to be tolerable. Others may desire more stability to thrive and want to ensure more of these thresholds are present.

Bottom line, if leaders are finding several of these thresholds (or lack thereof) are causing personal anxiety, fear, or hyper-concern, they should certainly address the situation and take steps to help individuals, families, and teams thrive. These thresholds and benchmarks can help leaders take measures intended to decrease the vulnerabilities of field workers allowing them to stay when threats increase, decide to relocate personnel to an area away from the immediate threat that allows the ministry to continue, or come to an agreement to evacuate completely to avoid tragedy.

To help with the departure/return process, my colleagues and I developed twenty-one thresholds and benchmarks for consideration. While not exhaustive, they do include:

1. Targeted Attacks: Has there been any targeting of expatriates in cities or the countryside in the past fourteen days?

---

[1] Used by permission. This material has been lightly edited for clarity.

2. Basic Services (water, sanitation, and electricity): Are potable water, sewer (if installed versus septic tank system), and electricity (as it is normally available) currently available, or restored?
3. Foodstuffs: Are the markets open and necessities stocked? Is food being rationed? Is there significant price gouging going on making key food stocks prohibitive? Have there been at least seven days of uninterrupted business with stores and vendors?
4. Fuel: Is fuel available? If so, is it rationed? Is there significant price gouging going on making daily life and ministry prohibitive?
5. General Medical: Are basic medical services available? Are the hospitals utilized by organization personnel open and operating?
6. Personal Health: Do members of your teams need a specific medication or medical support that must be replenished regularly? If so, is access to those items available from the local pharmacies or other vendors?
7. Communications: Are they better or worse than normal? Are mobile phone and internet networks operating as usual, or down? If down, is it due to vandalism or local government control? If due to government control, perhaps they are not finished with their control actions and still feel threatened.
8. Consular Services: Is the embassy or nearest consulate open, staffed, and functioning? If not, are there any of their services that you cannot thrive without (Passport renewal, Warden network information, evacuation assistance, etc.)?
9. Foreign Governments Concerns: Are foreign governments evacuating (or allowing the return) of non-essential diplomatic staff?
10. Host Government Concerns: Are very senior members of the government fleeing the country, or are senior members of the government publicly disavowing the senior leader?
11. Rebellion and Mutiny: Are military or law enforcement organizations (especially in the capital) rebelling or mutinying against the current government in light of a shifting balance of power (political shifts, tribal/ethnic shifts, civil war, etc.).
12. Local Relationships: What are the locals saying? Are they afraid to go out? Are they saying the situation is dangerous for them? Are they recommending you shelter-in-place, depart, or wait to return? Do they feel they can no longer protect you?

13. Overland Travel Safety: Are protesters blocking the roads and restricting travel between cities and, especially, to the airport or train stations? Have the roads been clear for at least ten days? Are there reports of criminal checkpoints being established on roads and nationals or expatriates being robbed or assaulted?
14. Urban Travel Safety: Are protesters blocking city streets? Is the government continuing the use of physical response (tear gas, pepper spray, rubber bullets, or live ammunition) against participants? Are protests in the immediate area deteriorating into looting, vandalism, and acts of arson? Are there reports of criminal checkpoints being established on city streets and nationals or expatriates being robbed or assaulted? Has it been at least seven days since this kind of activity took place in your area?
15. International Airport: Has the international airport (and/or small regional airports as appropriate) been open without restrictions for at least fourteen days?
16. Public Ground Transportation: Are the local, large city, and border crossing train stations open without restrictions for at least seven days? Are buses, taxis, and other local forms of transportation (Jeepney, Tuk-tuk, Rickshaw, other) operating without restriction for at least seven days?
17. Land Border Crossings: Are land border crossings open? Are there larger than normal numbers of people trying to leave (escape) the country causing greater lines and waiting? Are there political protests at the land border crossings inhibiting traffic flow? Are there reports of assaults, robbery, or other issues at or near border crossings presently? Are there other reasons related to the land borders to not attempt a land departure from, or return to the country?
18. General Safety: How do you and your family feel about daily routines? Can you go about daily routines without facing threats or direct hostility? Is it safe to go outside of homes back on the street as before? Have your families sensed a direct threat against them (versus general insecurity on the street)? How long has it been since your families sensed threats or direct hostility toward them? Can your personnel articulate how that threat has been abated or mitigated?
19. Work Security: Is it safe to conduct normal activities? Are your personnel's activities able to maintain a level of effectiveness like what was experienced before the crisis, environmental incident, protests, or before your organization's departure?

20. Work Relationships: Is your presence as an expat creating an undue burden on national partners? Are they (nationals) needing to watch out, care for, and help you more? Does their presence and involvement with you as an expat cause suspicion or interrogation of the national? Do the nationals think it would be better if the expats leave?

21. Prayer and Agreement: As field personnel and headquarters leadership pray, is there a sense of agreement on the departure or return? If not, what specifically is causing the division that needs to be addressed?

Personal and Spiritual Resection

Taken together, these twenty-one principles help us practice personal and spiritual resection.

Resection is a method for determining your position using at least two well-defined locations that can be pinpointed on a map. The more known locations available, the more accurately you can locate your position. Resection is most often done with a compass and topographic map.

When it comes to stay/go and return decisions for missionaries and gospel workers, a spiritual resection based on the aforementioned thresholds helps workers and their organizations reconcile subjective conviction with objective truth in critical and dangerous situations. This Romans 12:2 process helps us to better prove what God's "good, acceptable, and perfect will" is in these very subjective situations. This process requires finding "known points" in the Scriptures, circumstances (utilizing the aforementioned thresholds), wisdom, prayer, and agreement with our brothers and sisters in Christ (especially our supervisors and trusted colleagues).

As a security manager and crisis consultant, I have found this resection process to be very helpful in building margin in decision-making. The more margin an individual, family, or team has in their decision-making, the less stressful and emotionally charged decision-making becomes. Even before a crisis begins, when a situation is just beginning to "heat up," conducting a personal and spiritual resection before a critical incident begins can help us prepare to stay in place as we overcome fear through wise preparation and confidence in the Lord's provision, relocate in the country for a season to let a threat pass in a certain area as we continue our ministry from a nearby location, or choose to evacuate and avoid a tragedy that may otherwise end a ministry permanently.

Developing Congruency between Departure and Return

If a decision was made to depart, then when should a return be attempted? First, we need to establish a good memory as to why we left in order to develop reliable benchmarking for a successful return. What were the reasons for leaving? What specific thresholds/tripwires were met that triggered the departure? Have those specific issues now dissipated? Can they now be adequately abated or mitigated? Remember, there should be congruency in the assessment and analysis of why you left and why you should return. In other words, a similar decision-making process that justified departure should be applied in your justifications for return. That congruency in threshold benchmarking adds to consistency in decision-making for the individual, family, team, and ministry. This, in turn, allows individuals to have not only agreement but also buy-in with decision-making. Remember the wisdom of Proverbs 18:13: "If one gives an answer before he hears, it is his folly and shame." Instead, we must be of one mind and one heart in our desire to return. As Proverbs 11:14 says: "Where there is no guidance, a people falls, but in an abundance of counselors there is safety."

I believe that the Lord wants us to not only be wise in our decision-making—God wants us to be successful. For that success, God has laid out a seven step decision-making process in his word. Essentially:

- Clarify the Decision: I have been part of crisis discussions before where the team could not even agree on what exactly they wanted to do. Avoid that by quickly clarifying, "What is it exactly that we are trying to do?" and "What is the intended end goal/outcome?"

- Seek Biblical Wisdom: Are we making our decisions based more on our feelings and/or desires, or are we seeking biblical wisdom in this decision-making process? Seeking wisdom from God requires studying the Bible to understand what God has to say about your decisions. That said, it is indispensable to understand the difference between knowledge and wisdom. *Knowledge* is having the right information. If you have wrong or misleading information about what the Bible says, there is a real possibility of making poor decisions that are (at best) misinformed, or (worse) sinful. *Wisdom* is necessary to apply what the Bible has to say about your situation. Even then, biblical wisdom is not enough. We need to use the following steps to ensure we have good wisdom in our decision-making.

- Seek Godly Counsel: Godly council, including council from professionals outside the organization, is critical to avoid the "echo chamber" effect of listening to a group that already agrees with itself. While an outside opinion is valuable, I highly recommend that those you speak with not only be good security practitioners but also understand and share your values when it comes to calling and risk. Remember Proverbs 15:22, "Without counsel plans fail, but with many advisers they succeed."

- Prioritize Prayer and Agreement: Prayer and agreement within the body of Christ are critical to success. In the case of making stay/go and return decisions, both headquarters and field personnel must have an agreement through prayer.

- Consider the Alternatives: Are there choices available that will help us fulfill our mandate or mission? Instead of evacuation, are there relocation opportunities inside the country that allow us to mitigate risks and continue the mission? Likewise, are we called to a place or a people? Are there alternatives to returning to a dangerous place that allow us to fulfill our mission such as engaging a diaspora population of our people group located in another country?

- Hold Fast to Your Choices: Once a choice is made, hold fast to that decision. Far too many Christians "wade out into the water" only to turn around and return to the shore. Remember, calling does not change just because circumstances do.

- Trust the Lord: Regardless of the final decision, now is the time to trust the Lord with our decision. Trust leads to peace, empowerment, and fulfillment in our choices and our calling. Trust that the Holy Spirit will empower your obedience and make your path straight. Remember Proverbs 3:5, 6, "Trust in the LORD with all your heart, and do not lean on your understanding. In all your ways acknowledge him, and he will make straight your paths." Also, Isaiah 58:11, "And the LORD will guide you continually and satisfy your desire in scorched places and make your bones strong; and you shall be like a watered garden, like a spring of water, whose waters do not fail."

Closing Thoughts

Undoubtedly the stay/go and return decisions are stressful. The decision-making process can be filled with friction from disagreements and misunderstandings. Sometimes it seems that we may have made the wrong decisions. Regardless, we should draw comfort from the fact that the Lord is sovereign in our decision-making and loves us unconditionally. We must remember who we are and why we are doing what we are doing. Let the same values that led to your calling to go to the nations reinforce your priorities and steps along the path.

If you have any questions, Concilium stands ready to help. Please do not hesitate to reach out to us. May this document empower the gospel to reach every language, people, tribe, and nation! I hope this resource is helpful to you!

About the Author

SCOTT BRAWNER is a writer, speaker, President of Concilium, and the Executive Director of the Risk Management Network. He is an expert in the field of safety, security, and crisis management for gospel workers serving in open and closed countries with Christian missionary agencies, humanitarian organizations, and creative access entities. Scott is one of the most widely traveled and experienced leaders in his field with work and ministry in more than 110 countries around the world. Scott lives in the United States with his wife and three children.

Appendix B
Choosing to Stay
Processing How Our Desire to Risk Can Endanger Others

By Scott Brawner[1]

Part of my ministry is helping gospel workers and their organizations process stay/go decision-making. These are tough decisions to make and discerning God's will in these situations is often challenging. There can be genuine reasons to stay in places facing significant shifts in the old normal of a previous season of peace. However, we must also understand the liabilities and consequences if we do choose to stay as a shift takes place to a dangerous season and a new normal. Whether the normal is shifting because of social upheaval, civil war, invasion, occupation, or other reasons, we must weigh our decisions not only by how they impact us, but also how our decisions to stay impact our national brothers and sisters in the short and long term of a shifting normal.

Introduction

As I have said in the past, I am a fan of the "strategic vacation" for gospel workers facing new threats generated by violent conflict and acts of war (VCAW). When gospel workers have no experience serving in conflict zones or ministering in areas occupied by foreign control, there is a real need to prepare and adjust to this new environment in order to ensure ministry effectiveness. Thus, a strategic vacation is not an evacuation—it is an opportunity to depart a potential conflict zone for the express purpose of decompressing and strengthening emotionally and spiritually from a place of safety as one counts the cost of obedience and determines next steps for effective ministry in a potentially high-risk area.

Three Questions

Clearly there are many considerations to process when choosing to stay or to go. Listed below are the top three questions I try to help gospel workers process as they consider their desire to stay.

1. *Are You Prepared?*

Given the significance of the threat, are you prepared to support yourself, your family, or your team for a long season in a foreign-occupied location or

---
1 Used by permission. This material has been lightly edited for clarity.

territory? In situations where new incidents of VCAW are taking place, the likelihood that basic necessities will dry up and become extremely limited is high. Lacking basic necessities, then, will your presence become a burden to your local brothers and sisters? Worse, will those same brothers and sisters feel a burden to care for you while taking away from caring for themselves? Having a desire to support local believers with your presence is certainly noble. However, becoming a liability to your local partners (in Christ's name no less) because you are ill prepared for the circumstances is not what anyone wants to do. Therefore, make sure that if you are going to stay, you are prepared to be a blessing and not a liability.

2. *Is Your Presence a Liability?*

Is your presence as a foreign national going to cause more harm than good for your national brothers and sisters? While your desire to stay may be to forge solidarity with your co-laborers in Christ, you must be very careful not to put them at risk due to your nationality. In an area that is newly occupied by a foreign power, ideological fervor runs high. Therefore, you must be careful that your nationality does not create an ideological threat for your local partners. As a Westerner in a newly occupied area, you will (at best) be seen as an interloper by the occupiers. Worse, the authorities may consider you a spy. Either way, your relationships with your local partners could well place them at risk. Remember, it is one thing to suffer alongside your local brothers and sisters as a Christian for the sake of the gospel; it is an entirely separate issue to bring danger to them because they are seen as supporting interlopers or spies. Though your heart may be to stay with your partners, they may well be safer with your absence. This is a serious concern and should not be ignored.

3. *Prayer and Agreement?*

If you stay, is there prayer and agreement between family, team members, and your organizational leadership? Is there prayer and agreement between you and your local partners to accept the risk of your staying? Has God granted peace to all parties involved in your present course of action (to stay or to go)? What has the Lord told each of you after a time of concerted prayer in the word? In these situations, it is critical that there be agreement and peace with decision-making. To help individuals and teams process decision-making, Concilium teaches the principle: "Where the Bible is silent, you must follow your conscience as you submit it to God's will through God's word."

We would never ask you to violate your conscience. However, if your organization asks you to depart and you chose to stay, understand you have exceeded your organization's duty of care mandate and are now outside their legal and moral duty to help you in a time of need. Quite often, the decision to stay forces a person to resign from their organization in order to stay. There is much to consider here.

What's Next?

The intent of these recommendations is to help gospel workers build margin into their decision-making. It is always better to establish margin for decision-making before a crisis instead of during a crisis. Without margin, we often see decision-making happening in a panic, compounded by fear, and often exacerbated by communication interruption. This kind of poor decision-making can lead to disaster for those on the ground.

I hope this document is helpful in your decision-making to stay or go. These are hard decisions to make, no doubt. However, it is always better to make those decisions in agreement with all effected parties before a crisis begins because making stay/go decisions in the midst of a critical incident is never a good place to be.

For more information on stay/go decisions, including free resources for developing thresholds for departure and benchmarks for return, visit www.concilium.us/RESOURCES.

Appendix C
Risk Assessment and Management Training (RAM Training)

Hosted by Neal and Anna Hampton with Barnabas International:
ramworkshops@gmail.com

The two-day Risk Assessment and Management (RAM) Training (4-days via Zoom) is an adult-facilitated workshop experience. It is holistic, integrating faith and emotions and training in practical risk assessment and management tools. This training is a companion to *Facing Danger: A Guide through Risk* by Dr. Anna E. Hampton.

The graphic below illustrates the overlaps between the three significant risk preparation categories:

The RAM Training enhances all three categories by providing a framework for prayerful and Holy Spirit-guided implementation in each risk situation.

1. How is the RAM workshop unique from other crisis debrief training? RAM Training addresses the challenge of emotional-psychological-relational-spiritual preparation all field workers need at every leadership level. Because uncertainty is one of the most challenging aspects of living long term in increasingly risky field situations, the RAM Training addresses decision-making in risk.

Through RAM Training combined with the *Facing Danger* book, field workers learn how to analyze risk in uncertainty, how to address increasing anxiety, understand one's predictable responses to risk, and understand what holistic risk assessment and management look like. RAM Training provides a biblical foundation addressing the theology of risk exegetically and holistically, so workers better understand their thinking and emotions in the risk situation.

2. What will an attendee be able to do after attending the workshop?

   a. RAM Training equips participants with a scalable risk management protocol—one that is easily adapted to any risk environment.

   b. RAM Training provides a guide for using the Bible to discern risk rather than an anecdotal biblical model.

   c. RAM Training guides both leaders and individual team members in how to make sure they have responsibly and comprehensively calculated risk from rational, emotional, and spiritual perspectives.

   d. RAM Training equips workers with the key components of decision-making and discernment of risk.

   e. RAM Training augments other stress-resilience and security training by helping field workers discern which risks they are called to minister in—in short, when to stay and when to go.

   f. RAM participants will be equipped to better communicate about risk with other field workers, their children, their leadership, and sending partners.

For more about the Risk Assessment and Management Training, go to this web page: https://theologyofrisk.com.

Here's what others have said:

I am a very hands-on guy, and I love how you guys break down the training into very usable and understandable segments followed by putting all the pieces together and having us practice it.
                          —Global Servant working in Central Asia

> *I was tremendously challenged to re-evaluate my risk management and mitigation plan in light of the Word.*
> —Latin American Pastor serving in Eurasia

> *This is the first training like this I've taken that took a holistic view and was manageable to accomplish. I've enjoyed getting to work with my husband on our plans since the training.*
> —Global Servant working in North Africa

After the training you will leave with:

- Six ways of discovering God's voice in crisis
- Two easy tools to determine which risks need more forethought and which to let go of
- Four general ways to choose from when managing risk
- Knowledge of the difference between the theology of risk and your theology of suffering
- Awareness of ten myths in risk and the biblical truths to counter those myths
- An understanding of six dangerous attitudes in risk

You'll receive:

- Three scalable tools to make risk assessment more manageable and effective
- Four key biases global workers have in risk
- A biblical perspective on risk to help you when hearing God's voice for your direction in risk events
- Four ways to mitigate the effects of risk
- Five essential leadership skills during risk

Acknowledgments

I am grateful to the men and women of Concilium, Crisis Consulting International, and the Risk Management Network (RMN). They gave me the courage to speak up through their warm invitation, kind listening posture, willingness to engage in dialogue, humility, and friendship. I recognize brothers and sisters in RMN who have affirmed me, and your encouragement has given me the strength to grow in confidence. I appreciate Corey and his team who provided input on cybersecurity, and several other security specialists who requested to remain anonymous but gave their input and critical feedback on numerous aspects of this book.

Many others spent time discussing particular aspects of this book, and either took time to meet with me or wrote significant explanations to help me understand their areas of expertise. Specifically, Ted Witmer (Crossworld and *L'Université Shalom de Bunia*) who gave generous feedback on the Hebrew discussion in chapter three, Dr. Mary Ho (All Nations, Inc.), Dr. Frauke Schaefer (Barnabas International), Scott Brawner (Concilium), an individual on the Leadership Team (All Nations), Kate Ward (Gender and Religious Freedom), Brian Aho (Developing Shepherds International), Jim Law, Randy McAlister, Al Williams (SIL), Dr. Earnie Mangest (Reach Global), Dr. Stefan Henger (GEM), and Brian Lubinski (Visible Verse Outdoor Ministry) whose animal research was significant.

I want to acknowledge many other friends worldwide who did not want to be named for security reasons, but warmly consulted with me, patiently answering my many questions. *Thank you.* Good men and women are serving the body of Christ in multiple industries and will not become known publicly until Heaven. He knows the sacrifices you make for kingdom purposes. I hope my synthesis of your input within the content of this book is faithful to your witness and expertise.

I have utilized an interdisciplinary approach and synthesized thoughts from a broad range of researchers, authors, and practitioners. I've incorporated research from the disciplines of theology, spiritual formation, psychology of risk, business, systems science, neurotheology, cross-cultural intelligence, philosophy, psychiatry, animal and human biology, history, airplane engineering, aviation risk, security specialties, risk assessment and management, missiology, cultural anthropology, government research, war studies, and trauma resolution. While I have tried with careful integrity to accurately cite, represent, transliterate, and integrate the relevant yet esoteric, and often technical research and findings, any mistakes in synthesis and application in this book are mine.

Unless specifically identified, the examples used in this book are based on my own real-life experiences or those shared with me by eyewitnesses. Details have been carefully edited to protect locations, identities, and projects.

I'm thankful to be part of Barnabas International (BI) since 2010. Within BI, I've been given the space and freedom to live out God's calling on my life with Neal. I've felt accepted, affirmed, encouraged, and sharpened within the BI family.

Without our financial and prayer partners and our Bible study group, this book would not exist. You have been faithful to support us, pray for us, walk with us in our joys and pains, see us and our children, and cheer on our life's calling and the unique ministry entrusted to us for almost three decades.

I am deeply grateful to so many global workers and persecuted Christ-followers who generously and transparently shared their pain and suffering with Neal and me over the past twenty-five years. From their honest and vulnerable sharing and our own experiences, we've learned to formulate some of the difficult and painful questions being asked about God, life, and what it means to follow him in hard places in the twenty-first century. I hope that my careful listening to you rightly frames the pain, fear, loss, and grief so that you find a vast, thirst-quenching space in your soul as your experiences are named, validated, and affirmed in the following pages.

I treasure my children and their spouses for how your lives point me to Christ. I hope you can see, hear, and feel my mother's heart of love for you in these words. This book reveals my deepest longing for you to continue developing anti-fragile faith in Christ, growing from strength to strength in boldness as you follow Christ despite what happens in the world.

My spiritual director, Mary Maio, stood by me through 2021 as I was in the final stages of preparation and research for this book. The faith-shaking I experienced throughout that year was immensely destabilizing. The acrid bitterness of walking through dark valleys was made more endurable through her generous ministry. She has helped me learn deeper discernment, see and experience God's faithful intimate love for me, and keep moving forward with spiritual eyes. Thank you, Mary.

Without Neal, I could never have written this book. You know the price we've paid for me to write *Facing Fear* and its ongoing impact on us. We've had numerous discussions on almost every aspect of the ideas within—you challenged and sharpened my thinking. I love how you think, how you make me laugh, and how you love me. You are my safe harbor and home wherever we are in the world. I am forever in love with you.

May this book contribute to thoughtful engagement and discerning naming of reality, resulting in the soul-strengthening required to righteously and courageously face the horrors to come in the twenty-first century.

He is worthy.

Witness Risk Glossary

Actor Mapping: Actor mapping identifies all the key individuals, theology of risk, or other organizations that will affect your team or organization's functioning. Actors in any place of ministry can qualify as an adversary, a neutral, or a friend.[1] Actors can be an individual, a group of individuals acting together, paramilitary or military forces, communities, or a country's government.

Assessment: Risk Assessment asks two questions: (1) What could happen? and (2) How does it impact us?

Christ-Follower: A Christ-follower is anyone from any denomination or church tradition who walks in the way of Jesus as his Lord and Savior.

Crisis Management: The plan and procedures in place to mitigate the impact of a negative event.

Crisis Response: Crisis response is a holistic response to those impacted by trauma that promotes coping and flourishing. It encompasses practical, emotional, spiritual, and relational support provided by people with a variety of skills. There are many ways that peers can provide supportive and compassionate assistance to the traumatized. Sometimes professional psychological assistance is needed to help trauma victims.

Cross-Cultural Risk (CCR): The potential for loss and gain when following Christ and ministering cross-culturally.

Cybersecurity: Protecting digital information and how information is shared via phone, VHF radio, computer, and any other means.

Danger (Hazard): See *Risk*

Data: Factual, statistical information

Demographic Proximity: How likely is the risk event to impact people like us?

Frequency: How often is the risk event likely to happen?

Geographic Proximity: How likely is the risk event to happen close by?

Information Analysis: The process of collecting information and data, evaluating it, corroborating it, and then making a decision based on evaluated information.

Information Management: Who is allowed to receive the information and to what level of transparency?

---

[1] Headquarters, *Advanced Situational Awareness*, 10–12.

Intelligence: The "product" resulting from collecting, evaluating, interpreting, and analyzing all available data and information concerning the likelihood of the risk materializing or of the means, intent, and opportunity of a hostile entity carrying out their threat.

Inter-Cultural Risk: The potential for loss and gain when following Christ and living within one's home culture.

Liminality: A threshold, a state of ambiguity, a time of disorientation right before something that has the potential for major change or a new state.[2]

Mitigation: Addresses two questions: (1) How can we prevent the events from happening? and (2) How can we decrease the degree of impact on us?

Persecution: To be pursued. We are pursued by evil because of Christ within us; we are not choosing persecution. We are being pursued because the world hates Christ and hates us without cause (John 15:18, 25). It seems Jesus includes "all these things" in John 15:21 that fall into the category of rejection and persecution and are listed in chapter two.

Probability: In terms of risk, how likely is it that a specific risk event will happen? We can reduce uncertainty by subjective probability.

Risk: A danger or hazard which carries with it the potential for loss and gain.

Risk Assessment Process: Five parts. (1) Learn the environment; (2) identify the risks in that specific environment; (3) analyze the risks (frequencies, intensities, proximities); (4) evaluate and prioritize the risks by increasing threat levels; and (5) decide on risk mitigation strategies.

Risk Literacy: The basic knowledge required to assess various witness risks and mitigate them based on a mature discernment of Holy Spirit-led stewardship.

Severity: How likely is the risk event to have significant negative consequences?

Stewardship of Resources: Handling God's resources for God's purposes. It includes both pouring out and protecting.

Survivability: More than just physically surviving through some danger, but the ability to remain functional and continue our mission.

Theology of Risk: Consists of three critical elements. It asks, "What is my foundation?," "Who has been chosen for this specific risk?," and "How is he leading me to worship him through my risk response (staying or going)?"

---

2 Frost and Hirsch, *Faith of Leap*, 19.

Threat

Anonymous Threats: Direct, anonymous threats are rarely acted upon

Direct Threats: Direct and specific threats should be evaluated. When a person close to you makes a direct threat, the likelihood of them acting on the threat dramatically increases. This is described as the "Intimacy Effect." It should be taken very seriously and immediately mitigated.

Insider Threats: A person who has information and access to an organization greater than outsiders. It may be intentional or unintentional, violent, or non-violent. It may include government-sponsored espionage, fraud, sabotage, unauthorized dissemination of information, or poor security practices.

Blended Threats: some combination of threats against a person or team based on political unrest, terrorism, crime, gang activity, and religious persecution. It may be hard to sort out what the primary reason for the threat is.

Threat Assessment: Threat assessment is a fact-based process that incorporates multiple sources of information and practical experience to determine if a threat is likely to materialize.

Virtual Kidnappings: Virtual kidnappings are when someone makes a ransom demand by phone, text, or email by claiming to have taken the target's loved one hostage. As Artificial Intelligence (AI) technology improves, this risk is likely to increase.

Vulnerabilities: In terms of resources in the risk situation, see *Stewardship of Resources*

Vulnerability: In terms of survivability, vulnerability is the ability to withstand (or not succumb to) a threat.[3]

White Noise: A combination of an overload of uncorroborated and unevaluated information and data along with unevaluated verbal threats and risks.

Witness Risk: A witness is someone whose identity is in Christ, and witnesses to their relationship with Jesus, the Son of God. Witness risk is the potential for loss and gain when following Christ. It is what is faced by any Christ-follower working in hostile, dangerous situations, especially where the gospel is proclaimed.

---

3 Personal discussions with Scott Brawner—his definitions.

Witness Risk Assessment: See *Assessment*

Witness Risk Communication: Witness risk communication is sharing information to inform others what the actual assessed risks are and what risk mitigation will be implemented with different levels of stakeholders. It includes sharing what is happening with others so they can pray intelligently. It involves identifying the hardware necessary to maintain communication in risk and persecution.

Bibliography

Adamantius, Origen of Alexandria. *Homilies on Luke, Fragments on Luke.* Translated by Joseph Lienhard. Washington D.C.: Catholic University of America Press, 2009.

Allen, Jinan N. "What Is Risk Literacy? Accessed May 13, 2022. http://www.riskliteracy.org/.

Allender, Dan B., and Tremper Longman III. *Cry of the Soul: How Our Emotions Reveal Our Deepest Questions about God.* Colorado Springs: Navpress, 1994.

Aquinas, Thomas. 1274. *Summa Theologica, IIb, 123–128.* Accessed November 03, 2021. https://ccel.org/ccel/aquinas/summa/summa.

Asherman, Ira, John W. Bing, and Lionel Laroche. "Building Trust across Cultural Boundaries." *ITAP Intl.com.* Published February 6, 2005. https://asherman.com/downloads/article-btacb.pdf.

ASQ. *Failure Mode and Effects Analysis (FMEA).* ASQ Quality Press. Adapted from The Quality Toolbox. Accessed October 20, 2021. https://asq.org/quality-resources/fmea.

Assmuth, Timo, and Adam M. Finkel. "Choices and rationalities under radical uncertainty: Ideals and principles behind responses to risks and risk information." *Risk, Perception, and Response Conference.* Harvard: Harvard Center for Risk Analysis, 2014.

Ball, Robert E. *The Fundamentals of Aircraft Combat Survivability Analysis and Design.* 2nd ed. Reston: American Institute of Aeronautics and Astronautics, 2003.

Baxter, Keith. *What Is Groupthink? The Theory, Psychology, and Symptoms of a Risk Phenomenon.* Accessed 2022. https://www.de-risk.com/groupthink-and-risk/.

Becker, Gavin de. *The Gift of Fear: Survival Signals That Protect Us from Violence.* New York: Back Bay Books, 1997.

Beitzel, Walter A., and Barry J. Elwell. "Stoics, Stoicism." In *Baker Encyclopedia of the Bible.* Grand Rapids, MI: Baker Book House, 1988.

Blincoe, Robert. *Ethnic Realities and the Church: Lessons from Kurdistan. A History of Mission Work. 1668–1990.* Pasadena: Presbyterian Center for Mission Studies, 1998.

Bolsinger, Tod. *Canoeing the Mountains: Christian Leadership in Uncharted Territory.* Downers Grove: InterVarsity Press, 2018.

Bonhoeffer, Dietrich. *Ethics.* New York: Simon & Schuster, 1955. First Touchstone Edition 1995, Translated by Neville Horton Smith *Dietrich Bonhoeffer Works,* Volume 6, *Ethics.* Gen Editor Wayne Whitson Floyd Jr. 2005 by Fortress Press eBook.

Bowling, Andrew. *Theological Wordbook of the Old Testament.* Electronic ed. Edited by G. L. Archer Jr., B. K. Waltke, and R. L. Harris. Chicago: Moody Press, 1999.

Brackley, Dean. 2004. *The Call to Discernment: New Perspectives on the Transformative Wisdom of Ignatius of Loyola.* New York: Crossroad Publishing Company, 2004.

Bradshaw, Matt, Christopher G. Ellison, and Jack P. Marcum. "Attachment to God, Images of God, and Psychological Distress in a Nationwide Sample of Presbyterians." *International Journal for the Psychology of Religion* 20, no. 2 (2010): 130–47. Accessed April 23, 2022. doi: 10.1080/10508611003608049.

Brawner, Scott. "Decision Making in a Pandemic." Concilium, February 1, 2020.

Breakwell, Glynis M. *The Psychology of Risk*. 2nd ed. Cambridge: Cambridge University Press, 2014.

Brener, Anne. *Mourning & Mitzvah: A Guided Journal for Walking the Mourner's Path Through Grief to Healing*. Woodstock: Jewish Lights Publishing, 2004.

Brocker, Mark. "Boehoeffer's Appeal for Ethical Humility." *Journal of Lutheran Ethics* 3, no. 8 (2003). Accessed May 21, 2022. https://learn.elca.org/jle/bonhoeffers-appeal-for-ethical-humility/.

Brown, Eva, Helene Fisher, Elizabeth Lane Miller, and Rachel Morley. *Same Faith Different Persecution WWR 2021 GSRP Report*. Open Doors, 2 (2021). https://www.opendoors.org/Same_Faith_Different_Persecution_Report.pdf.

Brown Rat. Accessed April 30, 2022. https://animalia.bio/brown-rat.

Brueggeman, Walter. *The Prophetic Imagination*. Minneapolis: Fortress Press, 2018.

Buechner, Frederick. *Listening To Your Life: Daily Meditations with Frederick Buechner*. San Francisco: Harper Collins, 1992.

Bussie, Jacqueline. *The Laughter of the Oppressed: Ethical and Theological Resistance in Wiesel, Morrison, and Endo*. New York: T&T Clark, 2007.

Buth, Randall. *Living Biblical Hebrew: Selected Readings with 500 Friends*. Jerusalem: Biblical Language Center, 2007.

Calhoun, Frederick S., and Stephen W. Weston. "Perspectives on Threat Management." *Journal of Threat Assessment and Managment* (American Psychological Association) 2, no. 3–4 (2015): 258–67.

Cambridge Dictionary. "Obtuseness." Accessed March 3, 2022. https://dictionary.cambridge.org/dictionary/english/obtuseness.

Cambridge Dictionary. "Ritual." Accessed September 28, 2022. https://dictionary.cambridge.org/dictionary/english/ritual.

Cameron, Kim, and Robert McQuinn. *Diagnosing and Changing Organizational Culture Based on the Competing Values Framework*. San Francisco: Jossey-Bass, 2006.

Carr, Karen F. *Appendix A Crisis Response Packet of Tools*. Richmond, VA: Barnabas International, 2020.

Carr, Karen F. *Crisis Response Training Manual*. Barnabas International, 2020.

Cathi. "Lament and Hope." Birmingham: Women in Missions, June 6, 2018.

Chambers, Oswald. "Shallow and Profound." In *My Utmost for His Highest*, 377–78. Grand Rapids: Discovery House, 2017.

Childs, Brevard. *Biblical Theology of the Old and New Testaments: Theological Reflections on the Christian Bible*. Minneapolis: Fortress Press, 2012. https://skipmoen.com/2009/09/kingdom-ethics/.

Chussil, Mark. "Keep a List of Unethical Things You'll Never Do." *Harvard Business Review*, May 30, 2016.

Claassens, L. Juliana. "Tragic Laughter: Laughter as Resistance in the Book of Job." *Interpretation: A Journal of Bible and Theology* 69, no. 2 (2015): 143–55. doi:10.1177/0020964314564844.

Clines, D. J. A. *Word Biblical Commentary Job 1–20*. Vol. 17. Word Books, 1989.

Cloud, Henry. *Integrity: The Courage to Meet the Demands of Reality*. New York: Harper Collins, 2009.

Cochran, Gregory C. "What Kind of Persecution Is Happening to Christians Around the World?" *Southern Baptist Journal of Theology* 18, no. 1 (2014): 34.

Cokely, Felts, Ghazal, Allan, Petrova, Garcia-Retamero. "Skilled Decision Theory: From Intelligence to Numeracy and Expertise." In *Cambridge Handbook*, by www.RiskLiteracy.org, 476–504. Norman, OK: National Institute for Risk and Resiliency, 2017.

Cornerstone Ondemand Foundation. "Actor Mapping and Context Analysis." *Security Risk Tool Kit: Assessments*. Cornerstone OnDemand Foundation. Accessed February 18, 2022. https://gisf.ngo/wp-content/uploads/2020/03/Conducting-context-analysis-actor-mapping-and-risk-assessments.pdf.

Cornish, Charles John. *The Standard Library of Natural History*. Vol. 1. The University Society, Inc. 1908.

Crenshaw, Kitty, and Catherine Snapp. *The Hidden Life Awakened*. Jacksonville: Cairns Resources, 2016.

Cunningham, Scott. *Through Many Tribulations: The Theology of Persecution in Luke-Acts*. Sheffield Academic Press, 1997.

Davis, D. E. "The Characteristics of Rat Populations." *The Quarterly Review of Biology* 28 (1953): 373–401.

Davis, D. E., J. T. Emlen Jr., and A. W. Stokes. "Studies on home range in the brown rat." *Journal of Mammology* 29, no. 3 (1948): 207–25.

de Figueiredo, John M. "Distress, demoralization and psychopathology: Diagnostic boundaries." *The European Journal of Psychiatry* 28, no. 1 (2013). https://scielo.isciii.es/scielo.php?script=sci_arttext&pid=S0213-61632013000100008.

Devlon, Keith. *Confronting Context Effects in Intelligence Analysis: How Can Mathematics Help?* Stanford: CSLI, Stanford University, 2005.

Disparte, Dante. "Simple Ethics Rules for Better Risk Management." *Harvard Business Review*, published November 8, 2016. doi:https://hbr.org/2016/11/simple-ethics-rules-for-better-risk-management.

Dubay S.M., Thomas. *Authenticity: A Biblical Theology of Discernment.* San Francisco: Ignatius Press, 1977.

Elcoat, Donald. *Ancient Heresy and the Church Today.* The Banner of Truth, 1994. Accessed March 15, 2022. https://www.christianstudylibrary.org/article/ancient-heresy-and-church-today.

Ellis, Lisa D. "The Need for Effective Risk Communication Strategies in Today's Complex Information Environment." Published January 5, 2018. https://www.hsph.harvard.edu/ecpe/effective-risk-communication-strategies/.

Elverson, Tim. *Building Resilience: Eight simple activities to help you develop a resilient mind-set for facing adversity and change.* Steeple Claydon: Life Transitions Development, 2020.

Epstein, S. "Integration of the Cognitive and the Psychodynamic Unconscious." *American Psychologist* 49 (1994): 709–24.

Erickson, Angie. "Salt and Light." *Unpublished website.* March, 2022.

Federal Bureau of Investigation's Behavioral Analysis Unit. *Making Prevention a Reality: Identifying, Assessing, and Managing the Effect of Targeted Attacks.* Washington, D.C.: U.S. Department of Justice & Federal Bureau of Investigation.

Feinberg, Charles L. *Theological Wordbook of the Old Testament.* Electronic ed. Edited by G. L. Archer, Jr., B. K. Waltke, and R. L. Harris. Chicago: Moody Press, 1999.

Finucane, Melissa L., Paul Slovic, C. K. Mertz, James Flynn, and Terre D. Satterfield. "Gender, Race and Perceived Risk: The White-Male Effect." In *The Feeling of Risk: New Perspectives on Risk Perception*, 125–40. New York: Earthscan, 2010.

Fisher, Helene, and Elizabeth Miller. *Gendered Persecution: World Watch List 2018 Analysis and Implications.* Accessed January 29, 2022. https://www.opendoorsusa.org/christian-persecution/stories/gendered-persecution/.

Frankl, Viktor E. *The Doctor and the Soul: From Psychotherapy to Logotherapy.* Translated by Richard and Clara Winston. 3rd ed. New York: Vintage Books, 2019.

Frankl, Viktor E. *Man's Search for Meaning.* Boston: Beacon Press, 2006.

French, David. *Parenting Against the Spirit of Fear.* Email Newsletter. April 3, 2022.

Friedman, Edwin H. *A Failure of Nerve: Leadership in the Age of the Quick Fix.* New York: Seabury Books, 2007.

Frost, Michael, and Alan Hirsch. *The Faith of Leap: Embracing a Theology of Risk, Adventure, and Courage.* Grand Rapids: Baker Books, 2011.

Gallagher O.M.V., Timothy. *Teaching Discernment: A Pedagogy for Presenting Ignatian Discernment of Spirits.* Chestnut Ridge: Crossroad Publishing Company, 2020.

Gallagher O.M.V., Timothy. *Overcoming Spiritual Discouragement: The Wisdom and Spiritual Power of Venerable Bruno Lanteri.* Irondale: EWTN, 2019.

Galpin, Mark, Paul Bendor-Samuel, and David Greenlee. "Ethical Evangelism: Integrity, Truth, Timing, and Grace." In *Undivided Witness: Jesus Followers, Community Development, and Least-reached Communities,* 84. Oxford: Regnum Books International, 2020.

Gamhewage, Gaya. *An Introduction to Risk Communication.* World Health Organization, 1–6. Accessed March 2, 2022. https://www.who.int/risk-communication/introduction-to-risk-communication.pdf.

Gardner, Frank. *Jihadist Groups around the World.* Published June 19, 2014. https://www.bbc.com/news/world-middle-east-27930414.

Gardner, Laura Mae. "Escalating Stress Events." *Care Documents.* www.mmct.org.

Gelles, Michael. *Insider Threat Prevention, Detection, Mitigation, and Deterrence.* Cambridge: Butterworth-Heinemann, 2016.

Gigerenzer, Gerd. *Gut Feelings: The Intelligence of the Unconscious.* Penguin Books, 2007.

Gigerenzer, Gerd. *Rationality for Mortals: How People Cope with Uncertainty.* Oxford: Oxford University Press, 2008.

Gigerenzer, Gerd. *Risk Savvy: How to Make Good Decisions.* New York: Viking Penguin, 2014.

Gilchrist, Paul R. "859 לָחִי." In *Theological Wordbook of the Old Testament,* edited by R. Laird Harris, Gleason L. Archer, and Bruce K. Waltke, 373–74. Chicago: Moody Press, 1999.

Gloeckner, Erin. *The Optimism Bias.* Published October 16, 2015. https://nonprofitrisk.org/resources/e-news/the-optimism-bias/.

Greenburg, Moshe. *The Book of Job.* Accessed April 30, 2022. https://www.myjewishlearning.com/article/the-book-of-job/.

Gruber, Daniel. *The End from the Beginning: A Midrash on the First Three Verses.* Hanover: Elijah Publishing, 2014.

Haden, Jeff. *The 5 New Habits of the Most Effective Leaders, Backed by Considerable Science.* Published May 4, 2022. https://www.inc.com/jeff-haden/the-5-new-habits-of-most-effective-leaders-backed-by-considerable-science.html.

Haimovitch, Aviad Bar Guy, and Shai Meiri. *The Field Guide to Reptiles and Amphibians of Israel.* Frankfurt: Chimaira, 2021.

Hall, Wayne Michael, and Gary Cintrenbaum. *Intelligence Analysis: How to Think in Complex Environments.* Santa Barbara: ABC-CLIO, 2010.

Hampton, Anna E. *Facing Danger: A Guide Through Risk.* New Prague: Zendagi Press, 2016.

Hampton, Anna E. "Hampton Survey of RMN Security Personnel." *Top Fears within Mission Organizations.* Jan/Feb, 2022.

Hampton, Neal, and Anna Hampton. *RAM: A Workshop on Risk Assessment & Management*. Ankara: Zendagi, 2016.

Harter SJ, Michael, ed. *Hearts on Fire: Praying with the Jesuits*. Chicago: Loyola Press, 1993.

Head, George L. "Why Link Risk Management and Ethics." *Ethics*. Published February, 2005. https://www.irmi.com/articles/expert-commentary/why-link-risk-management-and-ethics.

Headquarters, Department of the Army. *Advanced Situational Awareness*. TC 3-22.69. Washington, D.C.: Department of the Army, 2021.

Hefner, R., and E. Geffen. "Group Size and Home Range of the Arabian Wolf (Canus Lupus) in Southern Israel." *Journal of Mammalogy* 80, no. 2 (1999): 611-19.

Henger, Stefan. "Risikomündigkeit in der Mission. Eine Beschreibung von Entscheidungskriterien deutscher Missionsleitungen über die Entsendung und Rückführung von Missionaren in risikoreiche Länder." *Doctor of Ministry Leadership*. Translated by Ability to Take Risks in the Mission. A description of the decision-making criteria of German mission leaders regarding the sending and repatriation of missionaries to high-risk countries. Columbia International University/European School for Culture and Theology, June, 2020.

Heschel, Abraham J. *The Prophets*. Peabody: Prince Press, 1962.

Heschel, Abraham J. *Who Is Man?* Stanford: Stanford University Press, 1965.

Heuer, Richards J. *The Psychology of Intelligence Analysis*. Washington, D.C.: Central Intelligence Agency, 1999.

Hofstede, Geert. *6-D Model of National Culture*. Accessed 2015. https://geerthofstede.com/culture-geert-hofstede-gert-jan-hofstede/6d-model-of-national-culture/.

Holcomb, Justin S. *Know the Heretics*. Grand Rapids: Zondervan, 2014.

Hubbard, Douglas. *How to Measure Anything: Finding the Value of Intangibles in Business*. 3. Hoboken: Wiley, 2014.

IBS. *Graham Staines Story*. Accessed February 22, 2022. http://ibsresources.org/articles/staines.shtml.

Inge, Denise. *A Tour of Bones: Facing Fear and Looking for Life*. London: Bloomsbury, 2014.

Jastrow, M. *In a Dictionary of the Targumim, the Talmud Babli and Yerushalmi, and the Midrashic Literature*. Vol. I. Luzac & Co.; G. P. Putnam's Sons, 1903.

Jenni, Ernst, and Claus Westermann. *Theological Lexicon of the Old Testament*. Electronic ed. Edited by G. L. Archer Jr., B. K. Waltke, and R. L. Harris. Chicago: Moody Press, 1999.

Jerajani, H. R., Bhagyashri Jaju, M. M. Phiske, and Nitin Lade. 2009. "Hematohidrosis—A Rare Clinical Phenomenon." *Indian Journal of Dermatology* 54, no. 3 (2009): 290-292. https://www.ncbi.nlm.nih.gov/pmc/articles/PMC2810702/.

Jerome, Christopher L. "Fixed-Wing Aircraft Combat Survivability Analysis for Operation Enduring Freedom and Operation Iraqi Freedom." *Airforce Institute of Technology*. Wright-Patterson Air Force Base, Ohio: Department of Aeronautics and Astronautics Graduate School of Engineering and Management. Published March 11, 2011. https://scholar.afit.edu/cgi/viewcontent.cgi?article=2334&context=etd.

Jethani, Skye. *The Real Meaning of Jesus Calming the Storm: Mark 4:35–40*. May 13, 2022.

Jones, Christine Brown. "When I Am Afraid: Fear in the Book of Psalms." *Review and Expositor* 115, no. 1 (2018): 15–25. doi:10.1177/0034637317752930.

Joshua Project. *Progress Scale Map*. Accessed November 01, 2021. https://joshuaproject.net/assets/media/maps/progress-scale-map-1040.pdf.

JTA. "Deadly Palestine Viper Declared Israel's National Snake." *The Times of Israel*. Published November 3, 2018. https://www.timesofisrael.com/deadly-palestine-viper-declared-israels-national-snake/.

Kahneman, Daniel. *Thinking Fast and Slow*. Farrar, Straus and Giroux, 2011.

Kalland, E. S. "398 קָבַד." In *Theological Wordbook of the Old Testament*, edited by R. L. Harris, G. L. Archer and B. K. Waltke. Chicago: Moody Press, 1999.

Kay, David. *Stress Inoculation Training*. Published March 14, 2020. https://krav-maga-self-defence.com/stress-inoculation-training/.

Kelly, Geffrey B., and F. Burton Nelson. *The Cost of Moral Leadership: The Spirituality of Dietrich Bonhoeffer*. Grand Rapids: Eerdmans, 2003.

Kessler, David. *Finding Meaning: The Sixth Stage of Grief*. New York: Scribner, 2019.

Kiev, Ari. *The Psychology of Risk: Mastering Market Uncertainty*. New York: John Wiley & Sons, 2002.

Kittel, G., G. Friedrich, and G. W. Bromily. *Theological Dictionary of the New Testament*. Grand Rapids, MI: Eerdmans, 1985.

Klama, R. B. *Malatya Murders: A 12-year Fight for Justice*. Published January 28, 2019. https://www.mnnonline.org/news/malatya-murders-a-12-year-fight-for-justice/.

Korkie, Yolande. *558 Days: A True Story*. Vereeniging: Christian Art Publishers, 2016.

Kutz, Karl V., and Rebekah L. Josberger. *Learning Biblical Hebrew: Reading for Comprehension—An Introductory Grammar*. Bellingham: Lexham Press, 2018.

Lan, Kwok Pui. "Discovering the Bible in the Non-Biblical World." In *Voices from the Margin: Interpreting the Bible in the Third World*, Ed. by R. S., Sugirtharajah, 289–305. Maryknoll: Orbis Books, 1995.

Lange, David H. "Exploring the Idol of Security." Master's thesis, Reformed Theological Seminary, 2019.

Leson, Col Joel. "Assessing and Managing the Terrorism Threat." Bureau of Justice Assistance, US Department of Justice, Washington, DC, 29 (2005). Accessed February 20, 2022. https://www.ojp.gov/pdffiles1/bja/210680.pdf.

LESS, Large Scale Scrum. *Systems Thinking*. Accessed May 12, 2022. https://less.works/less/principles/systems-thinking.

Levinson, Leila. *Gated Grief: The Daughter of a GI Concentration Camp Liberator Discovers a Legacy of Trauma*. Cable Publishing, 2011.

Lewis, C. S. *God in the Dock: Essays on Theology and Ethics*. New York: Harper Collins, 1970.

Lewis, C. S. *A Grief Observed*. New York: Harper Collins e-books, 2009.

Lewis, James, and James Bywater. "Leadership: What competencies does it take to remain engaged as a leader in a VUCA world?" *Assessment & Development Matters* 11, no. 3 (2019). https://ptc.bps.org.uk/sites/ptc.bps.org.uk/files/adm/2019_10_24_selected_article_web_vol11_no3_bywater_and_lewis.pdf.

Lewis, Rachel, Christian Ferragamo, Joanna Yarker, and Emma Donaldson-Feilder. "Keeping International Business Travelers Healthy, Happy, Engaged at Home and Away." *International SOS Foundation*. Accessed May 14, 2022. https://images.learn.internationalsos.com/Web/InternationalSOS/%7Bfede1ee9-1bbb-4562-9ff2-673717a309be%7D_Psychological_Study_with_Kingston___Affinity_FINAL.pdf.

Lewis, Richard D. *Cross-Cultural Communication: A Visual Approach*. 2. Hampshire: Transcreen Publications, 2008.

Lewis, Richard G. "How Cultures Work: A Roadmap for Intercultural Understanding in the Workplace." *Missio Nexus*. Published January 1, 2009. https://missionexus.org/how-cultures-work-a-roadmap-for-intercultural-understanding-in-the-workplace/.

Liebert, Elizabeth. *The Soul of Discernment: A Spiritual Practice for Communities and Institutions*. Louisville: Westminster John Knox Press, 2015.

Lingenfelter, Sherwood G., and Marvin K. Mayers. *Ministering Cross-Culturally: A Model for Effective Personal Relationships*. 3rd ed. Grand Rapids, MI: Baker Academic, 2016.

Litvin, Jay. "Spiritual Warrior." *The Tanya*. Chabad.org. Accessed December 9, 2015. www.chabad.org/library/tanya/tanya_cdo/aid/1281943/Jewish/Spiritual_Warrior.

Lloyd, Richard Raymond. "No one shall make them afraid." *Review and Expositor* 3, no. 4 (2014): 358–64.

Longman III, Tremper. "The 'Fear of God' in the Book of Ecclesiastes." *Bulletin for Biblical Research* 25, no. 1 (2015): 13–21.

Louw, J. P., and E. A. Nida. *Greek-English Lexicon of the New Testament: Based on Semantic Domains*. 2nd ed. United Bible Societies, 1996.

Lubinski, Brian. "Doves." March, 2022.

MacGill, Victor. "From Violence to Love: A systems wisdom workbook for living beyond violence." Unpublished manuscript, 2022.

Manges, Rev. E. "Bribery 30 Jan 2013." *Ethical Issues CGST L 4*. 2013.

Marin, Systems Thinking. *What Is Systems Thinking*. Accessed May 13, 2022. https://www.systemsthinkingmarin.org/about/what-is-systems-thinking/.

McBride, Duane C. "The Sociological Imagination and the Christian Worldview." *The Institute for Christian Teaching.* Vol. 18. Accessed April 14, 2022. https://christintheclassroom.org/vol_18/18cc_355-358.htm.

McCalister, Randy. "Insider Threats." 2022.

Mercer, Steve. "Crisis Leadership." *RMN Conference Presentation.* Orlando: Risk Management Network, 2022.

Mercer, Steve. "Risk and Security as Cultural Concepts: What Missionaries and Security Professionals Can Learn from Each Other." Research Paper, Southern Baptist Theological Seminary, 2021.

Mercer, Steve. "Crisis Leadership Lessons for Missionaries." Research Paper, Southern Baptist Theological Seminary, 2021.

Mermelstein, Ari. "Constructing Fear and Pride in the Book of Daniel: The Profile of a Second Temple Emotional Community." *Journal for the Study of Judaism* (2015): 449–83.

Meyer, Erin. *The Culture Map: Breaking Through the Invisible Boundaries of Global Business.* Philadelphia: PublicAffairs, 2014.

Miller, Mark. *Think Like a Green Beret: The PACE Plan.* Published June 3, 2018. https://sofrep.com/news/think-like-green-beret-making-pace-plan/.

Miller, William Ian. *The Mystery of Courage.* Cambridge: Harvard University Press, 2000.

Missio Nexus. *Global Missions and Risk.* Published April 20, 2022. https://missionexus.org/global-missions-and-risk/.

Moen, Skip. "Adhesive Qualities." *Hebrew Word Study | Skip Moen.* Published January 19, 2009. https://skipmoen.com/2009/01/adhesive-qualities/.

Moen, Skip. "Backup." *Hebrew Word Study | Skip Moen.* Published September 15, 2010. https://skipmoen.com/2010/09/backup/.

Moen, Skip. "Beneath Egypt." *Hebrew Word Study | Skip Moen.* Published June 12, 2014. https://skipmoen.com/2014/06/beneath-egypt/.

Moen, Skip. "Calm Terror." *Hebrew Word Study | Skip Moen.* Published March 28, 2008. https://skipmoen.com/2008/03/calm-terror/.

Moen, Skip. "Gods of War." *Hebrew Word Study | Skip Moen.* Published November 22, 2008. https://skipmoen.com/2008/11/gods-of-war/.

Moen, Skip. "Hidden Hope." *Hebrew Word Study | Skip Moen.* Published November 19, 2013. https://skipmoen.com/2013/11/hidden-hope/.

Moen, Skip. "In the Boat." *Hebrew Word Study | Skip Moen.* Published March 27, 2012. https://skipmoen.com/2008/03/in-the-boat/.

Moen, Skip. "An Incomplete Life." *Hebrew Word Study | Skip Moen.* Published November 8, 2012. https://skipmoen.com/2012/11/an-incomplete-life/.

Moen, Skip. "Kingdom Ethics." *Hebrew Word Study | Skip Moen.* Published September 5, 2009. https://skipmoen.com/2009/09/kingdom-ethics/.

Moen, Skip. "Kingdom Status." *Hebrew Word Study | Skip Moen.* Published August 20, 2015. https://skipmoen.com/2015/08/kingdom-status/.

Moen, Skip. "Parable Ethics." *Hebrew Word Study | Skip Moen.* Published April 17, 2018. https://skipmoen.com/2018/04/parable-ethics/.

Moen, Skip. "Personal Ethics." *Hebrew Word Study | Skip Moen.* Published August 18, 2017. https://skipmoen.com/2017/08/personal-ethics/.

Moen, Skip. "Stormy Monday." *Hebrew Word Study | Skip Moen.* Published June 21, 2008. https://skipmoen.com/2008/06/stormy-monday/.

Montgomery, John Warwick. "The New Age of Christian Martyrdom." *Global Journal for Classical Theology* 8, no. 3 (2011). https://www.galaxie.com/article/gjct08-3-01?highlight=persecution.

Moore, Charles E. *Perpetua: An Early Christian Martyr.* Published February 25, 2016. https://www.plough.com/en/topics/faith/witness/perpetua.

Morris, Leon. *The New International Commentary on the New Testament: The Gospel According to John.* Edited by F. F. Bruce. Grand Rapids: Eerdmans, 1971.

Mosebach, Martin. *The 21: A Journey into the Land of Coptic Martyrs.* Translated by Alta L. Price. Walden: Plough Publishing House, 2019.

Muller, Roland. *Honor and Shame: Unlocking the Door.* Xlibris, 2001.

Murphy, Sophia. *What Is Systems Thinking?* Published February 7, 2022. https://www.iatp.org/what-is-systems-thinking.

Musser, G. G., and M. D. Carleton. "Superfamily Muroidea." In *Mammal Species of the World: A Geographic and Taxonomic Reference*, by D. E. Wilson and D. A. Reeder, pp. 894–1531. Baltimore: The John Hopkins University Press, 2005.

Myers, Alicia D. "Introduction: Fear and Faith: Trusting God in a fear-filled world." *Review and Expositor* 115, no. 1 (2018): 8–12. doi:10.1177/0034637318754385.

Nash, A. J. "The Differences Between Data, Information, and Intelligence." April 2017. https://www.uscybersecurity.net/csmag/the-differences-between-data-information-and-intelligence/.

NCTC, DHS, FBI. *First Responder's Toolbox: Terrorist Attack Planning Cycle—A Homeland Case Study.* Unclassified and available on the Internet, NCTC, DHS, FBI, USA Homeland Security. 2017. https://info.publicintelligence.net/DHS-FBI-NCTC-TerroristPlanningCycle.pdf.

Newberg, Andrew, and Mark Robert Waldman. *How God Changes Your Brain: Breakthrough Findings from a Leading Neuroscientist.* New York: Ballantine Books, 2010.

Nisbett, Richard. *The Geography of Thought: How Asians and Westerners Think Differently...and Why.* Free Press, 2003.

Nouwen, Henri. *Wounded Healer.* New York: Doubleday, 1972.

O'Brien, Tim. *If I Die in a Combat Zone Box Me Up and Ship Me Home.* New York: Broadway Books, 1975.

Open Doors. *How the Scoring Works.* Accessed January 29, 2022. https://www.opendoorsusa.org/christian-persecution/world-watch-list/about-the-ranking/.

Open Doors. *The World Watch List: The Top 50 Countries Where Its Most Difficult to Follow Jesus.* Accessed November 01, 2021. https://www.opendoorsusa.org/christian-persecution/world-watch-list/.

Open Doors. *The 2022 World Watch List.* Open Doors, 2022.

Open Doors. *Complete World Watch List Methodology.* World Watch Research. Updated October, 2020. https://odusa-media.com/2021/01/Complete-WWL-Methodology-October-2020-FINAL.pdf.

OSAC. *Transnational Crime Fuels Spike in Ecuador Violence.* OSAC. Accessed March 22, 2022.

Oswalt, John N. "233 חָטַב." In *Theological Wordbook of the Old Testament*, edited by R. L. Harris, G. L. Archer, Jr., and B. K. Waltke, 101. Chicago: Moody Press, 1999.

Palmer, Parker J. *A Hidden Wholeness: The Journey Toward an Undivided Life.* San Francisco: Jossey-Bass, 2004.

Palmer, Parker J. *The Tragic Gap.* Accessed March 19, 2019. https://couragerenewal.org/library/chapter-10-standing-in-the-tragic-gap.

Palmieri, Lisa M. *Information vs. Intelligence: What Police Executives Need to Know.* International Association of Law Enforcement Intelligence Analysts, 2005. https://www.ialeia.org/docs/InformationvsIntelligence.pdf.

Parkes, Colin Murray. *Bereavement Studies of Grief in Adult Life.* New York: International Universities Press, 1972.

Penner, Glenn M. *In the Shadow of the Cross: A Biblical Theology of Persecution and Discipleship.* Bartlesville, OK: VOM Books, 2021.

Pennington, David A., Baxter Sawvel, and Brad R. Moon. "Debunking the Viper's Strike: Harmless Snakes Kill a Common Assumption." *Biology Letters.* March 1, 2016. doi:10.1098.

Peters, Ellen, Judith Hibbard, Paul Slovic, and Nathan Dieckmann. "Numeracy Skill and the Communication, Comprehension, and Use of Risk-Benefit Information." In *The Feeling of Risk: New Perspectives on Risk Perception*, by Paul Slovic, 351. New York: Earthscan, 2010.

Peterson, Jordan. "12 Rules That Will Change Your Life." Published January 18, 2022. https://www.youtube.com/watch?v=WLH6CPTQT9g.

Pires, Candace. *Don't Panic! Meet the experts with a steady hand when disaster strikes.* Published September 9, 2018. https://www.theguardian.com/world/2018/sep/09/dont-panic-meet-the-experts-with-a-steady-hand-when-disaster-strikes.

Plato. *Laches.* Translated by Benjamin Jowett. Accessed November 03, 2021. http://classics.mit.edu/Plato/laches.html.

Porter, Shirley. *What Is Stress Inoculation Training?* Published June 15, 2021. https://www.choosingtherapy.com/stress-inoculation-training/.

Qiaoying, Lu. "Aquinas' Transformation of the Virtue of Courage." *Frontiers of Philosophy in China* (Brill) 8, no. 3 (2013): 471–84. https://www.deepdyve.com/lp/brill/aquinas-s-transformation-of-the-virtue-of-courage-zRwUhcb23k?.

Quesenberry, Gary. *Spotting Danger Before It Spots You: Build Situational Awareness to Stay Safe*. Wolfeboro: YMAA Publication Center, 2020.

Rambo, Shelly. "Witnessing Holy Saturday." In *Spirit and Trauma: A Theology of Remaining* by Shelly Rambo, 45–80. Louisville: John Knox Press, 2010.

Religious Liberty Commission of the Evangelical Fellowship of India. "Hate and Targeted Violence Against Christians in India Yearly Report." Annual. Published February 15, 2022 https://efionline.org/2022/02/15/religious-liberty-commission-yearly-report-2021/.

Renfroe PSP, Nancy A., and Joseph L. Smith PSP. *Threat / Vulnerability Assessments And Risk Analysis*. Updated August 8, 2016. https://wbdg.org/resources/threat-vulnerability-assessments-and-risk-analysis.

Renita. "Accountable for Risks Not Taken." *Discipling Market Place Leaders.org*. Published January 3, 2022. renita@disciplingmarketplaceleaders.org.

Robson, David. *How East and West Think in Profoundly Different Ways*. Published January 19, 2017. https://www.bbc.com/future/article/20170118-how-east-and-west-think-in-profoundly-different-ways.

Robson, Sean, and Thomas Manacailli. *Enhancing Performance Under Stress: Stress Inoculation Training for Battlefield Airmen*. Rand Corporation, 2014. https://www.rand.org/pubs/research_reports/RR750.html.

Rohei. *Leadership Competencies That Matter Most in a VUCA World*. Published May 30, 2018. https://www.rohei.com/resources/leadership-competencies-that-matter-most-in-a-vuca-world.

Rolheiser, Ronald. *The Shattered Lantern: Rediscovering a Felt Presence of God*. New York: Crossroad Publishing, 2004.

Roskoski, John. "A Biblical Model of Human Dignity: Based on the Image of God and the Incarnation." *Contemporary Issues*. Published October 23, 2013. https://biblearchaeology.org/research/contemporary-issues/2405-a-biblical-model-of-human-dignity-based-on-the-image-of-god-and-the-incarnation.

Ruebusch, Pamel. "The Virtue of Courage: Why we need it in a time when there is so little of it." *The Human Edge*, September, 2004. www.ctl.ca.

Sacks, Rabbi Lord Jonathan. *To Heal a Fractured World: The Ethics of Responsibility*. New York: Schocken Books, 2005.

Sacks, Rabbi Lord Jonathan. *The Courage to Live with Uncertainty*. Accessed March 23, 2022. https://aish.com/the-courage-to-live-with-uncertainty/.

Sacks, Rabbi Lord Jonathan. *Covenant & Conversation, Genesis: The Book of Beginnings*. "Vayeshev." London: Koren Books, 2009.

Sauer, Christoff, and Richard Howell, eds. *Suffering, Persecution, and Martyrdom: Theological Reflections*, 2. Johannesburg: AcadSA, 2010.

Scazzero, Peter. *Emotionally Healthy Spirituality: It's impossible to be spiritually mature while remaining emotionally immature*. Grand Rapids: Zondervan, 2017.

Schaefer, Frauke C., Dan Blazer, and Harold Koenig. "Religious and Spiritual Factors and the Consequences of Trauma: A Review and Model of the Interrelationships." *International Journal of Psychiatry in Medicine* 38, no. 4 (2008): 507–24.

Schein, M. W., and H. Orgain. "A preliminary analysis of garbage as food for the Norway rat." *The American Journal of Tropical Medicine and Hygiene* 2 (1953): 1117–30.

Schirrmacher, Thomas. *Leadership and Ethical Responsibility: The Three Aspects of Every Decision*. Vol. 13. Bonn: Culture and Science, 2013.

Scholtz, Roger. "'I Had Heard of You . . . But Now My Eye Sees You': Re-Visioning Job's Wife." *Old Testament Essays* 26, no. 3 (2013): 819–39.

Schweitzer, Carol L. Schnabl. "A Lesson on Courage: Monks, Martyrs, and Muslims—but Strangers No Longer in Algeria." *Pastoral Psychology* 62 (2013): 759–74.

Seel, David John. *The New Copernicans: Millenials and the Survival of the Church*. Nashville: Thomas Nelson, 2018.

Segev, G., A. Shipov, E. Klement, S. Harrus, P. Kass, and I. Aroch. "Vipera palaestinae envenomation in 327 Dogs: A Retrospective Cohort Study and Analysis of Risk Factors for Mortality." *Toxicon* 43, no. 6 (2004): 691–99. doi:10.1016.

Seida, Caitlin. *My Broken Voice: Poetry from the Edge and Back*. "Hope Is Not a Bird, Emily, It's a Sewer Rat." Verdigris Visions Press, 2018.

Sermon Central. *Sermon Central*. Accessed January 10, 2021. https://www.sermoncentral.com/sermons/sermons-about-fear/?CheckedScriptureBookId=&keyword=fear&denominationFreeText=&maxAge=&searchPhrase=fear.

Simons, A., and R. F. Tunkel. "The Assessment of Anonymous Threatening Communications." In *The International Handbook of Threat Assessment*, edited by J. R. Meloy and J. Hoffman, 235–56. London: Oxford University Press, April 1, 2021. https://doi.org/10.1093/med-psych/9780190940164.003.0012.

Sittser, Gerald L. *Resilient Faith: How the Early Christian "Third Way" Changed the World*. Grand Rapids: Brazos Press, 2019.

Sittser, Gerald L. *A Grace Disguised: How the Soul Grows through Loss*. Grand Rapids: Zondervan, 2004.

Slovic, Paul. *The Perception of Risk*. London: Earthscan Publications, 2000.

Slovic, Paul. "Trust, Emotion, Sex, Politics, and Science: Surveying the Risk-Assessment Battlefield." *Risk Analysis* 19, no. 4 (1999).

Slovic, Paul, Baruch Fischhoff, and Sarah Lichtenstein. "Facts and Fears: Understanding Perceived Risks," 137–53, *The Perception of Risk*. London: Earthscan Publications, 2000.

Slovic, Paul, Melissa L. Finucane, Ellen Peters, and Donald G. MacGregor. "Risk as Analysis and Risk as Feelings: Some Thoughts about Affect, Reason, Risk, and Rationality." In *The Feeling of Risk: New Perspectives on Risk Perception*, edited by Paul Slovic. New York, NY: Earthscan, 2010.

Social Behavior. Accessed April 30, 2022. http://members.madasafish.com/~cj_whitehound/Rats_Nest/Norway_Rats/Social_behaviour.htm.

Society for Risk Analysis. *Core Subjects of Risk Analysis*. Updated August 2018.

Society for Risk Analysis. *Risk Analysis: Fundamental Principles*. Updated August 2018.

Soltes, Eugene. "Why It's So Hard to Train Someone to Make an Ethical Decision." *Harvard Business Review*, January 11, 2017.

SOS, International. *Travel Risks & Reality: The New Normal for Business*. Ipsos Global Reputation Centre, 2017. https://site.internationalsos.com/grmp/resources/white-papers.

Spencer, F. Scott. "To Fear and Not to Fear the Creator God: A Theological and Therapeutic Interpretation of Luke 12:4–34." *Journal of Theological Interpretation* 8, no. 2 (2014): 229–49.

Stigers, Harold G. In *Theological Wordbook of the Old Testament*. Edited by R. L. Harris, G. L. Archer, Jr., and B. K. Waltke. Chicago: Moody Press, 1999.

Stratfor Global Information. *The Terrorist Attack Cycle*. RANE, Updated October 3, 2012. https://worldview.stratfor.com/article/stratfor-terrorist-attack-cycle.

Stratfor. *How to Look for Trouble: A STRATFOR Guide to Protective Intelligence*. Austin: Walter H. Howerton Jr, 2010.

Swerdloff, Michael. "Six Types of Courage." Published September 18, 2020. https://www.michaelswerdloff.com/six-types-courage/.

Tahir, Uzma. "The Role of Globalization in Fuelling and Redressing Terrorism." *Al-mushir (The Counselor): Theological Journal of the Christian Study Centre* (Christian Study Centre, Rawalpindi, Pakistan) 47, no. 4 (2005): 3–17.

Taleb, Nassim Nicholas. *The Black Swan: Second Edition: The Impact of the Highly Improbable*. New York: Random House, 2010.

Taylor, J. Hudson. "A Retrospect, The Call to Service (1894)." In *Perspectives of the World Christian Movement*, by Steven C. Hawthorne (Editor) and Ralph D. Winter (Editor), Chapter 49, 319. Pasadena: William Carey Library, 2013.

Teiszen, Charles L. *Re-Examining Religious Persecution:Constructing a Theological Framework for Understanding Persecution*. Johannesburg: AcadSA, 2008.

TenBoom, Corrie. *Amazing Love*. Fort Washington: CLC, 2018.

Tetlow, Joseph A. *Making Choices in Christ: The Foundations of Ignatian Spirituality*. Chicago: Loyola Press, 2008.

Tetlow, Joseph A. *Always Discerning: An Ignatian Spirituality for the New Millennium*. Chicago: Loyola Press, 2016.

The American Heritage Dictionary of the English Language. 5. Accessed April 14, 2022. https://duckduckgo.com/?q=define+paradox&atb=v314-1&ia=definition.

Thistlethwaite, Susan Brooks. *Women's Bodies as Battlefields: Christian Theology and the Global War on Women*. New York: Palgrave Macmillan, 2017.

Thompson, Curt. *Anatomy of the Soul: Surprising Connections Between Neuroscience and Spiritual Practices That Can Transform Your Life and Relationships*. Tyndale House Publishers, 2010.

"Threat, Vulnerability, Risk: What Is the Difference?" *Lifars*. Published July 22, 2020. https://lifars.com/2020/07/threat-vulnerability-risk-what-is-the-difference/.

Thurman, Howard. *Jesus and the Disinherited*. Boston: Abingdon Press, 1976.

Thurman, Howard. *Deep Is the Hunger: Meditations for Apostles of Sensitiveness*. Muriwai Books, 2015.

Tierney, Kathleen. *The Social Roots of Risk: Producing Disasters, Promoting Resiliency*. Stanford: Stanford University Press, 2014.

Tigay, Jeffrey H. *Deuteronomy: The JPS Torah Commentary*. Philadelphia: Jewish Publication Society, 1996.

Tilton, Joshua N. *Jesus' Gospel: Searching for the Core of Jesus' Message*. Jerusalem: Jerusalem Perspectives, 2012.

Ton, Josef. *Suffering, Martyrdom, and Rewards in Heaven*. Wheaton: The Romanian Missionary Society, 2000.

Treverton, Gregory F., Seth G. Jones, Steven Boraz, and Phillip Lipscy. "Toward a Theory of Intelligence Workshop Report." *Rand Conference Proceedings*. Rand National Security Research Division, 25 (2006). Accessed April 10, 2022. https://www.rand.org/content/dam/rand/pubs/conf_proceedings/2006/RAND_CF219.pdf.

Tversky, Amos, and Daniel Kahneman. "The framing of decisions and the psychology of choice." *Science* (1981): 453–58.

van Breemen SJ, Peter G. *As Bread That Is Broken*. Denville: Dimension Books, 1974.

Västfjäll, Daniel, Ellen Peters, and Paul Slovic. "Affect, Risk Perception, and Future Optimism after the Tsunami Disaster." In *The Feeling of Risk: New Persepctives on Risk Perception*, by Paul Slovic, 109–24. New York: Earthscan, 2010.

Vinney, Cynthia. *What Is Cognitive Bias? Definition and Examples*. Updated October 31, 2018. https://www.thoughtco.com/cognitive-bias-definition-examples-4177684.

Voice of the Martyrs, The. *Wurmbrand: Tortured for Christ, The Complete Story*. Colorado Springs: David C. Cook, 2018.

Waldorf, Andrea C. "Principle 9: Shared Principles of Excellence." In *Undivided Witness: Jesus Followers, Community Development, and Least-reached Communities*, by Mark Galpin, Paul Bendor-Samuel and David Greenlee, 156. Oxford: Regnum Books International, 2020.

Waring, Sara. "Don't Panic!" Published September 9, 2018. https://www.theguardian.com/world/2018/sep/09/dont-panic-meet-the-experts-with-a-steady-hand-when-disaster-strikes.

Weaver, Pastor Patrick. *Faithhill Church USA*. Posted May 1, 2019. https://www.facebook.com/FaithhillChurchUSA/posts/your-calling-is-going-to-crush-you-if-youre-called-to-mend-the-brokenhearted-you/2272647579667230/.

Webb-Mitchel, Brett. "Open House: The American Family in the Household of God." *Theology Today* 52, no. 2 (1995): 250.

Weber, Carl Philip. *Theological Wordbook of the Old Testament*. Electronic ed. Edited by G. L. Archer Jr., B. K. Waltke, and R. L. Harris. Chicago: Moody Press, 1999.

Weingreen, J. *A Practical Grammar for Classical Hebrew*, 2nd ed. Oxford: Clarendon Press, 1959.

Wells, Lauren. *Unstacking Your Grief Tower: For Adult Third Culture Kids*. Fort Mill: Independent, 2021.

Weston, Christopher. "The Matrix's Red Pill Blue Pill Explained: Which Did Neo Swallow?" *Hitc*. Published October, 2021. https://www.hitc.com/en-gb/2021/09/08/matrix-red-pill-blue-pill/.

Wilder, Thorton. 1928. "The Angel That Troubled the Waters." *The Library of America: Story of the Week* (Library of America, 1928), 54–56. https://storyoftheweek.loa.org/2018/04/the-angel-that-troubled-waters.html.

Williams, Donald T. *Reflections from Plato's Cave*. Monroe: Lantern Hollow Press, 2012.

Wolde, Ellen van. *Mr. and Mrs. Job*. Trinity Press International, 1997.

Wolfe, Rabbi David. *Making Loss Matter: Creating Meaning in Difficult Times*. New York: Riverhead Books, 1999.

Wright, Christopher J. H. *Here Are Your Gods: Faithful Discipleship in Idolatrous Times*. Downers Grove: InterVarsity Press, 2020.

Yang, Zhiyong, Ritesh Saini, and Traci Freling. "How Anxiety Leads to Suboptimal Decisions Under Risky Choice Situations." *Risk Analysis: An International Journal* 35, no. 10 (2015): 1789–800. https://doi.org/10.1111/risa.12343.

Young, Francis. *Uncertainty in Theology*. Published June 12, 2017. https://theologyeverywhere.org/2017/06/12/uncertainty-in-theology.

About the Author

ANNA E. HAMPTON teaches God's word interwoven with personal experiences from living and working for almost a decade in war-torn Afghanistan, five years of living in Turkey, and from nearly thirty years of ministry experiences traveling in nearly seventy countries. She grew up as a farm girl in the Midwest and chose to follow Christ at age seven. At age fourteen, she was called to give the rest of her life to missions. By her mid-twenties, she was in full-time work leading teams of teenagers worldwide.

She and Neal began a long-distance courtship across three continents, and after marrying, they began raising their family in Afghanistan, where they lived and ministered for ten years. They and their three teenagers then lived in Turkey for five years and are now based in the USA. Neal and Anna focus their pastoral ministry primarily on Central Asia and the Middle East.

Anna writes, teaches, and speaks with realism and depth from her trials of facing overwhelming obstacles with faith and joy while living in extremist environments for almost two decades while raising three young children. She is the author of *Facing Danger: A Guide through Risk* and *Facing Fear: The Journey to Mature Courage in Risk and Persecution* and contributed to the Risk Assessment and Management (RAM) Training that Neal wrote based on her book. *Facing Danger* and the RAM Training have been translated into Spanish, Portuguese, Arabic, Traditional Chinese (in-process), and Simplified Chinese (in-process).

Professional affiliations include Overseas Security Advisory Council (OSAC), Risk Management Network, CernySmith, and the Society for Risk Assessment. She has been featured in podcasts such as *Quick to Listen* (Christianity Today), *Global Missions Podcast* (Send Canada), and *The Clarity Podcast*. She has written articles for Missio Nexus and *Evangelical Missions Quarterly* (*EMQ*).

Anna holds four degrees, including a Master of Educational Leadership from Bethel University and a Doctor of Religious Studies from Trinity Theological Seminary. She and her husband Neal serve with Barnabas International, and they work together as consultants and global risk specialists on a practical theology of witness-risk. Contact her at Theology of Risk (https://theologyofrisk.com/) or on Instagram: Theology.of.Risk.

Index

A

actor mapping 21, 162, 173, 299
adaptability xiv, 234, 244, 262
ambiguity 80–81, 92, 117, 129, 132, 178, 185, 231, 245, 254, 300
anger 37, 60, 181, 185, 202, 205–206, 218, 252, 254, 277
anxiety 17, 36, 55, 245, 284, 295
Aquinas 5, 213–214, 250
Aristotle 2–5, 122
artificial intelligence 24, 301
attachment 47–49, 51, 55, 227, 256, 268, 271, 279

B

balm of Gilead 53, 87–88, 259–260
baseline 139, 154–156, 158, 160, 164–165
behavioral 159–160, 174, 216
betrayal 26, 38, 266
bias 13, 81, 111, 122, 130–134, 136–137, 139. 171–172, 178–179, 183–185, 189, 195, 217, 229, 230, 237
   hindsight 81, 131, 179, 183, 237
black swan 80–81, 88
bribes 114–115
   transactional 115
   variance 115

C

Center for the Study of Globaly Christianity (CSGC) 8, 9
chaos 14, 44, 53, 58, 61, 66, 88, 90, 92, 121, 178, 187, 194, 216–218, 228, 268, 271, 273
Chau, John 9, 179
clarity xxvii, 13, 15, 52, 81, 149–150, 177, 199, 210, 212, 229, 234–245, 280, 282

Collateral Violence 21, 28
communication 13, 44–45, 55, 101, 144. 159, 174, 184, 186–188, 190, 192–199, 225, 236, 239, 243, 245–246, 282
   app 195–198
   device 144, 236
   ineffective 245
   secure 193, 195, 236
conceptual thinking xxiv, 142–143
Cooper's Color Code 157, 159
Copts 165, 221
courage 41, 52
   acquired 214, 218
   infused 214, 218
   mature i–ii, iv, xx–xxi, xxv, xxvii, 29, 45, 55–56, 104, 121, 152, 184, 228, 259, 275–279, 281
   moral 3, 44, 73, 80, 97, 100, 105, 108, 111, 117, 119–120, 199, 293
   resilient 127, 216–218, 221, 270, 293
COVID-19 5, 250
cowardice 2–3, 15, 35–36, 41, 52–53, 221
   moral 120
crisis response 15, 46, 79, 123, 129, 131, 159, 180, 186, 191–192, 198, 225, 228–229, 231–234, 236–237, 240, 244, 246–247
critical thinking 130, 137–138, 152
cunning 100, 197–198, 274
cybersecurity 22–23, 101, 193–194, 299

D

danger 19, 170, 175, 179, 187, 190, 193
Daniel xxiv, 46, 120, 143, 182, 197, 277, 307, 309, 311
darkness 65

data 7–9, 150, 164, 169
death threat xxv, 20, 22, 174–177
death-threat assessment 173
deception 22, 111, 171, 197
decision-making xxi, xxvii, 20, 29, 122, 146, 169, 173, 178, 180–187, 219, 228–229, 231, 233, 238, 243
  baseline 154
  biases 120–132, 134–136, 139
  discernment 97
  ethics 107–108
  individualism 71
  logframes 93
  Risk Axioms 146
  shrewd 101
de-escalate 161, 165, 187
deny 3, 27, 38, 45–46, 54, 60, 63–64, 75, 83, 86–87, 112, 123, 152, 200, 217
detainment 24
discernment ii, 26, 53, 65, 78, 89, 93, 95–96, 104, 109, 121, 137, 166, 178, 182, 184, 186, 201, 210, 217, 226, 228, 265, 295, 298, 300
discouragement 6, 27
  from family 78
Docetism 74–75
doves 76, 100, 102, 119

E

emotion 122–124, 146, 148, 154–155, 157, 171
endurance xx, 5, 14, 38, 88, 127, 213–214, 217
  wise 221
enemies 69
Epicureans 3
ethics 102, 111, 147
expectation 8, 21, 77, 80, 92, 96

F

failure 77, 83
faith 88, 142, 165, 201, 219
  anti-fragile 85, 88, 218, 257, 298
faithful 87, 94, 97, 241
fear 6, 12–14, 20–21, 29, 32–36, 41, 46–48, 55
  dread 4, 35–37, 39, 41, 54, 57, 59–60, 129–130, 217, 265, 270
  naming 54

G

Gender & Religious Freedom 8
Gender-Specific Religious Persecution (GSRP) 11
gendered persecution 24
Gideon 42
Global Risk Resource xxvi
Global Terrorism Database 9, 11
Gnosticism 74
gray man 155
gray woman. *See* gray man
grief 200, 203–204, 206
  gated 208–210
  meaning 210
  process 206
groupthink 134

H

hallucinations 220
hazard 19
heresies 72
hostility 8, 16, 21, 23, 27, 211, 213, 286

I

idols 69
Ignatian spirituality 154

impact 20
indifference 43, 103, 107, 203
inference 178
information 169
information management 187
interrogation 18, 24, 67, 113–114
Intimacy Effect 159, 175, 301

J

Jeremiah 82, 84, 86–87
Joan of Arc 3
Joshua Project 10
Judaizers 74
judgment 125, 178, 227, 236, 258
   bad 178

K

kidnappings 22, 301
   virtual 22

L

lament 205, 212
leadership 179–180, 192, 202, 225, 239, 242
   directive 243
   situational 180
   skills of, 234
limbic system 50
liminality 147
logframe 93

M

martyrdom vii, xxii, xxvii, 7–8, 14, 87, 98, 105, 180, 213–214, 219, 221

N

naming xxi, 7, 14, 15, 95, 130, 170, 201, 208, 226, 258–259, 271, 298
neuroplasticity 55
normal. *See* baseline

O

O'Brien, Tim 2
observation 44, 156, 164, 178
Observation 156
Open Doors 7–13, 21, 23, 147, 213, 306
openness 96
Origen 4–5

P

PACE 194, 311
panic 35, 40, 58–59, 198, 293, 313, 318
parenting 44
Pelagianism 73
Penner, Glenn M. 63
Perpetua 3
Peter 56, 86
Plato xx, 53
pray 66–67
probability 145
proselytizing 197
proximity
   demographic 20
   geographic 20
PTSD 35, 49, 209, 272

R

RAM Training xxi, 19
ransom 22, 116–117, 162, 301
reality
   discernment 97
   meaning of 6
reason 124
resignation 65
resilience 14, 29, 39, 52, 82, 88, 127, 181, 213–214, 216–218, 234, 242, 245, 266, 270, 295

response
  simplistic 220
  to fear 38, 42–43
rhomphaia 21, 26
risk 19–20
  agility 233
  aversion 227
  awareness 44, 106, 178
  axiom 16, 150
  detachment 181
  framing 186
  illiterate 225
  literatacy 225
  management 232
  meaning 93
  mitigation 13, 136, 150, 185, 187, 226, 233, 300, 302
  perception of 121–122, 125–126, 131, 187–188, 228, 233
  savvy system 234
  theology of xx– xxi, xxiii, xxv–xxvi, 22, 46, 96, 141, 224–226, 228, 295–296
  witness iii, xxii–xxiii, 20–21, 29, 73, 105, 122, 125–127, 130–131, 137, 141, 145, 150, 152, 161, 171, 174, 179, 185, 228, 236, 271
risk assessment xxiii, 13, 15, 19–21, 38, 73–75, 91, 108, 122–123, 126–127, 129, 133, 168, 177, 180, 224–226, 228–229, 231–233, 236–238, 240, 294, 295–296, 297
Risk Management Network (RMN) 12
Risk Management Team (RMT) 231–233
Rule of Three 159, 161

S

sanctification 148
Scazzero, Peter 60
security xxiii, xxvi, 12–13, 22, 70, 107
severity 20
shrewd 102
situational awareness 43
situational thinking 142
smash 15, 21, 25
snakes 100–101, 120
spiritual pride 69, 74
squeeze 21, 23
stakeholders 162, 179, 187
Stoic 3, 122
Stoicism 65
Stress Inoculation Training (SIT) 215
subjective probability 149
surveillance 23, 164–165
  digital 23
systems thinking 228, 230

T

technology 190
temptation 63
terror 60
terrorism 10, 12, 20, 22, 25, 176, 217, 231, 241, 243 , 301, 303
terrorist attack planning cycle 164
threat 19
  assessment 20, 174, 243
  probability 20
threats
  anonymous 21, 174, 301, 315
  blended 22, 301
  direct 21
  insider 22

torture 24–25, 114, 220
  psyschological 24
tragic laughter 217
trauma 79, 87, 144, 146, 199, 209

U

uncertainity 63, 77, 81, 185
unknowns 92, 138, 152

V

values 203
victim 8, 15, 22, 217
violence 6, 10, 12, 21, 24–25, 28, 105–106, 174, 176, 213, 218, 220, 273
volatility 231
VUCA environment 231, 234
vulnerability 20–21, 76, 135, 151–152, 236, 269, 235–236, 269

W

white noise 169, 224
wolf 27, 76
  behavior 76
worship 14, 96, 148–149, 201, 247
Wurmbrand, Richard 64, 97, 114, 220

visit us at missionbooks.org

Facing Danger (2nd Edition)

By Anna Hampton

COMING IN 2024!

Recovering from Traumatic Stress: A Guide for Missionaries

By Stephanie Laite Lanham & Joyce Hartwell Pelletier

Experiencing symptoms of traumatic stress can be debilitating. Post-Traumatic Stress Disorder (PTSD) is a normal reaction to an abnormal event. *Recovering from Traumatic Stress* provides information and resources for support that can lead to comfort and healing. This book teaches about the symptoms experienced after a traumatic incident and how to recognize them. It offers strength and ways to talk to children and others about traumatic experiences. With God's help, readers who have experienced traumatic situations can begin to regain a sense of peace for themselves and their families.

Global Member Care (Volume Two): Crossing Sectors for Serving Humanity

By Kelly O'Donnell and Michèle Lewis O'Donnell (Eds)

Global Member Care is part of an ongoing effort to help a diversity of colleagues keep current with a globalizing world and the global field of member care. This second volume in the Global Member Care series encourages readers to connect and contribute to various international sectors on behalf of mission/aid workers and humanity. The book's thirty-five chapters include a wealth of practical resources: guidelines, codes, resolutions, perspectives, principles, case examples, videos links, human rights instruments, and more. Get ready to venture into the heart of global issues and opportunities—from the trenches to the towers and everything in between!

www.ingramcontent.com/pod-product-compliance
Lightning Source LLC
Chambersburg PA
CBHW071229070526
44583CB00017B/2100